Beginning
OF THE END

Ellen G. White

Pacific Press® Publishing Association
Nampa, Idaho
Oshawa, Ontario, Canada
www.pacificpress.com

Cover design by Doug Church
Cover illustration by Eric Joyner
Inside design by Steve Lanto

Additional copies of this book are available by
calling toll-free 1-800-765-6955 or
online at www.adventistbookcenter.com

ISBN 13: 978-0-8163-2211-4
ISBN 10: 0-8163-2211-2

12 13 14 · 5 4 3

Contents

Foreword... 5

1. Why Was Sin Permitted?.. 7
2. Creation, God's Answer to Evolution 12
3. The Predicament of Our First Parents....................16
4. The Plan of Redemption Is Unveiled 22
5. The First Murderer and His Victim 26
6. Seth, When Men Turned to God 30
7. When the World Was Destroyed by Water 35
8. After the Flood, a New Beginning 42
9. The Beginning of the Literal Week 45
10. When Languages Were Changed............................ 48
11. Abraham, the Father of All Believers.....................52
12. Abraham, a Good Neighbor in Canaan.................. 56
13. The Offering of Isaac, Test of Faith....................... 63
14. The Sin of Sodom and Gomorrah 69
15. Isaac's Marriage, the Happiest in the Bible 76
16. Jacob and Esau 80
17. Jacob's Flight and Exile 84
18. Jacob's Terrible Night of Wrestling........................ 90
19. Jacob Comes Home 94
20. The Amazing Story of Joseph................................ 99
21. Joseph and His Brothers.......................................105
22. Moses, the Leader of God's People.......................116
23. The Ten Plagues of Egypt 124
24. The First Passover...133
25. The Israelites Leave Egypt 136
26. Israel Meets With Difficulties 140
27. God Gives His Law on Mount Sinai 146
28. Israel Worships a Golden Calf 153
29. Satan's Hatred of God's Law.................................161
30. The Sanctuary, God's Dwelling Place in Israel 167
31. The Sin of Nadab and Abihu 175
32. The Grace of Christ and the New Covenant............177
33. The Terrible Grumblings of God's People................183

34. Twelve Spies Survey Canaan..189
35. Korah Leads a Rebellion..194
36. Forty Years of Wandering in the Wilderness.....................200
37. Moses Fails on the Border of Canaan...............................203
38. Why the Long Journey Around Edom?.............................207
39. The Conquest of Bashan...213
40. Balaam Tries to Curse Israel...216
41. How Balaam Led Israel Into Sin.......................................224
42. God Teaches His Law to a New Generation......................229
43. The Death of Moses..233
44. Crossing the Jordan..239
45. The Miraculous Fall of Jericho..242
46. The Blessings and the Curses...248
47. A Canaanite Tribe Deceives Israel....................................251
48. Home at Last..254
49. The Last Words of Joshua...261
50. The Blessing of Tithes and Offerings................................264
51. God's Care for the Poor..266
52. Annual Feasts of Rejoicing...270
53. The Judges, Deliverers of Israel..273
54. Samson, the Strongest Yet Weakest Man.........................281
55. God Calls the Child Samuel...287
56. Eli and His Wicked Sons..290
57. Punishment, the Ark Taken..293
58. The Schools of the Prophets..300
59. Saul, the First King of Israel...304
60. Saul Makes a Terrible Mistake...311
61. Saul Rejected as King...316
62. David Anointed as King..321
63. David Kills Goliath...324
64. David Flees..328
65. The Largeheartedness of David..334
66. Saul Takes His Own Life...341
67. Ancient and Modern Spiritualism.....................................345
68. David's Heavy Trial..348
69. David at Last Crowned King...352
70. The Prosperous Reign of David..355
71. David's Sin of Adultery and His Repentance.....................362
72. The Rebellion of Absalom, David's Son............................367
73. A Man After God's Own Heart...377
Appendix...383

Foreword

This volume is an adaptation of *From Eternity Past,* the 1983 condensed edition of Ellen G. White's classic, *Patriarchs and Prophets.* The condensed volume included all the stories and major applications in the original book. Moreover, except for supplying a word here or there for a smooth transition, it rigidly retained Mrs. White's own words. *The Beginning of the End* has taken a step beyond that. It has substituted some modern words, expressions, and sentence constructions for twenty-first century readers. But it is not a paraphrase. It follows *From Eternity Past* sentence by sentence and maintains the force of Mrs. White's writing. It is hoped that new readers will thus develop a taste for Mrs. White's writings and will be led to read and enjoy the original books, though written in the style of an earlier time.

Except where noted, Scripture passages have been quoted from the New King James Version. It closely parallels the King James Version that Mrs. White usually used, but many people today find that they can read it more easily.

The Beginning of the End is rich in insight into the Bible stories of origins—the origin of sin, of this world, of the plan of salvation, and of the people of God. It makes the treasures of *Patriarchs and Prophets* accessible to more people. In this way it helps to make more widely known the beginning of "the great controversy" story that Mrs. White told so compellingly in the five-volume "Conflict of the Ages" series of books. That many more readers may experience the life-changing power of these books and their presentation of Bible themes is the hope and prayer of

The Trustees of
The Ellen G. White Estate

Why Was Sin Permitted?

God is love." His nature, His law, is love. It ever has been, and it ever will be. Every use of creative power is an expression of infinite love. The history of the great conflict between good and evil from the time it first began in heaven also reveals God's unchanging love.

The Sovereign of the universe was not alone in His work of doing good. He had an associate who could appreciate His purpose and share His joy in giving happiness to created beings. See John 1:1, 2.

Christ the Word was one with the eternal Father, one in nature, in character, in purpose. "His name will be called Wonderful, Counselor, Mighty God, Everlasting Father, Prince of Peace." Isaiah 9:6. His " 'goings forth have been from of old, from everlasting.' " Micah 5:2.

The Father worked by His Son in the creation of all heavenly beings. "By Him all things were created . . . , whether thrones or dominions or principalities or powers." Colossians 1:16. Angels are God's ministers, speeding to execute His will. But the Son, the "express image of His person," "the brightness of His glory," "upholding all things by the word of His power," holds supremacy over

them all. See Hebrews 1:3, 8.

From all His creatures, God wants the service of love—service that springs from an appreciation of His character. He takes no pleasure in forced obedience. He grants freedom of will to all, that they may give Him voluntary service. So long as all created beings were loyal through love, there was perfect harmony throughout the universe of God. There was no note of discord to mar heaven's harmonies.

But a change came over this happy state. There was one who used wrongly the freedom that God had granted to His creatures. Sin began with him who, next to Christ, had been most honored of God and was highest among the inhabitants of heaven. Lucifer, " 'son of the morning' " (Isaiah 14:12), was holy and undefiled. " ' "Thus says the Lord GOD: 'You were the seal of perfection, full of wisdom and perfect in beauty. . . . You were the anointed cherub who covers; I established you; you were on the holy mountain of God; you walked back and forth in the midst of fiery stones. You were perfect in your ways from the day you were created, till iniquity was found in you.' " ' "

Little by little, Lucifer indulged the desire to exalt himself. " ' " 'Your heart was lifted up because of your beauty; you corrupted your wisdom for the sake of your splendor.' " ' " Ezekiel 28:12-15, 17. " 'You have said in your heart: . . . "I will exalt my throne above the stars of God; . . . I will be like the Most High." ' " Isaiah 14:13, 14. Though honored above the heavenly host, he dared to covet worship due alone to the Creator. This prince of angels wanted power that was the right of Christ alone.

Now the perfect harmony of heaven was broken. In heavenly council the angels pleaded with Lucifer. The Son of God presented before him the goodness and justice of the Creator and the unchanging nature of His law. In departing from it, Lucifer would dishonor his Maker and bring ruin upon himself. But the warning given in infinite love and mercy only aroused resistance. Lucifer allowed his jealousy of Christ to prevail, and he became ever the more determined.

The king of the universe called for the heavenly hosts to come before Him, that in their presence He might set forth the true position of His Son and show His relationship to all created beings. The Son of God shared the Father's throne, and the glory of the eternal, self-existent One encircled both. Around the throne gathered the holy angels, "ten thousand times ten thousand, and thousands of thousands." Revelation 5:11. Before the inhabitants of heaven, the King declared that none but Christ could fully enter into His purposes and execute the mighty counsels of His will. Soon Christ was to exercise divine power in the creation of the earth and its inhabitants.

The Battle in Lucifer's Heart

The angels joyfully acknowledged Christ as supreme, and they poured out their love and adoration. Lucifer bowed with them; but in his heart there was a strange, fierce conflict. Truth and loyalty were struggling against envy and jealousy. The influence of the holy angels seemed for a time to carry him with them. As songs of praise ascended, the spirit of evil seemed overcome; unutterable love thrilled his entire being; his soul went out in harmony with the sinless worshipers in love to the Father and the Son. But again his desire to be supreme returned, and once more he indulged envy of Christ. The high honors given Lucifer called forth no gratitude to his Creator. He gloried in his brightness and wanted to be equal with God. Angels delighted to execute his commands, and he was clothed with glory above them all. Yet the Son of God was exalted above him. "Why," questioned this mighty angel, "should Christ have the supremacy?"

Lucifer went forth to spread the spirit of discontent among the angels. For a time he concealed his real purpose under an appearance of reverence for God. Subtly he planted doubts concerning the laws that governed heavenly beings, suggesting that angels needed no such rules, for their own wisdom was a sufficient guide. All their thoughts were holy; it was no more possible for them to do wrong than for God Himself to err. The exaltation of the Son of God as equal with the Father was represented as an injustice to Lucifer. If this prince of angels could only attain to his true, exalted position, great good would come to the entire host of heaven, for it was his purpose to secure freedom for all. Subtle deceptions through the wicked schemes of Lucifer were fast gaining ground in the heavenly courts.

The true position of the Son of God had been the same from the beginning. However, many of the angels were blinded by Lucifer's deceptions. He so artfully instilled into their minds his own distrust and discontent that they did not recognize what he was doing. Lucifer had presented the purposes of God in a false light to excite dissent and dissatisfaction. While he claimed to be perfectly loyal to God, he urged that changes were necessary for the stability of the divine government. While secretly stirring up discord and rebellion, he made it appear that his sole purpose was to promote loyalty and to preserve harmony and peace.

Though there was no open rebellion, division of feeling gradually grew up among the angels. Some looked with favor upon Lucifer's subtle criticisms and suggestions. They were discontented and unhappy, dissatisfied with God's purpose in exalting Christ. But angels who were loyal defended the wisdom and justice of the divine decree. Christ was the Son of God, one with Him before the angels were called into existence. He had ever stood at the right hand of the Father. So why should there now be discord?

God bore long with Lucifer. The spirit of discontent was a new element, strange, unaccountable. Lucifer himself did not see where he was drifting. But such efforts as only infinite love and wisdom could develop were made to convince him of his error. He was led to see what would be the result of persisting in revolt.

Lucifer was convinced that he was in the wrong. He saw that "the LORD is righteous in all His ways, gracious in all His works" (Psalm 145:17), that the divine statutes are just and that he ought to acknowledge them as such before all heaven. If he had done this, he might have saved himself and many angels. If he had been willing to return to God, satisfied to fill the place appointed him in God's great plan, he would have been reinstated in his office. The time had come for a final decision; he must yield to the divine sovereignty or place himself in open rebellion. He nearly reached the decision to return, but pride prevented him. It was too great a sacrifice for one who had been so highly honored to confess that he had been in error!

Lucifer pointed to the long-suffering of God as an evidence of his own superiority, an indication that the King of the universe would yet agree to his terms. If the angels would stand firmly with him, he declared, they could still get everything they wanted. He fully committed himself to the great controversy against his Maker. In this way Lucifer, "the light bearer," became Satan, "the adversary" of God and holy beings.

Satan Leads in Rebellion

Rejecting with scorn the appeals of the loyal angels, he called them deluded slaves. He would never again acknowledge the supremacy of Christ. He had determined to claim the honor that should have been given him. And he promised those who would enter his ranks a new and better government under which all would enjoy freedom. Great numbers of the angels declared their purpose to accept him as their leader. He hoped to win all the angels to his side, to become equal with God Himself, and to be obeyed by the entire host of heaven.

Still the loyal angels urged him and his sympathizers to submit to God, setting before them the inevitable result if they refused. They warned all to close their ears against Lucifer's deceptive reasoning and urged him and his followers to seek the presence of God without delay and confess the error of questioning His wisdom and authority.

Many were inclined to repent of their discontent and seek to be again received into favor with the Father and His Son. But Lucifer now declared that the angels who had joined with him had gone too far to return; God would not forgive. For himself, he was determined never again to acknowledge the authority of Christ. The only course remaining was to assert their liberty and gain by force the rights that had not been granted them.

God permitted Satan to carry forward his work until the spirit of discontent ripened into active revolt. It was necessary for his plans to be fully developed, that all might see their true nature. God's government included not only the inhabitants of heaven but all the world that He had created. Lucifer concluded that if he could carry the angels with him in rebellion, he could carry the worlds also. All his acts were so clothed with mystery that it was difficult to make clear the true nature of his work. Even the loyal angels could not fully discern his character or see to what his work was leading. Everything simple he shrouded in mystery, and by spinning the truth he cast doubt upon the plainest statements of God. And his high position gave greater force to his assertions.

Why God Did Not Destroy Satan

God could use only such methods as were consistent with truth and righteousness. Satan could use what God could not—flattery and deceit. It was therefore necessary to demonstrate before the inhabitants of heaven and all the worlds that God's government is just, His law perfect. Satan had made it seem that he himself was seeking to promote the good of the universe. His true character must be understood by all. He must have time to manifest himself by his wicked works.

He declared all evil to be the result of the divine administration; it was his own purpose to improve upon the statutes of God. Therefore God permitted him to demonstrate the nature of his claims, to show the working out of his proposed changes in the divine law. His own work must condemn him. The whole universe must see the deceiver unmasked.

Why Didn't God Destroy Satan?

Even when Satan was cast out of heaven, Infinite Wisdom did not destroy him. The loyalty of God's creatures must rest upon a conviction of His justice and love. At that time, the inhabitants of heaven and of the world could not have seen the justice of God in the destruction of Satan. Had he been immediately blotted out of existence, some would have served God from fear rather than from love. The influence of the deceiver would not have been fully destroyed, nor would the spirit of rebellion have been utterly eliminated. For the good of the entire universe through ceaseless ages he must more fully develop his principles, so that his charges against the divine government might be seen in their true light and that the justice of God and the unchangeable nature of His law might be forever placed beyond question.

Satan's rebellion was to be a lesson to the universe through all coming ages—a testimony forever to the nature of sin and its terrible results. Thus the history of this experiment of rebellion was to be an eternal safeguard to all holy beings to prevent them from being deceived as to the nature of transgression.

" 'His work is perfect; for all His ways are justice, a God of truth and without injustice; righteous and upright is He.' " Deuteronomy 32:4.

Creation, God's Answer to Evolution*

By the word of the LORD the heavens were made, and all the host of them by the breath of His mouth. . . . For He spoke, and it was done; He commanded, and it stood fast." Psalm 33:6, 9.

As the earth came forth from the hand of its Maker, it was unbelievably beautiful. Everywhere the fruitful soil produced luxuriant green vegetation. There were no foul swamps nor barren deserts. Graceful shrubs and delicate flowers greeted the eye at every turn. The air was clear and healthful. The entire landscape was more beautiful than the decorated grounds of the proudest palace.

After the earth had been called into existence, teeming with animal and vegetable life, human beings—the crowning work of the Creator—were brought upon the stage of action. "God said, 'Let Us make man in Our image, according to Our likeness; let them have dominion over . . . all the earth.' " "So God created man in His own image; . . . male and female He created them."

Here is set forth clearly the origin of the human race. God created us in His own image. There is no reason to suppose that we evolved by slow degrees from lower forms of animal or vegetable life. Inspiration traces the origin of our race, not to a line of developing germs, mollusks, and quadrupeds, but to the great Creator. Though formed from the dust, Adam was "the son of God." Luke 3:38.

The lower orders of being cannot grasp the concept of God, yet they were made capable of loving and serving human beings. "You have made him to have dominion over the works of Your hands; You have put all things under his feet, . . . the beasts of the field, the birds of the air." Psalm 8:6-8.

Christ alone is "the express image" (Hebrews 1:3) of the Father, but Adam and Eve were formed in the likeness of God. Their nature was in harmony with the will of God, their minds capable of comprehending divine things. Their affections were pure; their appetites and passions were under the control of reason. They were holy and happy in bearing the image of God and in obeying His will perfectly.

---

* This chapter is based on Genesis 1 and 2.

As our first parents came forth from the hand of their Creator, their faces glowed with the light of life and joy. Adam's height was much greater than that of men now living. Eve was somewhat less in stature, yet her form was noble and full of beauty. The sinless pair wore no artificial garments; they were clothed with a covering of light such as the angels wear.

The First Marriage

After the creation of Adam, "God said, 'It is not good that man should be alone; I will make him a helper comparable to him.' " God gave Adam a companion fitted for him, who would be one with him in love and sympathy. Eve was created from a rib taken from Adam's side. She was not to control him as the head, nor to be trampled under his feet as an inferior, but to stand by his side as an equal, loved and protected by him. She was his second self, showing the close union that should exist in this relationship. "For no one ever hated his own flesh, but nourishes and cherishes it." "Therefore a man shall leave his father and mother and be joined to his wife, and they shall become one." Ephesians 5:29; Genesis 2:24.

"Marriage is honorable." Hebrews 13:4. It is one of the two institutions that, after the Fall, Adam brought with him beyond the gates of Paradise. When the divine principles are recognized and obeyed, marriage is a blessing; it guards the purity and happiness of the race and elevates the physical, intellectual, and moral nature.

"The LORD God planted a garden eastward in Eden, and there He put the man whom He had formed." In this garden were trees of every variety, many of them heavy with delicious fruit. There were lovely vines, growing upright, their branches drooping under their load of tempting fruit. It was the work of Adam and Eve to train the branches of the vine to form bowers, thus making a home for themselves from living trees covered with foliage and fruit. In the middle of the garden stood the tree of life, surpassing in glory all other trees. Its fruit had the power to sustain life forever.

"The heavens and the earth, and all the host of them, were finished." "Then God saw everything that He had made, and indeed it was very good." No taint of sin or shadow of death marred the beautiful creation. "The morning stars sang together, and all the sons of God shouted for joy." Job 38:7.

The Blessing of the Sabbath

In six days the great work of creation had been accomplished. And God "rested on the seventh day from all His work which He had done. Then God blessed the seventh day and sanctified it, because in it He rested from all His work which God had created and made." All was perfect, worthy of its divine Author; and He rested, not as one weary, but as well pleased with the fruits of His wisdom and goodness.

After resting on the seventh day, God set it apart as a day of rest. Following the example of the Creator,

His human creatures were to rest upon this sacred day, that they might reflect upon God's work of creation and their hearts be filled with love and reverence for their Maker.

The Sabbath was given to the whole human family. In observing it, they would gratefully show that they recognized God as their Creator and rightful Ruler. They were the work of His hands, the subjects of His authority.

God saw that a Sabbath was essential for human beings, even in Paradise. They needed to lay aside their own interests for one day of the seven. They needed a Sabbath to remind them of God and to awaken gratitude because all that they enjoyed came from the hand of the Creator.

God designs that the Sabbath shall direct our minds to His created works. The beauty that clothes the earth is a token of God's love. The everlasting hills, the lofty trees, the opening buds and delicate flowers, all speak to us of God. The Sabbath, pointing to Him who made them all, bids us open the book of nature and trace in it the wisdom, power, and love of the Creator.

Our first parents were created innocent and holy, but they were not placed beyond the possibility of wrongdoing. God made them free moral agents. They could choose whether to obey or disobey. But before they could be eternally secure, their loyalty must be tested. At the beginning of human existence God placed a check upon self-indulgence, the fatal desire that lay at the foundation of Satan's fall. The tree of knowledge was to be a test of the obedience, faith, and love of our first parents. They were forbidden to taste the fruit of this tree, on pain of death. They were to be exposed to the temptations of Satan; but if they endured the trial successfully, they would be placed beyond his power, to enjoy unending favor with God.

The Beautiful Garden of Eden

God placed human beings under law, subjects of the divine government. God might have created them without the power to transgress; He might have prevented them from touching the forbidden fruit; but in that case Adam and Eve would have been mere robots. Without freedom of choice, their obedience would have been forced. Such a course would have been contrary to God's plan, unworthy of the intelligent beings He created, and would have sustained Satan's charge of God's arbitrary rule.

God made our first parents upright, with no bias toward evil. He presented before them the strongest possible motivations to be true. Obedience was the condition of eternal happiness and access to the tree of life.

The home of our first parents was to be a pattern for other homes as their children should go forth to occupy the earth. People today take pride and delight in magnificent and costly homes and glory in the works of their own hands, but God placed Adam in a garden. This was a lesson for all time—true happiness is found not by indulging in pride and luxury but by communing with God through His created works. Pride and ambition are never satisfied, but people who are truly wise will find pleasure in the enjoyment God has placed within the reach of all.

To the couple in Eden was committed the care of the garden, "to tend and keep it." God appointed work as a blessing, to occupy the mind, strengthen the body, and develop the abilities. In mental and physical activity Adam found one of the highest pleasures of his holy existence. It is an error to regard work as a curse, even though it bring weariness and pain. The rich often look down upon the working classes, but this is out of harmony with God's purpose in the creation. Adam was not to be idle. Our Creator, who understands what is for our happiness, appointed Adam his work. The true joy of life is found only by working men and women. The Creator has prepared no place for do-nothing laziness.

The holy pair were not only children under the fatherly care of God but students receiving instruction from the all-wise Creator. They were visited by angels and had the privilege of talking face to face with their Maker. They were full of vigor imparted by the tree of life, their intellectual power only slightly less than that of the angels. The laws of nature were opened to their minds by the infinite Creator and Upholder of all. With every living creature, from the mighty whale among the waters to the insect mote that floats in the sunbeam, Adam was familiar. He had given to each its name, and he was acquainted with the nature and habits of all. On every leaf of the forest, in every shining star, in earth and air and sky, God's name was written. The order and harmony of creation spoke of infinite wisdom and power.

So long as Adam and Eve remained loyal to the divine law, they constantly would be gaining new treasures of knowledge, discovering fresh springs of happiness, and obtaining clearer understandings of the immeasurable, unfailing love of God.

The Predicament of Our First Parents*

No longer free to stir up rebellion in heaven, Satan found a new field in plotting the ruin of the human race. Moved by envy, he determined to bring upon them the guilt and penalty of sin. He would change their love to distrust and their songs of praise to criticism of their Maker. Thus he would not only plunge these innocent beings into misery but cast dishonor upon God and cause grief in heaven.

Heavenly messengers opened to our first parents the history of Satan's fall and his plots for their destruction, unfolding the nature of the divine government that the prince of evil was trying to overthrow.

The law of God is a revelation of His will, a transcript of His character, the expression of divine love and wisdom. The harmony of creation depends upon perfect conformity to the law of the Creator. Everything is under fixed laws that cannot be disregarded. But human beings alone, of all that inhabits the earth, are responsible to moral law. To them God has given power to comprehend the justice and goodness of His law, and of them unswerving obedience is required.

Like the angels, the dwellers in Eden had been given time to show what they would do. They could obey and live or disobey and perish. He who spared not the angels that sinned could not spare them; transgression would bring upon them misery and ruin.

The angels warned them to be on guard against the schemes of Satan. If they firmly repelled his first subtle enticings, they would be secure. But if they once yielded to temptation, their nature would become so depraved that in themselves they would have no power and no inclination to resist Satan.

The tree of knowledge had been made a test of their obedience and love to God. If they should disregard His will in this particular, they would incur guilt. Satan was not to follow them with continual temptations; he could have access to them only at the forbidden tree.

To accomplish his work undetected, Satan employed a disguise. The serpent was one of the wisest and most beautiful creatures. It had dazzling brightness. Resting in the forbidden tree, feasting on the deli-

---

* This chapter is based on Genesis 3.

cious fruit, it was an object to arrest attention and delight the eye. Thus in the garden of peace lurked the destroyer.

The angels had warned Eve to beware of separating from her husband. With him she would be in less danger than if alone. But she unconsciously wandered from his side. Forgetting the angel's caution, she soon found herself gazing with mingled curiosity and admiration on the forbidden tree. The fruit was beautiful, and she wondered why God had withheld it from them.

Now was the tempter's opportunity. " 'Has God indeed said, "You shall not eat of every tree of the garden" ' "? Eve was startled to hear the echo of her thoughts. The serpent continued with subtle praise of her surpassing beauty, and his words were not displeasing. Instead of fleeing from the spot, she lingered. She didn't suspect that Satan was speaking through the fascinating serpent.

She replied: " 'We may eat the fruit of the trees of the garden; but of the fruit of the tree which is in the midst of the garden, God has said, "You shall not eat it, nor shall you touch it, lest you die." ' " "And the serpent said to the woman, 'You will not surely die. For God knows that in the day you eat of it your eyes will be opened, and you will be like God, knowing good and evil.' "

By partaking of this tree, he declared, they would reach a higher level of life. He himself had eaten and had acquired the power of speech. He implied that the Lord had jealously withheld it from them,

lest they be exalted to equality with Himself; because this fruit imparted wisdom and power, He had prohibited them from tasting or touching it. The divine warning was merely to intimidate them. How could it be possible for them to die? Had they not eaten of the tree of life? God had been seeking to prevent them from reaching a nobler development and finding greater happiness.

Such has been Satan's work from the days of Adam to the present. He tempts people to distrust God's love and doubt His wisdom. In their efforts to probe into what God has withheld, multitudes overlook truths that are essential to salvation. Satan tempts them to disobedience, to believe they are entering a wonderful field of knowledge. But this is all a deception. They are starting down the road that leads to degradation and death.

The Subtlety of Satan's Appeal

Satan told the holy pair that they would gain by breaking the law of God. Today many talk of the narrowness of those who obey God's commandments and claim that they themselves enjoy greater liberty. What is this but an echo of the voice from Eden? "In the day you eat of it"—transgress the divine requirement—"you will be like God." Satan did not let it appear that he had become an outcast from heaven. He concealed his own misery in order to draw others into the same position. So now the transgressors disguise their true character. But they are on the side of Satan, trampling upon the law of God and leading others to eternal ruin.

Eve disbelieved the words of God, and this was what led to her fall. In the judgment, people will not be condemned because they conscientiously believed a lie but because they did not believe the truth. We must set our hearts to know what is truth. Whatever contradicts God's Word comes from Satan.

The serpent plucked the fruit of the forbidden tree and placed it in the hands of the half-reluctant Eve. Then he reminded her of her own words, that God had forbidden them to touch it lest they die. Seeing no evil results, Eve grew bolder. When she "saw that the tree was good for food, that it was pleasant to the eyes, and a tree desirable to make one wise, she took of its fruit and ate." As she ate, she seemed to imagine herself entering upon a higher state of existence.

And now, having herself transgressed, she became Satan's agent to ruin her husband. In a state of strange, unnatural excitement, her hands filled with the forbidden fruit, she looked for and found him.

Adam appeared astonished and alarmed. To the words of Eve he replied that this must be the foe against whom they had been warned. Now, as God had said, she must die. In answer she urged him, "Eat," repeating the words of the serpent that they would not surely die. She felt no evidence of God's displeasure but sensed a delicious, exhilarating influence, thrilling every part of her body with new life.

Adam understood that his companion had disobeyed the command of God. There was a terrible struggle in his mind. He mourned that he had permitted Eve to wander from his side. But now the deed was done; he must be separated from her whose society had been his joy.

How could he endure this? Adam had enjoyed the companionship of God and of holy angels. He understood the high destiny opened to the human race if they remained faithful to God. Yet all these blessings were lost sight of in the fear of losing that one gift which, in his eyes, was of more value than every other. Love, gratitude, and loyalty to the Creator—all were swept aside by love to Eve. She was a part of himself, and he could not endure the thought of separation. If she must die, he would die with her. Might not the words of the wise serpent be true? No sign of death appeared in Eve, and he decided to brave the consequences. He seized the fruit and quickly ate.

After his transgression, Adam at first imagined himself entering upon a higher state of existence. But soon the thought of his sin filled him with terror. The love and peace that had been theirs was gone, and in its place they felt a sense of sin, a dread of the future, a nakedness of soul. The robe of light that had enshrouded them disappeared, and to supply its lack they tried to make for themselves a covering. They could not, while unclothed, meet the eye of God and holy angels.

They now began to see the true character of sin. Adam criticized his companion for leaving his side and permitting herself to be deceived by the serpent. But they both flattered themselves that the God who had given them so many evidences of His love would pardon this one transgression; they would not be subjected to so terrible a punishment as they had feared.

Satan gloated. He had tempted the woman to distrust God's love, to doubt His wisdom, and to transgress His law; and through her he had caused the overthrow of Adam!

The Sad Change That Sin Produced

The great Lawgiver was about to make known to Adam and Eve the result of their transgression. In their innocence and holiness they had joyfully welcomed the approach of their Creator; now they fled in terror. But "the LORD God called to Adam and said to him, 'Where are you?' So he said, 'I heard Your voice in the garden, and I was afraid because I was naked; and I hid myself.' And He said, 'Who told you that you were naked? Have you eaten from the tree of which I commanded you that you should not eat?' "

Adam blamed his wife and thus blamed God Himself: " 'The woman whom *You gave* to be with me, she gave me of the tree, and I ate.' " From love to Eve, he had deliberately chosen to give up the approval of God and an eternal life of joy; now he tried to make his companion, and even the Creator Himself, responsible for the transgression.

When the woman was asked, " 'What is this you have done?' " she answered, " 'The serpent deceived me, and I ate.' " "Why did You create the serpent? Why did You permit him to enter Eden?"—these were the questions implied in her first excuse. Self-justification was indulged by our first parents as soon as they yielded to the influence of Satan, and it has been exhibited by all the sons and daughters of Adam.

The Lord then passed sentence upon the serpent: " 'Because you have done this, you are cursed more than all cattle, and more than every beast of the field; on your belly you shall go, and you shall eat dust all the days of your life.' " From the most beautiful of the creatures of the field it was to become the most groveling and detested of all, feared and hated by both man and beast. The words next addressed to the serpent applied to Satan himself, pointing to his ultimate defeat and destruction: " 'I will put enmity between you and the woman, and between your seed and her Seed; He shall bruise your head, and you shall bruise His heel.' "

Eve was told of the sorrow and pain that she must have. " 'Your desire shall be for your husband, and he shall rule over you.' " God had made her the equal of Adam. But sin brought friction, and now their union could be maintained and harmony preserved only by submission on the part of one or the other. Eve had been the first in transgression. By her urging Adam sinned, and she was now placed in subjection to her husband. Man's abuse of the supremacy thus given him has too often rendered the lot of woman bitter and her life a burden.

Eve had been happy by her husband's side. But she was flattered with the hope of entering a higher sphere than God had assigned her. In attempting to rise above her original position, she fell far below it. In their efforts to reach positions for which God has not fitted them, many today leave vacant the place where they might be a blessing.

To Adam the Lord declared: " 'Because you have heeded the voice of your wife, and have eaten from the tree of which I commanded you, saying, "You shall not eat of it": Cursed is the ground for your sake; in toil you shall eat of it all the days of your life. Both thorns and thistles it shall bring forth for you, and you shall eat the herb of the field. In the sweat of your face you shall eat bread till you return to the ground, for out of it you were taken; for dust you are, and to dust you shall return.' "

God had freely given them good and had withheld evil. But they had eaten of the forbidden tree, and now they would have the knowledge of evil—all the days of their life. Instead of happy labor, anxiety and toil were to be their lot. They would be subject to disappointment, grief, and pain, and finally to death.

God made the first pair rulers over the earth and all living creatures. But when they rebelled against the divine law, the inferior creatures rebelled against their rule. Thus the Lord in mercy would show people the sacredness of His law and lead them to see the danger of setting it aside, even in the slightest degree.

A Plan of Recovery for Humanity

The life of toil and care henceforth to the lot of humanity was appointed in love, a discipline rendered needful by sin, to place a check upon the indulgence of appetite and passion, to develop habits of self-control. It was a part of God's great plan for the recovery of the human race.

The warning given to our first parents—"In the day that you eat of it you shall surely die"—did not mean that they were to die on the very day they partook of the forbidden fruit. But on that day the irrevocable sentence would be pronounced. That very day they would be doomed to death.

In order to possess endless existence, a person must continue to partake of the tree of life. Deprived of this, the vitality would gradually diminish until life should become extinct. It was Satan's plan that Adam and Eve would eat of the tree of life and thus perpetuate an existence of sin and misery. But holy angels were commissioned to guard the tree of life. Around these angels flashed the appearance of a glittering sword. None of the family of Adam were permitted to pass that barrier; this is why there are no immortal sinners.

Is God Too Severe?

Most people regard the tide of woe that flowed from the transgression of our first parents as too awful a consequence for so small a sin. But if they would look more deeply into this question, they might recognize their error. In His great mercy God appointed Adam no severe test. The very lightness of the prohibition made the sin exceedingly great. If some great test had been appointed Adam, then those whose hearts incline to evil would have excused themselves saying, "This is a trivial matter, and God is not so particular about little things."

Many who teach that the law of God is not binding upon us urge that it is impossible to obey its precepts. But if this were true, why did Adam suffer the penalty of transgression? The sin of our first parents brought guilt and sorrow upon the world, and had it not been for the goodness and mercy of God, it would have plunged the race into hopeless despair. Let none deceive themselves. "The wages of sin is death." Romans 6:23.

After their sin, Adam and Eve begged to remain in the home of their innocence and joy. They pledged that in the future they would yield strict obedience to God. But they were told that their nature had become depraved by sin. They had lessened their strength to resist evil. Now, in a state of conscious guilt, they would have less power to maintain their integrity.

In sadness they said Goodbye to their beautiful home and went out to dwell on the earth, where the curse of sin rested. The atmosphere was now subject to marked changes, and the Lord mercifully provided them with a garment of skins as a protection from the cold.

As they witnessed in drooping flower and falling leaf the first signs of decay, Adam and his companion mourned more deeply than people now mourn over their dead. When the beautiful trees dropped their leaves, the scene brought to mind the stern fact that death is the fate of every living thing.

The Garden of Eden remained upon the earth long after its first inhabitants had become outcasts from its pleasant paths. But when the wickedness of Adam and Eve's descendants determined their destruction by a flood of waters, the hand that had planted Eden withdrew it from the earth. When God finally sets all things right, when there shall be "a new heaven and a new earth," it is to be restored, more gloriously adorned than at the beginning. Revelation 21:1.

The Plan of Redemption Is Unveiled

The fall of Adam and Eve filled all heaven with sorrow. There appeared no escape for those who had transgressed the law. Angels ceased their songs of praise.

The Son of God was touched with pity for the fallen race as the woes of the lost world rose up before Him. Divine love had conceived a plan to save the helpless ones. The broken law of God demanded the life of the sinner. Only one equal with God could make atonement for its transgression. None but Christ could save sinners from the curse of the law and bring them again into harmony with Heaven. Christ would take upon Himself the guilt and shame of sin to rescue the ruined race.

The plan of salvation had been laid before the creation of the earth, for Christ is "the Lamb slain from the foundation of the world" (Revelation 13:8); yet it was a struggle for the King of the universe to give up His Son to die for the guilty race. But "God so loved the world that He gave His only begotten Son, that whoever believes in Him should not perish but have everlasting life." John 3:16. Oh, the mystery of redemption! the love of God for a world that did not love Him!

God was to be revealed in Christ, "reconciling the world to Himself." 2 Corinthians 5:19. Human beings had become so degraded by sin that it was impossible for them to bring themselves into harmony with God, whose nature is purity and goodness. But Christ could give divine power to unite with human effort. Thus by repentance toward God and faith in Christ, the fallen children of Adam might once more become "children of God." 1 John 3:2.

The angels did not feel happy as Christ opened before them the plan of redemption. In grief and wonder they listened as He told them how He must come in contact with the degradation of earth, to endure sorrow, shame, and death. He would humble Himself as a man and become acquainted with the sorrows and temptations that men and women would have to endure in order that He might be able to aid those who are tempted. Hebrews 2:18. When His mission as a teacher would end, He must be subjected to every insult and torture that Satan could inspire. He must die the cruelest of deaths as a guilty sinner. He must endure anguish of soul, the hiding of His Father's face, while the sins of the whole world were to be upon Him.

The angels offered to become a sacrifice for the human race. But only He who created man had power to redeem him. Christ was to be made "a little lower than the angels, for the suffering of death." Hebrews 2:9. As He would take human nature upon Him, His strength would not be equal to that of the angels, and they were to strengthen Him in His sufferings. They were also to guard the subjects of grace from the power of evil angels.

When the angels would witness the agony and humiliation of their Lord, they would wish to deliver Him from His murderers, but they were not to step in. It was a part of the plan that Christ should suffer the scorn and abuse of wicked people.

Christ assured the angels that by His death He would ransom many and recover the kingdom that had been lost by transgression. The redeemed were to inherit it with Him. Sin and sinners would be blotted out, nevermore to disturb the peace of heaven or earth.

Then inexpressible joy filled heaven. Through the celestial courts echoed the first strains of that song that was to ring out above the hills of Bethlehem, " 'Glory to God in the highest, and on earth peace, good will toward men.' " Luke 2:14. " 'The morning stars sang together, and all the sons of God shouted for joy.' " Job 38:7.

God Promises a Savior

In the sentence pronounced on Satan in the garden, the Lord de-clared, " 'I will put enmity between you and the woman, and between your seed and her Seed; He shall bruise your head, and you shall bruise His heel.' " Genesis 3:15. This was a promise that the power of Satan, the great adversary, would finally be broken. Adam and Eve stood as criminals before the righteous Judge, but before they heard of the hard work and sorrow that must be their portion or that they must return to dust, they listened to words that could not fail to give them hope. They could look forward to final victory!

Satan knew that his work of depraving human nature would be interrupted, that by some means men and women would be enabled to resist his power. Yet Satan rejoiced with his angels that, having caused humankind to fall, he could bring down the Son of God from His exalted position. When Christ would take upon Himself human nature, He also might be overcome.

Heavenly angels more fully opened to our first parents the plan for their salvation. Adam and his companion were not to be abandoned to Satan. Through repentance and faith in Christ they might again become the children of God.

Adam and Eve saw as never before the guilt of sin and its results. They pleaded that the penalty might not fall on Him whose love had been the source of all their joy; rather let it come on them and their descendants.

They were told that since the law of Jehovah is the foundation of His government, even the life of an angel could not be accepted as a sacrifice for transgression. But the Son of God, who had created them, could make an atonement for them. As Adam's transgression had brought misery and death, so the sacrifice of Christ would bring life and immortality.

At his creation Adam was placed in dominion over the earth. But by yielding to temptation he became Satan's captive. The dominion passed to the one who had conquered him. Thus Satan became "the god of this world." 2 Corinthians 4:4, KJV. But Christ by His sacrifice would not only redeem the human family but recover the dominion they had forfeited. All that was lost by the first Adam will be restored by the second. See Micah 4:8.

God created the earth to be the home of holy, happy beings. That purpose will be fulfilled when, renewed by the power of God and freed from sin and sorrow, it shall become the eternal home of the redeemed.

The Terrible Fruits of Sin

Sin brought separation between God and the human family, and the atonement of Christ alone could span the abyss. God would communicate with people through Christ and angels.

Adam was shown that while the sacrifice of Christ would be sufficient to save the whole world, many would choose a life of sin rather than of repentance and obedience. Crime would increase through successive generations. The curse of sin would rest more and more heavily on the human race and the earth. The days of men and women would be shortened by their own course of sin; they would deteriorate in physical, moral, and intellectual power until the world would be filled with misery. Through the indulgence of appetite and passion, people would become incapable of appreciating the great truths of the plan of redemption. Yet Christ would supply the needs of all who would come unto Him in faith. There would ever be a few who would preserve the knowledge of God and remain pure.

The sacrificial offerings were ordained to show repentance for sin and to be a confession of faith in the promised Redeemer. To Adam the first sacrifice was painful. His hand must be raised to take life, which only God could give. It was the first time he had witnessed death. He knew that if he had been obedient to God there would have been no death. He trembled at the thought that his sin must shed the blood of Christ, the spotless Lamb of God. This gave him a vivid sense of the greatness of his transgression, for which nothing but the death of God's dear Son could atone. A star of hope illumined the dark future.

The Wider Purpose of Redemption

But the plan of redemption had a yet broader and deeper purpose than the salvation of the human race. It was not merely that the inhabitants of this little world might regard the law of God as it should be regarded, but it was to vindicate the character of God before the universe. To this the Savior looked forward when just before His crucifixion He said: " 'Now is the judgment of this world; now the ruler of this world will be cast out. And I, if I am lifted up from the earth, will draw all peoples to Myself.' " John 12:31, 32. Christ dying for the salvation of humanity would justify God and His Son in their dealing with the rebellion of Satan, establish the law of God, and reveal the nature and results of sin.

From the beginning, the great controversy had been over the law of God. Satan had sought to prove that God was unjust, His law faulty, and that the good of the universe required it to be changed. In attacking the law he aimed to overthrow the authority of God, its Author.

When Satan overcame Adam and Eve, he thought he had gained possession of this world, "because," said he, "they have chosen me as their ruler." He claimed it was impossible for forgiveness to be granted; the fallen race were his rightful subjects, and the world was his. But God gave His own Son to bear the penalty of transgression. Thus sinners might be restored to His favor and brought back to their Eden home. The great controversy, which began in heaven, was to be decided in the very world, on the same field, that Satan claimed as his.

It was the marvel of all the universe that Christ would humble Himself to save fallen men and women. When Christ came to our world in the form of humanity, all were intensely interested in following Him as He traveled the blood-stained path from the manger to Calvary. Heaven noted the insult and mockery that He received and knew that it was at Satan's instigation. They watched the battle between light and darkness as it grew stronger. And as Christ upon the cross cried out, " 'It is finished!' " (John 19:30), a shout of triumph rang through every world and through heaven itself. The great contest was now decided, and Christ was conqueror. His death answered the question whether the Father and the Son had sufficient love for the human race to exercise self-denial and a spirit of sacrifice. Satan had revealed his true character as a liar and murderer. With one voice the loyal universe united in praising the divine administration.

But if the law was abolished at the Cross, as many claim, then the agony and death of God's dear Son were endured only to give to Satan just what he wanted; then the prince of evil triumphed, and his charges against the divine government were sustained. The fact that Christ bore the penalty for human disobedience is a mighty argument that the law is changeless; that God is righteous, merciful, and self-denying; and that infinite justice and mercy unite in the administration of His government.

The First Murderer and His Victim*

Cain and Abel, the sons of Adam, differed widely in character. Abel saw justice and mercy in the Creator's dealings with the fallen race, and he gratefully accepted the hope of redemption. But Cain permitted his mind to run in the same channel that led to Satan's fall—questioning the divine justice and authority.

These brothers were tested to prove whether they would believe and obey the word of God. They understood the system of offerings that God had ordained. They knew they were to express faith in the Savior whom the offerings typified and at the same time to acknowledge total dependence on Him for pardon. Without the shedding of blood, there could be no remission of sin. They were to show their faith in the blood of Christ as the promised atonement by offering the firstborn of the flock in sacrifice.

The two brothers erected their altars alike, and each brought an offering. Abel presented a sacrifice from the flock. "And the LORD respected Abel and his offering." Genesis 4:4. Fire flashed from heaven and consumed the sacrifice. But Cain, disregarding the Lord's direct command, presented only an offering of fruit. There was no sign from heaven to show that it was accepted. Abel pleaded with his brother to approach God in the divinely prescribed way, but his appeals made Cain the more determined to follow his own will. As the eldest, he despised his brother's counsel.

Cain came before God with resentment in his heart. His gift expressed no real sorrow for sin, for it would be an admission of weakness to follow the exact plan marked out by God, of trusting his salvation completely to the atonement of the promised Savior. He would come in his own merits. He would not bring the lamb and mingle its blood with his offering but would present *his* fruits, the products of *his* labor, as a favor done to God. Cain obeyed in building an altar, obeyed in bringing a sacrifice, but gave only partial obedience. The essence—recognition of the need of a Redeemer—was left out.

Both of these brothers were sinners, and both acknowledged the

---

* This chapter is based on Genesis 4:1-15.

claims of God to reverence and worship. To outward appearance their religion was the same up to a certain point, but beyond this the difference was great.

The Great Difference Between Cain and Abel

"By faith Abel offered to God a more excellent sacrifice than Cain." Hebrews 11:4. Abel saw himself a sinner, and he saw sin and its penalty—death—standing between his soul and God. He brought the slain lamb, thus acknowledging the claims of the law that had been violated. Through the shed blood he looked to Christ dying on the cross. Trusting in the atonement there to be made, he had the assurance that he was righteous and his offering accepted.

Cain had the same opportunity of accepting these truths as had Abel. God had not chosen one brother to be accepted and the other rejected. Abel chose faith and obedience; Cain, unbelief and rebellion.

Cain and Abel represent two classes that will exist till the close of time. One avail themselves of the appointed sacrifice for sin; the other depend on their own merits. Those who feel no need of the blood of Christ, who feel that they can secure the approval of God by their own works, are making the same mistake as did Cain.

Nearly every false religion has been based on the same principle—that man can depend upon his own efforts for salvation. It is claimed by some that the human race can refine, elevate, and regenerate itself. As Cain thought to secure divine favor by an offering that lacked the blood of a sacrifice, so do these expect to exalt humanity to the divine standard, independent of the atonement of Jesus. The history of Cain shows that humanity does not tend upward toward the divine but downward toward the satanic. Christ is our only hope. See Acts 4:12.

True faith will be shown by obedience to all the requirements of God. From Adam's day to the present the great controversy has been over obedience to God's law. In all ages there have been those who claimed a right to the favor of God while disregarding some of His commands. But by works "faith was made perfect," and without the works of obedience, faith "is dead." James 2:22, 17. Anyone who professes to know God "and does not keep His commandments, is a liar, and the truth is not in him." 1 John 2:4.

When Cain saw that his offering was rejected, he was angry that God did not accept his substitute in place of the sacrifice divinely ordained, and he was angry with his brother for choosing to obey God instead of joining in rebellion against Him.

God did not leave him to himself but stooped to reason with the man who had shown himself so unreasonable. " 'Why are you angry? And why has your countenance fallen? If you do well, will you not be accepted? And if you do not do well, sin lies at the door.' " If he would trust to the merits of the promised Savior and obey God's requirements, he would enjoy God's favor. But if he persisted in unbelief and sin, he would have no ground to complain that he was rejected by the Lord.

Instead of acknowledging his sin, Cain continued to complain of the injustice of God and to cherish jealousy and hatred of Abel. In meekness, yet firmly, Abel defended the justice and goodness of God. He pointed out Cain's error and tried to convince him that the wrong was in himself. He pointed to the compassion of God in sparing the life of their parents when He might have punished them with instant death. He urged that God loved them or He would not have given His Son, innocent and holy, to suffer the penalty that they had earned. All this caused Cain's anger to burn the hotter. Reason and conscience told him that Abel was in the right, but he was enraged that he could gain no sympathy in his rebellion. In fury he killed his brother.

So in all ages the wicked have hated those who were better than themselves. " 'Everyone practicing evil hates the light and does not come to the light, lest his deeds should be exposed.' " John 3:20.

The murder of Abel was the first example of the enmity between the serpent and the seed of the woman— between Satan and his subjects and Christ and His followers. Whenever through faith in the Lamb of God a person renounces the service of sin, Satan's anger is kindled. The holy life of Abel testified against Satan's claim that it is impossible for human beings to keep God's law. When Cain saw that he could not control

Abel, he was so enraged that he destroyed his life. And wherever anyone stands in defense of the law of God, the same spirit will be manifested. But every martyr of Jesus has died a conqueror. See Revelation 12:9, 11.

Cain the murderer was soon called to answer for his crime. "The LORD said to Cain, 'Where is Abel your brother?' And he said, 'I do not know. Am I my brother's keeper?' " He resorted to falsehood to conceal his guilt.

The Punishment of Cain

Again the Lord said to Cain, " 'What have you done? The voice of your brother's blood cries out to Me from the ground.' " Cain had had time to reflect. He knew the terrible nature of the deed he had done and the falsehood he had spoken to conceal it; but he was rebellious still, and sentence was no longer postponed. The divine voice pronounced the terrible words: " 'So now you are cursed from the earth, which has opened its mouth to receive your brother's blood from your hand. When you till the ground, it shall no longer yield its strength to you. A fugitive and a vagabond you shall be on the earth.' "

A merciful Creator still spared Cain's life and granted him opportunity for repentance. But Cain lived only to harden his heart, to encourage rebellion against divine authority, and to be the head of a line of bold sinners. His influence exerted demoralizing power until the earth became so corrupt and filled with violence that it needed to be destroyed.

The dark history of Cain and his descendants was an illustration of what would have been the result of permitting the sinner to live on forever, to carry out his rebellion against God. The patience of God made the wicked only more bold and defiant. Fifteen centuries after the sentence pronounced upon Cain, crime and pollution flooded the earth. It became clear that the sentence of death on the fallen race was just and merciful. The longer people lived in sin, the more degraded and reckless they became.

Satan is constantly at work to misrepresent the character and government of God and to hold the inhabitants of the world under his deception. God sees the end from the beginning. His plans were far-reaching and comprehensive, not merely to put down the rebellion but to demonstrate to all the universe its nature, fully establishing His wisdom and righteousness in His dealings with evil.

The inhabitants of other worlds were watching with the deepest interest the condition of the world before the Flood. They saw the results of the kind of rule that Lucifer had tried to establish in heaven in casting aside the law of God. The thoughts of human hearts were only evil continually (Genesis 6:5), at war with the divine principles of purity, peace, and love. It was an example of awful wickedness.

By the facts unfolded in the great controversy God carries with Him the sympathy of the whole universe, as step by step His great plan advances to its fulfillment in the final complete destruction of rebellion. It will be seen that all who have rejected the divine precepts have placed themselves on the side of Satan, in warfare against Christ. When the prince of this world shall be judged, and all who have united with him shall share his fate, the whole universe will declare, " 'Just and true are Your ways, O King of the saints!' " Revelation 15:3.

Seth, When Men Turned to God[*]

To Adam was given another son to be the heir of the spiritual birthright. The name Seth, given to this son, signified "appointed," or "compensation"; " 'for,' " said the mother, " 'God has appointed another seed for me instead of Abel, whom Cain killed.' " Seth resembled Adam more closely than did his other sons, a worthy character following in the steps of Abel. Yet he inherited no more natural goodness than did Cain. Seth, like Cain, inherited the fallen nature of his parents. But he also received the knowledge of the Redeemer and instruction in righteousness. He labored, as Abel would have done, to turn the minds of sinners to revere and obey their Creator.

"As for Seth, to him also a son was born; and he named him Enosh. Then men began to call on the name of the LORD." The distinction between the two classes became more marked—an open profession of loyalty to God on the part of one, contempt and disobedience on the part of the other.

Before the Fall, our first parents had kept the Sabbath, which was instituted in Eden, and after their expulsion from Paradise they continued to observe it. They had learned what everyone will sooner or later learn, that the divine laws are sacred and unchangeable and that the penalty of transgression will surely follow. The Sabbath was honored by all who remained loyal to God. But Cain and his descendants did not respect the day upon which God had rested.

Cain now founded a city and called it by the name of his eldest son. He had gone out from the presence of the Lord to seek possessions and enjoyment in the earth, standing at the head of that great class of people who worship the god of this world. In that which relates to mere earthly and material progress, his descendants became distinguished. But they were in opposition to the purposes of God for the human race. To the crime of murder, Lamech, the fifth in descent from Cain, added polygamy. Abel had led a pastoral life, and the descendants of Seth followed the same course, counting themselves "strangers and pilgrims on the earth," seeking "a better, that

---

[*] *This chapter is based on Genesis 4:25 to 6:2.*

is, a heavenly country." Hebrews 11:13, 16.

For some time the two classes remained separate. The race of Cain, spreading from their first settlement, scattered over the plains and valleys where the children of Seth had dwelt. The latter, in order to escape their contaminating influence, withdrew to the mountains and there continued the worship of God in its purity. But after some time they began to mingle with the inhabitants of the valleys. "The sons of God saw the daughters of men, that they were beautiful." The children of Seth displeased the Lord by intermarrying with them. Many of the worshipers of God were drawn into sin by the allurements constantly before them, and they lost their holy character. Mingling with the depraved, they became like them. The restrictions of the seventh commandment were disregarded, "and they took wives for themselves of all whom they chose." The children of Seth went "in the way of Cain." Jude 11. They fixed their minds on worldly prosperity and enjoyment and neglected the commandments of the Lord. Sin spread abroad in the earth.

Length of Adam's Life

For nearly a thousand years Adam tried to stop the spread of evil. He had been commanded to instruct his descendants in the way of the Lord, and he carefully treasured what God had revealed to him and repeated it to succeeding generations. For nine generations he described the holy and happy condi-

tions in Paradise and repeated the history of his fall. He told them of the sufferings by which God had taught him the necessity of strict adherence to His law and explained to them the merciful provisions for their salvation. Yet often he was met with bitter reproach for the sin that had brought such woe upon his descendants.

When he left Eden, the thought that he must die thrilled Adam with horror. Filled with sorrow for his own sin and mourning a double loss in the death of Abel and the rejection of Cain, Adam was bowed down with anguish. Though the sentence of death had appeared terrible at first, yet after beholding the results of sin for nearly a thousand years, he felt that it was merciful for God to bring to an end a life of suffering and sorrow.

The age before the Flood was not, as has often been supposed, an era of ignorance and barbarism. The people possessed great physical and mental strength, and their advantages were unrivaled. Their mental powers developed early, and those who cherished the fear of God continued to increase in knowledge and wisdom throughout their lives. Compared to them, famous scholars of our time would appear greatly inferior in mental and physical strength. As people's lifespan has decreased and their physical strength has diminished, so their mental capacities have lessened.

It is true that the people of modern times have the benefit of the accomplishments of others before them. Masterly minds have left their work for those who follow. But how much greater the advantages of the people of that time! For hundreds of years they had among them him who was formed in God's image. Adam had learned from the Creator the history of creation; he himself witnessed the events of nine centuries. The pre-Flood people had strong memories to retain what was communicated to them and to transmit it accurately to their descendants. For hundreds of years there were seven generations living on the earth at the same time, profiting by the knowledge and experience of all.

Far from being an era of religious darkness, that was an age of great light. All the world had opportunity to receive instruction from Adam, and those who feared the Lord also had Christ and angels for their teachers. And they had a silent witness to the truth, in the garden of God, which for many centuries remained on earth. Eden stood just in sight, its entrance barred by watching angels. The purpose of the garden and the history of its two trees were undisputed facts. And the existence and supreme authority of God were truths that people were slow to question while Adam was among them.

Despite the prevailing iniquity, a holy line of God's followers lived as in the companionship of heaven— people of massive intellect, of wonderful attainments. They had a great mission—to develop a character of righteousness, to teach a lesson of godliness, not only to the people of their time, but for future generations.

Only a few are mentioned in the Scriptures, but all through the ages God had faithful witnesses, true-hearted worshipers.

Enoch—The First Man Never to Die

Enoch lived sixty-five years and fathered a son. After that he walked with God three hundred years. He was one of the preservers of the true faith, the ancestors of the promised Seed. From the lips of Adam he had learned the story of the Fall and of God's grace as seen in the promise, and he relied upon the Redeemer to come.

But after the birth of his first son, Enoch reached a higher experience. As he saw the child's love for its father, its simple trust in his protection, as he felt the deep tenderness of his own heart for that firstborn son, he learned a precious lesson of the wonderful love of God in the gift of His Son. The boundless love of God through Christ became the subject of his meditations day and night, and he tried to reveal that love to the people around him.

Enoch's walk with God was not in a trance or vision but in all the duties of daily life. As a husband and father, a friend, a citizen, he was the unwavering servant of the Lord.

His heart was in harmony with God's will; for "can two walk together, unless they are agreed?" Amos 3:3. And this holy walk continued for three hundred years. Enoch's faith grew stronger, his love more ardent, with the passing of centuries.

Enoch was a man of vast knowledge, honored with special revelations from God, yet he was one of the humblest of men. He waited before the Lord. To him prayer was as the breath of the soul; he lived in the very atmosphere of heaven.

Through holy angels God revealed to Enoch His purpose to destroy the world by a flood. He also opened the plan of redemption more fully to him and showed him the great events connected with the second coming of Christ and the end of the world.

Enoch had been troubled in regard to the dead. It had seemed to him that the righteous and the wicked would go to the dust together and that this would be their end. He could not see the life of the just beyond the grave. In prophetic vision he was instructed concerning the death of Christ and His coming in glory, attended by all the holy angels, to ransom His people from the grave. He also saw the corrupt state of the world when Christ would appear the second time—that there would be a boastful, self-willed generation trampling upon the law and despising the atonement. He saw the righteous crowned with glory and honor and the wicked destroyed by fire.

Enoch became a preacher of righteousness, making known God's messages to all who would hear. In the land where Cain had tried to flee from the divine presence, the prophet made known the wonderful scenes that he had been shown. " 'Behold, ' " he declared, " 'the Lord comes with ten thousands of His saints, to execute judgment on all, to convict all

who are ungodly among them of all their ungodly deeds.' " Jude 14, 15.

While he preached the love of God in Christ, he rebuked the prevailing sins and warned that judgment would surely come upon the transgressor. It is not smooth things only that are spoken by holy men. God puts into the lips of His messengers truths that are sharp and cutting as a two-edged sword.

Some gave heed to the warning, but the multitudes went on more boldly in their evil ways. So will the last generation make light of the warnings of the Lord's messengers.

In the midst of a life of active labor, Enoch steadfastly maintained his fellowship with God. After remaining for a time among the people, he would spend time alone, hungering and thirsting for divine knowledge. Communing with God, Enoch came to reflect the divine image more and more. His face was radiant with the light that shines in the face of Jesus.

As year after year passed, deeper and deeper grew the tide of human guilt, darker and darker gathered the clouds of divine judgment. Yet Enoch kept on his way, warning, pleading, working to turn back the tide of guilt. Though his warnings were ignored by a sinful, pleasure-loving people, he had the assurance that God approved. He continued to battle against evil until God removed him from a world of sin to the pure joys of heaven.

Enoch Is Translated to Heaven

The people of that generation had mocked Enoch because he did not seek to build up possessions here. But his heart was upon eternal treasures. He had seen the King in His glory in the midst of Zion. His mind, his way of living, were in heaven. The greater the existing iniquity, the more earnest was his longing for the home of God.

For three hundred years Enoch had walked with God. Day by day he had longed for a closer union; nearer and nearer had grown the relationship, until God took him to Himself. Now the walk with God, which he had so long pursued on earth, continued, and he passed through the gates of the Holy City—the first from among earth's inhabitants to enter there.

His loss was felt on earth. Some, both righteous and wicked, had witnessed his departure. Those who loved him made diligent search, but without avail. They reported that he "was not," for God had taken him.

By the translation of Enoch the Lord designed to teach an important lesson. There was danger that men and women would yield to discouragement because of the fearful results of Adam's sin. Many were ready to exclaim, "What good is it that we have feared the Lord and have kept His laws, since a heavy curse is resting upon the race, and death is the reward of us all?" Satan was urging the belief that there was no reward for the righteous or punishment of the wicked and that it was impossible for human beings to obey the divine statutes. But in the case of Enoch, God shows what He will do for those who keep His commandments. People were taught that it is possible to obey the law of God, that they were able by grace to resist temptation and become pure and holy. His being taken to heaven was an evidence of the truth of his prophecy concerning the hereafter, with its award of immortal life to the obedient and of condemnation and death to the transgressor.

"By faith Enoch was translated so that he did not see death, . . . for before his translation he had this testimony, that he pleased God." Hebrews 11:5. The godly character of this prophet represents the state of holiness that must be attained by those who shall be "redeemed from the earth" (Revelation 14:3) at Christ's second advent. Then, as before the Flood, sin will prevail. Many will rebel against the authority of Heaven. But, like Enoch, God's people will seek for purity of heart and conformity to His will until they shall reflect the likeness of Christ. Like Enoch they will warn the world of the Lord's second coming and by their holy example will condemn the sins of the ungodly. As Enoch was translated to heaven, so the living righteous will be translated from the earth before its destruction by fire. See 1 Corinthians 15:51, 52; 1 Thessalonians 4:16-18.

When the World Was Destroyed by Water*

In the days of Noah a double curse was resting upon the earth as a result of Adam's sin and the murder committed by Cain. Yet the earth was still beautiful. The hills were crowned with majestic trees; the plains were sweet with the fragrance of a thousand flowers. The fruits of the earth were almost without limit. The trees far surpassed in size and perfect proportion any that now exist. Their wood was of fine grain and hard substance, resembling stone and hardly less enduring. Gold, silver, and precious stones existed in abundance.

The human race still retained much of its early vigor. There were many giants known for their wisdom, skillful in devising the most ingenious and wonderful works, but letting iniquity run loose.

God bestowed rich gifts on these pre-Flood people, but they used His bounties to glorify themselves and turned them into a curse by setting their affections on the gifts instead of the Giver. They tried to outdo one another in beautifying their dwellings with skillful workmanship. They reveled in scenes of pleasure and wickedness. Not wanting to keep God in their knowledge, they soon came to deny the He exists. They glorified human genius, worshiped the works of their own hands, and taught their children to bow down to graven images.

The psalmist describes the effect produced on the worshiper by the adoration of idols: "Those who make them are like them; so is everyone who trusts in them." Psalm 115:8. It is a law of the human mind that by beholding we become changed. If the mind is never raised above the level of humanity, if it is not uplifted to contemplate infinite wisdom and love, humankind will be constantly sinking lower and lower. "The LORD saw that the wickedness of man was great in the earth, and that every intent of the thoughts of his heart was only evil continually. . . . The earth also was corrupt before God, and the earth was filled with violence." His law was transgressed, and every imaginable sin was the result. Justice was trampled in the dust, and the cries of the oppressed reached to heaven.

---

* This chapter is based on Genesis 6 and 7.

Human Life Regarded With Indifference

Polygamy had been introduced early, though it was contrary to God's plan. The Lord gave one wife to Adam. But after the Fall people chose to follow their own sinful desires. As a result, crime and misery increased rapidly. Neither marriage nor the rights of property were respected. People reveled in violence. They delighted in destroying animals, and the use of flesh for food made them still more cruel and bloodthirsty, until they came to regard human life with indifference.

The world was in its infancy, yet evil had become so deep and widespread that God said, "I will destroy man whom I have created from the face of the earth." He declared that His Spirit would not always strive with the guilty race. If they did not cease their sins He would blot them from His creation; He would sweep away the beasts and the vegetation that furnished such an abundant supply of food and would transform the fair earth into one vast scene of ruin.

A Ship to Preserve Life

One hundred twenty years before the Flood, the Lord told Noah His plan and directed him to build an ark. He was to preach that God would bring a flood of water on the earth. Those who would believe the message and would prepare by repentance and reformation would find pardon and be saved. Methuselah and his sons, who lived to hear the preaching of Noah, assisted in building the ark.

God gave Noah the exact dimensions of the ark and instructed him how to build it. Human wisdom could not have designed a structure so strong and durable. God was the architect and Noah the master builder. It was three stories high, with only one door in the side. Light was admitted at the top, and the different apartments were so arranged that all were lighted. The material was cypress or gopher wood, which would be untouched by decay for hundreds of years. Building this huge structure was a slow process. Because of the size of the trees and the nature of the wood, much more work was required then than now to prepare timber. Everything humanly possible was done to make the work perfect, yet the ark on its own could not have withstood the storm. God alone could preserve His servants on the raging waters.

"By faith Noah, being divinely warned of things not yet seen, moved with godly fear, prepared an ark for the saving of his household, by which he condemned the world and became heir of the righteousness which is according to faith." Hebrews 11:7. While Noah gave his warning message, his faith was perfected and made evident, an example of believing just what God says. All that he possessed he invested in the ark. As he began to construct that immense boat, crowds came from every direction to see the strange sight and to hear the earnest words of the preacher.

At first, many appeared to receive the warning, yet they did not turn to God with true repentance. Overcome by the widespread unbelief, they finally joined their former associates in rejecting the solemn message. Some were convicted and would have heeded the warning, but so many people were ridiculing Noah that they entered into the same spirit, resisted the invitations of mercy, and were soon among the boldest scoffers. None go to such lengths in sin as do those who have once had light but have resisted the convicting Spirit of God.

Not all the people of that generation were idolaters. Many claimed to be worshipers of God. They said that their idols were representations of the Deity and that through them the people could obtain a clearer concept of the divine Being. Such people were leaders in rejecting the preaching of Noah, and they finally declared that the divine law was no longer in force and that it was contrary to the character of God to punish disobedience. Their minds had become so blinded by rejecting the light that they really believed Noah's message to be a delusion.

The world was set against God's justice and His laws, and Noah was regarded as a fanatic. Great men—worldly, honored and wise—said, "The threatenings of God are for the purpose of intimidating and will never come true. The destruction of the world by the God who made it and the punishment of the beings He has created will never take place. Fear not, Noah is a wild fanatic." They continued their disobedience and wickedness, as though God had not spoken through His servant.

But Noah stood like a rock in a storm. Connection with God made him strong in the strength of infinite power. For one hundred twenty years his solemn voice fell on the ears of that generation, warning of events which, as far as human wisdom could judge, were impossible.

Up to that time rain had never fallen; the earth had been watered by a mist or dew. The rivers had never yet passed their boundaries but had carried their waters safely to the sea. God's fixed decrees had kept the waters from overflowing their banks. See Job 38:11.

But time passed on; people whose hearts at times had trembled with fear began to be reassured. They reasoned that nature is above the God of nature. If the message of Noah were correct, nature would be turned out of her course. They showed their contempt for the warning of God by doing the same as they had done before the warning was given. They continued their festivities and gluttonous feasts. They ate and drank, planted and built, laying plans for the future. They claimed that if there were any truth in what Noah had said, the people of renown—the wise, the prudent, and the great people—would understand the matter.

The time of their probation was about to end. The ark was finished exactly as the Lord had directed and was stored with food for humans and animals. And now the servant of God made his last solemn appeal to the people. Noah pleaded with them to seek a refuge while there was still time. Again they rejected his words and raised their voices in scoffing.

Suddenly beasts of every description were seen coming from mountain and forest, quietly making their way toward the ark. Birds were flocking from all directions, and in perfect order passed to the ark. Animals "went into the ark to Noah" two by two, and the clean beasts by sevens. Philosophers were called upon to account for this unique event, but they could not explain it. The doomed race banished their rising fears by merriment and seemed to invite upon themselves the awakened wrath of God.

God commanded Noah, "Come into the ark, you and all your household, because I have seen that you are righteous before Me in this generation." His influence and example resulted in blessings to his family. God saved all the members of his family with him.

An Angel Shuts the Door

The beasts of the field and the birds of the air had entered the place of refuge. Noah and his household were within the ark, "and the LORD shut him in." The massive door, impossible for those inside to close, was slowly swung into place by unseen hands. Noah was shut in and the rejecters of God's mercy were shut out. So the door of mercy will be shut when Christ shall cease His ministry for guilty sinners before He comes in the clouds of heaven. Then divine grace will no longer restrain

the wicked, and Satan will have full control of those who have rejected mercy. They will try to destroy God's people; but as Noah was shut into the ark, so the righteous will be shielded by divine power.

For seven days after Noah and his family entered the ark, there was no sign of the coming storm. During this period their faith was tested. It was a time of triumph to the world outside. They continued making a joke of the exhibits of God's power. They gathered in crowds around the ark, making fun of its inmates with a reckless boldness that they had never dared to show before.

But on the eighth day dark clouds overspread the heavens. The muttering of thunder and the flash of lightning followed. Soon large drops of rain began to fall. The world had never witnessed anything like this, fear struck every heart. All were secretly inquiring, "Can it be that Noah was right and that the world is doomed?" The animals were roaming about in the wildest terror. Then "the fountains of the great deep were broken up, and the windows of heaven were opened." The clouds poured out rain like mighty waterfalls. Rivers broke away from their boundaries and overflowed the valleys. Jets of water burst from the earth with indescribable force.

The people first saw their splendid buildings and beautiful gardens and groves in which they had placed their idols destroyed by lightning from heaven. Altars on which human sacrifices had been offered were torn down, and the worshipers were made to tremble at the power of the living God.

As the violence of the storm increased, the terror of humans and animals was beyond description. Above the roar of the tempest was heard the wailing of men and women who had despised the authority of God. Satan himself, compelled to remain among the warring elements, feared for his own life. He now uttered curses against God. Many of the people, like Satan, blasphemed God. Others were frantic with fear, stretching their hands toward the ark, pleading to be let in. Conscience was at last aroused to know that there is a God who rules in the heavens.

They called upon Him earnestly, but His ear was not open to their cry. In that terrible hour they saw that transgression of God's law had caused their ruin. Yet they felt no true humility and sorrow, no horror of evil. They would have returned to their defiance of Heaven if the judgment had been removed.

Some clung to the ark until they were carried away by the surging waters or their hold was broken by colliding with rocks and trees. The massive ark trembled in every fiber as it was beaten by the merciless winds. The cries of animals within expressed their fear and pain. But the ark continued to ride safely. Angels were sent to preserve it.

Some of the people tied their children and themselves on powerful animals, knowing that these would climb to the highest points to escape the rising waters. Some fastened themselves to lofty trees on the hills or mountains, but the trees were uprooted and hurled into the waves. As the waters rose higher the people fled for refuge to the tallest mountains. Often people and animals struggled together for a foothold until both were swept away.

From the highest peaks the desperate people looked abroad upon a shoreless ocean. The solemn warnings of God's servant no longer seemed a subject for ridicule. Those doomed sinners pleaded for one hour's probation, one more call from the lips of Noah! But love, no less than justice, demanded that God's judgments should put a restraint on sin. The despisers of God perished in the black depths.

Conditions Before the Flood

The sins that called for vengeance upon the pre-Flood world exist today. The fear of God is banished from human hearts. His law is treated with indifference and contempt. " 'For as in the days before the flood, they were eating and drinking, marrying and giving in marriage, until the day that Noah entered the ark, and did not know until the flood came and took them all away, so also will the coming of the Son of Man be.' " Matthew 24:38, 39. God did not condemn the pre-Flood generation for eating and drinking. He had given the fruits of the earth to meet their physical wants. Their sin was in taking these gifts without gratitude to the Giver, indulging appetite without restraint. It was lawful to marry. He gave special directions concerning this relationship, clothing it with holiness and beauty. But marriage was perverted and made to serve passion.

Similar Conditions Today

A similar condition exists today. Appetite is indulged without restraint. Professed followers of Christ are eating and drinking with the drunken. Intemperance numbs the moral and spiritual powers and prepares for indulgence of the lower passions. Multitudes become slaves of lust, living for the sensual pleasures. Extravagance saturates society. People sacrifice integrity for luxury and display. Fraud, bribery, and theft go unrebuked. The media report many crimes so cold-blooded that it seems as though every instinct of humanity were blotted out. And these atrocities have become so common that they hardly produce surprise. The pent-up fires of lawlessness, having once escaped control, will fill the earth with woe and desolation. The pre-Flood world represents the condition to which modern society is rushing.

God sent Noah to warn the world, so that the people could be led to repentance and escape the threatened destruction. As the time of Christ's second coming draws near, the Lord sends His servants with a warning to prepare for that great event. Multitudes have been living in violation of God's law, and now in mercy He calls them to obey its sacred commands. All who will put away their sins by repentance and faith in Christ are offered pardon. But many reject His warnings and deny the authority of His law.

Out of the vast population of the earth before the Flood, only eight people believed and obeyed God's word through Noah. So before the Lawgiver shall come to punish the disobedient, sinners are warned to repent; but the majority will not heed these warnings. "Scoffers will come in the last days, walking according to their own lusts, and saying, 'Where is the promise of His coming? For since the fathers fell asleep, all things continue as they were from the beginning.' " 2 Peter 3:3, 4.

Jesus asked the significant question, " 'When the Son of man comes, will He really find faith on the earth?' " Luke 18:8. "The Spirit expressly says that in latter times some will depart from the faith, giving heed to deceiving spirits and doctrines of demons." 1 Timothy 4:1. "In the last days perilous times will come." 2 Timothy 3:1.

When Probation Closes

As the time for their salvation was closing, the people before the Flood gave themselves up to exciting amusements, filling their lives with mirth and pleasure. In our day the world is absorbed in pleasure-seeking. A constant round of excitement prevents the people from being impressed by the truths that alone can save them from coming destruction.

In Noah's day philosophers declared that it was impossible for the world to be destroyed by water. So now scientific minds try to show that the world cannot be destroyed by fire. But when everyone considered Noah's prophecy a delusion, then it was that God's time had come. The Lawgiver is greater than the laws of nature. " 'As it was in the days of Noah,' " " 'even so will it be in the day when the Son of Man is revealed.' " Luke 17:26, 30. "The day of the Lord will come as a thief in the night, in which the heavens will pass away with a great noise . . . ; both the earth and the works that are in it will be burned up." 2 Peter 3:10.

When religious teachers are pointing forward to ages of peace and prosperity and the people of the world are absorbed in planting and building, feasting and merrymaking, rejecting God's warnings and mocking His messengers—then it is that "sudden destruction comes upon them. . . . And they shall not escape." 1 Thessalonians 5:3.

After the Flood, a New Beginning*

The waters rose above the highest mountains. It often seemed to the family within the ark that they would die, as for five long months their boat was tossed about. It was a terrible ordeal, but Noah's faith did not waver.

As the waters began to subside, the Lord caused the ark to drift into a spot protected by a group of mountains preserved by His power. These mountains were only a little distance apart, and the ark moved about in this quiet area. This gave great relief to the weary, storm-tossed voyagers.

Noah and his family longed to go out again on the earth. Forty days after the tops of the mountains became visible, they sent out a raven to discover whether the earth had become dry. This bird, finding nothing but water, continued to fly to and from the ark. Seven days later a dove was sent forth. It found no footing and returned to the ark. Noah waited seven days longer and again sent forth the dove. When she returned at evening with an olive leaf in her mouth, there was great rejoicing. Still Noah waited patiently for special directions to leave the ark.

At last an angel opened the massive door and told the patriarch and his household to go out on the earth and take with them every living thing. Noah did not forget the One by whose gracious care they had been preserved. His first act was to build an altar and offer sacrifice, thus expressing his gratitude to God for deliverance and his faith in Christ, the great sacrifice. This offering was pleasing to the Lord, and a blessing resulted not only to Noah and his family but to all who would live upon the earth. "The LORD said in His heart, 'I will never again curse the ground for man's sake. . . . While the earth remains, seedtime and harvest, cold and heat, winter and summer, and day and night, shall not cease.' " Noah had come out onto a desolate earth, but before preparing a house for himself he built an altar to God. His stock of cattle was small, yet he cheerfully gave a part to the Lord to acknowledge that all was His. Likewise, we should acknowledge His mercy toward us by devotion and gifts to His cause.

---

* This chapter is based on Genesis 7:20 to 9:7.

The Rainbow—Sign of God's Kindness

So that people would not fear another flood, the Lord encouraged the family of Noah by a promise: " 'I establish My covenant with you: . . . never again shall there be a flood to destroy the earth. . . . I set My rainbow in the cloud, and it shall be for the sign of the covenant between Me and the earth. . . . When I bring a cloud over the earth, . . . the rainbow shall be seen in the cloud; . . . and I will look on it to remember the everlasting covenant between God and every living creature.' "

How great the condescension of God and His compassion for His wayward creatures!

This does not imply that God would ever forget, but He speaks to us in terms that we can understand. When the children would ask the meaning of the arch that spans the heavens, their parents were to repeat the story of the Flood and tell them that the Most High had placed it in the clouds as an assurance that the waters would never again overflow the earth. It would testify of divine love for humanity and strengthen their confidence in God.

In heaven a likeness of the rainbow encircles the throne and arches over the head of Christ. Ezekiel 1:28; Revelation 4:2, 3. When humanity's great wickedness invites divine judgments, the Savior, interceding with the Father, points to the bow in the clouds, to the rainbow around the throne, as a token of mercy toward the repentant sinner.

" 'As I have sworn that the waters of Noah would no longer cover the earth, so have I sworn that I would not be angry with you, nor rebuke you. . . . My kindness shall not depart from you, nor shall My covenant of peace be removed,' says the LORD, who has mercy on you." Isaiah 54:9, 10.

As Noah looked at the powerful beasts of prey as they came out of the ark, the Lord sent an angel with the assuring message: " 'The fear of you and the dread of you shall be on every beast of the earth, on every bird of the air, on all that move on the earth, and on all the fish of the sea. They are given into your hand. Every moving thing that lives shall be food for you. I have given you all things, even as the green herbs.' " Before this time God had given no permission to eat animals for food; but now that every green thing had been destroyed, He allowed them to eat the flesh of the clean animals that had been preserved in the ark.

The entire surface of the earth was changed at the Flood. Everywhere dead bodies lay on the ground. The Lord would not permit these to remain to decompose and pollute the air. A violent wind, which was caused to dry up the waters, moved them with great force. In some instances it even carried away the tops of mountains and heaped up trees, rocks, and earth above the bodies of the dead. By the same means the silver and gold, choice wood and precious stones, which had enriched the world before the Flood, were concealed. The violent action of the waters piled earth and rocks upon these treasures and even formed mountains above them. God saw that the more He enriched and prospered sinners, the more they would corrupt their ways before Him.

The mountains, once beautiful, had become broken and irregular. Ledges and ragged rocks were now scattered on the surface of the earth. Where once earth's richest treasures of gold, silver, and precious stones had been, the heaviest marks of the curse were seen. And on countries not inhabited and those where there had been the least crime, the curse rested more lightly.

More terrible manifestations than the world has yet seen will be witnessed at the second advent of Christ. As lightnings from heaven unite with the fire in the earth, the mountains will burn like a furnace and pour forth terrific streams of lava, overwhelming gardens and fields, villages and cities. Everywhere there will be dreadful earthquakes and eruptions.

Thus God will destroy the wicked from off the earth. But the righteous will be preserved, as Noah was preserved in the ark. Says the psalmist: "Because you have made the LORD, who is my refuge, even the Most High, your dwelling place, no evil shall befall you." Psalm 91:9, 10; see also verse 14 and Psalm 27:5.

The Beginning of the Literal Week

Like the Sabbath, the week had its beginnings at creation, and it has been preserved through Bible history. God Himself measured off the first week. It consisted of seven 24-hour days. Six days were employed in the work of creation. On the seventh God rested, then set it apart as a day of rest for humanity. " 'Remember the Sabbath day, to keep it holy. . . . For in six days the LORD made the heavens and the earth, the sea, and all that is in them, and rested the seventh day. Therefore the LORD blessed the Sabbath day and hallowed it.' " Exodus 20:8-11.

This reason appears beautiful and forcible when we understand the days of creation to be literal. The first six days of each week are given to us for labor. On the seventh day we are to refrain from labor to commemorate the Creator's rest.

But the teaching that the events of the first week required thousands upon thousands of years is godlessness in its most subtle and dangerous form. Its real character is so disguised that it is held and taught by many who profess to believe the Bible. "By the word of the LORD the heavens were made, and all the host of them by the breath of His mouth." Psalm 33:6. The Bible recognizes no long ages in which the earth slowly evolved from disorder. Of each successive day of creation, the sacred record declares that it consisted of the evening and the morning, like all other days that have followed.

Geologists claim to find evidence from the earth that it is very much older than the Bible teaches. Bones of men and animals much larger than any that now exist have been discovered, and from this many conclude that the earth was populated long before the time brought to view in the record of creation. Such reasoning has led many professed Bible believers to adopt the position that the days of creation were vast, indefinite periods.

But apart from Bible history, geology can prove nothing. Relics found in the earth do give evidence of conditions differing from the present in many respects, but the time when these conditions existed can be learned only from the Inspired Record. In the history of the Flood inspiration has explained that which geology alone could never discover. In the days of Noah, men, animals, and trees many times larger than now exist were buried and thus preserved as an evidence to later generations that the inhabitants perished by a flood. God designed that the discovery of these things should establish faith in inspired history. But many today, with their false reasoning, fall into the same error as did the people before the Flood—the things that God gave them as a benefit they turn into a curse by making a wrong use of them.

There is a constant effort to explain creation as the result of natural causes, and even professed Christians accept human reasoning in opposition to Scripture facts. Many oppose investigating the prophecies, especially Daniel and the Revelation, declaring that we cannot understand them. Yet these very persons eagerly receive the suppositions of geologists in contradiction of Moses' account. Just how God accomplished the work of creation He has never revealed to us; human science cannot search out the secrets of the Most High. See Deuteronomy 29:29.

Those who leave the Word of God and try to account for His created works on scientific principles are drifting without chart or compass on an unknown ocean. The greatest minds, if not guided by the Word of God in their research, become bewildered in their attempts to find the relationship between science and revelation. Those who doubt the records of the Old and New Testaments will be led to go a step further and doubt the existence of God. Then, having lost their anchor, they are left to beat about on the rocks of godless despair.

The Bible is not to be tested by human ideas of science. Skeptics, through an imperfect comprehension of either science or revelation, claim to find contradictions between them; but rightly understood they are in perfect harmony. Moses wrote under the guidance of the Spirit of God, and a correct theory of geology will never claim discoveries that cannot be harmonized with his statements.

True Science and the Bible Agree

In the Word of God many questions are raised that scholars can never answer. There is much among the common things of everyday life that human minds with all their boasted wisdom can never fully understand.

Yet scientists think they can comprehend the wisdom of God. The idea is widespread that He is restricted by His own laws. People either deny or ignore His existence or think to explain everything, even the operation of His Spirit on the human heart; and they no longer reverence His name.

Many teach that nature operates in harmony with fixed laws with which God Himself cannot interfere. This is false science. Nature is the servant of her Creator. God does not set aside His laws but is continually using them as His instruments. In nature there is the continual working of the Father and the Son. Christ says, " 'My Father has been working until now, and I have been working.' " John 5:17.

As regards this world, God's work

of creation is completed. "The works were finished from the foundation of the world." Hebrews 4:3. But His energy is still exerted in upholding the objects of His creation. Every breath, every beat of the heart, is an evidence of the universal care of Him in whom " 'we live and move and have our being.' " Acts 17:28. The hand of God guides the planets and keeps them in position. He "brings out their host by number; He calls them all by name, by the greatness of His might and the strength of His power; not one is missing." Isaiah 40:26. Through His power vegetation flourishes, the leaves appear, and the flowers bloom. He "makes grass to grow on the mountains" (Psalm 147:8), and by Him the valleys are made fruitful. "All the beasts of the forest . . . seek their food from God" (Psalm 104:20, 21), and every living creature, from the smallest insect to the full-gown human, is daily dependent upon His providential care.

All true science is in harmony with His works; all true education leads to obedience to His government. Science opens new wonders to our view; she soars high and explores new depths, but she brings nothing from her research that conflicts with divine revelation. The book of nature and the Written Word shed light on each other.

We may be ever searching, ever learning, and still there is an infinity beyond. The works of creation testify of God's power and greatness. See Psalm 19:1. Those who take the Written Word as their counselor will find in science an aid to understand God. "Since the creation of the world His invisible attributes are clearly seen, being understood by the things that are made, even His eternal power and Godhead." Romans 1:20.

When Languages Were Changed*

To repopulate the desolate earth God had preserved only one family, the household of Noah. To him God declared, " 'I have seen that you are righteous before Me in this generation.' " Genesis 7:1. Yet in the three sons of Noah—Shem, Ham, and Japheth—the character of their descendants was foreshadowed.

Noah, speaking by divine inspiration, foretold the history of the three great races that would be fathered by these three men. Tracing the descendants of Ham through the son rather than the father, He declared, " 'Cursed be Canaan; a servant of servants he shall be to his brethren.' " The unnatural crime of Ham revealed the corruption of his character. These evil characteristics continued in Canaan and his descendants.

On the other hand, the reverence shown by Shem and Japheth for God's laws promised a brighter future for their descendants. Concerning these sons it was declared, " 'Blessed be the LORD, the God of Shem, and may Canaan be his servant. May God enlarge Japheth, and may he dwell in the tents of Shem;

and may Canaan be his servant.' " The line of Shem was to be that of the chosen people. From him would descend Abraham, and the people of Israel, through whom Christ was to come. And Japheth will " 'dwell in the tents of Shem.' " The descendants of Japheth were especially to share in the blessings of the gospel.

The family line of Canaan descended to the most degrading forms of heathenism. Though the prophetic curse had doomed them to slavery, God bore with their corruption until they passed the limits of divine restraint. Then they became slaves to the descendants of Shem and Japheth.

The prophecy of Noah did not determine the character and destiny of his sons. But it showed what would be the result of the path they had chosen and the character they had developed. As a rule, children inherit the dispositions and tendencies of their parents and imitate their example. Thus the corruption and irreverence of Ham were reproduced in his posterity, bringing a curse upon them for many generations.

---

* *This chapter is based on Genesis 9:25-27; 11:1-9.*

On the other hand, how richly rewarded was Shem's respect for his father, and what a noble and honored line of holy men appears in his descendants!

For a time, the descendants of Noah continued to live among the mountains where the ark had rested. As their numbers increased, apostasy led to division. Those who wanted to forget their Creator and throw off the restraint of His law felt constantly annoyed by the teaching and example of their God-fearing associates. After a time they decided to separate. So they moved to Shinar on the banks of the Euphrates River, attracted by the beauty of the landscape and the fertility of the soil.

Here they decided to build a city and in it a tower so high that it would be the wonder of the world. God had directed people to disperse throughout the earth, but these Babel builders determined to keep their community united and to establish a kingdom that would embrace the whole earth. Thus their city would become the capital of a universal empire. Its glory would draw the admiration and praise of the world. The magnificent tower, reaching to the heavens, was meant to stand as a monument of the power and wisdom of its builders.

Those who settled on the plain of Shinar disbelieved God's covenant that He would not bring a flood upon the earth again. One purpose in erecting the tower was to secure their safety in case of another deluge. And because they would be able to go up to the region of the clouds, they hoped to learn the cause of the Flood. The whole undertaking was to exalt the pride of its developers and to turn future generations away from God.

When the tower had been partially completed, suddenly the work that had been advancing so well was stopped. Angels were sent to block the plan of the builders. The tower had reached a great height, and the workers were stationed at different points, each to receive and report to the one next below him the orders for needed material. As messages were passing from one to another, the language was confused so that the directions delivered were often the opposite of those that had been given. All work came to a standstill. The builders were completely unable to account for the strange misunderstandings among them. In their rage and disappointment they blamed one another. As an evidence of God's displeasure, lightnings from heaven broke off the upper portion of the tower and cast it to the ground.

God's Purpose in Changing Their Language

Up to this time, everyone had been speaking the same language. Now those who could understand one another's speech united in groups. Some went one way and some another. "The LORD scattered them abroad from there over the face of all the earth." This spread people all over the earth; and thus the Lord's plan was accomplished through the very means by which some had tried to prevent its fulfillment.

But at what a loss! It was God's plan that as people would go out to different parts of the earth they would carry with them the light of truth. Noah, the faithful preacher of righteousness, lived for three hundred fifty years after the Flood, and Shem for five hundred years; as a result, their descendants had opportunity to learn the requirements of God and the history of His dealings with the human race. But they had no desire to keep God in their knowledge; and by the confusion of languages they were largely shut out from communicating with those who might have given them light.

Satan was trying to bring contempt on the sacrificial offerings that pointed to the death of Christ. As the minds of the people were darkened by idolatry, he led them to counterfeit these offerings by sacrificing their own children on the altars of their gods. As people turned away from God, the divine traits of character—justice, purity, and love—were replaced by oppression, violence, and brutality.

The residents of Babel had determined to establish a government independent of God. Some among them, however, feared the Lord. For the sake of these faithful ones, the Lord delayed His judgments and gave the people time to reveal their true character. The followers of God tried to turn them from their plan, but the people were fully united in their Heaven-daring project. If they had gone on unhindered, they would have corrupted the world in its infancy. If this alliance had been permitted, a mighty power would have emerged to banish righteousness—and with it peace, happiness, and security—from the earth.

Those who feared the Lord cried out to Him to intervene. "But the Lord came down to see the city and the tower which the sons of men had built." In mercy to the world He defeated the plans of the tower-builders. In mercy He confused their speech, hindering their rebellion. God bears long with human wickedness, giving opportunity for repentance. From time to time His unseen hand is stretched out to restrain iniquity. The world receives unmistakable evidence that the Creator of the universe is the Supreme Ruler of heaven and earth. None can defy His power without reaping the results!

There are tower builders in our time. Humanists dare to pass sentence on God's moral government. They despise His law and boast of human reason. Then, "because the sentence against an evil work is not executed speedily, therefore the heart of the sons of men is fully set in them to do evil." Ecclesiastes 8:11.

Today's Tower of Babel

Many turn from the plain teachings of the Bible and build up a creed from human speculations and pleasing fables. They point to their "tower" as a way to climb up to heaven. Eloquent lips teach that the sinner will not die, that salvation may be had without obedience to the law of God. If the professed followers of Christ would accept God's standard, it would bring them into unity. But as long as human wisdom is exalted above God's Holy Word, there will be divisions and dissension. The existing confusion of conflicting beliefs and denominations is fitly represented by the term *Babylon*, which prophecy applies to the world-loving churches of the last days. See Revelation 14:8; 18:2.

The time of God's investigation is at hand. His sovereign power will be revealed; the works of human pride will be laid low.

Abraham, the Father of All Believers*

After Babel, idolatry again became nearly universal, and the Lord finally left the hardened sinners to follow their evil ways, while He chose Abraham, a descendant of Shem, and made him the keeper of His law for future generations. God has always had a remnant to preserve the precious revealings of His will. Abraham inherited this holy trust. Uncorrupted by the widespread apostasy, he faithfully persisted in worshiping God. The Lord communicated His will to Abraham and gave him a knowledge of His law and of salvation through Christ.

God promised Abraham, " 'I will make you a great nation; I will bless you and make your name great; and you shall be a blessing.' " To this was added the assurance that the Redeemer of the world would come from his descendants: " 'In you all the families of the earth shall be blessed.' " Yet, as the first condition of fulfillment, there was to be a test of faith; a sacrifice was demanded.

The message of God came to Abraham, " 'Get out of your country, from your family and from your father's house, to a land that I will show you.' " Abraham must be separated from the influence of relatives and friends. His character must be distinct, differing from all the world. He could not even explain his action so that his friends would understand. His idolatrous family did not comprehend his motives.

Abraham's unquestioning obedience is one of the most striking evidences of faith in all the Bible. See Hebrews 11:8. Relying on the divine promise, he abandoned home and family and native land and went out to follow where God would lead. "By faith he sojourned in the land of promise as in a foreign country, dwelling in tents with Isaac and Jacob." Hebrews 11:9.

There were strong ties to bind him to his country, his relatives, and his home. But he did not hesitate to obey the call. He asked no questions concerning the land of promise—whether the soil was fertile, the climate healthful. The happiest place on earth was the place where God wanted him to be.

Many are still tested as was Abraham. They do not hear the voice of God speaking directly from heaven,

---

This chapter is based on Genesis 12.

but He calls them by the teachings of His Word and the events of His leading. They may be required to abandon a career that promises wealth and honor and to separate from family in order to start out on what appears to be a path of self-denial and sacrifice. God has a work for them to do; the influence of friends and family would hinder it.

Who is ready, at the call of God, to renounce cherished plans, accept new duties, and enter unfamiliar fields? Those who will do this have the faith of Abraham and will share with him that "far more exceeding and eternal weight of glory." 2 Corinthians 4:17. See also Romans 8:18.

The call from heaven first came to Abraham in "Ur of the Chaldeans," and in obedience he moved to Haran. This far his father's family accompanied him. Here Abraham remained till the death of Terah.

Into the Unknown

But after his father died the divine voice called him to go forward. Besides Sarah, the wife of Abraham, only Lot chose to share the pilgrim life. Abraham possessed large flocks and many servants. He was never to return, and he took with him all that he had, "all their possessions that they had gathered, and the people whom they had acquired in Haran." In Haran both Abraham and Sarah had led others to the worship of the true God. These went with him to the land of promise, "the land of Canaan."

The place where they first stayed was Shechem. Abraham made his camp in a wide, grassy valley, with its olive groves and gushing springs. It was a beautiful and fertile country, " 'a land of brooks of water, . . . of wheat and barley, of vines and fig trees and pomegranates, a land of olive oil and honey.' " Deuteronomy 8:7, 8. But a heavy shadow rested on wooded hill and fruitful plain. In the groves were set up the altars of false gods, and human sacrifices were offered on nearby hills.

Then "the LORD appeared to Abram and said, 'To your descendants I will give this land.' " His faith was strengthened by this assurance. "And there he built an altar to the LORD, who had appeared to him." Still a traveler, he soon journeyed to a spot near Bethel and again built an altar and called on the name of the Lord.

Abraham set us a worthy example. His was a life of prayer. Wherever he pitched his tent, close beside he set up his altar, calling all within his camp to the morning and evening sacrifice. When he moved away, the altar remained. Roving Canaanites received instruction from Abraham, and wherever any of these came to that altar, they worshiped the living God there.

Why God Permitted Abraham to Suffer Famine

Abraham continued to travel southward, and again his faith was tested. The heavens withheld their rain, and the flocks and herds found no pasture. Starvation threatened the whole camp. All were eagerly watching to see what Abraham would do, as trouble after trouble came. As long as his confidence appeared unshaken, they felt that there was hope; they were assured that God was his friend and that He was still guiding him.

Abraham clung to the promise, " 'I will bless you and make your name great; and you shall be a blessing.' " He would not allow circumstances to shake his faith in God's word. To escape the famine he went down to Egypt. In his great trouble he did not turn back to the Chaldean land from which he came but looked for a temporary home as near as possible to the Land of Promise.

The Lord in His wisdom had brought this trial on Abraham to teach him lessons for the benefit of everyone after him who would be called to endure affliction. God does not forget or cast off those who put their trust in Him. The trials that test our faith most severely and make it seem that God has forsaken us are to lead us closer to Christ. We may lay all our burdens at His feet and experience in exchange the peace that He will give us.

The heat of the furnace is what separates the dross from the true gold of Christian character. By difficult, testing trials God disciplines His servants. He sees that some have powers that may be used in the advancement of His work. In His wisdom He brings them into positions that test their character and reveal weaknesses of which they were unaware. He gives them opportunity to correct these defects. He shows them

their own weakness and teaches them to lean on Him. In this way they are educated, trained, and disciplined, prepared to fulfill the grand purpose for which their powers were given to them. Heavenly angels can unite with them in the work to be accomplished on earth.

Abraham's Sad Mistake

In Egypt, Abraham showed that he was not free from human weakness. His wife, Sarah, was "very beautiful," and he was sure that the Egyptians would covet the lovely stranger and kill her husband. He reasoned that he was not guilty of lying in describing Sarah as his sister, for she was the daughter of his father, though not of his mother.

But this was deception. Through Abraham's lack of faith, Sarah was placed in great danger. The king of Egypt ordered her to be taken to his palace, intending to make her his wife. But the Lord, in His great mercy, protected Sarah by sending judgment on the royal household. By this means the king learned that he had been deceived. He reproved Abraham, saying, " 'What is this you have done to me? . . . Why did you say, "She is my sister"? I might have taken her as my wife. Now therefore, here is your wife; take her and go your way.' "

Pharaoh's dealing with Abraham was kind and generous, but he told him to leave Egypt. He had ignorantly been about to do Abraham a serious injury, but God had saved the monarch from committing such a great sin. Pharaoh saw in this stranger a man whom God honored. If Abraham remained in Egypt, his increasing wealth and honor would likely excite the envy or covetousness of the Egyptians, and some injury might be done to him which might again bring judgments on the royal house.

The matter could not be kept secret. It was seen that the God whom Abraham worshiped would protect His servant and that any harm done to him would be avenged. It is a dangerous thing to wrong one of the children of the King of heaven. The psalmist says that God "reproved kings for their sakes, saying, 'Do not touch My anointed ones, and do My prophets no harm.' " Psalm 105:14, 15.

Abraham, a Good Neighbor in Canaan*

Abraham returned to Canaan "very rich in livestock, in silver, and in gold." Lot was with him, and they came to Bethel and pitched their tents. Through hardships and trials they had lived together in harmony, but in their prosperity there was danger of conflict. There was not enough pasture for the flocks and herds of both. It was evident that they must separate.

Abraham was the first to propose plans for preserving peace. Although the whole land had been given to him by God Himself, he courteously chose not to demand this right. " 'Let there be no strife,' " he said, " 'between you and me, and between my herdsmen and your herdsmen; for we are brethren. Is not the whole land before you? Please separate from me. If you take the left, then I will go to the right; or, if you go to the right, then I will go to the left.' "

Many people under similar circumstances would cling to their individual rights and preferences. Many households and many churches have been divided, making the cause of truth a scandal and a disgrace among the wicked. The children of God all over the world are one family, and the same spirit of love and peacemaking should govern them. "Be kindly affectionate to one another with brotherly love, in honor giving preference to one another." Romans 12:10. A willingness to do to others as we would wish them to do to us would prevent or end half the troubles of life. The heart in which the love of Christ is cherished will possess that unselfish love that "does not seek its own." See also Philippians 2:4.

Lot showed no gratitude to his generous uncle. Instead, he selfishly tried to grasp all the advantages. He "lifted his eyes and saw all the plain of Jordan, that it was well watered everywhere, . . . like the garden of the Lord, like the land of Egypt." The most fertile region in all Palestine was the Jordan valley, reminding its viewers of the lost Paradise and equaling the beauty and productiveness of the Nile-enriched plains they had left. There were cities, wealthy and beautiful, inviting to profitable commerce. Dazzled with visions of worldly gain, Lot overlooked the moral evils found there.

---

* This chapter is based on Genesis 13 to 15; 17:1-16; 18.

He "chose for himself all the plain of Jordan," and "pitched his tent even as far as Sodom." Little did he foresee the terrible results of that selfish choice!

Soon after this, Abraham moved to Hebron. In the free air of those upland plains with their olive groves and vineyards, their fields of grain, and the wide pasture of the encircling hills, he settled, content with his simple life, leaving to Lot the perilous luxury of Sodom.

Abraham did not shut away his influence from his neighbors. In contrast to the worshipers of idols, his life and character exerted a telling influence in favor of the true faith. His loyalty to God was unswerving, and his friendliness and kindness inspired confidence and friendship.

While Christ is dwelling in the heart, it is impossible to conceal the light of His presence. It will grow brighter as the mists of selfishness and sin that envelop the soul are dispelled by the Sun of Righteousness.

The people of God are lights in the moral darkness of this world. Scattered in towns, cities, and villages, they are channels through which God will communicate to an unbelieving world the knowledge and wonders of His grace. It is His plan that all who receive salvation will be lights that shine brightly in the character, revealing the contrast with the selfish darkness of the natural heart.

Abraham was wise in diplomacy and brave and skillful in war. Three royal brothers, rulers of the Amorite plains in which he lived, showed friendship by inviting him to enter an alliance with them for greater security, for the country was filled with violence and oppression. An occasion soon arose for him to call on the help of this alliance.

Lot Rescued by Abraham

Chedorlaomer, king of Elam, had invaded Canaan years before and made it subject to him. Several of its princes now revolted, and the Elamite king again marched into the country to reduce them to submission. Five kings of Canaan fought the invaders, only to be completely defeated. The victors plundered the cities of the plain and left with rich spoils and many captives, among whom were Lot and his family.

From one who had escaped, Abraham learned the story of the calamity that had befallen his nephew. All his affection for him was awakened, and he determined to rescue Lot. Seeking divine counsel, Abraham prepared for war. From his own camp he called up three hundred eighteen trained servants, men trained in the fear of God, in the service of their master, and in the practice of arms. His allies, Mamre, Eshcol, and Aner, joined him, and together they started after the invaders. The Elamites had encamped at Dan, on the northern border of Canaan. Proud and excited with victory, they had given themselves up to celebrating. Abraham came upon the encampment by night. His attack, so vigorous and unexpected, resulted in speedy victory. The king of Elam was killed and his panic-stricken forces fled in defeat. Lot and his family, with all the prisoners and goods, were recovered, and the riches of the enemy fell into the hands of the victors.

Abraham had not only performed a great service for the country but had proved himself a man of valor. It was seen that Abraham's religion made him courageous in upholding the right and defending the oppressed. When Abraham returned, the king of Sodom came out to honor the conqueror, asking only that the prisoners be restored. The spoils belonged to the conquerors; but Abraham refused to take advantage of the unfortunate, only requiring that his allies receive the portion to which they were entitled.

If given such a test, few would have resisted the temptation to secure such rich plunder. Abraham's example is a rebuke to self-seeking. " 'I have raised my hand,' " he said, " 'to the LORD, God Most High, the Possessor of heaven and earth, that I will take nothing, from a thread to a sandal strap, and that I will not take anything that is yours, lest you should say, "I have made Abram rich." ' " God had promised to bless Abraham, and the glory should go to Him.

Another who came out to welcome victorious Abraham was Melchizedek, king of Salem. As "priest of God Most High," he pronounced a blessing on Abraham and gave thanks to the Lord, who had brought about deliverance by His servant. And Abraham "gave him a tithe of all."

Abraham Is Afraid

Abraham had been a man of peace, shunning strife as much as possible. With horror he recalled the carnage he had witnessed. The nations whose forces he had defeated would certainly renew the invasion and take special revenge on him. Furthermore, he had not begun to take possession of Canaan, nor could he now hope for an heir to whom the promise might be fulfilled.

In a vision of the night the divine voice was heard again. " 'Do not be afraid, Abram. I am your shield, your exceedingly great reward.' " But how was the covenant promise to be fulfilled while the gift of a son was withheld? " 'What will You give me,' " he said, " 'seeing I go childless? . . . Indeed one born in my house is my heir!' " He intended to make his trusty servant Eliezer his son by adoption. But he was assured that a child of his own was to be his heir. Then he was told to look up to the countless stars glittering in the heavens, and the words were spoken, " 'So shall your descendants be.' " " 'Abraham believed God, and it was accounted to him for righteousness.' " Romans 4:3.

The Lord stooped down to enter into a covenant with His servant. Abraham heard the voice of God, telling him not to expect immediate possession of the Promised Land, and pointing forward to the sufferings of his descendants before Canaan would be theirs. The plan of redemption was opened to him in the death of Christ, the great sacrifice, and His coming in glory. Abraham also saw the earth restored to Eden beauty, given for an everlasting inheritance as the final and complete fulfillment of the promise.

When Abraham had been nearly twenty-five years in Canaan, the Lord appeared to him and said, " 'Behold, My covenant is with you, and you shall be a father of many nations.' " In pledge of the fulfillment of this covenant, his name Abram was changed to Abraham, "father of a great multitude." Sarai's name became Sarah—"princess," for " 'she shall be a mother of nations; kings of peoples shall be from her.' "

At this time the rite of circumcision was given to Abraham, to be observed by him and his descendants as a sign that they were separated from idolaters and that God accepted them as His special treasure. They were not to marry the heathen, for by so doing they would be tempted to engage in the sinful practices of other nations and be drawn into idolatry.

Abraham Unwittingly Entertains Angels

God conferred great honor on Abraham. Angels walked and talked with him. When judgments were about to be visited on Sodom, the fact was not hidden from him, and he became an intercessor with God for sinners.

In the hot summer noontide Abraham was sitting in his tent door when he saw three travelers in the distance. Before they reached his tent, the strangers stopped. Without waiting for them to ask any favors, with the utmost courtesy Abraham urged them to honor him by staying for refreshment. With his own hands he brought water that they might wash the dust of travel from their feet. He selected food, and while they were resting under the cooling shade, he stood respectfully beside them while they ate and drank what he provided. Years later an inspired apostle referred to this act of courtesy: "Do not forget to entertain strangers, for by so doing some have unwittingly entertained angels." Hebrews 13:2.

Abraham had seen in his guests only three tired travelers, not thinking that among them One was divine, whom he might worship without sin. But the true character of the heavenly messengers was now revealed. They were on their way as agents of wrath, yet to Abraham they spoke first of blessings. God takes no delight in vengeance.

Abraham had honored God and the Lord honored him, revealing to him His purposes. " 'Shall I hide from Abraham what I am doing?' " said the Lord. " 'The outcry against Sodom and Gomorrah is great, and because their sin is very grave, I will go down now and see whether they have done altogether according to the outcry against it that has come to Me; and if not, I will know.' " God knew Sodom's guilt, but He expressed Himself in human terms that His justice might be understood. He would go Himself to conduct an examination of their course. If they had not passed the limits of divine mercy,

He would grant them opportunity for repentance.

Two of the heavenly messengers departed, leaving Abraham alone with the One whom he now knew to be the Son of God. And the man of faith pleaded for the inhabitants of Sodom. Once he had saved them by his sword; now he tried to save them by prayer. Lot and his household were still living there, and Abraham attempted to save them from the storm of divine judgment.

With deep humility he urged his plea: " 'I who am but dust and ashes have taken it upon myself to speak to the Lord.' " He did not claim favor because of his obedience or the sacrifices he had made in doing God's will. As a sinner, he pleaded in the sinner's behalf. Yet Abraham showed the confidence of a child pleading with a loved father. Though Lot had taken up residence in Sodom, he did not join in the sins of its inhabitants. Abraham thought that there must be other worshipers of the true God in that populous city. He pleaded, " 'Far be it from You. . . to slay the righteous with the wicked. . . . Shall not the Judge of all the earth do right?' " As his requests were granted, he gained the assurance that if even ten righteous persons could be found in Sodom, the city would be spared.

Abraham's prayer for Sodom shows that we should cherish hatred of sin but pity and love for the sinner. All around us people are going down to ruin. Every hour some are passing beyond the reach of mercy. Where are the voices of invitation, urging sinners to flee from this fearful doom? Where are those who are pleading with God for them?

Who Prays for "Sodom" Today?

The spirit of Abraham was the spirit of Christ, who is the great Intercessor in the sinner's behalf. Christ extended toward the sinner a love that infinite goodness alone could imagine. In the agonies of the crucifixion, burdened with the awful weight of the sins of the whole world, He prayed for His murderers, " 'Father, forgive them, for they do not know what they do.' " Luke 23:34.

The testimony of God is, " 'Abraham obeyed My voice and kept My charge, My commandments, My statutes, and My laws.' " " 'I have known him, in order that he may command his children and his household after him, that they keep the way of the LORD, to do righteousness and justice, that the LORD may bring to Abraham what He has spoken to him.' " It was a high honor to which Abraham was called—to be father of the people who were the guardians of the truth of God for the world, through whom all nations would be blessed in the coming of the Messiah. Abraham would keep the law and deal justly and righteously. And he would not only fear the Lord himself but would instruct his family in doing right.

Abraham's household numbered more than a thousand people. Here, as in a school, they received instruction that would prepare them to represent the true faith. He was training heads of families, and they would follow his methods of government in their own households.

It was necessary to bind the members of the household together, to build up a barrier against the widespread idolatry. Abraham worked to guard all those who were with him against mingling with the heathen and seeing their idol worship. He took care to impress the mind with the majesty and glory of the living God as the true object of worship.

God Himself had separated Abraham from his idolatrous relatives so that he might educate his family apart from the evil influences in Mesopotamia and preserve the true faith in its purity through his descendants.

The Influence of Daily Living

Abraham's children and household were taught that they were under the rule of the God of heaven. There was to be no oppression by the parents and no disobedience by the children. The silent influence of his daily life was a constant lesson. There was a fragrance about the life, a nobility of character, which revealed to everyone that he was connected with Heaven. He did not neglect the humblest servant. His household did not have one law for the master and another for the servant. He treated all with justice and compassion as heirs with him of the grace of life.

How few in our day follow this example! Too many parents show a blind and selfish sentimentalism, mistakenly called love, that leaves children to the control of their own will. This is cruelty to the youth and a great wrong to the world. Their parents' laxness strengthens the desire of young people to follow their own wishes instead of submitting to God's requirements. They then grow up to transmit their irreligious, rebellious spirit to their children and grandchildren. Obedience to parental authority should be taught as the first step in obedience to the authority of God.

The widespread teaching that God's laws are no longer binding has the same effect on the morals of the people as idolatry. Parents do not command their household to keep the way of the Lord. Children, as they make homes of their own, feel no obligation to teach their children what they themselves have never been taught. This is why there are so many godless families, and why wickedness is so widespread.

A reformation is needed, deep and broad. Parents and ministers need to reform; they need God in their households. They must bring His Word into their families and teach their children kindly and untiringly how to live in order to please God. The children of such a household have a foundation that cannot be swept away by the incoming tide of irreligion and doubt.

In many households parents feel they cannot spare a few moments to thank God for the sunshine and showers and for the protection of holy angels. They have no time for prayer. They go out to labor as the ox or the horse, without one thought of God or heaven. The Son of God gave His life to ransom them, but they have little more appreciation of His goodness than animals do.

If ever there was a time when every house should be a house of prayer, it is now. The father, as priest of the household, should offer to God a morning and evening sacrifice of prayer, while the wife and children unite with him in prayer and praise. Jesus will love to stay in such a household.

From every home love should flow out in thoughtful kindness, in gentle, unselfish courtesy. There are homes where God is worshiped and the truest love reigns. His mercies and blessings fall on these praying ones like morning dew.

A well-ordered household is a powerful argument in favor of the Christian religion. A noble influence at work in the family affects the children. The God of Abraham is with them. God speaks to every faithful parent: "I know him, that he will command his children and his household after him, and they shall keep the way of the LORD, to do justice and judgment" (KJV).

The Offering of Isaac, Test of Faith*

Abraham had accepted the promise of a son, but he did not wait for God to fulfill His word in His own time and way. God permitted a delay to test his faith, but he failed to endure the trial.

In her old age, Sarah suggested a plan by which the divine purpose might be fulfilled—that Abraham take one of her handmaidens as a secondary wife. Polygamy was no longer regarded as a sin, but it was a violation of the law of God and was fatal to the sacredness and peace of the family. Abraham's marriage with Hagar resulted in evil—not only to his own household but to future generations.

Flattered with her new position as Abraham's wife and hoping to be the mother of the great nation to descend from him, Hagar became proud. Jealousies between Sarah and Hagar disturbed the peace of the once happy home. Forced to listen to the complaints of both, Abraham tried to restore harmony, but without success. Though Sarah had urged him to marry Hagar, she now blamed him as the one at fault. She wanted to exile her rival. But Abraham refused to permit this, because Hagar was to be the mother of his child—as he dearly hoped, the son of promise. She was Sarah's servant, however, and he still left her to the control of her mistress. "When Sarai dealt harshly with her, she fled from her presence."

She made her way to the desert. As she rested, lonely and friendless, beside a spring, an angel appeared. Addressing her as "Hagar, Sarai's maid," he told her, " 'Return to your mistress, and submit yourself under her hand.' " Yet with the reproof were mingled words of comfort: " 'The Lord has heard your affliction.' " " 'I will multiply your descendants exceedingly, so that they shall not be counted for multitude.' " She was instructed to name her child Ishmael, "God shall hear."

When Abraham was nearly one hundred years old, the promise of a son was repeated: " 'Sarah your wife shall bear you a son, and you shall call his name Isaac; I will establish My covenant with him.' " " 'As for Ishmael,' " He said, " 'behold, I have blessed him, . . . and I will make him a great nation.' "

---

* This chapter is based on Genesis 16; 17:18-20; 21:1-14; 22:1-19.

Polygamy Brings Sorrow

The birth of Isaac filled the tents of Abraham and Sarah with gladness, but to Hagar this event was the overthrow of her deeply cherished ambitions. Everyone had thought of Ishmael as the heir of Abraham's wealth and the inheritor of the blessings promised to his descendants. Now he was suddenly set aside. Mother and son hated the child of Sarah.

The general rejoicing increased their jealousy, until Ishmael dared to mock openly the heir of God's promise. In Ishmael's stormy disposition Sarah saw an unending source of discord, and she appealed to Abraham to send Hagar and Ishmael away.

Abraham was thrown into great distress. How could he banish Ishmael his son, whom he still loved dearly? In his perplexity he pleaded for divine guidance. Through a holy angel the Lord directed him to grant Sarah's desire; in this way he could restore harmony and happiness to his family. The angel gave him the promise that God would not forsake Ishmael and that he would become the father of a great nation. Abraham obeyed, but not without keen suffering. The father's heart was heavy as he sent Hagar and his son away.

The sacredness of marriage was to be a lesson for all time. The rights and happiness of this relationship are to be carefully guarded, even at great sacrifice. Sarah was the only true wife of Abraham. No other person was entitled to share her rights. She was unwilling for Abraham to give his affections to another, and the Lord did not reprove her for requiring her rival to be sent away.

An Example for All Generations

Abraham was to stand as an example of faith to later generations. But his faith had not been perfect. He had shown distrust of God in marrying Hagar. So that he might reach the highest standard, God subjected him to another test, the most severe that any mortal was ever asked to endure. In a vision of the night he was directed to offer his son as a burnt offering on a mountain that God would show him.

Abraham had reached the age of one hundred twenty years. The strength of his youth had passed. In the vigor of manhood one may courageously meet difficulties and afflictions that would cause the heart to fail later in life. But God had reserved His most trying test for Abraham until the burden of years was heavy on him and he longed for rest.

Abraham was very rich and was honored as a mighty prince by the rulers of the land. Heaven seemed to have crowned with blessing his life of sacrifice and patient endurance.

Abraham Commanded to Offer Isaac

In faithful obedience, Abraham had left his native country and had wandered as a stranger in the land he was to inherit. He had waited long for the birth of the promised heir. At the command of God he had sent Ishmael away. And now, when it seemed his hopes were about to come true, a trial greater than all others was before him.

The command must have wrung that father's heart with anguish: " 'Take now your son, your only son Isaac, whom you love, . . . and offer him there as a burnt offering.' " Isaac was the light of his home, the comfort of his old age, the inheritor of the promised blessing, but he was commanded to shed the blood of that son with his own hand. It seemed a fearful impossibility.

Satan was there to suggest that he must be deceived, for God's law commands, "You shall not kill." God would not require what He had forbidden. Going outside his tent, Abraham remembered the promise that his descendants were to be as countless as the stars. If this promise was to be fulfilled through Isaac, how could he be put to death? Abraham bowed upon the earth and prayed as he had never prayed before for some confirmation of the command if he must perform this terrible duty. He remembered the angels who were sent to reveal God's purpose to destroy Sodom and who gave him the promise of this same son Isaac. He went to the place where he had met the heavenly messengers, hoping to receive some further direction; but none came. The command of God was sounding in his ears, " 'Take now your son, your only son Isaac, whom you love.' " That command he must obey. Day was approaching, and he must be on his journey.

Isaac lay sleeping the untroubled sleep of youth and innocence. For a moment the father looked upon the dear face of his son then turned away trembling. He went to Sarah, who also was sleeping. Should he awaken her? He longed to unburden his heart to her and share with her this terrible responsibility, but he did not dare. Isaac was her joy and pride; the mother's love might refuse the sacrifice.

Three Sad Days

Abraham at last awakened his son, telling him of the command to offer sacrifice on a distant mountain. Isaac had often gone with his father to worship, and this brought no surprise. The wood was made ready and put on the donkey, and with two servants they set out.

Father and son journeyed in silence, Abraham pondering his heavy secret. His thoughts were of the proud, adoring mother, and the day when he would have to return to her alone. He knew that the knife would pierce her heart when it took the life of her son.

That day—the longest Abraham had ever experienced—dragged slowly to its close. He spent the night in prayer, still hoping that some heavenly messenger might say that the youth could return unharmed to his mother. But no relief came to his tortured soul.

Another long day. Another night of humiliation and prayer. The command to slay his son was ringing in his ears. Satan was near to whisper doubts and unbelief, but Abraham resisted his suggestions.

As they were about to begin the journey of the third day, Abraham saw the promised sign, a cloud of glory hovering over Mount Moriah. He knew that the voice that had spoken to him was from heaven.

Even now he did not complain against God. This son had been given unexpectedly; didn't the One who bestowed the precious gift have a right to reclaim His own? Then faith repeated the promise, " 'In Isaac your seed shall be called' "—a seed numberless as the grains of sand on the shore. Isaac was the child of a miracle, and couldn't the power that gave him life restore it? Abraham grasped the divine word, "accounting that God was able to raise him up, even from the dead." Hebrews 11:19.

Yet none but God could understand how great was the father's sacrifice in yielding up his son to death. Abraham desired that none but God should witness the parting scene. He told his servants to remain behind, saying, " 'The lad and I will go yonder and worship, and we will come back to you.' "

The wood was laid upon Isaac, the father took a knife and the fire, and together they started up toward the mountain summit. The young man at last spoke, " 'My father, . . . look, the fire and the wood, but where is the lamb for a burnt offering?' "

What a test this was! How the endearing words, " 'my father,' " pierced Abraham's heart! Not yet—he could not tell him now. " 'My son,' " he said, " 'God will provide for Himself the lamb for a burnt offering.' "

At the appointed place they built the altar and laid the wood upon it. Then, with trembling voice, Abraham told Isaac the divine message.

Trained to Obey

With terror and amazement Isaac learned his fate, but he offered no resistance. He could have escaped if he had chosen. The old man, exhausted with the struggle of those three terrible days, could not have opposed the will of the vigorous youth. But Isaac had been trained from childhood to give ready obedience, and as the purpose of God was opened to him, he yielded a willing submission. He shared in Abraham's faith, and he felt honored in being called to give his life as an offering to God.

And now the last words of love were spoken, the last tears shed, the last embrace given. The father lifted the knife. Suddenly an angel of God called from heaven, " 'Abraham, Abraham!' " He quickly answered, " 'Here I am.' " Again the voice was heard: " 'Do not lay your hand on the lad, or do anything to him; for now I know that you fear God, since you have not withheld your son, your only son, from Me.' "

Then Abraham saw "a ram caught in a thicket," and quickly he offered it "instead of his son." In his joy and gratitude, Abraham gave a new name to the sacred spot—Jehovah-jireh, "the-Lord-Will-Provide."

The Promise to Abraham Repeated

On Mount Moriah, with a solemn oath, God again confirmed the blessing to Abraham and to his descendants: " 'Because you have done this thing, and have not withheld your son, your only son—blessing I will bless you, and multiplying I will multiply your descendants as the stars of the heaven and as the sand which is on the seashore; and your descendants shall possess the gate of their enemies. In your seed all the nations of the earth shall be blessed; because you have obeyed My voice.' "

Abraham's great act of faith stands like a pillar of light, illuminating the pathway of God's servants in all the ages since then. During that three days' journey Abraham had enough time to reason and to doubt God. He could have reasoned that killing his son would cause him to be looked upon as a murderer, a second Cain; it would cause his teaching to be rejected and despised and thus destroy his power to do good to others around him. He might have claimed that age should excuse him from obedience. But he did not take refuge in excuses. Abraham was human. His passions and attachments were like ours. But he did not stop to reason with his aching heart. He knew that God is just and righteous in all His requirements.

" 'Abraham believed God, and it was accounted to him for righteousness.' And he was called the friend of God." James 2:23. And Paul says, "Only those who are of faith are sons of Abraham." Galatians 3:7. But Abraham's faith was made manifest by his works. "Was not Abraham our father justified by works when he offered Isaac his son on the altar? Do you see that faith was working together with his works, and by works faith was made perfect?" James 2:21, 22.

Many fail to understand the relationship between faith and works. They say, "Only believe in Christ, and you are safe; it has nothing to do with keeping the law." But genuine faith will be demonstrated by obedience. The Lord declares concerning the father of the faithful, " 'Abraham obeyed My voice and kept My charge, My commandments, My statutes, and My laws.' " Genesis 26:5. Says the apostle James, "Faith by itself, if it does not have works, is dead." James 2:17. And John, who dwells so fully on love, tells us, "This is the love of God, that we keep His commandments." 1 John 5:3.

God "preached the gospel to Abraham beforehand." Galatians 3:8. And the patriarch's faith was fixed on the Redeemer to come. Christ said, " 'Your father Abraham rejoiced to see My day, and he saw it and was glad.' " John 8:56. The ram offered in place of Isaac represented the Son of God, who was to be sacrificed in our place. The Father, looking on His Son, said to the sinner, "Live: I have found a ransom."

The agony that Abraham endured during the dark days of that fearful trial was permitted so that he might understand something of the greatness of the sacrifice God made for our redemption. No other test could have caused Abraham such torture of soul as did the offering of his son. God gave His Son to a death of agony and shame. The angels were not permitted to interpose, as they did in the case of Isaac. There was no voice to cry, "It is enough." To save the fallen race, the King of glory yielded up His life.

"He who did not spare His own Son, but delivered Him up for us all, how shall He not with Him also freely give us all things?" Romans 8:32.

Lesson Book of the Universe

The sacrifice required of Abraham was not only for his good nor for the generations to come; it was also for the instruction of the sinless beings of heaven and other worlds. This earth, on which the plan of redemption is enacted, is the lesson book of the universe. Because Abraham had shown a lack of faith, Satan had accused him before angels and God. God desired to prove the loyalty of His servant before all heaven, to demonstrate that nothing less than perfect obedience can be accepted, and to open more fully before them the plan of salvation.

The test given Adam in Eden involved no suffering, but the command to Abraham demanded the most agonizing sacrifice. All heaven watched with wonder and admiration Abraham's unswerving obedience. All heaven admired his loyalty. Satan's accusations were shown to be false. God's covenant testified that obedience will be rewarded.

When the command was given to Abraham to offer his son, all heavenly beings watched with intense earnestness each step in the fulfillment of this command. Light was shed on the mystery of redemption, and even the angels understood more clearly the wonderful provision that God had made for our salvation. See 1 Peter 1:12.

The Sin of Sodom and Gomorrah*

Among the cities of the Jordan valley, Sodom was "like the garden of the LORD" (Genesis 13:10) in its fertility and beauty. Rich harvests clothed the fields, and flocks and herds covered the encircling hills all around. Art and commerce enriched the proud city. The treasures of the East decorated her palaces, and caravans brought supplies of precious things to her markets. With little thought or work, people there could live comfortably.

Idleness and riches harden the heart that has never been troubled by poverty or burdened by sorrow. The people gave themselves up to fulfilling their sensual desires. " 'This was the iniquity of your sister Sodom: She and her daughter had pride, fullness of food, and abundance of idleness; neither did she strengthen the hand of the poor and needy. And they were haughty and committed abomination before Me; therefore I took them away as I saw fit.' " Ezekiel 16:49, 50. Satan is never more successful than when he comes to people in their idle hours.

In Sodom there was laughter, partying, feasting, and drunkenness.

The most evil passions were unrestrained. People openly defied God and His law and delighted in violence. Though they had the example of the pre-Flood world and knew of their destruction, they followed the same course of wickedness.

When Lot settled in Sodom, corruption had not become universal, and in mercy God permitted rays of light to shine amid the moral darkness. Abraham was not a stranger to the people of Sodom, and his victory over much stronger forces prompted wonder and admiration. No one could avoid the conviction that a divine power had made him conqueror. His noble and unselfish spirit, so strange to the self-seeking inhabitants of Sodom, was another evidence that the religion he had honored was superior. God was speaking to that people by His providence, but the last ray of light was rejected, as all before had been.

Now the last night of Sodom was approaching, but no one was aware of it. While angels drew near on their mission of destruction, people were dreaming of prosperity and pleasure.

* This chapter is based on Genesis 19.

The last day was like every other that had come and gone. A landscape of unsurpassed beauty was bathed in the rays of the setting sun. Pleasure-seeking crowds were forgoing this way and that, intent on enjoying the hour.

In the twilight, two strangers approached the city gate. No one saw them as the mighty heralds of divine judgment. The careless multitude little dreamed that in mistreating these heavenly messengers, that very night they would reach the pinnacle of guilt that doomed their city.

Lot Entertains Angels Unwittingly

But one man showed kindly attention toward the strangers and invited them to his home. Lot did not know their true character, but being polite and hospitable was a habit with him—a lesson he had learned from Abraham. If he had not cultivated a spirit of courtesy, he might have been left to perish with Sodom. Many a household has closed its doors against a stranger and so has shut out God's messenger who would have brought blessing. God smiles on the humble, sincere acts of daily self-denial, performed with a cheerful, willing heart.

Knowing how strangers were abused in Sodom, Lot made it one of his duties to guard them by offering them room at his own house. He was sitting at the gate as the travelers approached and rose from his place to meet them. Bowing courteously, he said, " 'Here now, my lords, please turn in to your servant's house and spend the night.' " They seemed to decline, saying, " 'No, but we will spend the night in the open square.' " They had two reasons for answering this way—to test Lot's sincerity and to appear ignorant of the character of Sodom's inhabitants, as if they supposed it was safe to stay in the street at night. Lot urged his invitation until they yielded and went with him to his house.

Their hesitation and his persistent urging drew attention, and before they went to bed for the night, a lawless crowd gathered around the house, a huge company, youth and old men alike inflamed by the vilest passions. The strangers had been asking about the character of the city, when the mob started hooting and jeering, demanding that the men be brought out to them.

Lot went out to plead with them. " 'Please, my brethren,' " he said, " 'do not do so wickedly!' " He used the term "brethren" in the sense of neighbors, hoping to gain their goodwill. But their rage became like the roaring of a hurricane. They mocked Lot and threatened to deal worse with him than they had intended toward his guests. They would have torn him in pieces if he had not been rescued by the angels of God. The heavenly messengers "reached out their hands and pulled Lot into the house with them, and shut the door." "They struck the men who were at the doorway of the house with blindness, both small and great, so that they became weary trying to find the door." If they had not been afflicted with double blindness, being given up to hardness of heart, the stroke of God on them would have caused them to stop trying to do their evil work. That last night revealed no greater sins than many others before it, but mercy, so long ignored, had finally stopped pleading. The fires of God's vengeance were about to be kindled.

The angels revealed to Lot the purpose of their mission: " 'We will destroy this place, because the outcry against them has grown great before the face of the LORD, and the LORD has sent us to destroy it.' " The strangers whom Lot had tried to protect now promised to protect him and all his family who would flee with him from the wicked city. The mob had worn themselves out and left, and Lot went out to warn his children. " 'Get up, get out of this place; for the LORD will destroy this city!' " But they laughed at what they called his superstitious fears. His daughters were influenced by their husbands. They could see no sign of danger. They had great possessions and could not believe it possible that beautiful Sodom would be destroyed.

Lot Loses Everything Except His Life

Lot returned sorrowfully to his home and reported that his appeal had failed. Then the angels told him to take his wife and two daughters who were still in the house and leave. But Lot delayed. He had no true concept of the debasing vices practiced in that vile city. He did not realize the terrible necessity for God's judgments to put a restraint on sin. Some of his children clung

to Sodom, and the thought of leaving those whom he held dearest on earth seemed more than he could bear. It was hard to forsake his luxurious home and all the wealth of his whole life, to go out a poor, homeless wanderer. Stupefied with sorrow, he lingered. If it had not been for the angels, all of them would have perished. The heavenly messengers took him and his wife and daughters by the hand and led them out of the city.

In all the cities of the plain, even ten righteous persons had not been found. But in answer to Abraham's prayer, the one man who feared God was snatched from destruction. The command was given with startling intensity: " 'Escape for your life! Do not look behind you nor stay anywhere in the plain. Escape to the mountains, lest you be destroyed.' " To cast one lingering look on the city, to delay for one moment from regret to leave so beautiful a home, would cost their life. The storm of divine judgment was only waiting so that these poor fugitives could escape.

But Lot, confused and terrified, pleaded that he could not do what the two visitors had told him to do. Living in that wicked city, his faith had grown weak. The Prince of heaven was by his side, yet he pleaded for his own life as though God, who had shown such love for him, would not still take care of him. He should have trusted himself entirely to the divine Messenger. " 'See now, this city is near enough to flee to, and it is a little one; please let me escape there (is it not a little one?) and my soul shall live.' " Zoar was only a few miles from Sodom and, like it, was corrupt and doomed to destruction. But Lot asked for it to be spared, urging that this was just a small request. His desire was granted. The Lord assured him, " 'I have favored you concerning this thing also, in that I will not overthrow this city for which you have spoken.' "

Again the command was given to hurry, for the fiery storm would be delayed only a little longer. But one of the fugitives took a look backward to the doomed city, and she became a monument of God's judgment. If Lot himself had earnestly fled toward the mountains without one word of objection, his wife also would have made her escape. His example would have saved her from the sin that sealed her doom. But his reluctance caused her to regard the divine warning lightly. While her body was on the plain, her heart clung to Sodom, and she perished with it. She rebelled against God because His judgments involved her possessions and children in the ruin. She felt that God had dealt severely with her in requiring that the wealth that had taken years to accumulate be left to destruction. Instead of thankfully accepting deliverance, she looked back presumptuously, longing for the way of life of those who rejected the divine warning.

There are Christians who say, "I don't want to be saved unless my companion and children are saved."

They feel heaven would not be heaven without the presence of those who are so dear. But have those who cherish this feeling forgotten that they are bound by the strongest ties of love and loyalty to their Creator and Redeemer? Because our friends reject the Savior's love, shall we also turn away? Christ has paid an infinite price for our salvation, and no one who appreciates its value will despise God's mercy because others choose to do so. The fact that others ignore His claims should spur us on to be more diligent, that we may honor God and lead all whom we can to accept His love.

Sodom Destroyed

"The sun had risen upon the earth when Lot entered Zoar." The bright rays of morning seemed to promise only prosperity and peace to the cities of the plain. The stir of active life began in the streets; people were going their various ways, intent on the business or pleasure of the day. The sons-in-law of Lot were making fun of the fears and warnings of the weak-minded old man.

Suddenly and unexpectedly as thunder from a cloudless sky, the storm broke. The Lord rained brimstone and fire on the cities and the plain. Palaces and temples, costly homes, gardens, vineyards, and the pleasure-seeking crowds that only the night before had insulted the messengers of heaven—all were consumed. The smoke went up like a great furnace. The lovely Valley of Siddim became a place never to be built up or inhabited—a witness to all generations that God's judgments on transgression are certain.

There are greater sins than those for which Sodom and Gomorrah were destroyed. People who hear the gospel invitation calling to repentance, and pay no attention, are more guilty than the dwellers in the Valley of Siddim. The fate of Sodom is a solemn warning, not merely to those guilty of defiant sin, but to all who are not taking seriously their Heaven-sent light and privileges.

The Savior watches for a response to His offers of love and forgiveness with more tender compassion than that which moves the heart of an earthly parent to forgive a wayward child. " 'Return to Me, and I will return to you.' " Malachi 3:7. But anyone who persistently refuses that tender love will finally be left in darkness. The heart that has slighted God's mercy for a long time becomes hardened in sin, no longer able to respond to the influence of the grace of God. It will be more tolerable in the day of judgment for the cities of the plain than for those who have known the love of Christ and yet have turned away to the pleasure of sin. In the books of heaven God keeps a record kept of the sins of nations, of families, of individuals. Calls to repentance, offers of pardon may be given; yet a time will come when the account will be full. The individual's decision has been made. By his or her own choice, that person's destiny has been fixed. Then the signal will be given for judgment to be executed.

Another Sodom

In the religious world today God's mercy has been taken for granted and treated lightly. Multitudes make void the law, " ' "teaching as doctrines the commandments of men." ' " Matthew 15:9. Infidelity prevails in many churches, not infidelity in its broadest sense—an open denial of the Bible—but an infidelity undermining faith in the Bible as a revelation from God. Vital piety has been replaced by hollow formalism. As the result, apostasy and immorality prevail. Christ declared, " 'As it was also in the days of Lot: . . . Even so will it be in the day when the Son of man is revealed.' " Luke 17:28, 30. The world is fast becoming ripe for destruction.

Our Savior said, " 'Take heed to yourselves, lest your hearts be weighed down with carousing, drunkenness, and cares of this life, and that Day come on you unexpectedly. For it will come as a snare on all those who dwell on the face of the whole earth' "—all whose interests are centered in this world. " 'Watch therefore, and pray always that you may be counted worthy to escape all these things that will come to pass, and to stand before the Son of Man.' " Luke 21:34-36.

Before the destruction of Sodom, God sent a message to Lot, " 'Escape for your life!' " The same voice of warning was heard before the destruction of Jerusalem: " 'When you see Jerusalem surrounded by armies, then know that its destruction is near. Then let those in Judea flee to the mountains.' " Luke 21:20, 21.

They must not delay but must escape.

There was a coming out, a decided separation from the wicked, an escape for life. So it was in the days of Noah; so with Lot; so with the disciples before the destruction of Jerusalem; and so it will be in the last days. Again the voice of God is heard, calling His people to separate from the widespread iniquity.

The corruption and apostasy of the last days were presented to the prophet John in the vision of Babylon, " 'that great city which reigns over the kings of the earth.' " Revelation 17:18. Before its destruction the call from heaven is to be given, " 'Come out of her, my people, lest you share in her sins, and lest you receive of her plagues.' " Revelation 18:4. As in the days of Noah and Lot, there must be no compromise between God and the world, no turning back to get earthly treasures. See Matthew 6:24.

People are dreaming of prosperity and peace. The multitudes cry "Peace and safety" while Heaven declares that swift destruction is about to come on the transgressor. On the night before their destruction, the cities of the plain rioted in pleasure and scoffed at the warnings of the messenger of God. But that very night the door of mercy was forever closed to the careless inhabitants of Sodom. God will not always be mocked.

The great mass of the world will reject God's mercy and will be overwhelmed in swift and final ruin. But those who heed the warning will dwell "in the secret place of the Most High" and "abide under the shadow of the Almighty." Psalm 91:1.

Not long after, Zoar was consumed as God had seen necessary. Lot made his way to the mountains and lived in a cave.

But the curse of Sodom followed him even there. The sinful conduct of his daughters was the result of evil associations in that vile place. Lot had chosen Sodom for its pleasure and profit, yet he had retained the fear of God in his heart. He was saved at last as "a brand plucked from the fire" but without his possessions, mourning the loss of his wife and children, dwelling in caves, and covered with shame in his old age. And he gave to the world not a race of righteous people but two idolatrous nations, opposing God and warring with His people until, when their cup of iniquity was full, they were destroyed. How terrible the results that followed one unwise step!

"Labor not to be rich: cease from thine own wisdom." "He who is greedy for gain troubles his own house." "Those who desire to be rich fall into temptation and a snare, and into many foolish and harmful lusts which drown men in destruction and perdition." Proverbs 23:4 KJV; 15:27; 1 Timothy 6:9.

When Lot entered Sodom he fully intended to keep himself free from iniquity and command his household after him. But he failed. The result is there for us to see.

Like Lot, many see their children ruined, and they barely save their own souls. Their lifework is lost; their life is a sad failure. If they had exercised true wisdom, their children might have had less worldly prosperity, but they would have made sure of a claim to the immortal inheritance.

The heritage that God has promised is not in this world. Abraham "sojourned in the land of promise as in a foreign country, dwelling in tents with Isaac and Jacob, the heirs with him of the same promise; for he waited for the city which has foundations, whose builder and maker is God." We must live as pilgrims and strangers here if we intend to gain "a better, that is, a heavenly country." Hebrews 11:9, 10, 16.

Isaac's Marriage, the Happiest in the Bible*

Abraham had become an old man, yet one thing remained for him to do. God had appointed Isaac as the next keeper of the divine law and the father of the chosen people, but he was still unmarried.

The Canaanites were idol worshipers, and God had forbidden marriages between them and His people, knowing that such marriages would lead to apostasy. Isaac was gentle and yielding. If he united with someone who did not fear God, he would be in danger of sacrificing principle for the sake of harmony. To Abraham, the choice of a wife for his son was extremely important. He was anxious to have Isaac marry one who would not lead him from God.

In ancient times, marriage engagements were generally made by the parents, and this was the custom among those who worshiped God. None were required to marry those whom they could not love, but the youth were guided by the judgment of their God-fearing parents. It was a dishonor to parents, even a crime, to act contrary to this.

Trusting his father, Isaac was satisfied to commit the matter to him, believing also that God Himself would direct in the choice made. Abraham's thoughts turned to his father's relatives in Mesopotamia. They were not free from idolatry, but they had a knowledge of the true God. Isaac must not go to them, but it might be that one could be found among them who would leave her home and unite with him in maintaining the pure worship of the living God.

Abraham committed the important matter to Eliezer, his "oldest servant," a man of experience and sound judgment who had given him long and faithful service. He insisted that this servant make a solemn oath that he would not take a wife for Isaac from the Canaanites but would choose a maiden from the family of Nahor in Mesopotamia. If a young woman could not be found who would leave her home and family, then the messenger would be released from his oath. Abraham encouraged him with the assurance that God would crown his mission with success. " 'The LORD God of heaven,' " he said, " 'who took me from my father's house and from the

---

* *This chapter is based on Genesis 24.*

land of my family, . . . He will send His angel before you.' "

The messenger set out without delay. Taking ten camels for his own attendants and the bridal party that might return with him and also gifts for the intended wife and friends, he made the long journey beyond Damascus to the plains that border on the Euphrates, the great river of the East.

When he arrived at Haran, "the city of Nahor," he stopped outside the walls near the well where the women came at evening for water. His thoughts troubled him. Far-reaching results, not only to his master's household but to future generations, might follow from the choice he made. Remembering that God would send His angel with him, he prayed for clear guidance. In his master's family he was accustomed to constant kindness and hospitality, and now he asked that an act of courtesy might indicate the maiden whom God had chosen.

Hardly had he uttered the prayer before the answer was given. Among the women at the well, the courteous manners of one attracted his attention. As she came from the well, the stranger went to meet her, asking for some water from the pitcher on her shoulder. The request received a kind answer, and she offered to draw water for the camels also.

Thus the sign that he had asked for was given. The young woman "was very beautiful to behold," and her prompt courtesy gave evidence of a kind heart and an active, energetic nature. Thus far the divine

hand had been with him. The messenger asked whose daughter she was, and when he learned that her father was Bethuel, Abraham's nephew, he "bowed down his head, and worshiped the LORD."

The man told the young woman about his connection with Abraham. Returning home, she told what had happened, and Laban, her brother, at once hurried to bring the stranger to share their hospitality.

Eliezer would not eat any food until he had told his errand, his prayer at the well, and all the circumstances that went with it. Then he said, " 'Now if you will deal kindly and truly with my master, tell me. And if not, tell me, that I may turn to the right hand or to the left.' " The answer was, " 'The thing comes from the LORD; we cannot speak to you either bad or good. Here is Rebekah before you; take her and go, and let her be your master's son's wife, as the LORD has spoken.' "

Rebekah Believes God Has Spoken

Rebekah herself was asked whether she was willing to go so great a distance from her father's house to marry the son of Abraham. She believed that God had selected her to be Isaac's wife, and said, " 'I will go.' "

The servant, anticipating his master's joy, was impatient to be gone, and when morning came they set out on the homeward journey. Abraham was living at Beersheba, and Isaac, who had been tending the flocks in the adjoining country, had returned to his father's tent to wait for the messenger from Haran. "And Isaac went out to meditate in the field in the evening; and he lifted his eyes and looked, and there, the camels were coming. Then Rebekah lifted her eyes, and when she saw Isaac she dismounted from her camel; for she had said to the servant, 'Who is this man walking in the field to meet us?' The servant said, 'It is my master.' So she took a veil and covered herself. And the servant told Isaac all the things that he had done. Then Isaac brought her into his mother Sarah's tent; and he took Rebekah and she became his wife, and he loved her. So Isaac was comforted after his mother's death."

Abraham had noticed the result of intermarriage between those who feared God and those who did not, from the days of Cain to his own time. His own marriage with Hagar and the marriage connections of Ishmael and Lot were before him. Abraham's influence on his son Ishmael was counteracted by the influence of Hagar's idolatrous relatives and by Ishmael's connection with heathen wives. The jealousy of Hagar and of the wives whom she chose for Ishmael surrounded his family with a barrier that Abraham tried to overcome, but could not.

Abraham's early teachings had not failed to have an effect on Ishmael, but the influence of his wives resulted in establishing idolatry in his family. Separated from his father and embittered by the strife and contention of a home that lacked the love and fear of God, Ishmael was driven to choose the wild, marauding

life of a desert chief, "his hand . . . against every man, and every man's hand against him." Genesis 16:12. In later life he repented and returned to his father's God, but the stamp of character given to his descendents remained. The powerful nation that came from him were a turbulent, heathen people.

The wife of Lot was a selfish, irreligious woman, and she worked to separate her husband from Abraham. If he could have had his way, Lot would not have stayed in Sodom. The influence of his wife and the associations of that wicked city would have led him to apostatize from God if it had not been for the faithful instruction he had received in his youth from Abraham.

It is dangerous for one who fears God to connect himself with one who fears Him not. "Can two walk together, unless they are agreed?" Amos 3:3. The happiness and prosperity of marriage depends on the unity of the parties; but there is a radical difference of tastes, inclinations, and purposes between the believer and the unbeliever. However pure and correct one's principles, the influence of an unbelieving companion will tend to lead away from God.

Those who have entered marriage while unconverted and are later converted are under stronger obligation to be faithful to their companions, no matter how they may differ in religious faith. Yet the claims of God should be honored above every earthly relationship, even if this brings trials and persecution. The spirit of love and faithfulness may win the unbelieving one. But marriage with the ungodly is forbidden in the Bible. "Do not be unequally yoked together with unbelievers." 2 Corinthians 6:14, 17, 18.

Before One Marries

Isaac was the heir of the promises through which the world was to be blessed; yet when he was forty years old he let his father choose a wife for him. And the result of that marriage is a tender and beautiful picture of happiness at home: "Isaac brought her into his mother Sarah's tent; and he took Rebekah and she became his wife, and he loved her. So Isaac was comforted after his mother's death."

Young people too often feel that selecting a life partner is a matter on which to consult self alone. They think they are fully qualified to make their own choice, without the aid of their parents. A few years of married life usually show them their error, but too late. The same lack of wisdom and self-control that dictated the hasty choice makes matters worse, until marriage becomes a bitter burden. In this way many wreck their happiness in this life and their hope of the life to come.

If ever the Bible was needed as a counselor, if ever divine guidance should be sought in prayer, it is before taking a step that binds persons together for life.

Parents should never lose sight of their responsibility for the future happiness of their children. While Abraham required his children to respect parental authority, his daily life testified that this authority was not selfish or arbitrary but was rooted in love and had their well-being and happiness in view.

Fathers and mothers should guide the affections of youth so that they may place those affections on suitable companions. Mold the character of the children from their earliest years so that they will be pure and noble, attracted to the good and true. If love for truth, purity, and goodness is implanted in the soul early, the youth will seek the society of others who possess these characteristics.

Parents, try to be like our heavenly Father, who is love. Let home be full of sunshine. This will be worth more to your children than lands or money. Let the home love be kept alive in their hearts so that they may look back on the home of their childhood as a place of peace and happiness next to heaven.

True love is a high and holy principle, entirely different from that love which flashes up quickly but suddenly dies when severely tested. In their parents' home youth are to prepare themselves for homes of their own. Here they should practice self-denial, kindness, courtesy, and Christian sympathy.

The young man who goes out from such a household to stand at the head of a family will know how to promote the happiness of her whom he has chosen as a companion for life. Marriage, instead of being the end of love, will be only its beginning.

Jacob and Esau *

Jacob and Esau, the twin sons of Isaac, present a sharp contrast in character and in life. Before their birth, the angel of God foretold how unlike they would be. In answer to Rebekah's troubled prayer, he declared that two sons would be given her. He opened to her their future history, that each would become the head of a mighty nation but that one would be greater than the other, and the younger would have the preeminence.

Esau grew up loving to please himself, centering all his interest in living for today. Unhappy with restraint, he delighted in the chase and the life of a hunter. Yet he was his father's favorite. This elder son fearlessly ranged over mountain and desert, returning home with game and exciting accounts of his adventurous life.

Jacob, who was thoughtful, diligent, and always thinking more of the future than the present, was content to live at home, occupied in caring for the flocks and working the soil. His mother valued his patient perseverance, thrift, and foresight. His gentle attentions added more to her happiness than the boisterous, occasional kindnesses of Esau. To Rebekah, Jacob was the dearer son.

Esau and Jacob were taught to regard the birthright as a matter of great importance, for it included not only an inheritance of worldly wealth but spiritual preeminence. The one who received it was to be the priest of his family, and in the line of his descendants the Redeemer of the world would come.

On the other hand, certain obligations rested on the possessor of the birthright. The one who inherited its blessings must devote his life to the service of God. In marriage, in his family relations, in public life, he must consult the will of God.

Isaac made known to his sons these privileges and conditions and plainly stated that Esau as the eldest was the one entitled to the birthright. But Esau had no love for devotion, no inclination to a religious life. The requirements that accompanied the spiritual birthright were an unwelcome and even hateful restraint to him. Esau regarded the law of God, the condition of God's covenant with Abraham, as a yoke of bondage.

---

* This chapter is based on Genesis 25:19-34; 27.

Determined to indulge himself, he desired nothing so much as liberty to do as he pleased. To him power and riches, feasting and partying, were happiness. He gloried in the unrestrained freedom of his wild, roving life.

Rebekah remembered the words of the angel and read the character of their sons with clearer insight than her husband. Convinced that the heritage of divine promise was intended for Jacob, she repeated to Isaac the angel's words. But the father's affections were centered on the elder son, and he was unshaken in his decision to give him the birthright.

Jacob had learned from his mother that the birthright should fall to him, and he was filled with desire for the privileges it would confer. It was not his father's wealth that he craved; it was the spiritual birthright that he longed for. To commune with God as Abraham had, to offer the sacrifice of atonement, to be a forefather of the chosen people of the promised Messiah, to inherit the immortal possessions included in the covenant—these were the privileges and honor that he earnestly desired.

He listened to all that his father told concerning the spiritual birthright; he carefully treasured what he had learned from his mother. The subject became the focus of his life. But Jacob did not have a personal relationship with the God whom he revered. His heart had not been renewed by divine grace. He constantly studied to devise some way to get the blessing that his brother held

so lightly but which was so precious to himself.

Esau Sells His Treasure

Esau, coming home one day faint and weary from hunting, asked for the food that his brother was preparing. Jacob seized the advantage and offered to satisfy his brother's hunger at the price of the birthright. " 'Look, I am about to die,' " cried the reckless, self-indulgent hunter, " 'so what is this birthright to me?' " For a dish of red stew he gave up his birthright and confirmed the transaction by an oath. To satisfy the desire of the moment he carelessly traded the glorious heritage God Himself had promised his fathers. His whole interest was in the present. He was ready to sacrifice heavenly things for earthly pleasures, to exchange a future good for a momentary indulgence.

"Thus Esau despised his birthright." In giving it up he felt a sense of relief. Now he could do as he liked. For this wild pleasure, wrongly called freedom, many are still selling their birthright of an eternal inheritance in the heavens!

Esau took two Hittite wives. They worshiped false gods, and their idolatry was a bitter grief to Isaac and Rebekah. Esau had violated one of the conditions of the covenant, which prohibited intermarriage between the chosen people and the heathen; yet Isaac was still determined to bestow the birthright on him.

Years passed. Isaac, old and blind, soon to die, decided no longer to delay giving the blessing to his older son. But knowing the opposition of Rebekah and Jacob, he decided to perform the solemn ceremony in secret. He instructed Esau, " 'Go out to the field and hunt game for me. And make me savory food, . . . that my soul may bless you before I die.' "

Rebekah told Jacob what had taken place, urging immediate action to keep the blessing from going to Esau. She assured her son that if he would follow her directions, he would obtain the birthright as God had promised. Jacob did not consent right away. The thought of deceiving his father caused him great distress. Such a sin would bring a curse rather than a blessing.

But finally he gave in and proceeded to carry out his mother's suggestions. He did not intend to tell an outright lie, but once in the presence of his father he seemed to have gone too far to retreat, and he obtained the coveted blessing by fraud.

Consequences of Deception

Jacob and Rebekah succeeded in their plan but gained only trouble and sorrow by deception. God had declared that Jacob was to receive the birthright, and His word would have been fulfilled if they had waited in faith for Him to work. Rebekah bitterly regretted the wrong counsel she had given her son. Jacob was weighed down with self-condemnation. He had sinned against his father, his brother, his own soul, and against God. In one short hour he had provided material for lifelong repentance. This scene was vivid before him in later years when the wicked course of his own sons pained his soul.

No sooner had Jacob left his father's tent than Esau entered. Though he had sold his birthright, he was now determined to secure its blessing. With the spiritual was connected the temporal birthright, which would give him the headship of the family and a double portion of his father's wealth. " 'Let my father arise,' " he said, " 'and eat of his son's game, that your soul may bless me.' "

Trembling with surprise and distress, the blind old father learned the deception that had been practiced on him. He felt keenly the disappointment that must come upon his older son. Yet the conviction flashed into his mind that it was God's leading that had brought about the very thing he had determined to prevent. He remembered the words of the angel to Rebekah, and he saw in Jacob the one best fitted to accomplish the purpose of God. While the words of blessing were upon his lips, he had felt the Spirit of Inspiration upon him; and now he confirmed the benediction he had unwittingly pronounced on Jacob: " 'I have blessed him—and indeed he shall be blessed.' "

Esau Could Not Repent

Esau had lightly valued the blessing when it seemed within his reach, but now that it was gone from him his grief and rage were terrible. " 'Bless me—me also, O my father!' " " 'Have you not reserved a blessing for me?' " But the birthright that he had so carelessly bargained away he could not regain. "For one morsel of food," for a momentary gratification of his appetite that had never been restrained, Esau sold his inheritance.

But when he saw his folly, it was too late to recover the blessing. "He found no place for repentance, though he sought it diligently with tears." Hebrews 12:17. Esau was not shut out from seeking God's favor by repentance, but he could find no way to recover the birthright. His grief did not spring from conviction of sin; he did not desire to be reconciled to God. He sorrowed because of the results of his sin but not for the sin itself.

In Scripture Esau is called a "profane person." Verse 16. He represents those who lightly value the redemption Christ purchased for them and are ready to sacrifice their heavenly inheritance for the perishable things of earth. Multitudes live with no thought or care for the future. Like Esau they cry, " 'Let us eat and drink, for tomorrow we die.' " 1 Corinthians 15:32. The desires of appetite prevail, and God and heaven are virtually despised. When they are presented with the duty of cleansing themselves from all filthiness of the flesh and spirit, perfecting holiness in the fear of God, they are offended.

Multitudes are selling their birthright to indulge their senses. They sacrifice health, enfeeble their mental faculties, and forfeit heaven, all for temporary pleasure that both weakens and debases them. Esau awoke too late to recover his loss. So it will be in the day of God with those who have traded their status as heirs of heaven for selfish gratifications.

Jacob's Flight and Exile*

Threatened with death by Esau, Jacob went out from his father's home a fugitive but with the father's blessing. Isaac had renewed the covenant promise to him and had told him to look for a wife among his mother's family in Mesopotamia.

Yet it was with a deeply troubled heart that Jacob set out on his lonely journey. With only his staff in his hand, he must travel hundreds of miles through a country inhabited by wild, roving tribes. In his remorse and dread he tried to avoid people, to prevent his angry brother from following him. He feared that he had lost forever the blessing God had wanted to give him, and Satan was at hand to press temptations upon him.

The evening of the second day found him far away from his father's tents. He felt he was an outcast, and he knew that all his trouble had come upon him because of his own wrong actions. Despair pressed upon his soul, and he hardly dared to pray. But he was so lonely that he felt the need of protection from God as never before. With weeping he confessed his sin and asked earnestly for some

evidence that he was not utterly forsaken. He had lost all confidence in himself, and he feared that God had rejected him.

But God's mercy was still extended to His erring, distrustful servant. The Lord compassionately revealed just what Jacob needed—a Savior. He had sinned, but God revealed a way for him to be restored to divine favor.

Wearied, the wanderer lay down on the ground with a stone for his pillow. As he slept he saw a ladder whose base rested on the earth while the top reached to heaven. On this ladder angels were ascending and descending. Above it was the Lord of glory, and from the heavens His voice was heard: " 'I am the LORD God of Abraham your father and the God of Isaac.' " " 'In you and in your seed all the families of the earth shall be blessed.' " This promise had been given to Abraham and to Isaac, and now it was renewed to Jacob. Then the words of comfort and encouragement were spoken: " 'Behold, I am with you and will keep you wherever you go, and will bring you

---

back to this land; for I will not leave you until I have done what I have spoken to you.' "

The Lord in mercy opened up the future before the repentant fugitive so he might be prepared to resist the temptations that would come to him when alone among idolaters and schemers. The knowledge that the purpose of God was reaching its accomplishment through him would constantly prompt him to faithfulness.

In this vision Jacob saw the parts of the plan of redemption that were essential to him at that time. The mystic ladder revealed in his dream was the same to which Christ referred in His conversation with Nathanael: " 'You shall see heaven open, and the angels of God ascending and descending upon the Son of Man.' " John 1:51. The sin of Adam and Eve separated earth from heaven so that human beings could not have communion with their Maker. Yet the world was not left in hopelessness. The ladder represents Jesus, the appointed means of communication. Christ connects us in our weakness and helplessness with the source of infinite power.

All this was revealed to Jacob in his dream. Although his mind at once grasped a part of the revelation, its great and mysterious truths were the study of his lifetime, unfolding to his understanding more and more.

Jacob awoke in the deep stillness of night. The vision had disappeared. Only the dim outline of lonely hills and the heavens bright with stars now met his gaze. But he had a solemn sense that God was with him. " 'Surely the LORD is in this place,' " he said, " 'and I did not know it. . . . This is none other than the house of God, and this is the gate of heaven!' "

"Then Jacob rose early in the morning, and took the stone that he had put at his head, set it up as a pillar, and poured oil on top of it." He called the place Bethel, or "the house of God." Then he made the solemn vow, " 'If God will be with me, and keep me in this way that I am going, and give me bread to eat and clothing to put on, so that I come back to my father's house in peace, then the LORD shall be my God. And this stone which I have set as a pillar shall be God's house, and of all that You give me I will surely give a tenth to You.' "

Jacob was not trying to bargain with God. The Lord had already promised him prosperity, and this vow came from a heart filled with gratitude for the assurance of God's mercy. Jacob felt that the special evidences of divine favor demanded a return.

Christians should often recall with gratitude the precious deliverances that God has granted them, opening ways before them when all seemed dark and threatening, refreshing them when they were ready to faint. In view of countless blessings each one should often ask, "What shall I render to the LORD for all His benefits toward me?" Psalm 116:12.

Why the Tithe Is Sacred

Whenever we experience a special deliverance, or new and unexpected favors are granted us, we should acknowledge God's goodness by gifts or offerings to His cause. As we are continually *receiving* the blessings of God, so we are to be continually *giving*.

" 'Of all that You give me,' " said Jacob, " 'I will surely give a tenth to You.' " Shall we who enjoy the full light of the gospel be content to give less to God than was given by those who lived before Jesus came? Aren't our obligations even greater? But how useless to measure time, money, and love mathematically against a love so immeasurable and a gift of such incredible worth. Tithes for Christ! Oh, meager pittance, shameful response to that which cost so much! From the cross of Calvary Christ calls for total consecration of all that we have, all that we are.

With new faith and assured of the presence of heavenly angels, Jacob continued his journey to "the land of the people of the East." But how different was his arrival from that of Abraham's messenger nearly a hundred years before! Eliezer, the servant, had come with attendants riding on camels, with rich gifts of gold and silver; the son was a lonely, foot-sore traveler, with no possessions except his staff. Like Abraham's servant, Jacob stopped beside a well, and it was here that he met Rachel, Laban's younger daughter. On making known his kinship, he was welcomed to the home of Laban. A few weeks showed the worth of his diligence and skill, and he was urged to stay. It was arranged that he would give Laban seven years' service to be able to marry Rachel.

Jacob's Love for Rachel

In early times, custom required the bridegroom, before the marriage engagement, to pay a sum of money or its equivalent in other property, according to his financial circumstances, to the father of his wife. This was regarded as a safeguard to the marriage. Fathers did not think it safe to trust the happiness of their daughters to men who had not made provision for the support of a family. If they did not have sufficient thrift and energy to manage business and acquire cattle or lands, it was feared that their life would prove worthless. But provision was made to test those who had nothing to pay for a wife. They were permitted to work for the father whose daughter they loved. The length of time was regulated by the value of the dowry required. When the man was faithful and proved worthy, he obtained the daughter as his wife.

Generally the dowry that the father had received was given to the daughter at her marriage. In the case of both Rachel and Leah, however, Laban selfishly kept the dowry that should have been given them. They referred to this when they said, just before they left Mesopotamia, " 'He has sold us, and also completely consumed our money.' "

Requiring the suitor to render service to secure his bride prevented a hasty marriage. There was opportunity to test the depth of his affections as well as his ability to provide for a family. In our time it is often the case that persons have little opportunity before marriage to become acquainted with each other's habits and disposition. They are practically strangers when they unite their lives at the altar. Many find, too late, that they are not adapted to each other, and lifelong misery is the result. Often the wife and children suffer from the laziness or vices of the husband and father. If the character of the suitor had been tested before marriage according to the ancient custom, great unhappiness might have been prevented.

Jacob gave seven years of faithful service for Rachel, and the years that he served "seemed only a few days to him because of the love he had for her." But selfish Laban practiced a cruel deception in substituting Leah for Rachel. The fact that Leah herself cooperated in the cheat caused Jacob to feel that he could not love her. Angrily he rebuked Laban, who then offered him Rachel for another seven years' service. But Laban insisted that Leah should not be discarded. This placed Jacob in a most painful and trying position, but he finally agreed; he would keep Leah and marry Rachel. Rachel was always the one he loved best, but his life was made bitter by the rivalry between the sister-wives.

For twenty years Jacob stayed in Mesopotamia working for Laban, who was determined to secure to himself all the benefits of their connection. He demanded fourteen years of toil for his two daughters, and during the remaining period Jacob's wages were changed ten times.

Yet Jacob's service was diligent and faithful. During some parts of the year it was necessary for him to be constantly with the flocks in the fields, to guard them in the dry season against perishing from thirst and during the coldest months from becoming chilled with heavy night frosts. Jacob was the chief shepherd; the servants in his employ were the undershepherds. If any of the sheep were missing, the chief shepherd suffered the loss, and he called the servants to a strict account if the flock was not flourishing.

We Have a Faithful Shepherd

The shepherd's life of care-taking and compassion for the helpless creatures illustrates some precious truths of the gospel. Christ is compared to a shepherd. He saw His sheep doomed to die in the dark ways of sin. To save these wandering ones He left the honors and glories of His Father's house. He says, " 'I will seek what was lost and bring back what was driven away, bind up the broken and strengthen what was sick.' ". I will " 'save My flock, and they shall no longer be a prey.' " " 'Nor shall beasts of the land devour them.' " Ezekiel 34:16, 22, 28. His voice is heard calling them to His fold, a "shade in the daytime from the heat, for a place of refuge, and for a shelter from storm and rain." Isaiah 4:6. He strengthens the weak, relieves the suffering, gathers the lambs in His arms, and carries them next to His heart. His sheep love Him. " 'They will by no means follow a stranger, but will flee from him, for they do not know the voice of strangers.' " See John 10:1-15.

The church of Christ has been purchased with His blood, and every shepherd who has the spirit of Christ will imitate His self-denying example, constantly working for the good of his charge, and the flock will prosper under his care. "When the Chief Shepherd appears," says the apostle, "you will receive the crown of glory that does not fade away." 1 Peter 5:4.

Jacob, growing weary of working for Laban, proposed to return to Canaan. He said to his father-in-law, " 'Send me away, that I may go to my own place and to my country. Give me my wives and my children for whom I have served you, and let me go; for you know my service which I have done for you.' " But Laban urged him to stay, declaring, " 'I have learned by experience that the LORD has blessed me for your sake.' "

Said Jacob, " 'What you had before I came was little, and it has increased to a great amount.' " But as time passed, Laban became envious of the greater prosperity of Jacob, who "became exceedingly prosperous." Laban's sons shared their father's jealousy, and their malicious speeches came to Laban's ears. He " 'has taken away all that was our father's, and from what was our father's he has acquired all this wealth.' And Jacob saw the countenance of Laban, and

indeed it was not favorable toward him as before."

Jacob would have left his scheming relative long before except for the fear of meeting up with Esau. Now he felt that he was in danger from the sons of Laban, who, looking on his wealth as their own, might try to get it by violence. He was in great perplexity and distress. But he remembered the gracious promise at Bethel, and he carried his case to God. In a dream his prayer was answered: " 'Return to the land of your fathers and to your family, and I will be with you.' "

The flocks and herds were speedily gathered and sent forward, and with his wives, children, and servants, Jacob crossed the Euphrates River, hurrying on toward Gilead, on the borders of Canaan. After three days, Laban set out in pursuit, overtaking the company on the seventh day of their journey. He was hot with anger and determined to force them to return. The fugitives were indeed in great danger.

God himself intervened to protect His servant. " 'It is in my power to do you harm,' " said Laban, " 'but the God of your father spoke to me last night, saying, "Be careful that you speak to Jacob neither good nor bad." ' " That is, he should not force him to return or urge him by flattering promises.

Laban had withheld the marriage dowry of his daughters and treated Jacob with cunning and harshness, but he now reproved him for his secret departure which had given the father no opportunity to make a feast or even say Goodbye to his daughters and their children.

In reply, Jacob plainly set forth Laban's selfish and grasping conduct and appealed to him as a witness to his own faithfulness and honesty. " 'Unless the God of my father, the God of Abraham and the fear of Isaac, had been with me,' " said Jacob, " 'surely now you would have sent me away empty-handed. God has seen my affliction and the labor of my hands, and rebuked you last night.' "

Laban could not deny the facts and now proposed a covenant of peace. Jacob consented, and a pile of stones was erected to represent the agreement. To this pillar Laban gave the name Mizpah, "Watchtower," saying, " 'May the LORD watch between you and me when we are absent one from another. . . . The God of Abraham, the God of Nahor, and the God of their father judge between us.' And Jacob swore by the Fear of his father Isaac."

To confirm the treaty, the parties held a feast. The night was spent in friendly fellowship, and at dawn Laban and his company departed. With this separation all connection between the children of Abraham and the dwellers in Mesopotamia ended.

Jacob's Terrible Night of Wrestling*

With many misgivings Jacob retraced the road he had taken as a fugitive twenty years before. His sin of deceiving his father was always on his mind. He knew that his long exile was the direct result of that sin. He thought about these things day and night, his accusing conscience making his journey very sad. As the hills of his native land appeared before him in the distance, all the past rose vividly before him. With the memory of his sin came also the promises of divine help and guidance.

He thought of Esau with dread. Esau might be spurred to violence not only by revenge but to gain unchallenged possession of the wealth he had long looked upon as his own.

Again the Lord gave Jacob a sign of divine care; two camps, or armies, of heavenly angels advanced with his company, as if for their protection. Jacob remembered the vision at Bethel so long before, and his burdened heart grew lighter. The divine messengers who brought him hope and courage as he fled from Canaan were to be the guardians of his return. And he said, " 'This is God's camp.' "

Yet Jacob felt that he had something to do to secure his own safety. He therefore sent messengers to Esau with a greeting that he hoped his brother would receive with favor. The servants were sent to " 'my lord Esau.' " They were to refer to their master as " 'your servant Jacob.' " And to remove the fear that he was returning to claim the inheritance, Jacob was careful to state in his message, " 'I have oxen, donkeys, flocks, and male and female servants.' "

But Esau sent no response to the friendly message. It appeared certain that Esau was coming to seek revenge. Terror swept the camp. "Jacob was greatly afraid and distressed." His company, unarmed and defenseless, were completely unprepared for a hostile encounter. From his vast flocks he sent generous presents to Esau, with a friendly message. He did all in his power to atone for the wrong to his brother and to avert the threatened danger. Then he pleaded for divine protection: " 'I am not worthy of the least of all the

---

* This chapter is based on Genesis 32 and 33.

mercies and of all the truth which You have shown Your servant. . . . Deliver me, I pray, from the hand of my brother, from the hand of Esau; for I fear him, lest he come and attack me and the mother with the children.' "

Jacob decided to spend the night in prayer, alone with God. God could soften the heart of Esau. In Him was Jacob's only hope.

An Angel Wrestles With Jacob

It was a lonely, mountainous region, the haunt of wild beasts, robbers, and murderers. Unprotected, Jacob bowed in deep distress upon the earth. It was midnight. All who made life dear to him were exposed to danger and death. Bitter was the thought that his own sin had brought this peril on the innocent.

Suddenly a strong hand was laid on him. He thought that an enemy was seeking his life. In the darkness the two struggled for the mastery. Neither spoke a word, but Jacob put forth all his strength and did not relax his efforts for a moment. While he battled for his life, his guilt pressed upon his soul; his sins rose up to shut him out from God.

But in his terrible extremity he remembered God's promises. The struggle continued until near daybreak, when the stranger placed his finger on Jacob's thigh, and he was crippled instantly. Jacob now knew that he had been in conflict with a heavenly messenger. This was why his almost superhuman effort had not gained the victory. It was Christ, "the angel of the covenant." Jacob

was now disabled and suffering the sharpest pain, but he would not loosen his hold. Repentant and broken, he clung to the Angel. "He wept, and sought favor from Him," pleading for a blessing. He must have the assurance that his sin was pardoned. The Angel urged, " 'Let Me go, for the day breaks;' " but Jacob answered, " 'I will not let You go unless You bless me!' " He had the assurance of one who confesses his unworthiness yet trusts the faithfulness of a covenant-keeping God.

Jacob "struggled with the Angel and prevailed." Hosea 12:4. This sinful, erring mortal prevailed with the Majesty of heaven. He had fastened his trembling grasp on the promises of God, and the heart of Infinite Love could not turn away the sinner's plea.

Jacob's Name Becomes "Israel"

Jacob now clearly saw the error that had led to his sin in obtaining the birthright by fraud. He had not trusted God's promises but had tried by his own efforts to bring about what God would have accomplished in His own time and way. As an evidence that he had been forgiven, his name was changed to one designed to keep alive the memory of his victory. " 'Your name,' " said the Angel, " 'shall no longer be called Jacob [supplanter], but Israel; for you have struggled with God and with men, and have prevailed.' "

The crisis in his life was past. Doubt, perplexity, and remorse had made his existence bitter, but now all was changed. Sweet was the peace of being reconciled to God. Jacob no longer was afraid to meet his brother. God could move the heart of Esau to accept his humiliation and repentance.

While Jacob was wrestling with the Angel, another heavenly messenger was sent to Esau. In a dream, Esau saw his brother, for twenty years an exile; he witnessed his grief at finding that his mother was dead; he saw him surrounded by the hosts of God. The God of his father was with him.

The two companies at last approached each other, the desert chief leading his men of war and Jacob with his wives and children followed by long lines of flocks and herds. Leaning on his staff, Jacob went forward, pale and disabled from his recent conflict. He walked slowly and painfully, but his face was lighted up with joy and peace.

At the sight of that crippled sufferer, "Esau ran to meet him, and embraced him, . . . and they wept." Even the hearts of Esau's rough soldiers were touched. They could not account for the change that had come over their captain.

In his night of anguish Jacob had been taught how useless is human help, how groundless is trust in human power. Helpless and unworthy, he pleaded God's promise of mercy to the repentant sinner. That promise was his assurance that God would pardon and accept him.

The Future "Time of Jacob's Trouble"

Jacob's experience during that night of wrestling and anguish represents the trial through which the people of God must pass just before Christ's second coming. " ' "We have heard a voice of trembling, of fear, and not of peace. . . . Alas! for that day is great, so that none is like it; and it is the time of Jacob's trouble, but he shall be saved out of it." ' " Jeremiah 30:5-7.

When Christ ends His work as mediator in our behalf, this time of trouble will begin. Then the case of every person will have been decided, and there will be no atoning blood to cleanse from sin. The solemn announcement is made, " 'He who is unjust, let him be unjust still; he who is filthy, let him be filthy still; he who is righteous, let him be righteous still; he who is holy, let him be holy still.' " Revelation 22:11. As Jacob was threatened with death by his angry brother, so the people of God will be in peril from the wicked. The righteous will cry to God day and night for deliverance.

Satan had accused Jacob before the angels of God, claiming the right to destroy him because of his sin. He tried to force on him a sense of his guilt in order to discourage him and break his hold on God. When Jacob prayed fervently with tears, the heavenly Messenger, in order to test his faith, also reminded him of his sin and tried to escape from him. But Jacob had learned that God is merciful. As he reviewed his life, he was driven almost to despair, but he held tightly to the Angel, and with earnest, agonizing cries urged his request until he prevailed.

The Final Struggle

The experience of God's people will be like this in their final struggle with the powers of evil. God will test their faith, their perseverance, their confidence in His power. Satan will try to terrify them with the thought that their sins have been too great to receive pardon. As they review their lives, their hopes will sink. But remembering God's mercy and their own sincere repentance, they will cling to His promises. Their faith will not fail because their prayers are not immediately answered. The language of their souls will be, " 'I will not let You go unless You bless me.' "

If Jacob had not previously repented of his sin in obtaining the birthright by fraud, God could not have mercifully preserved his life. So in the time of trouble, if the people of God had unconfessed sins to appear before them while tortured with fear and anguish, despair would cut off their faith, and they could not have confidence to plead with God for deliverance. But they will have no concealed wrongs to reveal. Their sins will have been blotted out by the atoning blood of Christ, and they cannot remember them.

All who try to excuse or hide their sins and leave them on the books of heaven, unconfessed and unforgiven, will be overcome by Satan. The more exalted their profession is and the more honorable the position that they hold, the more certain is the triumph of the great adversary.

Jacob's history assures us that God will not cast off those who have been betrayed into sin but have returned to Him with true repentance. God taught His servant that divine grace alone could give him the blessing he craved. This is how it will be with those who live in the last days. In all our helpless unworthiness we must trust in the merits of the crucified and risen Savior. None will ever perish while they do this.

Jacob's experience testifies to the power of persistent, urgent prayer. It is now that we are to learn this lesson of unyielding faith. The greatest victories are not those gained by talent, education, wealth, or human favor; they are gained in the audience chamber with God, when earnest, agonizing faith lays hold upon the mighty arm of power.

All who will lay hold of God's promises as Jacob did, and be as earnest and persevering as he was, will succeed as he succeeded.

Jacob Comes Home*

Crossing the Jordan, "Jacob came safely to the city of Shechem, which is in the land of Canaan." Here he "bought the parcel of land, where he had pitched his tent, from the children of Hamor, Shechem's father, for one hundred pieces of money. Then he erected an altar there." It was here also that he dug the well to which Jesus came seventeen centuries later. Beside this well Jacob's Son and Savior rested during the noontide heat and told His amazed hearers of that " 'fountain of water springing up into everlasting life.' " John 4:14.

The time that Jacob and his sons spent at Shechem ended in bloodshed. One daughter of the household had been brought to shame and sorrow; two brothers were involved in the guilt of murder; a whole city had experienced ruin and slaughter in retaliation for the lawless deed of one rash youth. The beginning that led to results so terrible was the act of Jacob's daughter in going out to associate with the ungodly. Anyone who seeks pleasure among those who do not fear God is inviting temptations.

The treacherous cruelty of Simeon and Levi toward the Shechemites was a terrible sin. The news of their revenge filled Jacob with horror. Heartsick at the deceit and violence of his sons, he said, " 'You have troubled me by making me obnoxious among the inhabitants of the land, . . . and since I am few in number, they will gather themselves together against me and kill me. I shall be destroyed, my household and I.' "

Jacob felt that there was cause for deep humiliation. Cruelty and falsehood were in the character of his sons. False gods and idolatry had gained a foothold to some extent even in his household.

While Jacob was thus bowed down with trouble, the Lord directed him to journey southward to Bethel. The thought of this place reminded him not only of his vision of the angels and of God's promises of mercy but of the vow he had made there that the Lord would be his God. Determined that his household should be freed from the defilement of idolatry before going to this sacred spot, he gave direction to all, " 'Put away the foreign gods that are among you,

---

* This chapter is based on Genesis 34; 35; 37.

purify yourselves, and change your garments. Then let us arise and go up to Bethel; and I will make an altar there to God, who answered me in the day of my distress and has been with me in the way which I have gone.' "

Jacob Relates His Earlier Bethel Experience

With deep emotion, Jacob repeated the story of his first visit to Bethel and how the Lord had appeared to him in the night vision. His own heart was softened; his children also were touched by a subduing power. He had taken the most effective way to prepare them to join in the worship of God when they would arrive at Bethel. "So they gave Jacob all the foreign gods which were in their hands, and the earrings which were in their ears; and Jacob hid them under the terebinth tree which was by Shechem."

God caused a fear to come over the inhabitants of the land, so that they made no attempt to avenge the slaughter of Shechem. The travelers reached Bethel safely. Here the Lord appeared to Jacob again and renewed to him the covenant promise.

From Bethel it was only two days' journey to Hebron, but it brought a heavy grief to Jacob in the death of Rachel. Twice he had worked seven years for her sake, and his love had made the toil light. That love had been deep and abiding.

Before her death, Rachel gave birth to a second son. With her parting breath she named the child Benoni, "son of my sorrow." But his father called him Benjamin, "son of my right hand," or "my strength."

At last Jacob came to his journey's end, "to his father Isaac at Mamre, . . . (that is, Hebron)." Here he remained during the closing years of his father's life. To Isaac, weak and blind, the kind attentions of this long-absent son were a comfort during years of loneliness and bereavement.

Jacob and Esau met at the deathbed of their father. The elder brother's feelings had greatly changed. Jacob, well content with the spiritual blessings of the birthright, resigned to the elder brother the inheritance of their father's wealth, the only inheritance Esau sought or valued. No longer alienated, they parted, Esau settling in Mount Seir. God, who is rich in blessing, had given worldly wealth to Jacob in addition to the higher good that he had sought. This separation of Jacob and Esau was part of God's plan concerning Jacob. Since the brothers differed so greatly in regard to religious faith, it was better for them to live apart.

Both Esau and Jacob were free to walk in God's commandments and to receive His favor, but the two brothers had walked in different ways, and their paths would continue to diverge more and more widely.

There was no arbitrary choice on the part of God by which Esau was shut out from the blessings of salvation. There is no decision but one's own by which any may perish. In His Word God has set forth the conditions on which every soul will be chosen for eternal life—obedience to His commandments through faith in Christ. God has chosen a character in harmony with His law, and anyone who reaches the standard of His requirement will enter into the kingdom of glory. Concerning our final salvation, this is the only election brought to view in the Word of God.

Every person is elected who will work out his or her own salvation with fear and trembling, who will put on the armor and fight the good fight of faith. Every one is chosen who will pray earnestly, search the Scriptures, flee from temptation, have faith continually, and be obedient to every word that proceeds out of the mouth of God. The *provisions* of redemption are free to all; the *results* will be enjoyed by those who have complied with the conditions.

Esau had despised the blessings of the covenant. By his own deliberate choice he was separated from the people of God. Jacob had chosen the inheritance of faith. He had tried to obtain it by craftiness, treachery, and falsehood; but God had permitted his sin to work out its correction. Jacob never swerved from his purpose or renounced his choice. From that night of wrestling Jacob had come away a different man. Self-confidence had been uprooted. Ever after, in place of craft and deception, his life was marked by simplicity and truth. The baser elements of his character were consumed in the furnace fire; the true

gold was refined until the faith of Abraham and Isaac appeared undimmed in Jacob.

The sin of Jacob and the chain of events to which it led bore bitter fruit in the character of his sons. These sons developed serious faults. The household revealed the results of polygamy. This terrible evil tends to dry up the springs of love, and its influence weakens the most sacred ties. The jealousy of the several mothers had embittered the family relationships; the children had grown up ill-tempered, impatient of control. The father's life was darkened with anxiety and grief.

There was one, however, whose character was widely different—the elder son of Rachel, Joseph, whose rare personal beauty seemed to reflect an inward beauty of mind and heart. Pure, active, and joyous, the lad possessed moral earnestness and firmness. He listened to his father's instructions and loved to obey God. The qualities that later distinguished him in Egypt—gentleness, fidelity, and truthfulness—were already evident. His mother being dead, his affections clung the more closely to the father. Jacob's heart was bound up in this child of his old age. He "loved Joseph more than all his children."

But this affection was to become a cause of trouble and sorrow. Jacob unwisely showed his preference for Joseph, and this inflamed the jealousy of his other sons. Joseph tried gently to correct them, but this only increased their hatred and resentment. He could not endure to see them sinning against God and laid the matter before his father.

With deep emotion Jacob begged them not to bring reproach on his name and above all not to dishonor God by such disregard of His laws. Ashamed that their wickedness was known, the young men seemed to be repentant but only hid their real feelings, which became more bitter by this exposure.

The father's gift to Joseph of a costly coat, usually worn by persons of distinction, fueled a suspicion that he intended to bypass his older children to bestow the birthright on the son of Rachel.

The boy one day told them of a dream that he had had. " 'There we were, binding sheaves in the field. Then behold, my sheaf arose and also stood upright; and indeed your sheaves stood all around and bowed down to my sheaf.' "

" 'Shall you indeed reign over us? Or shall you indeed have dominion over us?' " exclaimed his brothers in envious anger.

Soon he had another dream, which he also related: " 'This time, the sun, the moon, and the eleven stars bowed down to me.' " The father, who was present, spoke reprovingly, " 'Shall your mother and I and your brothers indeed come to bow down to the earth before you?' " Despite the apparent severity of his words, Jacob believed that the Lord was revealing the future to Joseph.

As the lad stood before his brothers, his beautiful countenance lighted up with the Spirit of Inspiration. They could not help but admire him,

but they hated the purity that reproved their sins.

The brothers had to move from place to place to find pasture for their flocks. After the events just related, they went to Shechem. Some time passed bringing no news, and the father began to fear for their safety because of their former cruelty toward the Shechemites. He therefore sent Joseph to find them. If Jacob had known the real feeling of his sons toward Joseph, he would not have trusted him alone with them.

With a joyful heart, Joseph parted from his father, neither of them dreaming of what would happen before they would meet again. When Joseph arrived at Shechem, his brothers and their flocks were not there. He asked about them and was directed to Dothan. He hurried on, forgetting his weariness in the thought of relieving his father's worries and meeting the brothers whom he still loved.

His brothers saw him coming, but in their bitter hatred they took no thought of the long journey he had made to meet them, of his weariness and hunger, or of his right to their hospitality and brotherly love. The sight of the coat, the token of their father's love, filled them with frenzy. " 'Look, this dreamer is coming.' " Envy and revenge now controlled them. " 'Let us now kill him,' " they said, " 'and cast him into some pit; and we shall say, "Some wild beast has devoured him." We shall see what will become of his dreams!' "

But Reuben could not bear to think of murdering his brother and proposed that they throw Joseph alive into a pit and leave him there to die. He secretly intended, however, to rescue him and return him to his father. After persuading all to adopt his plan, Reuben left, fearing that his real intentions would be discovered.

Joseph arrived, not suspecting the danger. But instead of the expected greeting, he was terrified by the angry and revengeful glances that met him. His brothers grabbed him and stripped his coat from him. Their taunts and threats revealed a deadly purpose. He pleaded with them, but they refused to listen. Those hate-filled men dragged him roughly to a deep pit, pushed him in, and left him there to die.

Joseph Is Sold as a Slave

Soon a group of travelers approached—a caravan of Ishmaelites on their way to Egypt with merchandise. Judah now suggested they sell their brother instead of leaving him to die. While he would be effectively put out of their way, they would remain clear of his blood, " 'for,' " he urged, " 'he is our brother and our flesh.' " All agreed, and Joseph was quickly pulled up out of the pit.

As he saw the merchants, the dreadful truth flashed upon him. To become a slave was more to be feared than death. In an agony of terror he appealed to one and another of his brothers, but in vain.

Some were moved with pity, but all felt that they had now gone too far to retreat. Joseph would report them to their father. Steeling their hearts against his pleas, they delivered him into the hands of the heathen traders. The caravan moved on and was soon out of sight.

Reuben returned to the pit, but Joseph was not there. When he learned what had happened to Joseph, he was persuaded to go along with the attempt to conceal their guilt. Having killed a young goat, they dipped Joseph's coat in its blood and took it to their father, telling him that they had found it in the fields. " 'Do you know,' " they said, " 'whether it is your son's tunic or not?' " They were not prepared for the heart-rending anguish, the utter and unrestrained grief, that they were compelled to witness. " 'It is my son's tunic,' " said Jacob. " 'A wild beast has devoured him. Without doubt Joseph is torn to pieces.' " His sons and daughters tried to comfort him, But he "tore his clothes, put sackcloth on his waist, and mourned for his son many days." " 'I shall go down into the grave to my son in mourning,' " was his despairing cry.

The young men, terrified at what they had done, yet dreading their father's condemnation, still kept quiet about their guilt, which even to themselves seemed very great.

The Amazing Story of Joseph*

Meanwhile, Joseph was on the way to Egypt with his captors. In the distance the boy could discern the hills among which lay his father's tents. Bitterly he wept at the thought of that loving father in his loneliness and affliction. Ringing in his ears were the stinging, insulting words that had met his agonized pleadings at Dothan. With a trembling heart he looked forward to the future. Alone and friendless, what would be his destiny in the strange land to which he was going? For a time, Joseph gave himself up to uncontrolled grief and terror.

But even this experience was to be a blessing to him. He had learned things in a few hours that years might not otherwise have taught him. His father had done him wrong by his favoritism and lack of discipline. This had angered his brothers and provoked the cruel deed that had separated him from his home. In his character, faults had been encouraged. He was becoming self-sufficient and demanding. He felt that he was unprepared to cope with the difficulties facing him in the bitter, uncared-for life of a slave.

Then his thoughts turned to his father's God. Often he had listened to the story of the vision that Jacob saw as he fled from his home an exile and a fugitive. He had been told of the Lord's promises to Jacob and how, in the hour of need, angels had come to instruct, comfort, and protect him. He had learned of the love of God in providing a Redeemer. Now all these precious lessons came vividly before him. Joseph believed that the God of his fathers would be his God. Then and there he gave himself fully to the Lord and prayed that the Keeper of Israel would be with him in his exile.

His soul thrilled with the high resolve to prove true to God, to act as a subject of the King of heaven. He would meet the trials of his life with inner strength and perform every duty faithfully. One day's terrible calamity had changed him from a pampered child to a man, thoughtful, courageous, and self-possessed.

Arriving in Egypt, Joseph was sold to Potiphar, captain of the king's guard. For ten years here he was exposed to temptations in the

---

* *This chapter is based on Genesis 39 to 41.*

midst of idolatry, surrounded by all the pomp of royalty, the wealth and culture of the most highly civilized nation then in existence. Yet Joseph preserved his faithfulness to God. The sights and sounds of evil were all around him, but he was like someone who neither saw nor heard. He did not permit his thoughts to linger on forbidden subjects. The desire to gain the favor of the Egyptians could not cause him to conceal his principles. He made no effort to hide the fact that he was a worshiper of Jehovah.

"The LORD was with Joseph, and he was a successful man. . . . And his master saw that the LORD was with him and that the LORD made all he did to prosper in his hand." Potiphar's confidence in Joseph increased daily, and he finally promoted him to be his steward, with full control over all his possessions. "So he left all that he had in Joseph's hand, and he did not know what he had except for the bread which he ate."

Joseph's industry, care, and energy were crowned with the divine blessing; even his idolatrous master accepted this as the secret of his prosperity. God was glorified by His servant's faithfulness. He intended that the believer in God should appear in sharp contrast to the worshipers of idols. Thus the light of heavenly grace would shine out amid the darkness of heathenism.

The chief captain came to regard Joseph as a son rather than a slave. The youth was brought into contact with men of rank and learning, and he acquired a knowledge of science, languages, and public affairs—an education needful to the future prime minister of Egypt.

The Almost Overmastering Temptation

But Joseph's master's wife tried to entice the young man to transgress the law of God. He had remained pure of the corruption filling that heathen land, but this temptation, so sudden, so strong, so seductive—how should he deal with it?

Joseph knew well what refusing would bring. On the one hand were concealment, favor, and rewards; on the other, disgrace, imprisonment, perhaps death. His whole future life depended on the decision of the moment. Would Joseph be true to God? With inexpressible anxiety, angels looked on the scene.

Joseph's answer reveals the power of religious principle. He would not betray the confidence of his master on earth, and, whatever the consequences, he would be true to his Master in heaven. Joseph's first thought was of God. " 'How then can I do this great wickedness, and sin against God?' " he said.

Young people should always remember that wherever they are and whatever they do, they are in the presence of God. No part of our conduct escapes God's notice. We cannot hide our ways from the Most High. To every deed there is an unseen witness. Every act, every word, every thought is as distinctly noted as though there were only one person in the whole world.

Joseph suffered for his integrity.

His tempter took revenge by causing him to be put into prison. If Potiphar had believed his wife's charge against Joseph, the young Hebrew would have lost his life, but the modesty and uprightness that had characterized his conduct were proof of his innocence. Yet to save the reputation of his master's house, he was sent to disgrace and bondage.

At first Joseph was treated harshly by his jailers. The psalmist says, "They hurt his feet with fetters, he was laid in irons. Until the time that his word came to pass, the word of the LORD tested him." Psalm 105:18, 19.

Joseph in Prison

But Joseph's real character shone even in the dungeon. His years of faithful service had been most cruelly repaid, yet this did not turn him gloomy or make him distrustful. He had peace and trusted his case with God. He did not brood over his own wrongs but forgot his sorrow in trying to lighten the sorrows of others. He found a work to do, even in the prison. God was preparing him in the school of affliction for greater usefulness, and he did not refuse the needed discipline. He learned lessons of justice, sympathy, and mercy that prepared him to exercise power with wisdom and compassion.

Joseph gradually gained the confidence of the keeper of the prison, who finally entrusted him with the charge of all the prisoners. His conduct in the prison—his integrity and his sympathy for those in trouble and distress—opened the way for his future prosperity and honor. If prompted by a right motive, every kind word spoken to the sorrowful, every act to relieve the oppressed, and every gift to the needy, will result in blessings to the giver.

The king's chief baker and chief butler had been imprisoned for some offense, and they came under Joseph's responsibility. One morning, noting that they appeared very sad, he kindly inquired the cause and was told that each had had a remarkable dream, and they were anxious to learn the meaning. " 'Do not interpretations belong to God?' " said Joseph. " 'Tell them to me, please.' "

As each related his dream, Joseph made known its meaning. In three days the butler was to be restored to his position and place the cup in Pharaoh's hand as before, but the chief baker would be put to death by the king's command. Both events occurred as foretold.

The king's cupbearer had professed deep gratitude to Joseph for the cheering interpretation of his dream and for many acts of kind attention. In return Joseph, referring to his own unjust captivity, pleaded for his case to be brought before the king. " 'Remember me,' " he said, " 'when it is well with you, and please show kindness to me; make mention of me to Pharaoh, and get me out of this house. For indeed I was stolen away from the land of the Hebrews; and also I have done nothing here that they should put me into the dungeon.' "

The chief butler saw the dream

fulfilled in every particular; but when he was restored to royal favor, he forgot all about the one who had helped him. For two years longer, Joseph remained a prisoner. The hope that had been kindled in his heart gradually died out, and to all other trials was added the bitter sting of ingratitude.

But a divine hand was about to open the prison gates. The king of Egypt had two dreams in one night, apparently pointing to the same event and seeming to foreshadow some great calamity. The magicians and wise men could give no interpretation. The king's perplexity increased, and terror spread throughout his palace. The general agitation reminded the chief butler of his own dream; with it came the memory of Joseph and remorse for his forgetfulness and ingratitude. At once he informed the king how his own dream and that of the chief baker had been interpreted by a Hebrew captive and how the prediction had been fulfilled.

It was humiliating to Pharaoh to consult a slave, but he was ready to do so if his troubled mind might find relief. Joseph was immediately sent for; he put off his prison clothes and was taken to the king.

"And Pharaoh said to Joseph, 'I have dreamed a dream, and there is no one who can interpret it. But I have heard it said of you that you can understand a dream, to interpret it.' So Joseph answered Pharaoh, saying, 'It is not in me; God will give Pharaoh an answer of peace.' " Joseph modestly disclaimed the honor of possessing superior wisdom in himself. God alone can explain these mysteries.

Pharaoh then proceeded to relate his dreams: " 'Suddenly seven cows came up out of the river, fine looking and fat; and they fed in the meadow. Then behold, seven other cows came up after them, poor and very ugly and gaunt, such ugliness as I have never seen in all the land of Egypt. And the gaunt and ugly cows ate up the first seven, the fat cows. When they had eaten them up, no one would have known that they had eaten them, for they were just as ugly as at the beginning. So I awoke. Also I saw in my dream, and suddenly seven heads came up on one stalk, full and good. Then behold, seven heads, withered, thin, and blighted by the east wind, sprang up after them. And the thin heads devoured the seven good heads. So I told this to the magicians, but there was no one who could explain it to me.' "

The Interpretation of Pharaoh's Dream

Joseph said, " 'God has shown Pharaoh what He is about to do.' " There were to be seven years of great plenty. Field and garden would yield more abundantly than ever before. And this period was to be followed by seven years of famine. " 'So the plenty will not be known in the land because of the famine following, for it will be very severe.' " " 'Now therefore,' " he continued, " 'let Pharaoh select a discerning and wise man, and set him over the land of Egypt. Let Pharaoh do this, and let him appoint officers over the land, to collect one-fifth of the produce of the land of Egypt in the seven plentiful years. And let them gather all the food of those good years that are coming, and store up grain under the authority of Pharaoh, and let them keep food in the cities. Then that food shall be as a reserve for the land for the seven years of famine.' "

The interpretation was reasonable and consistent. The policy it recommended was sound and sensible. But who was to be entrusted with carrying out the plan? The nation's preservation depended on the wisdom of this choice.

For some time the matter of the appointment was under consideration. Through the chief butler the monarch had learned of Joseph's wisdom and good judgment in managing the prison. It was plain that he possessed superior administrative ability. In all the realm, Joseph was the only man gifted with wisdom to point out the danger that threatened the kingdom and the preparation necessary to meet it. There were none among the king's officers of state so well qualified to conduct the affairs of the nation at this crisis. " 'Can we find such a one as this, a man in whom is the Spirit of God?' " said the king to his counselors.

From Prisoner to Prime Minister

To Joseph came the astonishing announcement, " 'Inasmuch as God has shown you all this, there is no one as discerning and wise as you. You shall be over my house, and all my people shall be ruled according to your word; only in regard to the throne will I be greater than you.' " "Then Pharaoh took his signet ring off his hand and put it on Joseph's hand; and he clothed him in garments of fine linen and put a gold chain around his neck. And he had him ride in the second chariot which he had; and they cried out before him, 'Bow the knee!' "

From the dungeon, Joseph was exalted to be ruler over all the land of Egypt, a position of high honor, yet surrounded with peril. One cannot stand on a lofty height without danger. The tempest leaves the lowly flower of the valley unharmed while it uproots the stately tree on the mountaintop. So those who have maintained their integrity in humble life may be dragged down by the temptations that come with worldly success and honor. But Joseph's character bore the test of adversity and prosperity alike. He was a stranger in a heathen land, separated from his family, but he fully believed that the divine hand had directed his life. In constant reliance on God he faithfully discharged the duties of his position. The attention of the king and great men of Egypt was directed to the true God, and they learned to respect the principles revealed in Joseph as a worshiper of Jehovah.

In his early years Joseph had followed duty rather than inclination, and the integrity, the simple trust, the noble nature of the youth bore fruit in the deeds of the man.

The varied circumstances that we meet day by day are designed to test our faithfulness and qualify us for greater trusts. By sticking to principle the mind becomes accustomed to hold the claims of duty above pleasure and desire. Minds thus disciplined are not wavering between right and wrong like the reed trembling in the wind. By faithfulness in that which is least, they acquire strength to be faithful in greater matters.

An upright character is of greater value than the gold of Ophir. Without it none can rise to an honorable height. The formation of a noble character is the work of a lifetime. God gives opportunities; success depends on the use we make of them.

Joseph and His Brothers*

Under the direction of Joseph, huge buildings were erected throughout the land of Egypt in which to store the surplus of the expected harvest. During the seven years of plenty the amount of grain laid in store was beyond computing.

And now the seven years of famine began, according to Joseph's prediction. "The famine was in all lands, but in all the land of Egypt there was bread. So when all the land of Egypt was famished, the people cried to Pharaoh for bread. Then Pharaoh said to all the Egyptians, 'Go to Joseph; whatever he says to you, do.' The famine was over all the face of the earth, and Joseph opened all the storehouses and sold to the Egyptians."

The famine was severe in the country where Jacob lived. Hearing of the abundant provision made by the king of Egypt, ten of Jacob's sons journeyed there to buy grain. They were directed to the king's deputy and came to present themselves before the ruler of the land. And they "bowed down before him with their faces to the earth." "Joseph recognized his brothers, but they did not

recognize him." His Hebrew name had been changed, and there was little resemblance between the prime minister of Egypt and the youth they had sold to the Ishmaelites. As Joseph saw his brothers stooping and bowing down, his dreams and the scenes of the past rose vividly before him. His keen eye discovered that Benjamin was not among them. Had he also fallen victim to treacherous cruelty? He determined to learn the truth. " 'You are spies!' " he said sternly. " 'You have come to see the nakedness of the land!' "

They answered, " 'No, my lord, but your servants have come to buy food. . . . We are honest men; your servants are not spies.' " He wished to draw some information from them about their home, yet he knew how deceptive their statements could be. He repeated the charge, and they replied, " 'Your servants are twelve brothers, the sons of one man in the land of Canaan; and in fact, the youngest is with our father today, and one is no more.' "

Professing to doubt their story, the governor declared that he would require them to remain in Egypt till

* This chapter is based on Genesis 41:54-56; 42 to 50.

one of their number would go and bring their youngest brother. If they would not consent, they were to be treated as spies. But the sons of Jacob could not agree to this arrangement, since the time required would cause their families to suffer for food; and who among them would set out on the journey alone, leaving his brothers in prison? It seemed likely that they were to be put to death or made slaves, and if Benjamin were brought, it might be only to share their fate. They decided to remain and suffer together rather than bring additional sorrow on their father by the loss of his only remaining son. And so they were thrown into prison.

Wicked Men Had Learned Repentance

These sons of Jacob had changed in character. Envious, hot-headed, deceptive, cruel, and revengeful they had been; but now, tested by adversity, they were unselfish, true to one another, devoted to their father, and, even now as middle-aged men, subject to his authority.

Three days in the Egyptian prison were days of bitter sorrow as the brothers reflected on their sins. Unless Benjamin could be brought, their conviction as spies appeared certain.

On the third day, Joseph had the brothers brought before him. He dared not detain them longer. Already his father and the families with him might be suffering for food. " 'Do this and live,' " he said; " 'for I fear God: If you are honest men, let one of your brothers be confined to

your prison house; but you, go and carry grain for the famine of your houses. And bring your youngest brother to me; so your words will be verified, and you shall not die.' "

Joseph had communicated with them through an interpreter. Having no idea that the governor understood them, they talked freely with one another in his presence. " 'We are truly guilty concerning our brother, for we saw the anguish of his soul when he pleaded with us, and we would not hear; therefore this distress has come upon us.' " Reuben, who had formed the plan for delivering Joseph at Dothan, added, " 'Did I not speak to you, saying, "Do not sin against the boy"; and you would not listen? Therefore behold, his blood is now required of us.' "

Joseph, listening, could not control his emotions, and he went out and wept. When he returned, he commanded that Simeon be bound before their eyes and again committed to prison. In the cruel treatment of their brother, Simeon had been the instigator and chief actor.

Before permitting his brothers to leave, Joseph gave directions that they should be supplied with grain and that each man's money should be secretly placed in the mouth of his sack. On the way, one of the group, opening his sack, was surprised to find his bag of silver. The others were alarmed and said, " 'What is this that God has done to us?' "

Jacob was anxiously awaiting the return of his sons, and when they arrived, the whole encampment gathered eagerly around as they told their father all that had happened. Dread filled every heart. The conduct of the Egyptian governor seemed to imply some evil intent, and their fears were confirmed when, as they opened their sacks, the owner's money was found in each. In his distress the aged father exclaimed, " 'You have bereaved me . . . : Joseph is no more, Simeon is no more, and you want to take Benjamin away. All these things are against me.' " " 'My son shall not go down with you, for his brother is dead, and he is left alone. If any calamity should befall him along the way in which you go, then you would bring down my gray hair with sorrow to the grave.' "

But the drought continued, and the supply of grain from Egypt was nearly exhausted. Deeper and deeper grew the shadow of approaching famine. In the anxious faces of all in the encampment, the old man read their need. At last he said, " 'Go back, buy us a little food.' "

Judah answered, " 'The man solemnly warned us, saying, "You shall not see my face unless your brother is with you." If you send our brother with us, we will go down and buy you food. But if you will not send him, we will not go down; for the man said to us, "You shall not see my face unless your brother is with you." ' " Seeing that his father's resolve began to waver, he said, " 'Send the lad with me, and we will arise and go, that we may live and not die, both we and you and also our little ones.' " He offered to be responsible for his brother and to bear the blame forever if he failed to bring Benjamin back to his father.

Jacob could no longer withhold his consent. He instructed his sons to take to the ruler a present of such things as the famine-wasted country had—" 'a little balm and a little honey, spices and myrrh, pistachio nuts and almonds,' " and also a double quantity of money. " 'Take your brother also,' " he said, " 'and arise, go back to the man.' " As his sons were about to leave on their doubtful trip, the aged father arose, and raising his hands to heaven, uttered the prayer, " 'May God Almighty give you mercy before the man, that he may release your other brother and Benjamin.' "

Again they journeyed to Egypt and presented themselves before Joseph. As he looked at Benjamin, his own mother's son, he was deeply moved. He hid his emotion but ordered that they be taken to his house to dine with him. The brothers were greatly alarmed, afraid of being accused regarding the money found in their sacks. They thought that it might have been placed there to furnish a reason for making them slaves. In proof of their innocence they informed the steward of the house that they had brought back the money found in their sacks, also other money to buy food; and they added, " 'We do not know who put our money in our sacks.' " The man replied, " 'Peace be with you, do not be afraid. Your God and the God of your father has given you treasure in your sacks; I had your money.' " Their anxiety was relieved, and when

Simeon was released from prison and joined them, they felt that God was indeed gracious to them.

Joseph's Dreams Again Fulfilled

When the governor again met them, they presented their gifts and humbly "bowed down before him to the earth." Again his dreams came to his mind, and he quickly asked, " 'Is your father well, the old man of whom you spoke? Is he still alive?' " " 'Your servant our father is in good health; he is still alive,' " was the answer, as they again bowed down. Then his eye rested on Benjamin, and he said, " 'Is this your younger brother of whom you spoke to me?' " " 'God be gracious to you, my son,' " but overpowered by feelings of tenderness, he could say no more. "He went into his chamber and wept there."

When Joseph recovered his composure, he returned. By the laws of caste, the Egyptians were forbidden to eat with people of any other nation. For this reason the sons of Jacob had a table by themselves, while the governor, because of his high rank, ate by himself. The Egyptians also had separate tables. When all were seated, the brothers were surprised to see that they were arranged in exact order according to their ages. Joseph sent "servings to them from before him," but Benjamin's was five times as much as any of theirs. He hoped to find out if the youngest brother was regarded with the envy and hatred that the brothers had shown toward himself. Still supposing that Joseph did not understand their language, the brothers freely conversed with one another, giving him a good opportunity to learn their real feelings. Still he wanted to test them further. Before they left Egypt he ordered that his own drinking cup of silver be placed in the sack of the youngest.

Final Test of Their Repentance

Joyfully they set out on their return. Simeon and Benjamin were with them, their animals were well-burdened with grain, and all felt that they had safely escaped the perils that had seemed to surround them. But they had only reached the outskirts of the city when they were overtaken by the governor's steward, who inquired angrily, " 'Why have you repaid evil for good? Is not this the one from which my lord drinks, and with which he indeed practices divination? You have done evil in so doing.' " This cup was supposed to possess the power of detecting any poisonous substance placed in it. Cups of this kind were highly valued as a safeguard against murder by poisoning.

To the steward's accusation the travelers answered, " 'Why does my lord say these words? Far be it from us that your servants should do such a thing. Look, we brought back to you from the land of Canaan the money which we found in the mouth of our sacks. How then could we steal silver or gold from your lord's house? With whomever of your servants it is found, let him die, and we also will be my lord's slaves.' "

" 'Let it be according to your

words,' " said the steward; " 'he with whom it is found shall be my slave, and you shall be blameless.' "

The search began immediately. "Then each man speedily let down his sack to the ground," and the steward examined each, beginning with Reuben's, and taking them in order down to that of the youngest. In Benjamin's sack the cup was found.

The brothers tore their clothes in utter wretchedness and slowly returned to the city. By their own promise, Benjamin was doomed to slavery. They followed the steward to the palace, and finding the governor still there, fell to the ground before him.

" 'What deed is this you have done?' " he said. " 'Did you not know that such a man as I can certainly practice divination?' " Joseph intended to draw from them an acknowledgment of their sin.

Judah answered, " 'What shall we say to my lord? What shall we speak? Or how shall we clear ourselves? God has found out the iniquity of your servants; here we are, my lord's slaves, both we and he also with whom the cup was found.' "

" 'Far be it from me that I should do so,' " was the reply. " 'The man in whose hand the cup was found, he shall be my slave. And as for you, go up in peace to your father.' "

Judah's Plea

In his distress, Judah drew near the ruler. Eloquently he described his father's grief at the loss of Joseph and his reluctance to let Benjamin come with them to Egypt, as he was the only son left of his mother, Rachel, whom Jacob so dearly loved. " 'Now therefore,' " he said, " 'when I come to your servant my father, and the lad is not with us, since his life is bound up in the lad's life, it will happen, when he sees that the lad is not with us, that he will die. So your servants will bring down the gray hair of your servant our father with sorrow to the grave. For your servant became surety for the lad to my father, saying, "If I do not bring him back to you, then I shall bear the blame before my father forever." Now therefore, please let your servant remain instead of the lad as a slave to my lord, and let the lad go up with his brothers. For how shall I go up to my father if the lad is not with me, lest perhaps I see the evil that would come upon my father?' "

Joseph was satisfied. He had seen in his brothers the fruits of true repentance. He gave orders for all but these men to withdraw. Then, weeping aloud, he said, " 'I am Joseph; does my father still live?' "

Reconciliation!

His brothers stood motionless, silent with fear and amazement. The ruler of Egypt was their brother Joseph, whom they had envied and would have murdered, and finally sold as a slave! All their bad treatment of him passed before them. They remembered how long they had hated his dreams and had worked to prevent their fulfillment. Yet they had acted their part in fulfilling these dreams. Now that they were completely in his power, he would, no doubt, avenge the wrong that he had suffered.

Seeing their confusion, he said kindly, " 'Please come near to me,' " and as they came near, he continued, " 'I am Joseph your brother, whom you sold into Egypt. But now, do not therefore be grieved or angry with yourselves because you sold me here; for God sent me before you to preserve life.' " Feeling that they had suffered enough for their cruelty toward him, he nobly tried to banish their fears and lessen the bitterness of their self-condemnation.

" 'God sent me before you to preserve a posterity for you in the earth, and to save your lives by a great deliverance. So now it was not you who sent me here, but God; and He has made me a father to Pharaoh, and lord of all his house, and a ruler throughout all the land of Egypt. Hasten and go up to my father, and say to him, "Thus says your son Joseph: 'God has made me lord of all Egypt; come down to me, do not tarry. You shall dwell in the land of Goshen . . . lest you and your household, and all that you have, come to poverty; for there are still five years of famine.' " ' " "Then he fell on his brother Benjamin's neck and wept, and Benjamin wept on his neck. Moreover he kissed all his brothers and wept over them, and after that his brothers talked with him." They humbly confessed their sin and begged his forgiveness.

The news of what had taken place was quickly carried to the king. He confirmed the governor's invitation to his family, saying, " 'The best of all the land of Egypt is yours.' " The brothers were sent away abundantly supplied with food and everything necessary to bring all their families and servants to Egypt.

The sons of Jacob returned to their father with the joyful news. " 'Joseph is still alive, and he is governor over all the land of Egypt.' " At first the aged man was overwhelmed; he could not believe what he heard; but when he saw the long train of wagons and loaded animals, and when Benjamin was with him once more, he was convinced. In the fullness of his joy he exclaimed, " 'It is enough. Joseph my son is still alive. I will go and see him before I die.' "

Another act of humiliation remained for the ten brothers. They now confessed to their father the deceit and cruelty that had embittered his life and theirs for so many years. Jacob had not suspected them of such a vile sin, but he forgave and blessed his erring children.

The father and his sons, with their families, their flocks and herds, and numerous attendants, were soon on their way to Egypt. In a vision of the night the divine word came: " 'Do not fear to go down to Egypt, for I will make of you a great nation there. I will go down with you to Egypt, and I will also surely bring you up again.' "

The promise of descendants as numberless as the stars had been given to Abraham, but so far the chosen people had increased quite slowly. And the land of Canaan was in the possession of powerful heathen tribes that were not to be dispossessed until "the fourth generation." To become a numerous people, the descendants of Israel must either drive out the inhabitants of the land or disperse themselves among them. If they mingled with the Canaanites, they would be in danger of being drawn into idolatry. Egypt, however, offered the conditions necessary to fulfill God's plan. A section of country, well-watered and fertile, was open to them there, offering every advantage for their speedy increase. And they would remain a distinct and separate people, shut out from participating in the idolatry of Egypt.

When they reached Egypt, the company proceeded directly to the land of Goshen. Joseph came there in his chariot of state, accompanied by princely attendants. One thought alone filled his mind, one longing thrilled his heart. As he watched the travelers approaching, the love whose yearnings he had repressed for so many years would no longer be controlled. He sprang from his chariot and hurried to welcome his father. "And he presented himself to him, and fell on his neck and wept on his neck a good while. And Israel said to Joseph, 'Now let me die, since I have seen your face, because you are still alive.' "

Joseph wished to save his brothers from the temptations to which they would be exposed at a heathen court, so he counseled them to tell the monarch frankly their occupation. The sons of Jacob followed this counsel, being careful also to state

that they had come to stay in the land temporarily, not to become permanent dwellers, thus reserving the right to leave if they chose.

Jacob's Sunset Years

Not long after their arrival, Joseph brought his father to be presented to the king. Jacob was a stranger in royal courts, but amid the grand scenes of nature he had communed with a mightier Monarch. Now, in conscious superiority, he raised his hands and blessed Pharaoh.

In his first greeting to Joseph, Jacob had spoken as if, with this joyful ending to his long anxiety and sorrow, he was ready to die. But seventeen years were yet to be granted him in the peaceful retirement of Goshen. These years were in happy contrast to those that had preceded them. In his sons he saw evidence of true repentance. He saw his family surrounded by all the conditions they would need to develop into a great nation. And his faith grasped the sure promise that they would be established in Canaan in the future. He himself was surrounded with every token of love and favor that the prime minister of Egypt could bestow.

Jacob Adopts Joseph's Sons

Another matter demanded attention—the sons of Joseph were to be formally instated among the children of Israel. Joseph, coming for a last interview with his father, brought with him Ephraim and Manasseh. Through their mother, these youths were connected with the highest order of the Egyptian priesthood, and the position of their father opened to them the paths to wealth and distinction, if they chose to connect themselves with the Egyptians. It was Joseph's desire, however, that they would unite with their own people. He showed his faith in the covenant promise, renouncing in behalf of his sons all the honors that the court of Egypt offered, for a place among the despised shepherd tribes who had been entrusted with the oracles of God.

Said Jacob, " 'Your two sons, Ephraim and Manasseh, who were born to you in the land of Egypt before I came to you in Egypt, are mine; as Reuben and Simeon, they shall be mine.' " They were to be adopted as his own and to become the heads of separate tribes.

As they came nearer, the patriarch embraced and kissed them, solemnly laying his hands on their heads in blessing. Then he prayed, " 'God, before whom my fathers Abraham and Isaac walked, the God who has fed me all my life long to this day, the Angel who has redeemed me from all evil, bless the lads.' " There was no complaint of the evil days in the past. He no longer regarded its trials and sorrows as things against him. Memory recalled only the mercy and loving-kindness of God, who had been with Jacob throughout his pilgrimage.

All the sons of Jacob were gathered around his deathbed. "And Jacob called his sons and said, 'Gather together, that I may tell you what shall befall you in the last days.' "

Jacob Foretells the Future of His Sons

The Spirit of Inspiration rested on him, and in prophetic vision the future of his descendants was unfolded before him. One after another the names of his sons were mentioned, the character of each was described, and the future history of the tribe was briefly foretold.

"Reuben, you are my firstborn,
My might and the beginning of my strength,
The excellency of dignity and the excellency of power."

But Reuben's terrible sin at Edar had made him unworthy of the birthright blessing. Jacob continued,

"Unstable as water, you shall not excel."

The priesthood was given to Levi, the kingdom and the Messianic promise to Judah, and the double portion of the inheritance to Joseph. The tribe of Reuben never rose to any prominence in Israel; it was not as numerous as Judah, Joseph, or Dan and was among the first to be carried into captivity.

Next were Simeon and Levi. They had been united in cruelty toward the Shechemites and had been the most guilty in the selling of Joseph.

"I will divide them in Jacob
And scatter them in Israel."

Moses, in his last blessing to Israel before entering Canaan, made no reference to Simeon. In the settlement of Canaan, this tribe received only a small portion of Judah's lot, and any families that afterward became powerful formed different colonies and settled in territory outside the borders of the Holy Land. Levi also received no inheritance except forty-eight cities. However, their faithfulness when the other tribes apostatized secured their appointment to the sacred service of the sanctuary. In this way the curse was changed into a blessing.

The crowning blessings of the birthright were transferred to Judah:

"Judah, you are he whom your
    brothers shall praise;
Your hand shall be on the neck of
    your enemies;
Your father's children shall bow
    down before you. . . .
The scepter shall not depart from
    Judah,
Nor a lawgiver from between his
    feet,
Until Shiloh comes;
And to Him shall be the obedience
    of the people."

The lion, king of the forest, is a fitting symbol for this tribe, from which came David, and the Son of David, Shiloh, the true "Lion of the tribe of Judah," to whom all powers shall finally bow and all nations give honor.

For most of his children, Jacob foretold a prosperous future. At last he reached the name of Joseph, and the father's heart overflowed as he invoked blessings upon " 'the head of him who was separate from his brothers' ":

"Joseph is a fruitful bough,
A fruitful bough by a well;
His branches run over the wall.
The archers have bitterly grieved
    him,
Shot at him and hated him.
But his bow remained in strength,
And the arms of his hands were
    made strong
By the hands of the mighty God of
    Jacob . . . .
The blessings of your father
Have excelled the blessings of my
    ancestors,
Up to the utmost bound of the
    everlasting hills.
They shall be on the head of
    Joseph,
And on the crown of the head of
    him who was separate from his
    brothers."

Jacob was a man of deep affection; his love for his sons was strong and tender. He had forgiven them all, and he loved them to the last. His fatherly tenderness would have found expression only in words of encouragement and hope, but the power of God rested on him. Under the influence of Inspiration he was led to declare the truth, however painful.

Jacob's last years brought an evening of tranquillity and rest after a troubled and weary day. Dark clouds had gathered above his path, yet his sun set clear, and the radiance of heaven lighted up his parting hours. Says the Scripture, "At evening time it shall . . . be light." Zechariah 14:7. "Mark the blameless man, and observe the upright; for the future of that man is peace." Psalm 37:37.

Inspiration faithfully records the faults of good people who were distinguished by the favor of God. This has given the infidel occasion to scoff at the Bible. But it is one of the strongest evidences of the truth of Scripture that it does not gloss over the facts or suppress the sins of its chief characters. If the Bible had been written by uninspired persons, it would surely have presented its honored characters in a more flattering light.

Seeing where others struggled through discouragements like our own, where they fell when tempted as we have done and yet took heart again and conquered through the grace of God, we are encouraged in our quest for righteousness. Though sometimes they were beaten back, they recovered their ground and were blessed of God. So we, too, may be overcomers in the strength of Jesus. On the other hand, the record of their lives may serve as a warning to us. God sees sin in His most favored ones, and He deals with it in them even more strictly than in those who have less light and responsibility.

After the death and burial of Jacob, fear again filled the hearts of Joseph's brothers. They were conscious of their guilt, and this made them distrustful and suspicious that Joseph would now inflict on them the long-deferred punishment for their crime. They dared not appear before him but sent a message, " 'Before your father died he commanded, saying, "Thus you shall say to Joseph: 'I beg you, please forgive the trespass of your brothers and their sin; for they did evil to you.' " Now, please, forgive the trespass of the servants of the God of your father.' "

This message touched Joseph, bringing him to tears. Encouraged by this, his brothers came and fell down before him with the words, " 'Behold, we are your servants.' " Joseph was pained that they could think he would cherish a spirit of revenge. " 'Do not be afraid,' " he said; " 'for am I in the place of God? But as for you, you meant evil against me; but God meant it for good, in order to bring it about as it is this day, to save many people alive. Now therefore, do not be afraid; I will provide for you and your little ones.' "

Seeing Christ in Joseph

The life of Joseph illustrates the life of Christ. It was envy that moved the brothers of Joseph to sell him as a slave; they hoped to prevent him from becoming greater than they themselves. They felt certain that they were to be troubled no more with his dreams, that they had removed all possibility of their fulfillment. But God overruled their course to bring about the very event they intended to hinder. Similarly, the priests and elders were jealous of Christ. They put Him to death to prevent Him from becoming king, but in doing so they brought about this very result.

Through his bondage in Egypt, Joseph became a savior to his father's family, yet this fact did not lessen the guilt of his brothers. So the crucifixion of Christ by His enemies made Him the Redeemer of humankind, the Savior of the fallen race, and Ruler over the whole world; but the crime of His murderers was just as dreadful as though God's guiding hand had not controlled events.

Joseph was falsely accused and thrown into prison because of his virtue; so Christ was despised and rejected because His righteous, self-denying life was a rebuke to sin; and though guilty of no wrong, He was condemned on the testimony of false witnesses. And Joseph's patience under injustice, his ready forgiveness and noble graciousness toward his unnatural-behaving brothers represent the Savior's uncomplaining endurance of the hate and abuse of wicked men and His forgiveness of all who come to Him confessing their sins and seeking pardon.

Joseph lived to see the increase and prosperity of his people, and through all the years his faith in God to restore Israel to the Land of Promise was unshaken.

When he saw that his end was near, his last act was to show that his lot was cast with Israel. His last words were, " 'God will surely visit you, and bring you out of this land to the land of which He swore to Abraham, to Isaac, and to Jacob.' " And he took a solemn oath from the children of Israel that they would carry his bones with them back to the land of Canaan. "So Joseph died, being one hundred and ten years old; and they embalmed him, and he was put in a coffin in Egypt."

Through the following centuries of toil, that coffin testified to Israel that they were only staying in Egypt temporarily. It called them to keep their hopes fixed on the Land of Promise, for the time of deliverance would surely come.

Moses, the Leader of God's People *

In recognition of the service that Joseph had rendered the Egyptian nation, the children of Jacob were not only granted a part of the country as a home but were exempted from taxes and liberally supplied with food during the famine. The king publicly acknowledged that it was through the God of Joseph that Egypt enjoyed plenty while other nations were dying from famine. He saw, too, that Joseph's management had greatly enriched the kingdom, and his gratitude surrounded the family of Jacob with royal favor.

But as time rolled on, the great man to whom Egypt owed so much passed to the grave. And "there arose a new king over Egypt, who did not know Joseph." Not that he was ignorant of Joseph's services to the nation, but he did not wish to recognize them. As far as possible, he wanted them to be forgotten. "And he said to his people, 'Look, the people of the children of Israel are more and mightier than we; come, let us deal wisely with them, lest they multiply, and it happen, in the event of war, that

they also join our enemies and fight against us, and so go up out of the land.' "

The Israelites already "were fruitful and increased abundantly, multiplied and grew exceedingly mighty; and the land was filled with them." But they had kept themselves a distinct race, having nothing in common with the Egyptians in customs or religion, and their increasing numbers now fueled the fears of the king and his people.

Many of them were able and skilled workmen, and they added greatly to the wealth of the nation. The king needed such workers in erecting his magnificent palaces and temples. He therefore ranked them with Egyptians who had sold themselves and their possessions to the kingdom. Soon taskmasters were set over them, and their slavery became complete. "The Egyptians made the children of Israel serve with rigor. And they made their lives bitter with hard bondage—in mortar, in brick, and in all manner of service in the field." "But the more they afflicted them, the more they multiplied and grew."

---

* This chapter is based on Exodus 1 to 4.

The king and his counselors had hoped to subdue the Israelites with hard labor, decrease their numbers, and crush their independent spirit. Orders were now issued to the women, whose jobs gave them opportunity, to destroy the Hebrew male children at their birth. Satan knew that a deliverer was to come from among the Israelites, and by leading the king to destroy their children he hoped to defeat the divine plan. But the women feared God and did not dare to carry out the cruel command.

The king, angry at the failure of his plot, made the orders more urgent and extensive. "Pharaoh commanded all his people, saying, 'Every son who is born you shall cast into the river, and every daughter you shall save alive.' "

Moses Born in the Worst of Times

While this command was in full force, a boy baby was born to Amram and Jochebed, Israelites of the tribe of Levi. The parents, believing that the time for Israel to be set free was drawing near and that God would raise up a deliverer for His people, determined that their little one should not be sacrificed. Faith in God strengthened their hearts, "and they were not afraid of the king's command." Hebrews 11:23.

The mother hid the child for three months. Then, finding that she could no longer keep him safely, she prepared a little ark of rushes, making it watertight by means of asphalt and pitch; and, laying her baby in it, she placed it among the reeds at the river's edge. His sister Miriam lingered near, anxiously watching to see what would become of her little brother.

And there were other watchers. The mother had committed her child to the care of God; and angels, unseen, hovered above his lowly resting place. Angels directed Pharaoh's daughter to that spot. The little basket aroused her curiosity, and as she looked at the beautiful child within, his tears awakened her compassion; her sympathies went out to the unknown mother who had tried in this way to preserve her precious little one. She determined that he would be saved; she would adopt him as her own.

Miriam, seeing that the child was being received tenderly, dared to go closer, and at last said, " 'Shall I go and call a nurse for you from the Hebrew women, that she may nurse the child for you?' " Permission was given.

The sister hurried to her mother with the happy news and without delay returned with her to Pharaoh's daughter. " 'Take this child away and nurse him for me, and I will give you your wages,' " said the princess.

Twelve Short Years

God had heard the mother's prayer. With deep gratitude she took up her now safe and happy task, to educate her child for God. She knew that she must soon give him up to his royal "mother," to be surrounded with influences that would tend to lead him away from God. She worked to instill in his mind the fear of God and the love of truth and justice. She showed him the folly and sin of idolatry and taught him from his early days to bow down and pray to the living God, who alone could hear him and help him in every emergency.

She kept the boy as long as she could but had to give him up when he was about twelve years old. From his humble cabin home he was taken to the royal palace, to the daughter of Pharaoh, "and he became her son." Yet even here he could not forget the lessons learned at his mother's side. They kept him from the pride, the unbelief, and the vice that flourished in the splendor of the court.

The whole future life of Moses, the great mission that he fulfilled as the leader of Israel, testifies to the importance of a mother's work. No other work can equal this. The mother is dealing with developing minds and characters, working not just for time but for eternity. She is sowing seed that will spring up and bear fruit, either for good or for evil. Her work is not to paint a figure of beauty on canvas or to chisel it from marble but to impress upon a human soul the image of the divine. The impressions made on developing minds will remain all through life. Children are placed in our care to be trained, not as heirs to the throne of an earthly empire but as kings and queens to God, to reign through unending ages.

In the judgment day it will be found that many crimes have resulted from the ignorance and neglect of those whose duty it was to guide children's feet in the right way. Then it will be found that many who have blessed the world with the light of genius and truth and holiness owe their success to a praying mother.

At the court of Pharaoh, Moses received the highest civil and military training. The monarch determined to make his adopted grandson his successor on the throne, and young Moses was educated for this high position. " 'And Moses was learned in all the wisdom of the Egyptians, and was mighty in words and deeds.' " Acts 7:22. His ability as a military leader made him a favorite with the armies of Egypt, and he was generally regarded as a remarkable character. Satan's purpose had been defeated. The very decree condemning the Hebrew children to death had been overruled by God for the training of His people's future leader.

Angels taught the elders of Israel that the time for them to be set free was near and that Moses was the man God would use. Angels instructed Moses also that Jehovah had chosen him to break the bondage of His people. Moses supposed that they were to obtain their freedom in battle, and he expected to lead the Hebrew host against the armies of Egypt.

How Young Moses Was Tested

By the laws of Egypt, all who occupied the throne of the Pharaohs must become members of the priestly caste. Moses, as the heir apparent, was to be inducted into the mysteries of the national religion. But he could not be persuaded to participate in the worship of the gods. He was threatened with the loss of the crown and warned that he would be disowned by the princess if he persisted in the Hebrew faith. But he was unshaken in his determination to worship none but the one God, the Maker of heaven and earth. He reasoned with priests and worshipers, showing the folly of their superstitious reverence for senseless objects. For a while his firmness was tolerated because of his high position and the favor with which both the king and the people regarded him.

"By faith Moses, when he became of age, refused to be called the son of Pharaoh's daughter, choosing rather to suffer affliction with the people of God than to enjoy the passing pleasures of sin, esteeming the reproach of Christ greater riches than the treasures in Egypt; for he looked to the reward." Hebrews 11:24-26. Moses was fitted to take first place among the great people of the earth, to shine in the courts of its most glorious kingdom, and to wield its scepter of power. As historian, poet, philosopher, general of armies, and legislator, he stands without an equal. Yet with the world before him, he had the moral strength to refuse wealth, greatness, and fame, "choosing rather to suffer affliction with the people of God."

The magnificent palace of Pharaoh and the throne were held out as an enticement to Moses; but he knew that in its lordly courts were the sinful pleasures that make people forget God. He looked beyond the palace, beyond a monarch's crown, to the high honors that the saints of the Most High will receive in a kingdom untainted by sin. By faith he saw an imperishable crown that the King of heaven would place on the head of the overcomer. This faith led him to join the humble, poor, despised nation that had chosen to obey God rather than to serve sin.

Moses remained at the royal court until he was forty years old. He visited his brethren in their slavery and encouraged them with the assurance that God would work for their deliverance. One day, seeing an Egyptian beating an Israelite, he sprang forward and killed the Egyptian. Other than the Israelite, no one had witnessed the deed, and Moses immediately buried the body in the sand. He had now shown himself ready to take up the cause of his people, and he hoped to see them rise to recover their liberty. " 'He supposed that his brethren would have understood that God would deliver them by his hand, but they did not understand.' " Acts 7:25. They were not yet prepared for freedom.

The next day Moses saw two Hebrews fighting together, one of them evidently at fault. Moses reproved the offender, who at once retaliated on him, saying that he had no right to interfere, and rudely accusing him of a crime: " 'Who made you a prince and a judge over us?' " he said. " 'Do you intend to kill me, as you killed the Egyptian?' "

The whole matter soon reached the ears of Pharaoh. The king was told that this act meant much, that

Moses planned to lead his people against the Egyptians, to overthrow the government, and to seat himself on the throne. The monarch at once determined that he should die, but Moses became aware of his danger and fled toward Arabia.

The Lord directed his course, and he found a home with Jethro, the priest and prince of Midian, who was a worshiper of God. After a time Moses married one of Jethro's daughters; and here, as keeper of his flocks, he remained forty years.

It was not God's will to deliver His people by warfare, as Moses thought, but by His own mighty power, so that the glory might be given to Him alone. Moses was not prepared for his great work. He still had to learn the same lesson of faith that Abraham and Jacob had been taught—not to rely on human strength or wisdom but on the power of God to fulfill His promises. In the school of self-denial and hardship he was to learn patience, to control his passions. His own heart must be fully in harmony with God before he could teach the knowledge of His will to Israel and exercise a fatherly care over all who needed his help.

Doing God's Work the Wrong Way

In Egypt Moses had learned much that he must unlearn. The influences that had surrounded him had left deep impressions on his developing mind and to some extent had molded his habits and character. Time could remove these impressions. It would require a life-and-

death kind of struggle for Moses to renounce error and accept truth, but God would be his helper when the conflict would be too severe for human strength.

"If any of you lacks wisdom, let him ask of God, who gives to all liberally and without reproach, and it will be given to him." James 1:5. But God will not give people divine light while they are content to remain in darkness. In order to receive God's help, they must realize their weakness and lack; they must apply their own minds to the great change God wants to work in them; they must be aroused to earnest, unwavering prayer and effort.

Shut in by the high mountain walls, Moses was alone with God. In the solemn grandeur of the everlasting hills he saw the majesty of the Most High, and in contrast he realized how powerless the gods of Egypt were. Here his pride and self-sufficiency were swept away. The results of Egypt's luxury disappeared. Moses became patient, reverent, and "very humble, more than all men who were on the face of the earth" (Numbers 12:3), yet strong in faith.

As the years rolled on, his prayers for Israel arose by day and by night. Here, under the inspiration of the Holy Spirit, he wrote the book of Genesis. The long years spent in the desert solitude have richly blessed the world in all ages.

The Time for Freedom Comes!

"In the process of time . . . the king of Egypt died. Then the children of Israel groaned because of the bondage, and they cried out; and their cry came up to God. . . . And God looked upon the children of Israel, and God acknowledged them." The time for deliverance had come.

God would accomplish His plan in a way to pour contempt on human pride. The deliverer was to go forth as a humble shepherd, with only a rod in his hand, but God would make that rod the symbol of His power.

Leading his flocks one day near Horeb, "the mountain of God," Moses saw a bush in flames, yet not consumed. When he drew near, a voice from out of the flame called him by name. With trembling lips he answered, " 'Here I am.' " He was warned not to approach irreverently: " 'Take your sandals off your feet, for the place where you stand is holy ground. . . . I am the God of your father—the God of Abraham, the God of Isaac, and the God of Jacob.' " And Moses hid his face, for he was afraid to look upon God."

As Moses waited in awe before God, the words continued: " 'I have surely seen the oppression of My people who are in Egypt, and have heard their cry because of their taskmasters, for I know their sorrows. So I have come down to deliver them out of the hand of the Egyptians, and to bring them up from that land to a good and large land, to a land flowing with milk and honey. . . . Come now, therefore, and I will send you to Pharaoh that you may bring My people, the children of Israel, out of Egypt.' "

Amazed and terrified, Moses stepped back, saying, " 'Who am I that I should go to Pharaoh, and that I should bring the children of Israel out of Egypt?' "

Moses thought of the blindness, ignorance, and unbelief of his people. Many knew almost nothing about God. " 'Indeed,' " he said, " 'when I . . . say to them, "The God of your fathers has sent me to you, and they say to me, 'What is His name?' what shall I say to them?" ' " The answer was, " 'I AM WHO I AM. . . . "I AM has sent me to you." ' "

God commanded Moses first to assemble the elders of Israel who had long mourned because of their bondage and to declare to them a message from Him. Then he was to go before the king and say, " 'The LORD God of the Hebrews has met with us; and now, please, let us go three days' journey into the wilderness, that we may sacrifice to the LORD our God.' "

Moses was forewarned that Pharaoh would resist the appeal. Yet the courage of God's servant must not fail. The Lord would manifest His power. " 'I will stretch out My hand and strike Egypt with all My wonders which I will do in its midst; and after that he will let you go.' "

The Lord declared, " 'It shall be, when you go, that you shall not go empty-handed. But every woman shall ask of her neighbor, namely, of her who dwells near her house, articles of silver, articles of gold, and clothing.' " The Egyptians had been enriched by the labor unjustly required from the Israelites, and it was right for the latter to claim the reward of their years of work. God would give them favor in the sight of the Egyptians. The requests of the slaves would be granted.

What proof could Moses give his people that God had indeed sent him? " 'But suppose,' " he said, " 'they will not believe me or listen to my voice; suppose they say, "The LORD has not appeared to you." ' " He was told to throw his rod on the ground. As he did so, "it became a serpent; and Moses fled from it." He was commanded to grab it, and in his hand it became a rod. He was told to put his hand into his bosom. He obeyed, and "when he took it out, behold, his hand was leprous, like snow." Being told to put it again into his bosom, he found when he drew it out that it had become like the other. By these signs his own people, as well as Pharaoh, would be convinced that One mightier than the king of Egypt was surely among them.

Moses Is Reluctant

But in his distress and fear the servant of God now pleaded as an excuse a lack of ready speech: " 'O my Lord, I am not eloquent. . . . I am slow of speech and slow of tongue.' " He had been away from the Egyptians so long that he could not speak their language as easily as when he was among them.

Moses asked that a more competent person be chosen. But after the Lord had promised to remove all difficulties and give him final success, any further complaining about his unfitness showed distrust of God. It implied a fear that God was unable to qualify him or that He had made a mistake in His choice of the man.

Aaron, his older brother, having used the language of the Egyptians daily, was able to speak it perfectly. God told Moses that Aaron was coming to meet him. The next words from the Lord were an unqualified command.

" 'You shall speak to him and put the words in his mouth. . . . So he shall be your spokesman to the people. And he himself shall be as a mouth for you, and you shall be to him as God. And you shall take this rod in your hand, with which you shall do the signs.' " Moses could resist no further, for all ground for excuse was removed.

Having once accepted the work, Moses entered into it with his whole heart, putting all his trust in the Lord. God blessed his prompt obedience, and he became eloquent, hopeful, self-possessed, and well fitted for the greatest work ever given to a human being.

A person will gain power and efficiency by accepting the responsibilities that God places on him or her. However humble the position or limited one's ability, that person will attain true greatness who seeks to perform the work faithfully. Feeling one's weakness is at least some evidence of recognition that the appointed work is great. Such a person will make God his counselor and strength.

Moses secretly dreaded Pharaoh and the Egyptians, whose anger had been kindled against him forty years before; this made him reluctant to return to Egypt. But after he had set out to obey the divine command, the Lord revealed to him that his enemies were dead.

On the way from Midian, an angel appeared to Moses in a threatening manner, as if to destroy him. No explanation was given, but Moses remembered that he had disregarded one of God's requirements. He had neglected to perform the rite of circumcision on their youngest son. Such a neglect on the part of Israel's chosen leader would certainly lessen the force of God's instructions on the people. Zipporah, fearing that her husband would be killed, performed the rite herself, and the angel then permitted Moses to continue on his journey. His life could be preserved only through the protection of holy angels. But while he lived in neglect of a known duty, he would not be secure, for he could not be shielded by the angels of God.

In the time of trouble just before the coming of Christ, the righteous will be preserved through the intervention of angels, but there will be no security for the person who breaks God's law. Angels cannot protect those who are disregarding any of the divine precepts.

The Ten Plagues of Egypt*

Instructed by angels, Aaron went forth to meet his brother in the solitude of the desert near Horeb. Here Moses told Aaron "all the words of the LORD who had sent him, and all the signs which He had commanded him." Exodus 4:28. Together they journeyed to Egypt to assemble the elders of Israel. "The people believed; and when they heard that the LORD had visited the children of Israel and that He had looked on their affliction, then they bowed their heads and worshiped." Exodus 4:31.

With a message for the king, the two brothers entered the palace of the Pharaohs as ambassadors from the King of kings: " 'Thus says the LORD God of Israel: "Let My people go, that they may hold a feast to Me in the wilderness." ' "

" 'Who is the LORD, that I should obey His voice to let Israel go?' " demanded the monarch; " 'I do not know the LORD, nor will I let Israel go.' "

Their answer was, " 'The God of the Hebrews has met with us. Please, let us go three days' journey into the desert and sacrifice to the LORD our God, lest He fall upon us with pestilence or with the sword.' "

The king's anger was kindled. " 'Moses and Aaron, why do you take the people from their work?' " he said. " 'Get back to your labor.' " Already the kingdom had suffered loss through the interference of these strangers. At the thought of this he added, " 'Look, the people of the land are many now, and you make them rest from their labor!' "

To some extent, in their bondage the Israelites had lost the knowledge of God's law, and they had generally disregarded the Sabbath. The demands of their taskmasters made keeping it seem impossible. But Moses had shown his people that obedience to God was the condition of their deliverance. The efforts made to restore Sabbath observance had come to the notice of their oppressors. (See Appendix, Note 1.)

The king, thoroughly upset, suspected the Israelites of a plot to revolt from his service. He would make sure that no time was left to them for dangerous scheming. At once he took steps to make their service

---

* This chapter is based on Exodus 5 to 10.

harder and crush their independent spirit. The most common building material was sun-dried brick, and brick-making employed great numbers of the slaves. Because they mixed cut straw with the clay to hold it together, large quantities of it were required. The king now ordered that no more straw be supplied; the workers must find it for themselves, but the same amount of brick must be made.

The Egyptian taskmasters appointed Hebrew officers to oversee the work. When the requirement of the king was put in force, the people scattered to gather stubble instead of straw, but they found it impossible to produce the usual amount of brick. For this failure the Hebrew officers were cruelly beaten.

These officers went to the king with their grievances. Pharaoh met their complaint with a taunt: " 'You are idle! You are idle! Therefore you say, "Let us go and sacrifice to the LORD." ' " He ordered them back to their work; their burdens were not to be lightened at all. Returning, they met Moses and Aaron, and cried out to them, " 'Let the LORD look on you and judge, because you have made us abhorrent in the sight of Pharaoh and in the sight of his servants, to put a sword in their hand to kill us.' "

Moses was distressed. The sufferings of the people had been increased. All over the land a cry of despair went up from old and young. All united in blaming him for the disastrous change in their condition. In bitterness of soul he went before

God. " 'Lord, why have You brought trouble on this people? Why is it You have sent me? For since I came to Pharaoh to speak in Your name, he has done evil to this people; neither have You delivered Your people at all.' "

The answer was, " 'Now you shall see what I will do to Pharaoh. For with a strong hand he will let them go, and with a strong hand he will drive them out of his land.' "

The elders of Israel tried to encourage the sinking faith of their brethren by repeating the promises made to their fathers and the prophetic words of Joseph foretelling their deliverance from Egypt. Some listened and believed. Others refused to hope. The Egyptians, having been told of what was reported among their slaves, mocked their expectations and scornfully denied the power of their God. They taunted, "If your God is just and merciful and possesses power greater than that of the Egyptian gods, why doesn't He make you a free people?" They worshiped deities that the Israelites called false gods, yet they were a rich and powerful nation. Their gods had blessed them with prosperity and had given them the Israelites as servants. Pharaoh himself boasted that the God of the Hebrews could not deliver them from his power.

Words like these destroyed the hopes of many of the Israelites. True, they were slaves, their children had been slaughtered, and their own lives were a burden; yet they were worshiping the God of heaven. Surely He would not leave them like this in bondage to idolaters. But those who were true to God understood that it was because of Israel's departure from Him, because of their inclination to marry with heathen nations and thus be led into idolatry, that the Lord had permitted them to become slaves. They confidently assured the others that He would soon break their bondage.

But the Hebrews were not yet prepared for deliverance. They had little faith in God. Many were content to remain in slavery rather than face the difficulties of moving to a strange land; and the habits of some had become so much like those of the Egyptians that they preferred to stay in Egypt. So the Lord overruled events to develop the tyrannical spirit of the Egyptian king more fully and also to reveal Himself to His people. Moses' work would have been much less difficult if many of the Israelites had not become so corrupted that they were unwilling to leave Egypt. The Bible says, "They did not heed Moses, because of anguish of spirit and cruel bondage."

Again the divine message came to Moses, " 'Go in, speak to Pharaoh king of Egypt, that he must let the children of Israel go out of his land.' " In discouragement he replied, " 'The children of Israel have not heeded me. How then shall Pharaoh heed me?' " He was told to take Aaron with him and go before Pharaoh and again demand that he " 'bring the children of Israel out of the land of Egypt.' "

Pharaoh Could Yet Save Egypt

Moses was informed that the monarch would not yield until God would inflict judgments on Egypt and bring out Israel by the dramatic manifestation of His power. Before each plague came, Moses was to describe its nature and effects so that the king might save himself from it if he chose. Every punishment rejected would be followed by one more severe, until his proud heart would be humbled and he would acknowledge the Maker of heaven and earth as the true and living God. The Lord would punish the people of Egypt for their idolatry and silence their boasting so that other nations might tremble at His mighty acts and His people be led to turn from idolatry and offer Him pure worship.

Again Moses and Aaron entered the lordly halls of the king of Egypt. There stood the two representatives of the enslaved race, surrounded by tall columns, glittering adornments, amid the rich paintings and sculptured images of heathen gods. The king demanded a miracle as evidence of their divine commission. Aaron now took the rod and threw it down before Pharaoh. It became a serpent. The monarch then sent for his "wise men and the sorcerers," and "every man threw down his rod, and they became serpents. But Aaron's rod swallowed up their rods." The king, more determined than before, declared that his magicians were equal in power with Moses and Aaron. He accused the servants of the Lord as being impostors, yet was restrained by divine power from doing them harm.

Satan's Counterfeits

The magicians did not really cause their rods to become serpents; but by magic, helped by the great deceiver, they were able to produce this appearance. The prince of evil possesses all the wisdom and might of a fallen angel, but he has no power to create or to give life; this is God's right alone. Satan produced a counterfeit.

To human sight the rods had changed to serpents. This is what Pharaoh and his court believed them to be. Though the Lord caused the real serpent to swallow up the false ones, Pharaoh did not regard this as a work of God's power, but as the result of a kind of superior magic.

Pharaoh was seeking some excuse to disregard the miracles that God had performed through Moses. Satan gave him just what he wanted. He made it appear that Moses and Aaron were only magicians and sorcerers and that the message they brought could not claim respect as coming from a superior being. Thus Satan's counterfeit caused Pharaoh to harden his heart against conviction. Satan hoped also to shake the faith of Moses and Aaron.

The prince of evil knew very well that Moses prefigured Christ, who was to break the reign of sin over the human family. He knew that when Christ would appear, mighty miracles would be an evidence to the world that God had sent Him. By counterfeiting the work of God through Moses, Satan hoped not only to prevent the deliverance of Israel but through future ages to destroy faith in the miracles of Christ by making them appear to be only the result of human power.

The Plagues Strike Egypt

Moses and Aaron were directed to go to the riverside next morning. Because the overflowing of the Nile was the source of food and wealth for all Egypt, the river was worshiped as a god, and the monarch came to its banks daily for his personal devotions. The two brothers again repeated the message to him and then stretched out the rod and struck the water. The sacred stream turned to blood, the fish died, and the river smelled bad. The water in the houses and the supply in the cisterns was likewise changed to blood. But "the magicians of Egypt did so with their enchantments," and "Pharaoh turned and went into his house. Neither was his heart moved by this." For seven days the plague continued, but without changing Pharaoh's mind.

Again Aaron stretched out the rod, and frogs came up from the river. They overran the houses, occupied the bedchambers, and even got into the ovens and kneading troughs. The Egyptians regarded the frog as sacred, and they would not destroy it; but the slimy pests now swarmed even in the palace of the Pharaohs, and the king was impatient to have them removed. The magicians had seemed to produce frogs, but they could not remove them.

When he saw this, Pharaoh was somewhat humbled. He sent for Moses and Aaron and said, " 'Entreat the LORD that He may take away the frogs from me and from my people; and I will let the people go, that they may sacrifice to the LORD.' " They asked him to appoint a time when they should pray for the removal of the plague. He set the next day, secretly hoping that the frogs might disappear on their own and thus save him from the bitter humiliation of submitting to the God of Israel. The plague, however, continued till the time specified, when throughout all Egypt the frogs died. But their putrid bodies remained and polluted the atmosphere.

The Lord could have caused them to return to dust in a moment; but He did not do this, so that the king and his people could not declare it to be the result of enchantment like the work of the magicians. The frogs died and were then gathered together in piles, evidence that this work was not accomplished by magic but was a judgment from the God of heaven.

"When Pharaoh saw that there was relief, he hardened his heart." At the command of God, Aaron stretched out his hand with the rod, and the dust of the earth became lice throughout all the land of Egypt. Pharaoh called for the magicians to do the same, but they could not. The magicians acknowledged, " 'This is the finger of God.' " But the king was still unmoved.

Another judgment followed. Flies filled the houses, so that "the land was corrupted because of the swarms of flies." These flies were large and poisonous, and their bite was extremely painful. As foretold, this plague did not extend to the land of Goshen.

Pharaoh Hardens His Heart

Pharaoh now offered the Israelites permission to sacrifice in Egypt, but they refused. " 'It is not right to do so,' " said Moses. " 'If we sacrifice the abomination of the Egyptians before their eyes, then will they not stone us?' " The animals that the Hebrews would be required to sacrifice were among those the Egyptians regarded as sacred. To kill one even accidentally was a crime punishable with death.

Moses again proposed to go three days' journey into the wilderness. The monarch agreed and begged the servants of God to ask God to remove the plague. They promised to do this but warned him against dealing deceitfully with them. The plague was stopped, but the king's heart had become hardened by persistent rebellion, and he still refused to yield.

A more terrible stroke followed—a plague of disease came upon all the Egyptian cattle. Both the sacred animals and the beasts of burden—cows and oxen and sheep, horses and camels and donkeys—were destroyed. It had been distinctly stated that the Hebrews were to be exempt; and Pharaoh, on sending messengers to the home of the Israelites, confirmed the truth of this. "Of the livestock of the children of Israel, not one died." Still the king refused to yield.

Moses was next directed to take ashes from a furnace and " 'scatter it toward the heavens in the sight of Pharaoh.' " The fine particles spread over the land of Egypt, and wherever they settled, they produced boils that broke out "in sores on man and beast." The priests and magicians had encouraged Pharaoh in his stubbornness, but now a judgment had reached even them. Struck with a repulsive and painful disease, they were no longer able to fight against the God of Israel. The magicians were not able to protect even their own bodies.

Still the heart of Pharaoh grew harder. And now the Lord sent a message to him, " 'At this time I will send all My plagues to your very heart, and on your servants and on your people, that you may know that there is none like Me in all the earth. . . . But indeed for this purpose I have raised you up, that I may show My power in you.' " God's providence had overruled events to place him on the throne at the very time appointed for Israel's deliverance.

Although this haughty tyrant had forfeited the mercy of God, his life had been preserved so that through his stubbornness the Lord could reveal His wonders in Egypt. God's people were permitted to experience the grinding cruelty of the Egyptians so that they would not be deceived concerning the degrading influence of idolatry. In His dealing with Pharaoh, the Lord showed His hatred of idolatry and His determination to punish cruelty and oppression.

God had declared concerning Pharaoh, " 'I will harden his heart, so that he will not let the people go.' " Exodus 4:21. No supernatural power hardened the heart of the king, but the seeds of rebellion that he sowed when he rejected the first miracle produced their harvest. As he dared to continue from one degree of stubbornness to another, his heart became more and more hardened, until he was called to look upon the cold, dead faces of the firstborn.

How Stubbornness Develops

God speaks to us through His servants, rebuking sin. If a person refuses to be corrected, divine power does not intervene to prevent the results of one's own action. Such people are hardening the heart against the influence of the Holy Spirit.

Anyone who has once yielded to temptation will yield more easily the second time. Every repetition lessens the power to resist, blinds the eyes, and stifles conviction. God works no miracle to prevent the harvest. "Whatever a man sows, that he will also reap." Galatians 6:7. In this way multitudes grow to listen with stony indifference to the truths that once stirred their souls. They sowed neglect and resistance to the truth, and this is the harvest they reap.

Some people quiet a guilty conscience with the thought, "I can change my evil course whenever I choose." They think that after casting their influence on the side of the great rebel, they will change leaders when danger surrounds them. But this is not easily done. A life of sinful indulgence has so molded the character that they cannot then receive the image of Jesus. If no light had shone on their pathway, mercy might intervene. But after light has been long despised, it will finally be withdrawn.

Next a plague of hail was threatened upon Pharaoh. " 'Therefore send now and gather your livestock . . . , for the hail shall come down on every man and every beast which is found in the field and is not brought home, and they shall die.' " No one had ever seen such a storm as this would be. The report spread rapidly, and all who believed the word of the Lord gathered in their cattle, while those who despised the warning left them in the field. So in the midst of judgment the mercy of God was displayed, and it was shown how many had been led to fear God.

The storm came—thunder and hail, and fire mingled with it, "so very heavy that there was none like it in all the land of Egypt since it became a nation. And the hail struck throughout the whole land of Egypt, all that was in the field, both man and beast; and the hail struck every herb of the field and broke every tree of the field." Ruin and desolation marked the path of the destroying angel. The land of Goshen alone was spared.

Pharaoh at Last Relents

All Egypt trembled under the divine judgment. Pharaoh quickly sent for the two brothers: " 'I have sinned this time. The LORD is righteous, and my people and I are wicked. Entreat the LORD, that there may be no more mighty thundering and hail, for it is enough. I will let you go, and you shall stay no longer.' "

Moses knew that the struggle was not over. Pharaoh's confessions and promises were not the result of any radical change in his mind but were wrung from him by terror and anguish. Moses promised, however, to grant his request, because he wanted to give him no occasion for further stubbornness. The prophet went out, ignoring the fury of the storm, and Pharaoh and all his attendants were witnesses to the power of Jehovah to preserve His messenger. Moses "spread out his hands to the LORD; then the thunder and the hail ceased, and the rain was not poured on the earth." But no sooner had the king recovered from his fears than his heart returned to its rebellion.

Then the Lord set out to give unmistakable evidence of the difference He placed between Israel and the Egyptians. He would cause all nations to know that the Hebrews were under the protection of the God of heaven. Moses warned the monarch that a plague of locusts would be sent, which would cover the earth and eat up every green thing that remained. They would fill the houses, even the palace itself. He said that this would be a disaster such as

" 'neither your fathers nor your fathers' fathers have seen, since the day that they were on the earth to this day.' "

The counselors of Pharaoh were horrified. The nation had suffered great loss in the death of the cattle. Many of the people had been killed by the hail. The forests were broken down and the crops destroyed. The Egyptians were quickly losing all that they had gained by the work of the Hebrews. The whole land was threatened with starvation. Princes and officials crowded around the king and demanded, " 'How long shall this man be a snare to us? Let the men go, that they may serve the LORD their God. Do you not yet know that Egypt is destroyed?' "

Pharaoh summoned Moses and Aaron again and said to them, " 'Go, serve the LORD your God. But who are the ones that are going?' "

Pharaoh Again Hardens His Heart

The answer was, " 'We will go with our young and our old; with our sons and our daughters, with our flocks and our herds we will go, for we must hold a feast to the LORD.' "

The king was filled with rage. He cried, " 'Not so! Go now, you who are men, and serve the LORD, for that is what you desired.' And they were driven out from Pharaoh's presence." Pharaoh pretended to have deep interest in their welfare and a tender care for their little ones, but his real intent was to keep the women and children as a way to guarantee the return of the men.

Moses now stretched his rod over the land, and an east wind brought locusts. "They were very severe; previously there had been no such locusts as they, nor shall there be such after them." They filled the air till the sky was darkened, and they devoured every green thing remaining.

Pharaoh quickly sent for the prophet and said, " 'I have sinned against the LORD your God and against you. . . . Entreat the LORD your God, that He may take away from me this death only.' " They did so, and a strong west wind carried away the locusts toward the Red Sea. Still the king kept on in his stubborn purpose.

The people of Egypt were ready to despair, and they were filled with fear for the future. The nation had worshiped Pharaoh as a representative of their god; but many were now convinced that he was battling against One who made all the powers of nature the agents of His will. The Hebrew slaves were becoming confident of deliverance. Throughout Egypt there was a secret fear that the enslaved race would rise and avenge their wrongs. People everywhere were asking, "What will come next?"

Suddenly a darkness settled on the land, so thick and black that it seemed to be a "darkness which may even be felt." Breathing was difficult. "They did not see one another; nor did anyone rise from his place for three days. But all the children of Israel had light in their dwellings." The sun and moon were objects of worship to the Egyptians.

This mysterious darkness struck the people and their gods alike. (See Appendix, Note 2.) Dreadful as it was, this judgment was an evidence of God's compassion and unwillingness to destroy. He would give the people time for reflection and repentance before bringing upon them the last and most terrible of the plagues.

At the end of the third day of darkness Pharaoh summoned Moses and agreed to allow the people to leave, provided the flocks and herds were permitted to remain. " 'Not a hoof shall be left behind,' " Moses replied firmly. The king's anger burst forth uncontrollably. " 'Get away from me!' " he cried. " 'Take heed to yourself and see my face no more! For in the day you see my face you shall die!' "

Moses answered, " 'You have spoken well. I will never see your face again.' "

"The man Moses was very great in the land of Egypt, in the sight of Pharaoh's servants and in the sight of the people." The king did not dare harm him, for the people looked upon him as the only one who possessed power to remove the plagues. They wanted the Israelites to be permitted to leave Egypt. It was the king and the priests who opposed the demands of Moses to the very end.

The First Passover*

When Moses first presented the demand for Israel's release to the king of Egypt, he gave warning of the most terrible of the plagues. " 'Thus says the LORD: "Israel is My son, My firstborn. So I say to you, let My son go that he may serve Me. But if you refuse to let him go, indeed I will kill your son, your firstborn." ' " Exodus 4:22, 23.

God has a tender care for the beings formed in His image. If the loss of their harvests and their flocks and herds had brought Egypt to repentance, the children would not have been harmed. But the nation had stubbornly resisted the divine command. Now the final blow was about to fall.

Moses had been forbidden, on pain of death, to appear again in Pharaoh's presence; but again Moses came before him, with the terrible announcement: " 'Thus says the LORD: "About midnight I will go out into the midst of Egypt; and all the firstborn in the land of Egypt shall die, from the firstborn of Pharaoh who sits on his throne, even to the firstborn of the maidservant who is behind the handmill, and all the

firstborn of the beasts. Then there shall be a great cry throughout all the land of Egypt, such as was not like it before, nor shall be like it again. But against none of the children of Israel shall a dog move its tongue, against man or beast, that you may know that the LORD does make a difference between the Egyptians and Israel." ' "

Before executing this sentence the Lord gave direction through Moses to the children of Israel about leaving Egypt and how to be preserved from the coming judgment. Each family, alone or with others, was to slaughter a lamb or a kid "without blemish," and with a bundle of hyssop sprinkle its blood on "the two doorposts and on the lintel" of the house, so that the destroying angel at midnight would not enter that dwelling. They were to eat the flesh roasted, with unleavened bread and bitter herbs, at night, as Moses said, "with a belt on your waist, your sandals on your feet, and your staff in your hand. So you shall eat it in haste. It is the LORD's Passover."

The Lord declared, " 'I will pass through the land of Egypt on that

---

This chapter is based on Exodus 11; 12:1-32.

night, and will strike all the firstborn in the land of Egypt, both man and beast; and against all the gods of Egypt I will execute judgment. . . . Now the blood shall be a sign for you on the houses where you are. And when I see the blood, I will pass over you; and the plague shall not be on you to destroy you.' "

To remind them of this great deliverance, Israel was to observe a feast yearly in all future generations—"the Passover sacrifice of the LORD, who passed over the houses of the children of Israel in Egypt when he struck the Egyptians and delivered our households."

The Passover Points to Christ

The Passover was to be both commemorative and symbolic, not only pointing back to the deliverance from Egypt but forward to the greater deliverance that Christ was to accomplish in freeing His people from the bondage of sin. The sacrificial lamb represents "the Lamb of God," in whom is our only hope of salvation. The apostle Paul wrote, "Christ, our Passover, was sacrificed for us." 1 Corinthians 5:7. It was not enough that the Passover lamb be killed; its blood must be sprinkled on the doorposts. Likewise, the merits of Christ's blood must be applied to the soul. We must believe not only that He died for the world but that He died for us individually.

The hyssop symbolized purification. "Purge me with hyssop, and I shall be clean; wash me, and I shall be whiter than snow." Psalm 51:7.

The lamb was to be prepared whole, with not a bone broken; so not a bone was to be broken of the Lamb of God, who was to die for us. See John 19:36.

The flesh was to be eaten. It is not enough that we believe on Christ for the forgiveness of sin; by faith we must be constantly receiving spiritual nourishment from Him through His Word. Said Christ, " 'Unless you eat the flesh of the Son of Man and drink His blood, you have no life in you. Whoever eats My flesh and drinks My blood has eternal life.' " " 'The words that I speak to you are spirit, and they are life.' " John 6:53, 54, 63. The followers of Christ must take the Word of God into themselves so that it will become the driving force of life and action. By the power of Christ they must be changed into His likeness and reflect the divine characteristics.

The lamb was to be eaten with bitter herbs, as pointing back to the bitterness of the bondage in Egypt. So when we feed upon Christ, it should be with repentance of heart, because of our sins. The use of unleavened bread—bread without yeast—also was significant. All who would receive life and nourishment from Christ must put away the leaven of sin. So Paul writes to the Corinthian church, "Therefore purge out the old leaven, that you may be a new lump. . . . Let us keep the feast, not with old leaven, nor with the leaven of malice and wickedness, but with the unleavened bread of sincerity and truth." 1 Corinthians 5:7, 8.

Before obtaining freedom, the slaves must show their faith in the great deliverance. They must place the blood on their houses, and they must separate themselves and their families from the Egyptians and gather within their own dwellings. All who failed to follow the Lord's directions would lose their firstborn by the hand of the destroyer.

How Faith Must Be Shown

By obedience the people were to give evidence of their faith. So all who hope to be saved by the blood of Christ should realize that they have something to do themselves in securing their salvation. We are to turn from sin to obedience. We are to be saved by faith, not by works; yet our faith must be shown by our works. We must appreciate and use the helps that God has provided; we must believe and obey all the divine requirements.

As Moses told Israel God's provisions for their deliverance, "the people bowed their heads and worshiped." Many of the Egyptians had been led to acknowledge the God of the Hebrews as the only true God, and these now begged to find shelter in the homes of Israel when the destroying angel would pass through the land. They were welcomed gladly, and they pledged to serve God and go forth from Egypt with His people.

The Israelites obeyed the directions God had given. Their families were gathered, the Passover lamb killed, the flesh roasted with fire, the unleavened bread and bitter herbs prepared. The father and priest of the household sprinkled the blood on the doorpost. In haste and silence the people ate the Passover lamb. Fathers and mothers clasped their loved firstborn in their arms, as they thought of the fearful stroke that was to fall that night. The sign of blood—the sign of a Savior's protection—was on their doors, and the destroyer did not enter.

At midnight "there was a great cry in Egypt, for there was not a house where there was not one dead." All the firstborn in the land, "from the firstborn of Pharaoh who sat on his throne to the firstborn of the captive who was in the dungeon, and all the firstborn of livestock," had been struck. The pride of every household had been laid low. Shrieks and wails filled the air. King and officers trembled at the overwhelming horror. With his Heaven-daring pride humbled in the dust, Pharaoh "called for Moses and Aaron by night, and said, 'Rise and go out from among my people, both you and the children of Israel. And go, serve the LORD as you have said. . . . Be gone; and bless me also.' "

The Israelites Leave Egypt*

Before daybreak, the people of Israel were on their way. During the plagues the Israelites had gradually assembled in Goshen. To make some provision for the necessary organization and control of the moving multitudes, they had already been divided into companies under appointed leaders.

And they went out, "about six hundred thousand men on foot, besides children. A mixed multitude went up with them also"—not only those motivated by faith in the God of Israel but also a far greater number who only wanted to escape from the plagues. This group were a constant problem and a snare to Israel.

The people took with them "flocks and herds—a great deal of livestock." Before leaving Egypt, the people claimed compensation for their unpaid work, and the slaves went out with much treasure from their oppressors.

"So it came to pass . . . that the LORD brought the children of Israel out of the land of Egypt according to their armies." The Israelites carried with them the bones of Joseph, which, during the dark years of bondage, had reminded them of Israel's promised deliverance.

Instead of taking the direct route to Canaan through the country of the Philistines, the Lord directed their course southward toward the shores of the Red Sea. "For God said, 'Lest perhaps the people change their minds when they see war, and return to Egypt.' " The Philistines regarded them as slaves escaping from their masters and would not have hesitated to make war on them. The Israelites had little knowledge of God and little faith in Him, and they would have become terrified and discouraged. They were unarmed and not used to war, their spirits were depressed by long slavery, and they had the added responsibility of women and children, flocks and herds. In leading them by the Red Sea, the Lord showed Himself to be a God of compassion.

The Pillar of Cloud

"So they took their journey from Succoth and camped in Etham at the edge of the wilderness. And the LORD went before them by day in a

---

* *This chapter is based on Exodus 12:34-51; 13 to 15.*

pillar of cloud to lead the way; and by night in a pillar of fire to give them light, so as to go by day and night. He did not take away the pillar of cloud by day or the pillar of fire by night from before the people." Says the psalmist, "He spread a cloud for a covering, and fire to give light in the night." Psalm 105:39. See also 1 Corinthians 10:1, 2. It served as a protection from the burning heat, and its coolness and moisture provided welcome refreshment in the parched, thirsty desert. By night it became a pillar of fire, illuminating their encampment and constantly assuring them of the divine presence.

Across a dreary, desertlike expanse they journeyed. Already they were becoming weary with the difficult terrain, and some began to be afraid that the Egyptians would come after them. But the cloud went forward, and they followed. Now the Lord directed Moses to turn aside into a rocky gorge and make camp beside the sea. God revealed to him that Pharaoh would pursue them but that God would be honored in their deliverance.

Pharaoh's counselors told the king that their slaves had fled, never to return. Their great men, recovering from their fears, claimed that the plagues were the result of natural causes. "Why have we done this, that we have let Israel go from serving us?" was the bitter cry.

Pharaoh collected his forces, "six hundred choice chariots, and all the chariots of Egypt," horsemen, captains, and foot soldiers. The king himself, attended by the great men of his realm, led the attacking army. The Egyptians were afraid that their forced submission to God would make other nations ridicule them. If they could now go out with a great show of power and bring back the fugitives, they would redeem their glory as well as recover the services of their slaves.

The Hebrews were camped beside the sea, which seemed an impassable barrier before them, while on the south a rugged mountain blocked their further progress. Suddenly in the distance they saw flashing armor and moving chariots. Terror filled the hearts of Israel. Most of them rushed to Moses with their complaints: " 'Because there were no graves in Egypt, have you taken us away to die in the wilderness? . . . It would have been better for us to serve the Egyptians than that we should die in the wilderness.' "

True, there was no possibility of deliverance unless God Himself intervened for their release; but since they had been brought to this position by obeying the divine direction, Moses felt no fear of the consequences. His calm, assuring reply to the people was, " 'Do not be afraid. Stand still, and see the salvation of the LORD, which He will accomplish for you today. For the Egyptians whom you see today, you shall see again no more forever. The LORD will fight for you, and you shall hold your peace.' "

Lacking discipline and self-control, the hosts of Israel became violent and unreasonable. Their wailings and laments were loud and deep. They had followed the wonderful pillar of cloud as the signal of God to go forward, but now had it not led them on the wrong side of the mountain, into an impassable way? To their deluded minds the angel of God appeared as an omen of disaster.

As the Egyptian army approached them, the cloudy column rose majestically into the heavens, passed over the Israelites, and came down between them and the armies of Egypt. The Egyptians could no longer see the camp of the Hebrews and were forced to halt. But as night deepened, the wall of cloud became a great light to the Hebrews.

Then hope returned to the hearts of Israel. "And the LORD said to Moses, . . . 'Tell the children of Israel to go forward. But lift up your rod, and stretch out your hand over the sea and divide it. And the children of Israel shall go on dry ground through the midst of the sea.' "

As Moses stretched out his rod, the waters divided, and Israel went into the midst of the sea on dry ground, while the waters stood like a wall on each side. The light from God's pillar of fire lighted the road and cut like a groove through the waters.

The End of Pharaoh's Army

"The Egyptians pursued and went after them into the midst of the sea, all Pharaoh's horses, his chariots, and his horsemen. Now it came to pass, in the morning watch, that the LORD looked down upon the army of the Egyptians through the pillar of fire and cloud, and He troubled the army of the Egyptians."

Thunders pealed and lightning flashed. The Egyptians became confused. They tried to turn around and go back to the shore, but Moses stretched out his rod, and the piled-up waters rushed together and swallowed the Egyptian army in their black depths.

As morning broke, Israel could see all that remained of their mighty foes—armor-clad bodies thrown up on the shore. From the most terrible danger, Jehovah had brought complete deliverance, and their hearts were turned to Him in gratitude and faith. The Spirit of God rested on Moses, and he led the people in a triumphant song of thanksgiving, the earliest and one of the most sublime known to humanity.

It was taken up by the women of Israel. Miriam, the sister of Moses, led the way as they went out with timbrel and dance. Far over the desert and sea rang the joyful chorus, and the mountains re-echoed the words of their praise, "Sing to the LORD, for He has triumphed gloriously."

That song does not belong to the Jewish people alone. It points forward to the destruction of all the enemies of righteousness and the final victory of the Israel of God. The prophet of Patmos saw the white-robed multitude that "have the victory," standing on the "sea of glass mingled with fire," having "harps of God. And they sing the song of Moses, the servant of God, and the song of the Lamb." Revelation 15:2, 3.

In freeing us from the bondage of sin, God has worked a deliverance for us greater than that of the Hebrews at the Red Sea. Like them, we should praise the Lord with heart, soul, and voice for His "wonderful works to the children of men!" What compassion, what matchless love, God has shown in connecting us with Himself, to be a special treasure to Him! What a sacrifice our Redeemer has made, that we may be called children of God!

The Redeemed Will Sing

" 'Whoever offers praise,' " says the Creator, " 'glorifies Me.' " Psalm 50:23. All the inhabitants of heaven unite in praising God. Let us learn the song of the angels now, so that we may sing it when we join their radiant ranks.

God brought the Hebrews into the mountain strongholds before the sea that He might show His power and unmistakably humble the pride of their oppressors. He chose this method to test their faith and strengthen their trust in Him. If the people had held back when Moses called them to advance, God would never have opened the path for them. It was "by faith" that "they passed through the Red Sea as by dry land." Hebrews 11:29. In marching down to the very water they showed that they believed the word of God spoken by Moses. Then the Mighty One of Israel divided the sea to make a path for their feet.

Often life is plagued by dangers, and duty seems hard to perform. We imagine that we are on the verge of ruin. Yet the voice of God speaks clearly, "Go forward." We should obey this command, even though our eyes cannot see through the darkness, and we feel the cold waves about our feet. Those who put off obeying till every uncertainty disappears and there remains no risk of failure or defeat will never obey at all; but faith courageously urges us to advance. The path where God leads may lie through the desert or the sea, but it is a safe path.

Israel Meets With Difficulties *

From the Red Sea the people of Israel again set out on their journey under the guidance of the pillar of cloud. They were full of joy in their new sense of freedom, and every discontented thought was hushed.

But for three days, as they journeyed, they could find no water. The supply which they had taken with them was gone. There was nothing to quench their burning thirst as they dragged wearily over the sun-burnt plains. Moses, who was familiar with this region, knew what the others did not: at Marah, where springs were found, the water was unfit for use. With a sinking heart he heard the glad shout, "Water! water!" echo along the line. Men, women, and children in joyous haste crowded to the oasis, when suddenly a cry of anguish erupted—the water was bitter!

In their despair the people blamed Moses, not remembering that God's presence in that mysterious cloud had been leading him as well as them. Moses did what they had forgotten to do; he called earnestly to God for help. "And the LORD showed him a tree; and when he cast it into the waters, the waters were made sweet." Here God gave the promise to Israel: " 'If you diligently heed the voice of the LORD your God and do what is right in His sight, give ear to His commandments and keep all His statutes, I will put none of the diseases on you which I have brought on the Egyptians. For I am the LORD who heals you.' "

From Marah the people journeyed to Elim, where they found "twelve wells of water." Here they remained several days.

When they had been gone from Egypt for a month, their stock of food had begun to fail. How could such a large number of people be fed? Even the rulers and elders joined in complaining against the leaders God had appointed: " 'Oh, that we had died by the hand of the LORD in the land of Egypt, when we sat by the pots of meat and when we ate bread to the full! For you have brought us out into this wilderness to kill this whole assembly with hunger.' "

They had not yet actually gone hungry, but they feared for the future. In imagination they saw their children starving. The Lord permitted difficulties to surround them and their sup-

---

This chapter is based on Exodus 15:22-27; 16 to 18.

ply of food to be cut short, so that their hearts might turn to Him who had been their Deliverer. If they would call on Him in their need, He would still grant them evidence of His love and care. It was sinful unbelief on their part to think that they or their children might die of hunger.

They needed to encounter difficulties and endure hardships. God was bringing them from corruption and shame to occupy an honorable place among the nations and to receive sacred trusts. If they had possessed faith in Him, in view of all that He had done for them, they would cheerfully have borne inconvenience, lack of food, and even real suffering. But they forgot the goodness and power of God in delivering them from bondage. They forgot how their children had been spared when the destroying angel killed all the firstborn of Egypt. They forgot the grand display of divine power at the Red Sea. They forgot that their enemies, in trying to follow them, had been overwhelmed by the waters of the sea.

Instead of saying, "God has done great things for us; we were slaves, but He is making a great nation of us," they talked of how hard the journey was and wondered when their weary pilgrimage would end.

God wants His people in these days to review the trials through which ancient Israel passed, in order to learn how to prepare for the heavenly Canaan. Many look back to the Israelites and marvel at their unbelief. They feel that they themselves would not have been so ungrateful.

But when their faith is tested even by little trials, they reveal no more faith or patience than ancient Israel did. They complain about the process by which God has chosen to purify them. Though their present needs are supplied, many constantly fear that poverty will come on them, and their children will be left to suffer. Obstacles, instead of leading them to seek help from God, separate them from Him because they awaken unrest and discontent.

Why should we be ungrateful and distrusting? Jesus is our friend. All heaven is interested in our welfare. Anxiety and fear grieve the Holy Spirit of God. It is not God's will for His people to be weighed down with care.

Our Lord does not tell us there are no dangers in our path, but He points us to a never-failing refuge. He invites the weary and care-burdened, " 'Come to Me, all you who labor and are heavy laden, and I will give you rest.' " Take off the yoke of anxiety and care that you have placed on your own neck, and " 'take My yoke upon you and learn from Me, for I am gentle and lowly in heart, and you will find rest for your souls.' " Matthew 11:28, 29. Instead of grumbling and complaining, the language of our hearts should be, "Bless the LORD, O my soul, and forget not all His benefits." Psalm 103:2.

God knew all about Israel's needs. He said to their leader, " 'I will rain bread from heaven for you.' " God directed that the people gather a daily supply, with a double amount on the sixth day, to maintain the sacred observance of the Sabbath.

Moses assured the congregation that their needs would be supplied, that the Lord would give them " 'meat to eat in the evening, and in the morning bread to the full.' " And he added, " 'What are we? Your murmurings are not against us but against the LORD.' " They must learn that the Most High, not merely Moses, was their leader.

At nightfall the camp was surrounded by vast flocks of quails, enough to supply the entire company. In the morning there lay upon the ground "a small round substance, . . . like white coriander seed." The people called it "Manna." Moses said, " 'This is the bread which the LORD has given you to eat.' " The people found that there was an abundant supply for all. They "ground it on millstones or beat it in the mortar, cooked it in pans, and made cakes of it." "And the taste of it was like wafers made with honey." Numbers 11:8; Exodus 16:31.

They were directed to gather an omer each day for every person and not to leave any of it until the morning. The provision for the day must be gathered in the morning, because all of it that remained on the ground was melted by the sun. "He who gathered much had nothing over, and he who gathered little had no lack."

How the Sabbath Was Honored

On the sixth day the people gathered two omers for every person. The rulers quickly told Moses what had been done. His answer was, " 'This is what the LORD has said: "Tomorrow is a Sabbath rest, a holy Sabbath to the LORD. Bake what you will bake today, and boil what you will boil; and lay up for yourselves all that remains, to be kept until morning." ' " They did so and found that it remained unchanged. And Moses said, " 'Eat that today, for today is a Sabbath to the LORD; today you will not find it in the field. Six days you shall gather it, but on the seventh day, which is the Sabbath, there will be none.' "

God requires that His holy day be kept as sacredly now as in the time of Israel. We should make the day before the Sabbath a day of preparation, so that everything may be in readiness for its sacred hours. In no case should our own business be allowed to encroach on holy time. God has directed that the sick should be cared for; the labor required to make them comfortable is a work of mercy and no violation of the Sabbath; but all unnecessary work should be avoided. Work that is neglected until the beginning of the Sabbath should remain undone until after sundown at its close.

The Israelites witnessed a threefold miracle to impress their minds with the sacredness of the Sabbath: a double quantity of manna fell on the sixth day, none on the seventh, and the portion needed for the Sabbath stayed sweet and pure.

Sabbath Before Sinai

In the way God gave the manna, we have conclusive evidence that the

Sabbath did not originate when the law was given at Sinai. Before the Israelites came to Sinai, they understood that God expected them to keep the Sabbath. When every Friday they had to gather a double portion of manna in preparation for the Sabbath, the sacred nature of the day of rest was continually impressed upon them. And when some of the people went out on the Sabbath to gather manna, the Lord asked, " 'How long do you *refuse* to keep My commandments and My laws?' "

"The children of Israel ate manna forty years, . . . until they came to the border of the land of Canaan." For forty years they were daily reminded of God's unfailing care and tender love. God gave them "of the bread of heaven. Men ate angels' food" (Psalm 78:24, 25)—that is, food provided for them by the angels. They were taught each day that they were as secure from want as if surrounded by fields of waving grain on the fertile plains of Canaan.

The manna was a symbol of Him who came from God to give life to the world. Jesus said, " 'I am the bread of life. Your fathers ate the manna in the wilderness, and are dead. This is the bread which comes down from heaven. . . . If anyone eats of this bread, he will live forever; and the bread that I shall give is My flesh, which I shall give for the life of the world.' " John 6:48-51.

After leaving the Wilderness of Sin, the Israelites made camp in Rephidim. Here there was no water, and again they distrusted the providence of God. The people came to Moses with the demand, " 'Give us water, that we may drink.' " They shouted in anger, " 'Why is it you have brought us up out of Egypt, to kill us and our children and our livestock with thirst?' " When they had been so abundantly supplied with food, they remembered with shame their unbelief and promised to trust the Lord in the future; but they failed at the first test of their faith. The pillar of cloud that was leading them seemed to conceal a frightening mystery. And Moses—who was he? What could be his purpose in bringing them from Egypt? Suspicion and distrust filled their hearts, and in the storm of rage they were about to stone him.

Water From a Rock

In distress Moses cried out to the Lord, " 'What shall I do with this people?' " He was directed to take the elders of Israel and the rod with which he had worked wonders in Egypt and to go on ahead of the people. And the Lord said to him, " 'Behold, I will stand before you there on the rock in Horeb; and you shall strike the rock, and water will come out of it, that the people may drink.' " He obeyed, and the waters gushed out in a living stream that abundantly supplied the encampment. In His mercy, the Lord made the rod His instrument to accomplish their deliverance.

It was the Son of God who, veiled in the cloudy pillar, stood beside Moses and caused the life-giving water to flow. All the congregation saw the glory of the Lord; but if the cloud had been removed, they would have been killed by the terrible brightness of Him who was hidden in it.

The people's unbelief was criminal, and Moses feared that the judgment of God would fall on them. He called the name of the place Massah, "tempted," and Meribah, "contention," as a memorial of their sin.

War With Amalek

A new danger now threatened them. Because of their complaining against Him, the Lord permitted them to be attacked by their enemies. The Amalekites came out against them and struck those who, faint and weary, had fallen behind. Moses directed Joshua to choose a body of soldiers from the different tribes and lead them against the enemy, while he himself would stand on a hill nearby with the rod of God in his hand. So the next day Joshua and his company attacked the enemy, while Moses, Aaron, and Hur were on a hill overlooking the battlefield. With arms outstretched toward heaven and holding the rod of God in his right hand, Moses prayed for the success of the armies of Israel. It was observed that as long as his hands were reaching upward, Israel was winning; but when they were lowered, the enemy was victorious. As Moses became tired, Aaron and Hur held up his hands until sunset, when the enemy was defeated.

The act of Moses was significant, showing that God held their destiny in His hands. While they put their trust in Him, He would fight for them

and conquer their enemies. But whenever they let go their hold on Him and trusted in their own power, they would be weak and their foes would prevail against them.

Divine strength is to be combined with human effort. Moses did not believe that God would overcome their foes while Israel remained inactive. While the great leader was pleading with the Lord, Joshua and his brave followers were putting forth their utmost efforts to defeat the enemies of Israel and of God.

Just before his death Moses delivered to his people the solemn charge: " 'Remember what Amalek did to you on the way as you were coming out of Egypt, how he met you on the way and attacked your rear ranks, all the stragglers at your rear, when you were tired and weary; and he did not fear God. . . . You will blot out the remembrance of Amalek from under heaven. You shall not forget.' " Deuteronomy 25:17-19. Concerning this wicked people the Lord declared, "The hand of Amalek is against the throne of Jehovah." Exodus 17:16, KJV margin.

The Amalekites were not ignorant of God's character or of His supreme authority, but they had set themselves to defy His power. They made the wonders performed by Moses before the Egyptians a subject of mockery. They had taken an oath by their gods that they would destroy the Hebrews and boasted that Israel's God would be powerless to resist them. The Israelites had not threatened them. Their assault was unprovoked. To show their defiance of God they tried to destroy His people. The Amalekites had long been bold sinners, yet God's mercy had still called them to repentance; but when the men of Amalek attacked the wearied and defenseless ranks of Israel, they sealed their nation's doom. Over all who love and fear Him, God's hand extends as a shield; let all beware that they not strike that hand, for it wields the sword of justice.

Jethro, the father-in-law of Moses, now set out to visit the Hebrews and restore to Moses his wife and two sons. Moses, the great leader, went out with joy to meet them and brought them to his tent.

Jethro's Wise Advice

As Jethro remained in the camp, he soon saw what heavy burdens rested on Moses. Not only the general interests and duties of the people, but the controversies that arose among them, were referred to him. He said, " 'I make known the statutes of God and His laws.' " But Jethro protested, saying, " 'This thing is too much for you; you are not able to perform it by yourself.' " He counseled Moses to appoint proper persons as rulers of thousands, others as rulers of hundreds, and others of tens. These were to judge in all minor matters, while the most difficult and important cases should still be brought before Moses. This counsel was accepted, and it brought not only relief to Moses but more perfect order among the people.

The fact that he had been chosen to instruct others did not lead Moses to conclude that he himself needed no instruction. The chosen leader of Israel listened gladly to the suggestions of the godly priest of Midian and adopted his plan.

From Rephidim the people continued their journey, following the movement of the cloudy pillar. Their route had led across barren plains, over steep slopes, and through rocky gorges. Now Mount Sinai lifted its massive front before them in solemn majesty. The cloudy pillar rested on its summit, and the people spread their tents on the plain beneath. Here was to be their home for nearly a year. At night the pillar of fire assured them of divine protection, and while they were deep in slumber, the bread of heaven fell gently on the encampment.

Here Israel was to receive the most wonderful revelation ever made by God to humanity. Here the Lord had gathered His people that He might impress them with the sacredness of His requirements by declaring His holy law with His own voice. They were to undergo radical changes, for the degrading influences of slavery and idolatry had left their mark on the people's habits and character. God was working to lift them to a higher moral level by giving them a knowledge of Himself.

God Gives His Law
on Mount Sinai*

S oon after making camp at Sinai, Moses was called up into the mountain to meet with God. Israel was now to be taken into a close and special relationship to the Most High—to be organized as a church and a nation under the government of God. " 'You have seen what I did to the Egyptians, and how I bore you on eagles' wings and brought you to Myself. Now therefore, if you will indeed obey My voice and keep My covenant, then you shall be a special treasure to Me above all people; for all the earth is Mine. And you shall be to Me a kingdom of priests and a holy nation.' "

Moses returned to the camp, and he repeated the divine message to the elders of Israel. Their answer was, " 'All that the LORD has spoken we will do.' " In this way they entered into a solemn covenant with God, pledging themselves to accept Him as their ruler, becoming in a special sense the subjects of His authority.

God intended to make the occasion of speaking His law a scene of awe-inspiring grandeur. Everything connected with the service of God must be regarded with the greatest reverence. The Lord said to Moses, " 'Go to the people and consecrate them today and tomorrow, and let them wash their clothes. . . . For on the third day the LORD will come down upon Mount Sinai in the sight of all the people.' " All were to spend the time in solemn preparation to appear before God. Their person and their clothing must be free from impurity. They were to devote themselves to self-examination, fasting, and prayer, that their hearts might be cleansed from iniquity.

On the morning of the third day, Sinai's summit was covered with a thick cloud, black and dense, sweeping downward until the entire mountain was shrouded in darkness and mystery. Then a sound like a trumpet was heard, calling the people to meet with God. From the thick darkness lightnings flashed, while peals of thunder echoed among the surrounding heights. "Now Mount Sinai was completely in smoke, because the LORD descended upon it in fire . . . and the whole mountain quaked greatly." The hosts of Israel shook with fear and fell on their

* *This chapter is based on Exodus 19 to 24.*

faces before the Lord. Even Moses exclaimed, " 'I am exceedingly afraid and trembling.' " Hebrews 12:21.

Now the thunder stopped; the trumpet was no longer heard; the earth was still. There was a period of solemn silence; then the voice of God was heard. Speaking out of the thick darkness as He stood on the mountain, surrounded by angels, the Lord made known His law.

" 'I am the LORD your God, who brought you out of the land of Egypt, out of the house of bondage.' " He who had brought them out of Egypt, making a way for them through the sea and overthrowing Pharaoh and his army—He it was who now spoke His law.

God honored the Hebrews by making them the guardians and keepers of His law, but they were to hold it as a sacred trust for the whole world. The laws of the Ten Commandments are adapted to people everywhere, and they were given for the instruction and government of all. Ten precepts, brief, comprehensive, and authoritative, cover our duty to God and to other people, and all based on the great fundamental principle of love. " ' "You shall love the LORD your God with all your heart, with all your soul, with all your strength, and with all your mind," and "your neighbor as yourself." ' " Luke 10:27. In the Ten Commandments these principles are applied to our lives.

(1) " 'You shall have no other gods before Me.' " Whatever we cherish that tends to lessen our love for God or to interfere with the service that is rightfully His—of that we make a god.

(2) " 'You shall not make for yourself any carved image or any likeness of anything that is in heaven above, or that is in the earth beneath, or that is in the water under the earth; you shall not bow down to them nor serve them.' "

Concepts of God Affect Human Behavior

Many heathen nations claimed that their images were only symbols by which the Deity was worshiped, but God has declared such worship to be sin. The attempt to represent the Eternal One by material objects would lower our concepts of God. Our minds would be attracted to the creature rather than to the Creator. As our concepts of God were lowered, so the human race would become degraded.

" 'I, the LORD your God, am a jealous God.' " The close relation of God to His people is represented by the illustration of marriage. Since idolatry is spiritual adultery, the displeasure of God against it is fittingly called jealousy.

" 'Visiting the iniquity of the fathers on the children to the third and fourth generations of those who hate Me.' " Children are not punished for their parents' guilt, except as they take part in their sins. Usually, however, by inheritance and example the children become partakers of the parents' sin. Wrong tendencies, perverted appetites, and debased morals, as well as physical disease and decline, are passed along from parent to child, to the third and fourth generation.

" 'Showing mercy to thousands, to those who love Me and keep My commandments.' " To those who are faithful in His service, God promises mercy, not merely to the third and fourth generation like the wrath threatened against those who hate Him, but to thousands of generations.

(3) " 'You shall not take the name of the LORD your God in vain, for the LORD will not hold him guiltless who takes His name in vain.' "

This commandment forbids us to use the name of God in a light or careless manner. By the thoughtless mention of God in common conversation, and by frequent, thoughtless repetition of His name, we dishonor Him. "Holy and awesome is His name." Psalm 111:9. We should speak it with reverence and solemnity.

(4) " 'Remember the Sabbath day, to keep it holy. Six days you shall labor and do all your work, but the seventh day is the Sabbath of the LORD your God. In it you shall do no work: you, nor your son, nor your daughter, nor your manservant, nor your maidservant, nor your cattle, nor your stranger who is within your gates. For in six days the LORD made the heavens and the earth, the sea, and all that is in them, and rested the seventh day. Therefore the LORD blessed the Sabbath day and hallowed it.' "

The Sabbath is not introduced as a new institution but as having been established at Creation. Pointing to God as the Maker of the heavens and the earth, it distinguishes the true God from false gods. Thus the Sabbath is the sign of our allegiance to God. The fourth commandment is the only one of the ten in which we find both the name and the title of the Lawgiver, the only one that shows by whose authority the law is given. Thus it contains the seal of God.

God has given us six days in which to work, and He requires that we do our work in those six days. Acts of necessity and mercy are permitted on the Sabbath. The sick and suffering are always to be cared for; but we should strictly avoid unnecessary labor. To keep the Sabbath holy, we should not even allow our minds to dwell on things of a worldly character. And the commandment includes all within our "gates." All the members of the household are to lay aside their worldly business during the sacred hours. All should unite to honor God by their willing service on His holy day.

(5) " 'Honor your father and your mother, that your days may be long upon the land which the LORD your God is giving you.' "

Parents are entitled to a degree of love and respect owed to no other person. To reject the rightful authority of one's parents is also to reject the authority of God. The fifth commandment requires children not only to respect, submit to, and obey their parents but also to give them love and tenderness, to lighten their cares, to guard their reputation, and to care for and comfort them in old age. It also requires respect for ministers and rulers.

(6) " 'You shall not murder.' "

All acts of injustice that tend to shorten life; the spirit of hatred and revenge, or indulging any passion that leads to injurious acts toward others (even to wish them harm, for "whoever hates his brother is a murderer"); a selfish neglect of caring for the needy; self-indulgence or overwork that tends to injure health—all these are, to a greater or less degree, violations of the sixth commandment.

(7) " 'You shall not commit adultery.' "

God's law demands purity not only in the outward life but in the secret intents and emotions of the heart. Christ, who taught the far-reaching obligation of the law of God, declared that the evil thought or look is as truly sin as is the unlawful deed.

(8) " 'You shall not steal.' "

This prohibition condemns kidnapping and slave dealing, wars of conquest, theft and robbery. It demands strict integrity in the smallest details of life. It forbids shady business dealings and requires the payment of rightful debts or wages. Every attempt to gain advantage by the ignorance, weakness, or misfortune of another is registered as fraud in the books of heaven.

(9) " 'You shall not bear false witness against your neighbor.' "

An intention to deceive is what makes a falsehood. By a glance of the eye, a motion of the hand, an expression of the face, we may tell a lie as effectively as by words. It is falsehood even to state the facts in such a way as to mislead. Every effort to injure our neighbor's reputation by misrepresentation, slander, or gossip, and even hiding truth in order to injure others, is a violation of the ninth commandment.

(10) " 'You shall not covet your neighbor's house; you shall not covet your neighbor's wife, nor his manservant, nor his maidservant, nor his ox, nor his donkey, nor anything that is your neighbor's.' "

The tenth commandment strikes at the very root of all sins; it prohibits the selfish desire, from which springs the sinful act. The person who refuses to indulge even a sinful desire for something that belongs to another will not be guilty of a wrong act toward anyone else.

God proclaimed His law with demonstrations of His power and glory so that His people would never forget the scene. He wanted to show everyone the sacredness and permanence of His law.

God's Law Is a Law of Love

As God's great rule of right was presented before them, the people realized as never before how offensive sin is to a holy God and how guilty they were in His sight. They cried out to Moses, " 'You speak with us, and we will hear; but let not God speak with us, lest we die.' " The leader answered, " 'Do not fear; for God has come to test you, and that His fear may be before you, so that you may not sin.' "

Blinded and depraved by slavery and heathenism, the people were not prepared to understand fully the far-reaching principles of God's ten precepts. Additional instruction was given, illustrating and applying the principles of the Ten Commandments. These laws were called "judgments" because the magistrates were to give judgment according to them. Unlike the Ten Commandments, they were delivered privately to Moses.

The first of these related to servants. A Hebrew could not be sold as a slave for life. His service was limited to six years; on the seventh he was to be set free. The holding of non-Israelites as slaves was permitted, but their life and person were strictly guarded. The murderer of a slave was to be punished; an injury inflicted on a slave by his master, even if no more than the loss of a tooth, entitled him to his freedom.

The Israelites were to beware of indulging the spirit of cruelty like that from which they had suffered under their Egyptian taskmasters. The memory of their own bitter experience should enable them to put themselves in the servant's place, to be kind and compassionate.

The rights of widows and orphans were specially guarded. " 'If you afflict them in any way,' " the Lord declared, " 'and they cry at all to Me, I will surely hear their cry; and My wrath will become hot, and I will kill you with the sword; your wives shall be widows, and your children fatherless.' " Aliens who united themselves with Israel were to be protected from wrong or oppression. " 'You shall not oppress a stranger, for you know the heart of a stranger, because you were strangers in the land of Egypt.' "

Charging interest on a loan to the poor was forbidden. A poor person's garment or blanket taken as a pledge for a loan must be given back at nightfall. Judges were warned against perverting justice, aiding a false cause, or receiving bribes. Slander was prohibited, and acts of kindness were required even toward personal enemies.

The people were reminded of the sacred obligation of the Sabbath. Yearly feasts were appointed, at which all the men of the nation were to assemble before the Lord, bringing to Him their offerings of gratitude and the firstfruits of His provision of crops. The purpose of all these regulations was stated: all were given for the good of Israel. The Lord said, " 'You shall be holy men to Me.' "

These laws were to be recorded by Moses and carefully treasured as the foundation of the national law and, with the ten precepts, as the condition of God's fulfilling His promises to Israel.

The message was now given, " 'Behold, I send an Angel before you to keep you in the way and to bring you into the place which I have prepared. Beware of Him and obey His voice; do not provoke Him.' " Christ in the pillar of cloud and of fire was their Leader. While there were symbols or "types" pointing to a Savior to come, there was also a present Savior, who gave commands to Moses for the people and was set forth before them as the only channel of blessing.

How the "Old Covenant" Was Made

After coming down from the mountain, "Moses came and told the people all the words of the LORD and all the judgments. And all the people answered with one voice and said, 'All the words which the LORD has said we will do.' "

Then they ratified the covenant. An altar was built at the foot of the mountain, and beside it twelve pillars were set up, "according to the twelve tribes of Israel," as a testimony that they accepted the covenant. Moses "took the Book of the Covenant and read in the hearing of the people." All were free to choose whether they would comply with the covenant's conditions. They had heard God's law proclaimed, and its principles had been applied to various situations, so that they could know how much this covenant involved. Again the people answered together, " 'All that the LORD has said we will do, and be obedient.' " "When Moses had spoken every precept to all the people according to the law, he took the blood . . . and sprinkled both the book itself and all the people, saying, 'This is the blood of the covenant which God has commanded you.' " Hebrews 9:19, 20.

Moses had received the command, " 'Come up to the LORD, you and Aaron, Nadab and Abihu, and seventy of the elders of Israel.' " The seventy elders were to assist Moses in governing Israel, and God put His Spirit on them. "And they saw the God of Israel. And there was under His feet as it were a paved work of sapphire stone, and it was like the very heavens in its clarity." They did not see God Himself, but they saw the glory of His presence. They had been thinking about His glory, purity, and mercy, until they could come nearer to Him.

Moses and "his assistant Joshua" were now summoned to meet with God. The leader appointed Aaron and Hur, assisted by the elders, to act in his place. Moses waited to be called into the presence chamber of the Most High. His patience and obedience were tested, but he did not forsake his post. Even this favored servant of God could not immediately approach into His presence and endure His glory. For six days he must devote himself to God by searching of heart, meditation, and prayer.

On the seventh day, which was the Sabbath, Moses was called up into the cloud. "So Moses went into the midst of the cloud. . . . And Moses was on the mountain forty days and forty nights." He fasted during the entire forty days.

God Exalts a Race of Slaves

During his stay on the mountain, Moses received directions for building a sanctuary in which the divine Presence would be specially revealed. "Let them make Me a sanctuary, that I may dwell among them," was the command of God. For the third time keeping the Sabbath was commanded: " 'It is a sign between Me and the children of Israel forever,' " the Lord declared, " 'that you may know that I am the LORD who sanctifies you. You shall keep the Sabbath, therefore, for it is holy to you. . . . Whoever does any work on it, that person shall be cut off from among his people.' " Exodus 31:17, 13, 14.

From then on the people were to be honored with the abiding presence of their King. " 'I will dwell among the children of Israel and will be their God,' " " 'and the tabernacle shall be sanctified by My glory.' " Exodus 29:45, 43.

From a race of slaves the Israelites had been exalted above all peoples to be the special treasure of the King of kings. God had separated them from the world, He had made them the holders of His law, and through them He intended to preserve on earth the knowledge of Himself.

Thus the light of heaven was to shine out to a world in darkness. A voice was to be heard appealing to all peoples to turn from idolatry to serve the living God. If the Israelites would be true to their trust, God would be their defense, and He would exalt them above all other nations.

Israel Worships a Golden Calf*

While Moses was away on the mountain, it was a time of waiting and suspense for Israel. The people waited eagerly for his return. In Egypt they had become accustomed to material objects representing deity, and it had been hard for them to trust in an invisible being. They had come to rely on Moses to sustain their faith. Now he was taken from them. Week after week passed, and still he did not return. It seemed to many in the camp that their leader had deserted them or that he had been consumed by the devouring fire.

During this period of waiting, there was time to meditate on the law of God which they had heard and to prepare their hearts to receive any further revelations that He might make to them. If they had been seeking a clearer understanding of God's requirements and humbling their hearts before Him, they would have been shielded from temptation. But soon they became careless, inattentive, and lawless, especially the "mixed multitude." They were impatient to be on their way to the land flowing with milk and honey. That goodly land was promised to them only on condition of obedience, but they had forgotten this. Some suggested they return to Egypt; but whether forward to Canaan or backward to Egypt, most of the people were determined to wait no longer for Moses.

The "mixed multitude" had been the first to indulge in complaining and impatience, and they were the leaders in apostasy. Among the objects the Egyptians regarded as symbols of deity was the ox or calf. At the suggestion of those who had practiced idolatry in Egypt, a calf was now made and worshiped. The people wanted some image to represent God and to go before them in the place of Moses. The mighty miracles in Egypt and at the Red Sea were intended to establish faith in God as the invisible, all-powerful Helper of Israel. The people's desire for some visible display of His presence had been granted in the pillar of cloud and of fire, and in the revealing of His glory on Mount Sinai. But with the cloud of the Presence still before them, in their hearts they turned back to the idolatry of Egypt.

This chapter is based on Exodus 32 to 34.

In Moses' absence, the judicial authority had been delegated to Aaron, and a vast crowd gathered about his tent. The cloud, they said, now rested permanently on the mountain; it would no longer direct their travels. They must have an image in its place. And if, as some had suggested, they should return to Egypt, they would find favor with the Egyptians by carrying this image ahead of them as their god. (See Appendix, Note 3.)

Instead of Leading, Aaron Follows

Aaron protested feebly with the people, but his indecision and his timid response at the critical moment only made them the more determined. A blind, unreasoning frenzy seemed to possess the crowd. Some remained true to their covenant with God, but most of them joined in the apostasy. A few who dared to denounce the proposed image-making as idolatry were beaten and finally lost their lives.

Aaron feared for his own safety, and instead of nobly standing up for the honor of God, he yielded to the demands of the crowd. They willingly gave him their ornaments, and from these he made a molten calf in imitation of the gods of Egypt.

The people proclaimed, " 'This is your god, O Israel, that brought you out of the land of Egypt!' " And Aaron basely permitted this insult to Jehovah. He did even more. Seeing how pleased the people were with the golden god, he built an altar before it and proclaimed, " 'Tomorrow is a feast to the LORD.' Then they rose early on the next day, offered burnt offerings, and brought peace offerings; and the people sat down to eat and drink, and rose up to play." They gave themselves up to gluttony and sinful reveling.

A religion that permits people to devote themselves to selfish or sensual gratification is as pleasing to the multitudes now as it was in the days of Israel. There are still weak-willed Aarons in the church who will yield to the desires of the unconverted and thus encourage them in sin.

Israel Broke Their Solemn Promise

Only a few days had passed since the Hebrews had stood trembling before Mount Sinai, listening to the words of the Lord, " 'You shall have no other gods before Me.' " The glory of God still hovered above the mountain in the sight of the congregation; but "they made a calf in Horeb, and worshiped the molded image. Thus they changed their glory into the image of an ox." Psalm 106:19, 20.

On the mountain, Moses was warned of the apostasy in the camp. " 'Go, get down!' " were the words of God; " 'your people whom you brought out of the land of Egypt have corrupted themselves. They have turned aside quickly out of the way which I commanded them.' "

God's covenant with His people had been broken, and He declared to Moses, " 'Let Me alone, that My wrath may burn hot against them and I may consume them. And I will make of you a great nation.' " The people of Israel, especially the "mixed multitude," would be constantly inclined to rebel against God, complain about their leader, and bring sorrow to him by their unbelief and stubbornness. Their sins had already lost for them the favor of God.

If God had decided to destroy Israel, who could plead for them? But Moses saw ground for hope where there appeared only discouragement and divine fury. The words of God, "Let Me alone," he understood not to forbid but to encourage him to plead their case; if he asked earnestly, God would spare His people.

God had implied that He had disowned His people. He had spoken of them to Moses as "your people whom *you* brought out of Egypt." But Moses disclaimed the leadership of Israel. They were not his, but God's—" 'Your people whom *You* have brought out . . . with great power and with a mighty hand.' " " 'Why,' " Moses urged, " 'should the Egyptians speak, and say, "He brought them out to harm them, to kill them in the mountains"?' "

During the few months since Israel had left Egypt, the report of their amazing deliverance had spread to all the surrounding nations. Terrible dread rested on the heathen. All were watching to see what the God of Israel would do for His people. If they now were to be destroyed, their enemies would triumph. The Egyptians would claim that their accusations were true—instead of leading His people into the wilderness to sacrifice, He had caused them to be sacrificed. The destruction of the people whom He had honored would bring a slur on His name. How great is the responsibility on those whom God has highly honored, to make His name a praise in the earth!

As Moses interceded for Israel, the Lord listened to his pleadings and granted his unselfish prayer. God had proved his love for that ungrateful people, and Moses had nobly endured the trial. The well-being of God's people was more important to him than becoming the father of a mighty nation. God was pleased with his faithfulness and integrity and committed to him the great responsibility of leading Israel to the Promised Land.

As Moses and Joshua came down from the mountain and neared the camp, they saw the people shouting and dancing around their idol—a scene of heathen riot, an imitation of the idolatrous feasts of Egypt. How unlike the solemn and reverent worship of God! Moses was overwhelmed. He had just come from the presence of God's glory, and he was unprepared for that dreadful display of Israel's degraded condition. To show his horror at their crime, he threw down the tablets of stone, and they were broken in view of all the people, signifying that as they had broken their covenant with God, so God had broken His covenant with them.

Moses Punishes the Wrongdoers

Taking hold of the idol, Moses threw it into the fire. Afterward he ground it to powder and scattered it on the stream that came down from the mountain. In this way he showed the utter worthlessness of the god they had been worshiping.

The great leader summoned his guilty brother. Aaron tried to defend himself by relating the clamors of the people, stating that if he had not done as they asked he would have been put to death. " 'They said to me, "Make us gods that shall go before us; as for this Moses, the man who brought us out of the land of Egypt, we do not know what has become of him." And I said to them, "Whoever has any gold, let them break it off." So they gave it to me, and I cast it into the fire, and this calf came out.' " He wanted Moses to believe that a miracle had taken place, that the gold changed to a calf by supernatural power. But his excuses made no difference. He was properly dealt with as the chief offender.

It was Aaron, "the saint of the LORD" (Psalm 106:16), who had made the idol and announced the feast. He had failed to stop the idolaters in their heaven-defying plan. He was not stirred to action by the proclamation before the molten image, " 'This is your god, O Israel, that brought you out of the land of Egypt.' " He had been with Moses on the mountain and there had seen the glory of the Lord. It was he who had changed that glory into the image of an ox. God had committed to him the government of the people in Moses' absence, but he had permitted rebellion. " 'The LORD was very angry with Aaron and would have destroyed him.' " Deuteronomy 9:20. But in answer to Moses' intercession, his life was spared; he repented for his great sin and was restored to the favor of God.

How Aaron Encouraged Rebellion

If Aaron had had courage to stand for the right, he could have prevented the apostasy. If he had firmly maintained his own loyalty to God and had reminded the people of their solemn covenant with God, the evil would have been stopped. But his willingness to cooperate with them emboldened the people to go to greater lengths in sin than they had ever thought of before.

To justify himself, Aaron tried to make the people responsible for his weakness in yielding to their demand; but despite this, they were filled with admiration of his gentleness and patience. But Aaron's yielding spirit and desire to please had blinded his eyes to the enormity of the crime he was permitting. His actions cost the life of thousands. In contrast was the course of Moses. While faithfully executing God's judgments, he showed that the welfare of Israel was more precious to him than prosperity, honor, or life.

God wants His servants to prove their loyalty by faithfully rebuking transgression, however painful that act may be. Those who are honored with a divine commission are not to exalt themselves or shun disagreeable duties but to perform God's work with unswerving faithfulness.

If not quickly crushed, the rebellion that Aaron had permitted would escalate in wickedness and bring the nation to ruin. By terrible severity the evil must be put away. Moses called to the people, " 'Whoever is on the LORD's side, let him come to me!' " Those who had not joined the apostasy were to take their position at the right; those who were guilty but repentant, at the left. It was found that the tribe of Levi had taken no part in the idolatrous worship. From among other tribes there were great numbers who now expressed their repentance. But a large company, mostly the "mixed multitude," persisted in their rebellion. In the name of "the LORD God of Israel," Moses now commanded those who had kept themselves clear of idolatry to put on their swords and kill all who persisted in rebellion. "And about three thousand men of the people fell that day." The ringleaders in wickedness were cut off, but all who repented were spared.

People are to be careful how they judge and condemn others. But when God commands them to execute His sentence on evil, He is to be obeyed. Those who performed this painful act thus demonstrated their abhorrence of rebellion and idolatry. The Lord honored their faithfulness by bestowing special distinction on the tribe of Levi.

Justice had to be visited on the traitors to maintain the divine government. Yet even here God's mercy was displayed: He granted freedom of choice and opportunity for repentance to all. Only those who persisted in rebellion were cut off.

Why Israel's Idolatry Must Be Punished

It was necessary that this sin should be punished as a warning to surrounding nations of God's displeasure against idolatry. Whenever the Israelites would later condemn idolatry, their enemies would throw back the charge that the people who claimed Jehovah as their God had made a calf and worshiped it in Horeb. Though they had to acknowledge the disgraceful truth, Israel could point to the terrible fate of the transgressors as evidence that their sin had not been excused.

Love no less than justice demanded that judgment be inflicted. God cuts off those who are determined to rebel, that they may not lead others to ruin. In sparing the life of Cain, God had demonstrated the result of permitting sin to go unpunished. His life and teaching led to the corrupt conditions that demanded the destruction of the whole world by a flood. The history of the pre-Flood people testifies that God's great patience and restraint did not curb their wickedness.

So at Sinai. If transgression had not been speedily punished, the same results would have appeared again. The earth would have become as corrupt as in the days of Noah. Evils would have followed, greater than those that resulted from sparing Cain's life. It was the mercy of God that thousands should suffer, to prevent the need for visiting judgments on millions. To save the many He must punish the few.

Furthermore, as the people had forfeited divine protection, the whole nation was exposed to the power of their enemies. They would soon have fallen prey to their many powerful foes. It was necessary for the good of Israel that crime should be promptly punished.

And it was no less a mercy to the sinners themselves to be cut short in their evil course. If their lives had been spared, the same spirit that led them to rebel against God would have resulted in hatred and strife among themselves. They would eventually have destroyed one another.

Moses' Christlike Love for Israel

As the people began to see how great their guilt was, they feared that every offender was to be cut off. Moses promised to plead with God for them once more.

" 'You have sinned a great sin,' " he said. " 'So now I will go up to the LORD; perhaps I can make atonement for your sin.' " In his confession before God he said, " 'Oh, these people have sinned a great sin, and have made for themselves a god of gold! Yet now, if You will forgive their sin—but if not, I pray, blot me out of Your book which You have written.' "

The prayer of Moses directs our minds to the heavenly records in which the names of all are inscribed and their deeds, good or evil, are registered. The book of life contains the names of all who have entered the service of God. If by stubborn persistence in sin any of these become finally hardened against His Holy Spirit, in the judgment their names will be blotted from the book of life.

If the people of Israel were to be rejected by the Lord, Moses wanted his name to be blotted out with theirs; he could not bear to see the judgments of God fall on those who had been graciously delivered. Moses' intercession on behalf of Israel illustrates Christ's mediation for sinners. But the LORD did not permit Moses to bear the guilt of the transgressor, as Christ did. " 'Whoever has sinned against Me,' " He said, " 'I will blot him out of My book.' "

In deep sadness the people buried their dead. Three thousand had fallen by the sword; soon after, a plague had broken out in the camp; and now the message came to them that the divine Presence would no longer go with them in their journey: " 'I will not go up in your midst, lest I consume you on the way for you are a stiffnecked people.' " And God commanded, " 'Take off your ornaments, that I may know what to do to you.' " In penitence and humiliation, "the children of Israel stripped themselves of their ornaments by Mount Horeb."

By divine command, the tent that had served as a temporary place of worship was taken "far from the camp." This was further evidence that God had withdrawn His presence from them. The people felt the rebuke keenly, and to the conscience-stricken multitudes it seemed to foretell greater calamity.

But they were not left without hope. The tent was pitched outside the camp, but Moses called it "the tabernacle of meeting." All who were truly repentant and wanted to return to the Lord were told to go there to confess their sins and seek His mercy. When they returned to their tents, Moses entered the tabernacle. The people watched for some sign that his intercessions for them were accepted. When the cloudy pillar came down and stood at the entrance of the tabernacle, the people wept for joy, and they "rose and worshiped, each man in his tent door."

Help From God, a Necessity

Moses had learned that in order to lead the people successfully, he must have help from God. He pleaded for an assurance of God's presence: " 'Now therefore, I pray, if I have found grace in Your sight, show me now Your way, that I may know You and that I may find grace in Your sight. And consider that this nation is Your people.' "

The answer was, " 'My Presence will go with you, and I will give you rest.' " But Moses was not yet satisfied. He prayed that the favor of God might be restored to His people and that the visible evidence of His presence might continue to direct their journeyings: " 'If Your presence does not go with us, do not bring us up from here. For how then will it be known that Your people and I have found grace in Your sight, except that You go with us?' "

And the Lord said, " 'I will also do this thing that you have spoken; for you have found grace in My sight, and I know you by name.' " Still the prophet did not cease pleading. He now made a request that no human being had ever made before: " 'Please, show me Your glory.' "

Moses Sees God's Glory

The gracious words were spoken, " 'I will make all My goodness pass before you.' " Moses was called to the mountain summit; then the hand that made the world, that hand that " 'removes the mountains, and they do not know' " (Job 9:5), took this creature of the dust and placed him in a cleft of the rock, while the glory of God and all His goodness passed before him.

To Moses, this experience was an assurance that was worth infinitely more to him than all the learning of Egypt or all his achievements as a statesman or military leader. No earthly power or skill of learning can substitute for God's abiding presence.

Moses stood alone in the presence of the Eternal One, and he was not afraid, for his soul was in harmony with his Maker. "If I regard iniquity in my heart, the LORD will not hear." Psalm 66:18. But "the secret of the LORD is with those who fear Him, and He will show them His covenant." Psalm 25:14.

The Deity proclaimed Himself " 'The LORD, the LORD God, merciful and gracious, longsuffering, and abounding in goodness and truth, keeping mercy for thousands, forgiving iniquity and transgression and sin, by no means clearing the guilty.' "

"Moses made haste and bowed his head toward the earth, and worshiped." The Lord graciously promised to renew His favor to Israel and to do marvels such as had not been done " 'in all the earth, nor in any nation.' " During all this time, as at the first, Moses was miraculously sustained. At God's command he had prepared two tablets of stone and had taken them with him to the summit; and again the Lord "wrote on the tablets the words of the covenant, the Ten Commandments." (See Appendix, Note 4.)

Moses' face radiated with a dazzling light when he descended from the mountain. Aaron as well as the people "were afraid to come near him." Seeing their terror, he held out to them the pledge of God's reconciliation. They heard nothing in his voice but love and appeal, and at last one man dared to approach him. Too awed to speak, he silently pointed to the face of Moses and then toward heaven. The great leader understood his meaning. In their conscious guilt, they could not endure the heavenly light which would have filled them with joy if they had been obedient to God.

Moses put a veil on his face and continued to do so after this whenever he returned to the camp from communion with God.

By this brightness, God intended to impress on Israel the exalted character of His law and the glory of the gospel revealed through Christ. While Moses was on the mountain, God presented to him not only the tablets of the law but also the plan of salvation. He saw the sacrifice of Christ prefigured by all the types and symbols of the Jewish age; and it was the heavenly light streaming from Calvary, no less than the glory of the law of God, that caused such radiance on the face of Moses.

The glory reflected in the countenance of Moses testifies that the closer is our communion with God and the clearer our knowledge of His requirements, the more fully we will be conformed to the divine image.

As Israel's intercessor veiled his face, so Christ, the divine Mediator, veiled His divinity with humanity when He came to earth. If He had come clothed with the brightness of heaven, sinful human beings could not have endured the glory of His presence. So He humbled Himself, and was made "in the likeness of sinful flesh" (Romans 8:3), that He might reach the fallen race and lift them up.

Satan's Hatred of God's Law

The first effort of Satan to overthrow God's law—begun among the sinless inhabitants of heaven—seemed for a time to succeed. A vast number of the angels were deceived. But Satan's apparent triumph resulted in defeat and loss, separation from God, and banishment from heaven.

When the conflict was renewed on earth, Satan again seemed to win an advantage. By transgression, the human race became his captive. Now the way seemed open for Satan to establish an independent kingdom and to defy the authority of God and His Son. But the plan of salvation made it possible for sinners to be brought back into harmony with God.

Again Satan was defeated, and again he resorted to deception in the hope of converting defeat into victory. He now portrayed God as unjust in having permitted our first parents to transgress His law. The tempter said, "When God knew what would be the result, why did He permit His creatures to be given a test and bring in misery and death?" The children of Adam willingly listened to the tempter and complained against the only Being who could save them from Satan's destructive power.

Thousands today are echoing the same rebellious complaint against God. They do not see that to deprive human beings of freedom of choice would make them no more than robots. Like the inhabitants of all other worlds, we must undergo the test of obedience; but we are never brought into a position where yielding to evil becomes necessary. No temptation or trial is permitted that we are unable to resist.

As the population increased, almost the whole world joined the ranks of rebellion. Once more Satan seemed to have gained the victory, but the earth was cleansed by the Flood from its moral pollution.

Why God Chose Israel

Says the prophet, "Let grace be shown to the wicked, yet he will not learn righteousness; . . . and will not behold the majesty of the LORD." Isaiah 26:10. This is how it was after the Flood. The inhabitants of the earth again rebelled against the Lord. The world had twice rejected God's covenant. Both the people before the Flood and the descendants of Noah cast off the divine authority. Then God entered into covenant with Abraham and took to Himself a people to become the guardians of His law.

To lure and destroy this people, Satan began at once to lay his snares. The children of Jacob were tempted to enter marriages with the heathen and worship their idols. But Joseph's faithfulness was a testimony to the true faith. To quench this light Satan worked through Joseph's brothers to cause him to be sold as a slave. But God overruled. Both in the house of Potiphar and in the prison, Joseph received an education that, with the fear of God, prepared him for his position as prime minister of the nation. His influence was felt throughout the land, and the knowledge of God was spread far and wide. The idolatrous priests were filled with alarm. Inspired by Satan's hostility toward the God of heaven, they set themselves to quench the light.

After Moses fled from Egypt, idolatry seemed to conquer. Year by year the hopes of the Israelites grew fainter. Both king and people mocked the God of Israel. This spirit grew until it ripened fully in the Pharaoh whom Moses confronted. When the Hebrew leader came before the king with a message from "the LORD God of Israel," it was not ignorance of the true God but defiance of His power that prompted the answer, " 'Who is the LORD, that I should obey His voice . . . ? I do not know the LORD.' " From first to last, Pharaoh's opposition resulted from hatred and defiance.

In the days of Joseph, Egypt had been a refuge for Israel. God had been honored in the kindness shown His people; and now the long-suffering One, full of compassion, gave each judgment time to do its work. The Egyptians had evidence of the power of Jehovah, and all who were willing could submit to God and escape His judgments. The stubbornness of the king resulted in spreading the knowledge of God and bringing many Egyptians to give themselves to His service.

The extreme idolatry of the Egyptians and their cruelty during the latter part of the Hebrew stay there should have inspired the Israelites to recoil from idolatry and flee for refuge to the God of their fathers. But Satan darkened their minds, leading them to imitate the practices of their heathen masters.

When the time came for Israel's deliverance, Satan determined to hold that great people, numbering more than two million, in ignorance, superstition, obscurity, and bondage, so that he could obliterate the remembrance of God from their minds.

When Moses performed the miracles before the king, Satan tried to counterfeit the work of God and resist His will. This only prepared the way for greater exhibitions of divine power and glory.

God "brought out His people with joy, His chosen ones with gladness . . . that they might observe His statutes and keep His laws." Psalm 105:43-45.

During the bondage in Egypt, to a great extent many of the Israelites had lost the knowledge of God's law and had mingled its principles with heathen customs and traditions. God brought them to Sinai, and there with His own voice He declared His law.

Even while God was proclaiming His law to His people, Satan was plotting to tempt them to sin. By leading them into idolatry, he would destroy the value of all worship, for how can anyone be elevated by adoring what may be symbolized by his own handiwork? If people could so forget their own relationship to God that they would bow down to these revolting and senseless objects, then the evil passions of the heart would be unrestrained, and Satan would have full control.

At the very foot of Sinai, Satan began to plan for overthrowing the law of God, thus carrying forward the same work he had begun in heaven. During the forty days Moses was on the mountain with God, Satan was stirring up doubt, apostasy, and rebellion. When Moses came from the presence of divine glory with the law they had pledged to obey, he found God's covenant people bowing in adoration before a golden image.

Satan had planned to cause their ruin. Since they had proved themselves so completely degraded, Satan believed that the Lord would divorce them from Himself. Thus would be secured the extinction of the seed of Abraham that was to preserve the knowledge of the living God and through whom the true Seed was to come to conquer Satan. But the great rebel again was defeated. While those who stubbornly placed themselves on the side of Satan were cut off, the people, humbled and repentant, were mercifully pardoned. The whole universe had been witness to the scenes at Sinai; all had seen the contrast between the government of God and that of Satan.

The True Sign of Loyalty to God—The Sabbath

God's claim to reverence and worship above the gods of the heathen is based on the fact that He is the Creator. Says the prophet Jeremiah, "The living God . . . has made the earth by His power, He has established the world by His wisdom, and has stretched out the heavens at His discretion." "Everyone is dull-hearted, without knowledge; every metalsmith is put to shame by the graven image; for his molded image is falsehood, and there is no breath in them. They are futile, a work of errors; in the time of their punishment they shall perish." Jeremiah 10:10-12, 14, 15. The Sabbath, as a memorial of God's creative power, points to Him as the maker of the heavens and the earth. It is a constant witness to His greatness, wisdom, and love. If the Sabbath had always been sacredly observed, there could never have been an atheist or an idolater.

The Sabbath originated in Eden; it is as old as the world itself. It was observed by all the patriarchs, from creation onward. When the law was proclaimed at Sinai, the first words of the fourth commandment were, "Remember the Sabbath day, to keep it holy," showing that the Sabbath was not just then instituted. We are pointed back to Creation for its origin. Satan aimed to tear down this great memorial. If people could be led to forget their Creator, they would make no effort to resist the power of evil, and Satan would take them captive.

Satan's hatred against God's law had driven him to war against every principle of the Ten Commandments. Contempt for the authority of parents will soon lead to contempt for the authority of God, so Satan has worked to lessen the obligation of the fifth commandment. In many heathen nations parents were abandoned or put to death as soon as they were too old to provide for themselves. The mother was treated with little respect, and when her husband died, she was required to submit to the authority of her eldest son. Moses commanded obedience by sons and daughters; but as the Israelites strayed from the Lord, the fifth commandment, with others, came to be disregarded.

Satan was "a murderer from the beginning" (John 8:44), and as soon as he got power over the human race, he not only prompted them to hate and kill one another but made the violation of the sixth commandment a part of their religion.

Heathen nations were led to believe that human sacrifices were necessary to secure the favor of their gods, and the most horrible cruelties have been committed under various forms of idolatry. Among these was the practice of causing their children to pass through the fire before their idols. When one came through unharmed, the people believed their offerings were accepted. They regarded the one thus delivered as specially favored by the gods. They heaped benefits on that child and held it in high esteem from then on. However terrible the favored one's crimes, no punishment ever followed. But if a child were burned in passing through the fire, his fate was sealed; the anger of the gods could be appeased only by taking the life of the victim. In times of great apostasy these abominations existed to some extent among the Israelites.

The violation of the seventh commandment also was early practiced in the name of religion. Abominable sexual rites became a part of the heathen worship. The gods themselves were impure, and their worshipers unleashed their baser passions. Religious festivals were characterized by universal, open impurity.

Polygamy was one of the sins that brought the wrath of God upon the pre-Flood world. Yet after the Flood it again became widespread. It was Satan's studied effort to pervert marriage, to weaken its obligations and lessen its sacredness. In no surer way could he deface the image of God in humanity and open the door to misery and vice.

God Will Win the Battle

Multitudes welcome Satan's deceptions and set themselves against God. But amid the working of evil, God's plans move steadily forward to their accomplishment. He is unveiling His justice and benevolence to all created intelligences. The whole human race have become transgressors of God's law, but by the sacrifice of His Son they may return to God. Through the grace of Christ they may be enabled to obey the Father's law. In every age God gathers out a people " 'in whose heart is My law.' " Isaiah 51:7.

God's dealings with rebellion will fully unmask the work so long carried on under cover. The fruits of setting aside the divine laws will be laid open to the view of all created intelligences. All will admit that the law of God is completely good and right. In the presence of the witnessing universe, Satan himself will confess the justice of God's government and the righteousness of His law.

The terrors of Sinai were to represent to the people the scenes of the judgment. The sound of a trumpet summoned Israel to meet with God. The voice of the Archangel and the trump of God shall summon both the living and the dead from the whole earth to the presence of their Judge. At the great judgment day, Christ will come " 'in the glory of His Father with His angels.' " Matthew 16:27. All nations will be gathered in His presence.

When Christ comes in glory with His holy angels, the whole earth will be ablaze with the terrible light of His presence. "Our God shall come, and shall not keep silent; a fire shall devour before Him, and it shall be very tempestuous all around Him. He shall call to the heavens from

above, and to the earth, that He may judge His people." Psalm 50:3, 4. "The Lord Jesus is revealed from heaven with His mighty angels, in flaming fire taking vengeance on those who do not know God, and on those who do not obey the gospel." 2 Thessalonians 1:7, 8.

When Moses came from the divine Presence on the mountain, guilty Israel could not endure the light that glorified his face. How much less can sinners look on the Son of God when He will appear in the glory of His Father, surrounded by all the holy angels, to execute judgment on the transgressors of His law and the rejecters of His atonement. "The kings of the earth, the great men, the rich men, the commanders, the mighty men" shall hide themselves "in the caves and in the rocks of the mountains," and they shall say to the mountains and rocks, " 'Fall on us and hide us from the face of Him who sits on the throne. . . . For the great day of His wrath has come, and who is able to stand?' " Revelation 6:15-17.

Satan has claimed that good would result from transgression, but it will be seen that "the wages of sin is death." Romans 6:23. " 'For behold, the day is coming, burning like an oven, and all the proud, yes, all who do wickedly will be stubble. And the day which is coming shall burn them up,' says the LORD of hosts, 'that will leave them neither root nor branch.' " Malachi 4:1.

But amid the tempest of divine judgment, the children of God will not be afraid. "The LORD will be a shelter for His people, and the strength of the children of Israel." Joel 3:16.

The great plan of redemption results in fully bringing the world back into God's favor. All that was lost by sin is restored. Not only the human race but the earth is redeemed, to be the eternal home of the obedient. Now God has accomplished His original purpose in its creation. "The saints of the Most High shall receive the kingdom, and possess the kingdom forever, even forever and ever." Daniel 7:18.

The sacred laws of God, which Satan has hated and tried to destroy, will be honored throughout a sinless universe. "The Lord GOD will cause righteousness and praise to spring forth before all the nations." Isaiah 61:11.

The Sanctuary, God's Dwelling Place in Israel[*]

The command came to Moses while he was on the mountain with God, " 'Let them make Me a sanctuary, that I may dwell among them.' " Exodus 25:8. Full directions were given for constructing the tabernacle. By their apostasy, the Israelites gave up their right to the divine Presence, but after God took them into favor again, the great leader proceeded to carry out the divine command.

God Himself gave Moses the plan for the sanctuary, its size and form, the materials to be used, and every article of furniture it was to contain. The holy places made with hands were "copies of the true," "copies of the things in the heavens" (Hebrews 9:24, 23), a miniature representation of the heavenly temple where Christ, our great High Priest, was to minister in the sinner's behalf. God gave Moses a view of the heavenly sanctuary and commanded him to make everything according to the pattern shown him.

For building the sanctuary, a large amount of the most costly material was required, yet the Lord accepted only freewill offerings.

All the people responded. "Then everyone came whose heart was stirred, and everyone whose spirit was willing, and they brought the LORD's offering for the work of the tabernacle of meeting. . . . They came, both men and women, as many as had a willing heart, and brought earrings and nose rings, rings and necklaces, all jewelry of gold."

While the sanctuary was being built, men, women, and children continued to bring their offerings until those in charge of the work found that they had more than could be used. And Moses issued a proclamation throughout the camp, " 'Let neither man nor woman do any more work for the offering of the sanctuary.' And the people were restrained from bringing." The Israelites' devotion, zeal, and liberality are an example worthy to imitate. All who love the worship of God will show the same spirit of sacrifice in preparing a house where He may meet with them. We should freely give enough to accomplish the work, so that the builders may be able to say, as the builders of the tabernacle did, "Bring no more offerings."

---

[*] *This chapter is based on Exodus 25 to 40; Leviticus 4 and 16.*

The tabernacle was small, not more than fifty-five feet long and eighteen wide and high. Yet it was magnificent. The wood was from the acacia tree, less likely to decay than any other at Sinai. The walls consisted of upright boards, set in silver sockets, and held firm by pillars and connection bars. All overlaid with gold, they looked like solid gold.

Two Apartments Symbolize Two Phases of Ministry

The building was divided into two apartments by a beautiful veil, and a similar veil closed the entrance of the first apartment. These were of magnificent colors—blue, purple, and scarlet—with cherubim woven in with threads of gold and silver to represent the angelic host.

The sacred tent was surrounded by an open space called the court. The entrance was at the eastern end, closed by curtains of beautiful workmanship but not as spectacular as those of the sanctuary. People outside the court could see the building plainly. In the court stood the bronze altar of burnt offering. On this altar were consumed all the sacrifices made by fire to the Lord, and its horns were sprinkled with the atoning blood. Between the altar and the door of the tabernacle was the laver, the large bronze basin made from the mirrors that had been the freewill offering of the women of Israel. At the laver the priests were to wash their hands and feet whenever they went into the sacred tabernacle or approached the altar to offer a burnt offering to the Lord.

In the tabernacle's first apartment, the Holy Place, were the table of showbread, the lampstand, and the altar of incense. The table of showbread stood on the north; it was overlaid with pure gold. On this table each Sabbath the priests were to place twelve cakes, arranged in two piles. On the south was the seven-branched lampstand, its branches decorated with exquisitely made flowers, all crafted from one solid piece of gold. The lamps were never all extinguished at one time but shed their light by day and night.

Just in front of the veil separating the Holy Place from the Most Holy and the immediate presence of God stood the golden altar of incense. Every morning and evening the priest was to burn incense on this altar; on the great Day of Atonement its horns were touched with the blood of the sin offering and sprinkled with blood. God Himself kindled the fire on this altar. Day and night the holy incense spread its fragrance throughout the sacred apartments and far around the tabernacle.

Beyond the inner veil was the Holy of Holies, the focal point of the symbolic service of atonement and intercession, the connecting link between heaven and earth. In this apartment was the ark, overlaid with gold inside and out, the container for the tablets of stone, the Ten Commandments. It was called the ark of God's testament, the ark of the covenant, since the Ten Commandments were the basis of the covenant made between God and Israel.

The cover of the chest was called the mercy seat. This was made of one solid piece of gold, with golden cherubim mounted on each end. The position of the cherubim, with their faces turned toward each other and looking reverently downward toward the ark, represented the reverence that the heavenly host have for the law of God and their interest in the plan of redemption.

Above the mercy seat was the Shekinah, the manifestation of the divine Presence. Divine messages were sometimes communicated to the high priest by a voice from the cloud.

The law of God within the ark was the great rule of righteousness and judgment. That law pronounced death on the lawbreaker, but above the law was the mercy seat. On the basis of the atonement, pardon was granted to the repentant sinner. "Mercy and truth have met together; righteousness and peace have kissed." Psalm 85:10.

A Dim Reflection of Heavenly Glory

No language can describe the glory within the sanctuary. The gold-plated walls reflecting light from the golden lampstand; the table, and altar of incense, glittering with gold; beyond the second veil the sacred ark, and above it the holy Shekinah, the manifestation of Jehovah's presence—all were no more than a dim reflection of the glories of the temple of God in heaven, the great center of the work for our redemption.

Building the tabernacle took about half a year. When it was completed, Moses examined all the work of the builders. "As the LORD had commanded, just so had they done it. And Moses blessed them." The people of Israel crowded around to look at the sacred structure. The pillar of cloud floated over the sanctuary, and "the glory of the LORD filled the tabernacle." There was a display of the divine majesty, and for a time even Moses could not enter. With deep emotion the people gazed at the sign that God had accepted the work of their hands. A solemn awe rested on all. The gladness of their hearts welled up in tears of joy. God had stooped to abide with them.

In the days of Abraham, the priesthood was the birthright of the oldest son. Now, instead of the first-born, the Lord accepted the tribe of Levi for the work of the sanctuary. However, only Aaron and his sons were permitted to serve as actual priests before the Lord; the rest of the tribe were entrusted with responsibilities for the tabernacle and its furniture.

Special clothing was worn by the priests. The robe of the common priest was of white linen, woven in one piece, held at the waist by a white linen belt embroidered in blue, purple, and red. On his head was a linen turban or miter. This completed his outer attire. The priests were to leave their shoes in the court before entering the sanctuary and also to wash both their hands and feet before ministering in the tabernacle. This made clear the lesson that those who would approach the presence of God must put away all defilement.

The garments of the high priest were made of costly material and revealed beautiful workmanship. In addition to the linen clothing of the common priest, he wore a robe of blue, also woven in one piece. Around the skirt it was decorated with golden bells and pomegranates of blue, purple, and scarlet. The ephod, a shorter garment, was held by a belt of the same colors. The ephod was sleeveless, and on its shoulder pieces were two onyx stones containing the names of the twelve tribes of Israel.

Over the ephod was the square-shaped breastplate, suspended from the shoulders by a cord of blue. The border was formed of a variety of precious stones, the same that form the twelve foundations of the City of God. The Lord directed, " 'Aaron shall bear the names of the sons of Israel on the breastplate of judgment over his heart, when he goes into the holy place, as a memorial before the LORD continually.' " Exodus 28:29. So Christ, the great High Priest, pleading His blood in the sinner's behalf, bears on His heart the name of every repentant, believing soul.

At the right and left of the breastplate were two large stones known as the Urim and Thummim. When questions were brought before the Lord, a halo of light encircling the stone at the right was a sign of God's approval, while a cloud shadowing the stone at the left was evidence of denial.

Everything connected with the clothing and conduct of the priests was to impress the people with the holiness of God and the purity required of those who come into His presence.

The Sanctuary Ministry Foreshadowed Heavenly Things

Not only the sanctuary but the ministry of the priests was to serve as a "copy and shadow of the heavenly things." Hebrews 8:5. The ministration consisted of two divisions—daily and yearly services. The daily service took place at the altar of burnt offering in the court of the tabernacle and in the Holy Place, while the yearly service was in the Most Holy.

No mortal eye but that of the high priest was to see the inner apartment of the sanctuary. Only once a year could he enter there. In reverent silence the people awaited his return, their hearts uplifted in prayer for the divine blessing. At the mercy seat the high priest made the atonement for Israel, and God, in the cloud of glory, met with him. If the high priest stayed longer than the accustomed time, the people were filled with fear that because of their sins or his own he had been killed by the glory of the Lord.

The Daily Service

Every morning and evening a year-old lamb was burned on the altar, symbolizing the daily consecration of the nation and their constant dependence on the atoning blood of Christ. Only an offering "without blemish" could be a symbol of the perfect purity of Jesus, who was to offer Himself as "a lamb without blemish and without spot." 1 Peter 1:19. The apostle Paul says, "I beseech you therefore, brethren, by the mercies of God, that you present your bodies a living sacrifice, holy, acceptable to God, which is your reasonable service." Romans 12:1. Those who love Him with all the heart will give Him the best service of the life and will constantly seek to bring every power of their being into harmony with His will.

When the priest offered incense, he came more directly into the presence of God than in any other act of the daily ministry. The glory of God that appeared above the mercy seat was partially visible from the first apartment. When the priest offered incense before the Lord, he looked toward the ark, and as the divine glory descended on the mercy seat and filled the most holy place, often the priest had to retreat to the door of the tabernacle. As the priest looked by faith to the mercy seat, which he could not see, so the people of God are now to direct their prayers to Christ, their great High Priest, who is pleading in their behalf in the sanctuary above.

The incense represents the merits and intercession of Christ, His perfect righteousness, which through faith is credited to His people and which is the only thing that can make the worship of sinful beings acceptable to God. By blood and by incense God was to be approached—symbols pointing to the great Mediator, the only one through whom mercy and salvation can be granted to the repentant soul.

As the priests entered the holy place morning and evening, the daily sacrifice was ready to be offered on the altar in the court. This was a time of intense interest; the worshipers at the tabernacle were to search their hearts and confess their sins. Their requests rose with the cloud of incense, while faith clung to the merits of the promised Savior that the atoning sacrifice prefigured. In later times the Jews, scattered as captives in distant lands, still turned their faces toward Jerusalem at the appointed hour and offered their prayers to the God of Israel. In this custom Christians have an example for morning and evening prayer. God looks with great pleasure on those who bow morning and evening to seek pardon and to present their requests for blessings.

The showbread was a perpetual offering, part of the daily sacrifice. It was always in the presence of the Lord (Exodus 25:30), acknowledging human dependence on God for both physical and spiritual food, received only through Christ's mediation. God had fed Israel with bread from heaven, and they were still dependent on His gifts, both for physical food and spiritual blessings. Both the manna and the showbread pointed to Christ, the living Bread. He Himself said, "I am the living Bread which came down from heaven." John 6:48-51. The bread was removed every Sabbath and replaced with fresh loaves.

The most important part of the daily ministry was the service in behalf of individuals. The repentant sinner brought his offering to the door of the tabernacle and, placing his hand upon the victim's head, confessed his sins, thus symbolically transferring the sins from himself to the innocent sacrifice. By his own hand the animal was then killed, and the priest carried the blood into the holy place and sprinkled it in front of the veil, behind which was the ark containing the law that the sinner had transgressed. By this ceremony the sin was transferred symbolically to the sanctuary through the blood. In some cases the blood was not taken into the holy place (see Appendix, Note 5), but the flesh was eaten by the priest, as Moses directed, saying, " 'God has given it you to bear the guilt of the congregation.' " Leviticus 10:17. Both ceremonies symbolized the transfer of sin from the repentant one to the sanctuary.

This work went on day by day throughout the year. With the sins of Israel having been transferred to the sanctuary, the holy places were defiled, and a special work became necessary to remove the sins. God commanded that an atonement be made for each of the sacred apartments, as for the altar, to "cleanse it, and hallow it from the uncleanness of the children of Israel." Leviticus 16:19.

Once a year, on the great Day of Atonement, the high priest entered the most holy place for the cleansing of the sanctuary. He brought two kids of the goats to the door of the tabernacle and cast lots for them, "one lot for the LORD and the other lot for the scapegoat." The goat on which the first lot fell was killed as a sin offering for the people. The priest was to bring its blood within the veil and sprinkle it on the mercy seat. " 'So he shall make atonement for the Holy Place, because of the uncleanness of the children of Israel, and because of their transgressions, for all their sins; and so he shall do for the tabernacle of meeting.' "

" 'Aaron shall lay both his hands on the head of the live goat, confess over it all the iniquities of the children of Israel, and all their transgressions, concerning all their sins, putting them on the head of the goat, and shall send it away into the wilderness by the hand of a suitable man. The goat shall bear on itself all their iniquities to an uninhabited land.' " Not until the goat had been led away did the people regard themselves as free from the burden of their sins. All Israel were to afflict their souls while the work of atonement was going forward. All business was laid aside, and the whole congregation of Israel spent the day in solemn humiliation before God with prayer, fasting, and deep searching of heart.

Truths Taught by the Day of Atonement

This yearly service taught important truths concerning the atonement. In the sin offerings presented during the year, a substitute had been accepted in the sinner's place, but the blood of the victim had not made full atonement for the sin. It had only provided a means of transferring the sin to the sanctuary. By offering the blood, the sinner confessed the guilt of his transgression and expressed faith in Him who was to take away the sin of the world. But the sinner was not entirely released from the condemnation of the law. On the Day of Atonement the high priest, having offered a sacrifice for the congregation, went into the Most Holy Place with the blood and sprinkled it on the mercy seat, above the tablets of the law.

In this way the claims of the law, which demanded the sinner's life, were satisfied. Then in his role of mediator the priest took the sins upon himself and, leaving the sanctuary, bore with him the burden of Israel's guilt. He laid his hands on the head of the scapegoat and confessed over it " 'all the iniquities of the children of Israel, and all their transgressions, concerning all their sins, putting them on the head of the goat.' " When the goat was sent away, these sins were regarded as forever separated from the people. This service was performed as a "copy and shadow of the heavenly things." Hebrews 8:5.

The True Heavenly Sanctuary

The earthly sanctuary was "symbolic for the present time in which both gifts and sacrifices are offered"; its two holy places were "copies of the things in the heavens." Christ, our great High Priest, is "a Minister of the sanctuary and of the true tabernacle which the Lord erected, and not man." Hebrews 9:9, 23; 8:2.

The apostle John was given a view of the temple of God in heaven. He saw there "seven lamps of fire" that "were burning before the throne." He saw an angel "having a golden censer . . . . He was given much incense, that he should offer it with the prayers of all the saints upon the golden altar which was before the throne." Revelation 4:5; 8:3. Here the prophet was permitted to look into the first apartment of the sanctuary in heaven. Again, "the temple of God was opened in heaven," and within the inner veil he looked on the Holy of Holies. Here he saw "the ark of His covenant" (Revelation 11:19), represented by the sacred chest that Moses constructed to contain the law of God.

Paul declares that "the tabernacle and all the vessels of the ministry," when completed, were "the copies of the things in the heavens." Hebrews 9:21, 23. And John says that he saw the sanctuary in heaven. That sanctuary, in which Jesus ministers in our behalf, is the great original. The sanctuary Moses built was a copy.

The earthly sanctuary and its services were to teach important truths concerning the heavenly sanctuary and the work done there for man's redemption.

After His ascension, our Savior was to begin His work as our High Priest. "Christ has not entered the holy places made with hands, which are copies of the true, but into heaven itself, now to appear in the presence of God for us." Hebrews 9:24. Christ's priestly ministry was to consist of two great divisions, each occupying a period of time and having a distinctive place in the heavenly sanctuary. So the symbolic, earthly ministry consisted of two divisions— the daily and the yearly service—and an apartment of the tabernacle was devoted to each.

At His ascension, Christ appeared in the presence of God to plead His blood for repentant believers. To symbolize this, the priest in the daily ministration sprinkled the blood of the sacrifice in the Holy Place on the sinner's behalf.

Though the blood of Christ was to release the repentant sinner from the condemnation of the law, it was not to conceal the sin, which would stand on record in the sanctuary until the final atonement. So in the symbolic services of the sanctuary, the blood of the sin offering removed the sin from the penitent one, but it remained in the sanctuary until the Day of Atonement.

In the great day of final award, the dead will be "judged according to their works, by the things which were written in the books." Revelation 20:12. Then the sins of all the truly repentant ones will be blotted from the books of heaven. Thus the sanctuary will be freed, or cleansed, from the record of sin. In the symbolic service this great work of blotting out of sins was represented by the services of the Day of Atonement, the cleansing of the earthly sanctuary by removing the sins that had polluted it.

In the final atonement the sins of the truly penitent are to be blotted from the records of heaven, no more to be remembered or come into mind. So in the symbolic service they were carried away into the wilderness, forever separated from the congregation.

Since Satan is the one responsible for all the sins that caused the death of the Son of God, justice demands that Satan suffer the final punishment. Christ's work to redeem men and women and to purify the universe from sin will be closed by placing these sins on Satan, who will bear the final penalty. So in the earthly service, the yearly cycle of services closed by purifying the sanctuary and confessing the sins on the head of the scapegoat.

Thus in the services of the tabernacle the people were taught each day the great truths regarding Christ's death and ministration, and once each year their minds were carried forward to the closing events of the great controversy between Christ and Satan, the final purifying of the universe from sin and sinners.

The Sin of Nadab and Abihu*

After the dedication of the tabernacle, the priests were consecrated to their sacred office. These services filled seven days; on the eighth day Aaron offered the sacrifices that God required. All had been done as God commanded, and He revealed His glory in a dramatic way—fire came and burned up the offering on the altar. In unison the people raised a shout of praise and adoration and fell on their faces.

But soon afterward a terrible calamity fell on the family of Aaron, the high priest. Two of his sons each took his censer and burned fragrant incense before the Lord. But they violated God's command by using "profane fire." They took common fire instead of the sacred fire that God Himself had provided. For this sin, fire from the Lord devoured them in the sight of the people.

Next to Moses and Aaron, Nadab and Abihu had stood highest in Israel. They had been especially honored by the Lord, having been permitted with the seventy elders to behold His glory on the mountain. All this made their sin more serious. If people have received great light, if

like the princes of Israel they have ascended the mountain and been privileged to have communion with God in the light of His glory, they should not think that they can sin with no consequences, that God will not be strict to punish their iniquity. Great privileges require virtue and holiness that correspond to the light given. Great blessings never give license to sin.

Nadab and Abihu had not been trained to exercise self-control. Their father's gentle disposition had led him to neglect to discipline his children. He had permitted his sons to follow their own desires. Habits of self-indulgence gained a hold on them that even the responsibility of the most sacred office did not have power to break. They did not realize the need of exact obedience to the requirements of God. Aaron's mistaken indulgence of his sons prepared them to become the subjects of divine judgment.

Partial Obedience Not Acceptable

God cannot accept partial obedience. It was not enough that in this solemn worship *nearly* everything

---

* *This chapter is based on Leviticus 10:1-11.*

was done as He had directed. No one should deceive himself with the belief that any of God's commandments are nonessential or that He will accept a substitute for what He has required. God has placed no command in His Word that we may obey or disobey as we choose and not suffer the consequences.

"Moses said to Aaron, and to Eleazar and Ithamar, his sons, 'Do not uncover your heads nor tear your clothes, lest you die, . . . for the anointing oil of the LORD is upon you.' " The great leader reminded his brother of the words of God, " 'Before all the people I must be glorified.' " Aaron was silent. The death of his sons in so terrible a sin—a sin that he now saw to be the result of his own neglect of duty—wrung the father's heart with anguish. But he must not by any show of grief seem to sympathize with sin. The congregation must not be led to find fault with God.

The Lord wanted to teach His people to acknowledge the justice of His corrections, so that others might fear. God rebukes that false sympathy for the sinner that tries to excuse sin. Wrongdoers do not realize the enormity of transgression, and without the convicting power of the Holy Spirit they remain partially blind to their sin. It is the duty of Christ's servants to show these erring ones their danger. Many have gone down to ruin as the result of false and deceptive sympathy.

Nadab and Abihu would never have committed that fatal sin if they had not first become partially drunk by freely using wine. They were disqualified for their holy office by their intemperance. Their minds became confused and their moral senses dulled so that they could not tell the difference between the sacred and the common. God gave the warning to Aaron and his surviving sons, " 'Do not drink . . . when you go into the tabernacle of meeting, lest you die.' " The use of alcoholic drinks prevents people from realizing the sacredness of holy things or the binding force of God's requirements. All who occupied positions of responsibility were to maintain strict temperance so that their minds might be clear to know the difference between right and wrong.

The same obligation rests on every follower of Christ. "You are a chosen generation, a royal priesthood, a holy nation, His own special people." 1 Peter 2:9. When alcoholic drinks are used, the same effects will follow as in the case of those priests of Israel. The conscience will lose its sensitivity to sin and a hardening will take place, till the difference between the common and the sacred will not seem important. "Therefore, whether you eat or drink, or whatever you do, do all to the glory of God." 1 Corinthians 10:31. The solemn and fearful warning is addressed to the church of Christ in all ages: "If anyone defiles the temple of God, God will destroy him. For the temple of God is holy, which temple you are." 1 Corinthians 3:17.

The Grace of Christ and the New Covenant

At their creation Adam and Eve had a knowledge of the law of God. They were acquainted with its claims, and its principles were written on their hearts. When they fell by transgression, the law was not changed but God gave the promise of a Savior. Sacrificial offerings pointed to the death of Christ as the great sin offering.

The law of God was handed down from father to son through successive generations. Yet only a few people obeyed. The world became so vile that it was necessary to cleanse it from its corruption by the Flood. Noah taught his descendants the Ten Commandments. As they again departed from God, the Lord chose Abraham, of whom He said, " 'Abraham obeyed My voice and kept My charge, My commandments, My statutes, and My laws.' " Genesis 26:5. God gave him the rite of circumcision, a pledge to be separate from idolatry and obey the law of God. The failure of Abraham's descendants to keep their pledge was the cause of their slavery in Egypt. In their contact with idolaters and their forced submission to the Egyptians, the divine principles became still more corrupted with the vile teachings of heathenism. Therefore the Lord came down on Sinai and spoke His law in awesome majesty in the hearing of all the people.

He did not even then trust His laws to the memory of a people so likely to forget but wrote them on tablets of stone. And He did not stop with giving them the Ten Commandments. He commanded Moses to write judgments and laws giving detailed instruction about what He required. These directions only amplified the principles of the Ten Commandments in a specific manner, designed to guard their sacredness.

If Abraham's descendants had kept the covenant, of which circumcision was a sign, there would have been no need for God's law to be proclaimed from Sinai or engraved on tablets of stone.

The sacrificial system also was perverted. Through long contacts with idolaters, Israel had mingled many heathen customs with their worship; therefore the Lord gave them definite instructions concerning the sacrificial service. The ceremonial law was given to Moses, and he wrote it in a book. But the law of Ten Commandments had been written by God Himself on tablets of stone and preserved in the ark.

Two Laws: Moral and Ceremonial

Many try to blend these two systems, using the texts that speak of the ceremonial law to prove that the moral law has been abolished, but this is a perversion of the Scriptures. The ceremonial system consisted of symbols pointing to Christ, to His sacrifice and priesthood. The Hebrews were to perform this ritual law with its sacrifices and ordinances until type met antitype—symbol met fulfillment—in the death of Christ. Then all the sacrificial offerings were to cease. It is this law that Christ "has taken . . . out of the way, having nailed it to the cross." Colossians 2:14.

But speaking about the law of Ten Commandments the psalmist wrote, "Forever, O LORD, Your word is settled in heaven." Psalm 119:89. And Christ Himself says, " 'Do not think that I came to destroy the Law. . . . For assuredly, I say to you, till heaven and earth pass away, one jot or one tittle will by no means pass from the law till all is fulfilled.' " Matthew 5:17, 18. Here Jesus teaches that the claims of God's law will hold as long as the heavens and the earth remain.

Concerning the law proclaimed from Sinai, Nehemiah says, " 'You came down also on Mount Sinai, and spoke with them from heaven, and gave them *just ordinances and true laws, good statutes and commandments.' "* Nehemiah 9:13. And Paul, the "apostle to the Gentiles,"

declares, "the law is holy, and the commandment holy and just and good." Romans 7:12.

While the Savior's death brought to an end the law of types and shadows, it did not reduce the obligation of the moral law. The very fact that Christ had to die in order to atone for the breaking of that law proves it to be unchangeable.

Christ the Mediator of the New Covenant

Some people claim that Christ came to do away with the Old Testament. They present the religion of the Hebrews as nothing but forms and ceremonies. But this is an error. Through all the ages after the Fall, "God was in Christ reconciling the world to Himself." 2 Corinthians 5:19. Christ was the foundation and center of the sacrificial system. Since the sin of our first parents, the Father has given the world into the hands of Christ, that through His work as Mediator He may redeem lost humanity and confirm the authority of God's law. All communication between heaven and the fallen race has been through Christ. It was the Son of God who gave our first parents the promise of redemption. Adam, Noah, Abraham, Isaac, Jacob, and Moses understood the gospel. These holy men of old had fellowship with the Savior who was to come to our world in human flesh.

Christ was the leader of the Hebrews in the wilderness, the Angel who went before them, veiled in the cloudy pillar. It was He who gave the law to Israel. (See Appendix, Note

6.) Amid the glory of Sinai Christ declared the Ten Commandments of His Father's law. He gave the law to Moses, engraved on tablets of stone.

Christ spoke to His people through the prophets. The apostle Peter says that the prophets "prophesied of the grace that would come to you, searching what, or what manner of time, the *Spirit of Christ* who was in them was indicating when He testified beforehand the sufferings of Christ and the glories that would follow." 1 Peter 1:10, 11. It is the voice of Christ that speaks through the Old Testament. " 'The testimony of Jesus is the spirit of prophecy.' " Revelation 19:10.

While personally on earth, Jesus directed the minds of the people to the Old Testament. " 'You search the Scriptures, for in them you think you have eternal life; and these are they which testify of Me.' " John 5:39. At that time the books of the Old Testament were the only part of the Bible in existence.

The ceremonial law was given by Christ. Even after it was no longer to be followed, the great apostle Paul pronounced this law glorious, worthy of its divine Originator. The cloud of incense ascending with the prayers of Israel represents His righteousness, the only thing that can make the sinner's prayer acceptable to God. The bleeding victim on the altar testified of a Redeemer to come. Thus through darkness and apostasy, faith was kept alive in human hearts until the coming of the promised Messiah.

Jesus was the Light of the world before He came in the form of humanity. The first gleam of light that pierced the gloom came from Christ. From Him has come every ray of heaven's brightness that has fallen on the inhabitants of the earth.

Since the Savior shed His blood and went back to heaven "to appear in the presence of God for us" (Hebrews 9:24), light has been streaming from the cross of Calvary and from the heavenly sanctuary. The gospel of Christ gives significance to the ceremonial law. As truths are revealed, we see more keenly the character and purposes of God. Every additional ray of light gives a clearer understanding of the plan of redemption. We find new beauty in the inspired Word and study its pages with ever-increasing interest.

God did not intend for Israel to build up a wall of partition between themselves and others. The heart of Infinite Love was reaching out toward all of earth's inhabitants, seeking to make them enjoy and benefit by His love and grace. He gave his blessing to the chosen people so that they might bless others.

Abraham did not shut himself away from the people around him. He maintained friendly relations with the kings of the surrounding nations, and through him the God of heaven was revealed.

God manifested Himself to the people of Egypt through Joseph. Why did the Lord choose to exalt Joseph so highly among the Egyptians? He wanted to put him in the palace of the king so that the heavenly light could extend far and near. Joseph was a representative of Christ. The Egyptians were to see in their benefactor the love of their Creator and Redeemer. In Moses also God placed a light beside the throne of earth's greatest kingdom so that all could learn of the true and living God.

In Israel's deliverance from Egypt, a knowledge of the power of God spread far and wide. Centuries after the Exodus, the priests of the Philistines reminded their people of the plagues of Egypt and warned them against resisting the God of Israel.

Why God Worked With Israel

God called Israel in order to reveal Himself through them to all of earth's inhabitants. For this purpose He commanded them to keep themselves distinct from the idolatrous nations around them.

It was just as necessary then as it is now for God's people to be pure, "unspotted from the world." But God did not want His people to shut themselves away from the world so that they could have no influence on it. It was their evil heart of unbelief that led them to hide their light instead of letting it shine on the peoples around them, to shut themselves away in proud exclusiveness as if God's love and care were for them alone.

The covenant of grace was first made in Eden. After the Fall, God promised that the seed of the woman would bruise the serpent's head. To everyone this covenant offered pardon and the assisting grace of God

to obey through faith in Christ. It also promised eternal life on condition of loyalty to God's law. Thus the patriarchs received the hope of salvation.

God renewed this same covenant to Abraham in the promise, " 'In your seed all the nations of the earth shall be blessed.' " Genesis 22:18. Abraham trusted in Christ for the forgiveness of sins. It was this faith that was credited to him for righteousness. The covenant with Abraham also upheld the authority of God's law. The testimony of God was, " 'Abraham obeyed My voice and kept My charge, My commandments, My statutes, and My laws.' " Genesis 26:5. Though this covenant was made with Adam and renewed to Abraham, it could not be ratified until the death of Christ. It had existed by the promise of God; it had been accepted by faith; yet, when ratified by Christ, it is called a new covenant. The law of God was the basis of this covenant, which was simply an arrangement for bringing sinners into harmony again with the divine will, placing them where they could obey God's law.

Another covenant—called in Scripture the "old" covenant—was made between God and Israel at Sinai and was then ratified by the blood of a sacrifice. The covenant with Abraham, ratified by the blood of Christ, is called the "second," or "new" covenant, because the blood by which it was sealed was shed after the blood of the first covenant.

But if the Abrahamic covenant contained the promise of redemption, why was another covenant made at Sinai? In their slavery the people had largely lost the knowledge of the principles of the Abrahamic covenant. In delivering them from Egypt, God intended to reveal His power and mercy so that they might be led to love and trust Him. He bound them to Himself as their Deliverer from physical slavery.

But they had no true concept of God's holiness, of the exceeding sinfulness of their own hearts, their complete inability in themselves to obey God's law, and their need of a Savior.

God gave them His law with the promise of great blessings on condition of obedience: " 'If you will indeed obey My voice and keep My covenant, . . . you shall be to Me a kingdom of priests and a holy nation.' " Exodus 19:5, 6. The people did not realize the sinfulness of their own hearts and that without Christ it was impossible for them to keep God's law. Feeling able to establish their own righteousness, they declared, " 'All that the LORD has said we will do, and be obedient.' " Exodus 24:7. They readily entered into covenant with God. Yet only a few weeks passed before they broke their covenant and bowed down to worship the image of a calf. Now, seeing their sinfulness and their need of pardon, they were brought to feel their need of the Savior revealed in the Abrahamic covenant and symbolized in the sacrificial offerings. Now they were prepared to appreciate the blessings of the new covenant.

The New Covenant and Justification by Faith

The terms of the "old covenant" were, Obey and live: " 'If a man *does,* he shall live by them.' " Ezekiel 20:11. But " ' "cursed is the one who does not confirm all the words of this law" ' " to do them. Deuteronomy 27:26. The "new covenant" was established upon "better promises," the promise of forgiveness and the grace of God to change the heart and bring it into harmony with God's law. " 'This is the covenant that I will make with the house of Israel: After those days, says the LORD, I *will put My law* in their minds, *and write it on their hearts*; . . . I will *forgive* their iniquity, and their sin I will remember no more.' " Jeremiah 31:33, 34.

The same law that was engraved on tablets of stone is written by the Holy Spirit on the heart. We accept the righteousness of Christ. His blood atones for our sins. His obedience is accepted for us. Then through the grace of Christ we will walk even as He walked. Through the prophet He declared concerning Himself, " 'I delight to do Your will, O My God, and Your law is within My heart.' " Psalm 40:8.

Paul clearly presents the relation between faith and the law under the new covenant: "Having been *justified by faith,* we have peace with God through our Lord Jesus Christ." "Do we then make void the law through faith? Certainly not! On the contrary, we establish the law." "For what the law could not do in that it was weak through the flesh [it could not justify the sinner, who in the sinful nature could not keep the law], God did by sending His own Son in the likeness of sinful flesh, on account of sin: He condemned sin in the flesh, that *the righteous requirement of the law* might be fulfilled in us who do not walk according to the flesh but according to the Spirit." Romans 5:1; 3:31; 8:3, 4.

Beginning with the first gospel promise and coming down through the patriarchal and Jewish ages to the present time, there has been a gradual unfolding of the intentions of God in the plan of redemption. The clouds have rolled back, the mists and shades have disappeared, and Jesus, the world's Redeemer, stands revealed. He who proclaimed the law from Sinai is the same who spoke the Sermon on the Mount. The great principles of love to God are only a restating of what He had spoken through Moses. The Teacher is the same in both Old Testament and New Testament times.

The Terrible Grumblings of God's People*

The government of Israel had thorough organization, amazingly complete and simple. God was the center of government, the ruler of Israel. Moses stood as leader to administer the law in His name. Later, a council of seventy was chosen to assist Moses in the general business of the nation. Next came the priests, who consulted the Lord in the sanctuary. Chiefs, or princes, ruled over the tribes. Under these were " 'leaders of thousands, leaders of hundreds, leaders of fifties, leaders of tens.' " Deuteronomy 1:15.

The Hebrew camp was separated into three great divisions. In the center was the tabernacle, the abiding place of the invisible King. Around it the priests and Levites were stationed. Beyond these were camped all the other tribes.

Each tribe was assigned a position. Each was to march and to encamp beside its own banner, as the Lord had commanded. Numbers 2:2, 17. The mixed multitude that had accompanied Israel from Egypt were to stay on the outskirts of the camp, and their children were to be excluded from the community until the third generation. Deuteronomy 23:7, 8.

Strict order and thorough sanitary regulations were enforced, rules essential to preserving health among so large a group of people. It was necessary also to maintain perfect order and purity. God declared: " 'The LORD your God walks in the midst of your camp, to deliver you and give your enemies over to you; therefore your camp shall be holy.' " Deuteronomy 23:14.

In all of Israel's traveling, "the ark of the covenant of the LORD went before them . . . to search out a resting place for them." Priests with silver trumpets were stationed near it. These priests received directions from Moses, which they communicated to the people by the trumpets. It was the duty of the leaders of each company to give definite directions concerning all the movements to be made, as indicated by the trumpets.

God is a God of order. Everything connected with heaven is in perfect order; thorough discipline marks the movements of all the angels. Success can only attend order and harmonious action; God requires

---

This chapter is based on Numbers 10 to 12.

this now no less than in the days of Israel.

God Himself directed the Israelites in their travels. The descent of the pillar of cloud indicated the place they were to camp; and so long as they were to remain in camp, the cloud rested over the tabernacle. When they were to continue their journey, it rose high above the sacred tent.

Only eleven days' journey lay between Sinai and Kadesh, on the borders of Canaan. With the prospect of speedily entering the land, the hosts of Israel resumed their march when the cloud gave the signal. What blessings might they not expect, now that they had officially been acknowledged as the chosen people of the Most High?

With reluctance many left the place where they had camped. The scene was so closely associated with the presence of God and holy angels that it seemed too sacred to be left thoughtlessly, or even gladly. At the signal from the trumpeters, however, all eyes turned anxiously to see in what direction the cloud would lead. As it moved toward the east, where only black and desolate mountain masses huddled together, a feeling of sadness and doubt arose in many hearts.

As they advanced, the way became more difficult. Their route lay through stony ravines and barren wastes, "a land of deserts and pits, . . . a land of drought and the shadow of death, . . . a land that no one crossed and where no one dwelt." Jeremiah 2:6. Their prog-ress was slow and hard, and the multitudes were not prepared to endure the dangers and discomforts of the way.

The People Demand a Meat Diet

After three days' journey open complaints were heard. These started with the mixed multitude, many of whom were always finding fault with the way in which *Moses* was leading them, though they knew that he was following the cloud. Dissatisfaction is contagious, and it soon spread in the camp.

Again they began to demand flesh to eat. Many of the Egyptians among them had been used to a rich diet, and these were the first to complain.

God might have provided them with flesh as easily as with manna, but His aim was to supply food better suited to their needs. The perverted appetite was to be brought into a more healthy state so that they could enjoy the food originally provided for the human family, the fruits of the earth which God gave to Adam and Eve in Eden. For this reason the Israelites had been largely deprived of animal food.

Satan tempted them to think of this as unjust and cruel. He saw that filling every desire of appetite would tend to produce sensuality, and by this means the people could be brought under his control more easily. From the time he induced Eve to eat of the forbidden fruit, he has, to a large extent, led men into sin through appetite. Intemperance in eating and drinking prepares the way to disregard all moral standards.

God brought the Israelites from Egypt so that He could establish them in the land of Canaan as a pure, holy, and happy people. If they had been willing to deny appetite, feebleness and disease would have been unknown among them. Their descendants would have possessed physical and mental strength, clear perceptions of truth and duty, keen discernment, and sound judgment.

Says the psalmist: "They tested God in their heart by asking for the food of their fancy. Yes, they spoke against God: they said, 'Can God prepare a table in the wilderness? . . . Can He provide meat for His people?' Therefore the LORD heard this and was furious." Psalm 78:18-21. They had been witnesses to the majesty, power, and mercy of God, and their unbelief and discontent brought on them the greater guilt. They had made a covenant to obey His authority. Their grumbling was now rebellion, and as such it must receive prompt punishment if Israel was to be preserved from anarchy and ruin. "The fire of the LORD burned among them, and consumed some in the outskirts of the camp." The most guilty of the complainers were killed by lightning from the cloud.

Their Demands Become Rebellious

In terror the people begged Moses to plead with the Lord for them. He did so, and the fire was quenched. But instead of leading the survivors to be humble and repent, this fearful judgment seemed only to increase their complaints. In all directions the people gathered at the doors of their tents, weeping and lamenting. "The mixed multitude who were among them yielded to intense craving; so the children of Israel also wept again and said: 'Who will give us meat to eat? We remember the fish which we ate freely in Egypt, the cucumbers, the melons, the leeks, the onions, and the garlic; but now our whole being is dried up; there is nothing at all except this manna before our eyes!' " Yet, despite the hardships, there was not a feeble one in all their tribes.

The heart of Moses sank. In his love for them, he had prayed that his name might be blotted from the book of life rather than for them to perish, and this was their response. They blamed him for all their hardships and even their imaginary sufferings. In his distress he was tempted even to distrust God. His prayer was almost a complaint: " 'Why have You afflicted Your servant . . . that You have laid the burden of all these people on me? . . . they weep . . . saying, "Give us meat, that we may eat." I am not able to bear all these people alone, because the burden is too heavy for me.' "

The Lord responded to his prayer and directed him to appoint seventy men possessing sound judgment and experience to share his responsibilities. Their influence would help put down rebellion, yet serious evils would eventually result from their promotion. They would never have been chosen if Moses had manifested faith corresponding to the evidences of God's power and goodness that he had witnessed. If he had relied fully on God, the Lord would have guided him continually and given him strength for every emergency.

Moses announced the appointment of the seventy elders. The great leader's instruction to these chosen men could well serve as a model of judicial integrity for the judges and lawmakers of modern times: " 'Hear the cases between your brethren, and judge righteously between a man and his brother or the stranger who is with him. You shall not show partiality in judgment; you shall hear the small as well as the great; you shall not be afraid in any man's presence, for the judgment is God's.' " Deuteronomy 1:16, 17.

"Then the LORD came down in the cloud, and spoke to him, and took of the Spirit that was upon him, and placed the same upon the seventy elders; and . . . they prophesied, although they never did so again." Like the disciples on the Day of Pentecost, they were filled with "power from on high." The Lord wished to honor them in the presence of the congregation, to establish confidence in them.

A strong wind blowing from the sea now brought flocks of quails, "about a day's journey on this side and about a day's journey on the other side, all around the camp, and about two cubits above the surface of the ground."

All that day and night and the following day, the people worked to gather the food miraculously provided. Immense quantities were secured. All that they did not need for present use they preserved by drying, so that the supply, as promised, was sufficient for a whole month.

God gave the people what was not for their highest good because they persisted in wanting it. But they were left to suffer the result. They feasted without restraint, and their gluttony was speedily punished. "The LORD struck the people with a very great plague." The most guilty among them were stricken as soon as they tasted the food for which they had lusted.

At Hazeroth, the next encampment after leaving Taberah, a still more bitter trial awaited Moses. Aaron and Miriam had occupied a position of high honor and leadership in Israel. Both had been associated with Moses in the deliverance of the Hebrews. Miriam, who was richly endowed with gifts of poetry and music, had led the women of Israel in song and dance on the shore of the Red Sea. In the hearts of the people and the honor of Heaven she stood second only to Moses and Aaron.

But in the appointment of the seventy elders, Moses had not consulted Miriam and Aaron, and they became jealous. They felt that their position and authority had been ignored. They thought of themselves as sharing the burden of leadership equally with Moses, and they considered the appointment of further assistants as uncalled for.

Sin of Jealousy

Moses realized his own weakness and made God his counselor. But Aaron thought of himself more highly, trusted less in God, and had failed in the matter of the idol worship at Sinai. Miriam and Aaron, blinded by jealousy and ambition, said, " 'Has the LORD indeed spoken only through Moses? Has He not spoken through us also?' "

Miriam found reason to complain in events that God had especially overruled. The marriage of Moses had been displeasing to her. It was an offense to her family and national pride that he would choose a woman of another nation instead of taking a wife from among the Hebrews. She treated Zipporah with poorly disguised contempt.

Though called a "Cushite woman," the wife of Moses was a Midianite and thus a descendant of Abraham. She differed from the Hebrews in having a somewhat darker complexion. Though not an Israelite, Zipporah was a worshiper of the true God. She had a timid, retiring disposition and was greatly distressed at the sight of suffering. For this reason Moses, on his way to Egypt, had agreed to have her return to Midian.

When Zipporah rejoined her husband in the wilderness, she saw that his burdens were wearing away his strength, and she expressed her fears to Jethro, who suggested measures for his relief. Here was the chief reason for Miriam's dislike of Zipporah. She regarded Moses' wife as the cause of the supposed neglect shown to her and Aaron. If Aaron had stood firmly for the right, he might have stopped the evil; but instead of showing Miriam the sinfulness of her conduct, he sympathized with her and thus came to share her jealousy.

Moses bore their accusations in uncomplaining silence. Moses "was very humble, more than all men who were on the face of the earth," and this is why he was granted divine wisdom and guidance above all others.

God had chosen Moses. Miriam and Aaron, by their complaining, were guilty of disloyalty not only to their appointed leader but to God Himself. "Then the LORD came down in the pillar of cloud and stood in the door of the tabernacle, and called Aaron and Miriam." Their claim to the prophetic gift was not denied. But a nearer communion had been granted to Moses. With *him* God spoke face to face. " 'Why then were you not afraid to speak against My servant Moses?' So the anger of the LORD was aroused against them, and He departed." As evidence of God's displeasure, Miriam "became leprous, as white as snow." Aaron was spared but was severely rebuked in Miriam's punishment. Now, their pride humbled in the dust, Aaron confessed their sin and pleaded that his sister might not be left to die of that hideous, deadly plague.

In answer to the prayers of Moses, the leprosy was cleansed. But Miriam was shut out of the camp for seven days. The whole company stayed in Hazeroth, awaiting her return.

This display of the Lord's displeasure was designed to halt the growing spirit of discontent and rebellion. Envy is one of the most satanic traits that can exist in the human heart. Envy is what first caused discord in heaven, and indulging it has produced measureless evil in the world.

The Bible teaches us not to bring accusations lightly against those whom God has called to act as His ambassadors. "Do not receive an accusation against an elder except from two or three witnesses." 1 Timothy 5:19. He who has placed on some the responsibility of being leaders and teachers of His people will hold the people accountable for the way they treat His servants. The judgment imposed on Miriam should be a rebuke to all who yield to jealousy and complain against those on whom God lays the burden of His work.

Twelve Spies Survey Canaan*

The Israelites camped at Kadesh, in the wilderness of Paran, which was not far from the borders of the Promised Land. Here the people proposed that spies be sent out to survey the country. Moses presented the matter to the Lord, and permission was granted. The men were chosen and Moses told them to go and see the country and the people, whether they were strong or weak, few or many; also to evaluate the soil and its productivity and to bring some of the fruit of the land.

They went and surveyed the whole land, returning after forty days. The news of the spies' return was met with rejoicing. The people rushed out to greet the messengers who had safely escaped the dangers of their risky undertaking. The spies brought specimens of the fruit, showing the fertility of the soil. They brought a cluster of grapes so large that it was carried between two men. They also brought figs and pomegranates which grew there abundantly.

The people listened intently as the report was brought to Moses. " 'We went to the land where you sent us,' " the spies began. " 'It truly flows with milk and honey, and this is its fruit.' " The people were enthusiastic; they would eagerly obey the voice of the Lord and go up at once to possess the land.

But all but two of the spies enlarged on the dangers and voiced the feelings of their unbelieving hearts, which were filled with discouragement prompted by Satan. Their unbelief threw a gloomy shadow over the congregation. The mighty power of God, so often shown in behalf of the chosen nation, was forgotten. The people did not call to mind how wonderfully God had delivered them from their oppressors, cutting a path through the sea and destroying the pursuing armies of Pharaoh. They left God out of the question, as though they must depend only on human power.

In their unbelief they repeated their earlier error of complaining against Moses and Aaron. "This, then, is the end of all our high hopes," they said. They accused their leaders of deceiving the people and bringing trouble on Israel.

---

* This chapter is based on Numbers 13 and 14.

A wail of agony arose, mingled with the confused murmur of voices. Bold to stand in defense of the word of God, Caleb did all in his power to counteract the evil influence of his unfaithful associates. He did not contradict what the others had said; the walls were high and the Canaanites strong. But God had promised the land to Israel. " 'Let us go up at once and take possession,' " urged Caleb, " 'for we are well able to overcome it.' "

But the ten, interrupting him, listed the obstacles. " 'We are not able to go up against the people,' " they declared, " 'for they are stronger then we. . . . All the people whom we saw in it are men of great stature . . . and we were like grasshoppers in our own sight, and so we were in their sight.' "

Revolt and Open Mutiny

These men, having started on a wrong course, stubbornly set themselves against Caleb and Joshua, against Moses, and against God. They distorted the truth in order to sustain their evil influence. It is a land that " 'devours its inhabitants,' " they said. This was not only a bad report; it was a lying one. The spies had declared the country to be fruitful and the people of giant stature, which would be impossible if the climate were so unhealthful that the land could be said to "devour its inhabitants."

Revolt and open mutiny quickly followed. The people seemed to lack all reason. They cursed Moses and Aaron, forgetting that the Angel of God's presence, enshrouded in the cloudy pillar, was witnessing their terrible outburst of anger. Then their feelings rose against God: " 'Why has the Lord brought us to this land to fall by the sword, that our wives and children should become victims?' So they said to one another, 'Let us select a leader and return to Egypt.' " Thus they accused not only Moses but God Himself of deception in promising them a land they were not able to possess.

Caleb and Joshua tried to quiet the ruckus. They rushed in among the people, and their ringing voices sounded above the tempest of rebellious grief: " 'If the Lord delights in us, then He will bring us into this land and give it to us, "a land which flows with milk and honey." Only do not rebel against the Lord, nor fear the people of the land, for they are our bread; their protection has departed from them, and the Lord is with us. Do not fear them.' "

By the covenant of God, the land was guaranteed to Israel. But the false report of the unfaithful spies was accepted. The whole congregation was deceived. The traitors had done their work. If just the two men had brought the evil report and all the ten had encouraged them to possess the land in the name of the Lord, they still would have taken the advice of the two over that of the ten, because of their wicked unbelief.

The cry went up to stone Caleb and Joshua. The insane mob rushed forward with yells of madness, when suddenly the stones dropped from their hands, and they shook with fear. God stepped in. The glory of His presence, like a flaming light, lighted up the tabernacle. None dared continue their resistance. The spies who brought the evil report crouched terror-stricken and hurried to their tents.

Moses now rose and entered the tabernacle. The Lord declared to him, " 'I will strike them with the pestilence and disinherit them, and I will make of you a nation greater and mightier than they.' " But again Moses pleaded for his people. " 'I pray, let the power of my LORD be great, just as You have spoken, saying, "The LORD is longsuffering and abundant in mercy." . . . Pardon the iniquity of this people, I pray, according to the greatness of Your mercy, just as You have forgiven this people, from Egypt even until now.' "

The Lord promised to spare Israel from immediate destruction, but because of their unbelief and cowardice He could not exercise His power to subdue their enemies. Therefore in His mercy He had them turn back toward the Red Sea.

In their rebellion the people had exclaimed, " 'If only we had died in this wilderness!' " Now this prayer would be granted: " 'Just as you have spoken in My hearing, so I will do to you: The carcasses of you who have murmured against me shall fall in this wilderness, all of you who were numbered, according to your entire number, from twenty years old and above. . . . But your little ones, whom you said would be victims, I will bring in, and they shall know the land

which you have despised.' " And of Caleb He said, " 'My servant Caleb, because he has a different spirit in him and has followed Me fully, I will bring into the land where he went, and his descendants shall inherit it.' " As the spies had spent forty days in their journey, so the people of Israel were to be nomads in the wilderness forty years.

An Example of False Repentance

When Moses told the people the divine decision, they knew that their punishment was just. The ten unfaithful spies, struck by God with the plague, perished in the sight of all Israel, and in their fate the people read their own doom.

Now they seemed to repent sincerely, but they were sorry for the result of their evil course rather than from a sense of their ingratitude and disobedience. When they found that the Lord did not change His decree, their self-will again arose and they declared that they would not return into the wilderness. In telling them to go back, God tested their apparent submission and proved it was not real. Their hearts were unchanged, and they only needed an excuse to start a similar outbreak. If they had mourned for their sin when it was faithfully laid before them, this sentence would not have been pronounced; but they mourned over the judgment. Their sorrow was not repentance and could not gain them a reversing of their sentence.

The people spent that night sorrowing, but in the morning they resolved to redeem their cowardice.

When God had told them to go up and take the land, they had refused; and now when He directed them to retreat, they were equally rebellious.

God had made it their privilege and duty to enter the land at the time He had appointed, but through their willful neglect that permission had been withdrawn. Now, in the face of divine prohibition, Satan urged them on to do the very thing that they had refused to do when God required it, leading them to rebel the second time. " 'We have sinned against the LORD,' " they cried. " 'We will go up and fight, just as the LORD our God commanded us.' " Deuteronomy 1:41. So terribly blinded had they become! The Lord had never commanded them to "go up and fight." He did not intend them to gain the land by warfare but by strict obedience to His commands.

"We have sinned," they confessed, acknowledging that the fault was in themselves, not in God, whom they had wickedly charged with failing to fulfill His promises. Though their confession did not spring from true repentance, it served to confirm the justice of God.

The Lord still works in a similar way to glorify His name by bringing people to acknowledge His justice. God uses opposition and setbacks to reveal the works of darkness. Though the spirit that prompted to evil is not radically changed, confessions are made that establish the honor of God and justify His faithful reprovers who have been opposed and misrepresented. This is how it will be when the wrath of God shall be poured out at the end. Every sinner will be brought to see and acknowledge the justice of being condemned.

How Rebellion Made Their Situation Worse

Regardless of the divine sentence, the Israelites prepared to set out to conquer Canaan. In their own estimation, they were fully prepared for conflict. Contrary to the command of God and the solemn prohibition of their leaders, they went out to meet the armies of the enemy.

Moses hurried after them with the warning, " 'Now why do you transgress the command of the LORD? For this will not succeed. Do not go up, lest you be defeated by your enemies, for the LORD is not among you.' "

The Canaanites had heard of the mysterious power that seemed to be guarding this people, and they now gathered a strong force to repel the invaders. The attacking army had no leader. No prayer was offered that God would give them the victory. Though untrained in war, they hoped by a fierce assault to crush all opposition. Presumptuously they challenged the enemy that had not dared to attack them.

The Canaanites had stationed themselves on a rocky plateau reached only by a steep and dangerous incline. The immense numbers of the Hebrews could only make their defeat more terrible. Massive rocks came thundering down, marking their path with the blood of the slain. Those who reached the summit, exhausted with their climb, were fiercely repulsed and driven back with great loss. The army of Israel was utterly defeated.

The enemies of Israel, who had awaited with trembling the approach of that mighty host, were inspired with confidence to resist them. All the reports they had heard concerning the marvelous things that God had done for His people, they now considered to be false; there was no cause for fear. By inspiring the Canaanites with courage and resolve, that first defeat of Israel had made the conquest much more difficult.

Israel had no choice but to fall back from the face of their victorious foes, into the wilderness, knowing that there a whole generation must die.

Korah Leads a Rebellion*

The judgments inflicted on the Israelites restrained their complaining and rebellion for a while, but the spirit of rebellion was still in their hearts. Now a deep-laid conspiracy was formed to overthrow the authority of the leaders appointed by God Himself.

Korah, the leading spirit in this movement, a cousin of Moses, was a man of ability and influence. He had become dissatisfied with his position and wanted the dignity of the priesthood. For some time Korah had been secretly opposing the authority of Moses and Aaron, though He had not dared to rebel openly. He finally devised the bold plan of overthrowing both the civil and the religious authority. Dathan and Abiram, two princes, readily joined in his ambitious schemes and determined to divide the honors of the priesthood with Korah.

The feeling among the people favored Korah. In the bitterness of their disappointment, their former doubts, jealousy, and hatred returned, and again they directed their complaints against their patient leader. They forgot that they were under divine guidance, that the presence of Christ went before them, and that Moses received directions from Him.

Unwilling to die in the wilderness, they were ready to believe that it was not God but Moses who had pronounced their doom. Although the evidence of God's displeasure at their rebellious nature was still before them, they did not take the lesson to heart.

He who reads the secrets of all hearts had given His people warning and instruction that could have enabled them to escape the deception of these scheming men. They had seen the judgment of God on Miriam because of her jealousy and complaints against Moses. The Lord had declared, " 'I speak with him face to face.' " " 'Why then,' " He added, " 'were you not afraid to speak against My servant Moses?' " Numbers 12:8. These instructions were intended not for Aaron and Miriam alone but for all Israel.

Korah and his coconspirators were among those who went up with Moses into the mountain and saw the divine glory. But they had har-

---

* This chapter is based on Numbers 16 and 17.

bored a temptation, though small at first, until their minds were controlled by Satan. They first whispered their discontent to one another and then to leading men of Israel. At last they really believed that they were driven by zeal for God.

They were successful in recruiting two hundred fifty princes. With these influential supporters they felt confident of greatly improving the administration of Moses and Aaron.

Jealousy had given rise to envy, and envy to rebellion. And they deceived themselves and one another into thinking that Moses and Aaron had themselves assumed the positions they held, that these two leaders had exalted themselves by taking the priesthood and government. They were no more holy than the people, and it should be enough for them to be on a level with their brethren, who were equally favored with God's presence and protection.

Korah's Method: Praise the People

Korah and his associates appealed for the support of the congregation. They declared it a mistake to charge that the complaints of the people had brought God's anger on them. They said that the congregation were not at fault, since they desired nothing more than their rights; but Moses was an overbearing ruler; he had found fault with the people as sinners when they were a holy people.

Korah's hearers thought they saw clearly that their troubles might have been prevented if Moses had followed a different course. Their ex-

clusion from Canaan was a result of mismanagement by Moses and Aaron. If Korah were their leader and he encouraged them by dwelling on their good deeds instead of pointing out their sins, they would have a very fruitful journey. Instead of wandering in the wilderness they would proceed directly to the Promised Land.

Korah's success with the people increased his confidence. He claimed that God had authorized him to make a change in the government before it was too late.

Unfair Attack on Moses

But many were not ready to accept Korah's accusations against Moses. They remembered his patient, self-sacrificing labors, and their consciences were disturbed. So Korah found it necessary to assign some selfish motive; the old charge was repeated that Moses had led them out to die in the wilderness so that he might seize their possessions.

As soon as the movement gained sufficient strength to support an open break, Korah publicly accused Moses and Aaron of usurping authority. " 'You take too much upon yourselves,' " said the conspirators, " 'for all the congregation is holy, every one of them, and the LORD is among them. Why then do you exalt yourselves above the congregation of the LORD?' "

Moses had not suspected this carefully-laid plot, and he fell on his face in silent appeal to God. He rose up calm and strong. Divine guidance had come. " 'Tomorrow morning,' " he said, " 'the LORD will show who is His and who is holy, and . . . whom He chooses He will cause to come near to Him.' " Those who thought they should be priests were to come each with a censer and offer incense at the tabernacle. Even the priests, Nadab and Abihu, had been destroyed for daring to offer "strange fire" contrary to a divine command. Yet Moses challenged his accusers to refer the matter to God if they dared risk making such an appeal.

Singling out Korah and his fellow Levites, Moses said, " 'Is it a small thing to you that the God of Israel has separated you from the congregation of Israel, to bring you near to Himself, to do the work of the tabernacle of the LORD . . . and that He has brought you near to Himself, you and all your brethren, the sons of Levi, with you? And are you seeking the priesthood also? Therefore you and all your company are gathered together against the LORD. And what is Aaron that you murmur against him?' "

Dathan and Abiram had not taken as bold a stand as Korah had, and Moses called them to appear before him, that he might hear their charges against him. But they rudely refused to acknowledge his authority: " 'Is it a small thing that you have brought us up out of a land flowing with milk and honey, to kill us in the wilderness, that you should keep acting like a prince over us? Moreover you have not brought us into a land flowing with milk and honey, nor given us inheritance of fields and

vineyards. Will you put out the eyes of these men? We will not come up!' "

In this way they declared that they would no longer submit to be led around like blind men, now toward Canaan, and now toward the wilderness, to fit Moses' ambitious plans. They portrayed him as the worst tyrant and power-grabber. They blamed him for their exclusion from Canaan.

Moses did not try to defend himself. He solemnly appealed to God in the presence of the congregation and begged Him to be his judge.

The Great Test: Whom Would God Acknowledge?

The next day the two hundred fifty princes, with Korah leading them, presented themselves with their censers, while the people gathered to await the result. It was not Moses who assembled the congregation to see the defeat of Korah and his company. The rebels, in their blind presumption, had called them together to witness their victory. A large part of the congregation openly sided with Korah.

Korah had left the assembly to join Dathan and Abiram when Moses, with the seventy elders, went down with a last warning to the men who had refused to come to him. At God's direction, Moses told the people, " 'Depart now from the tents of these wicked men! Touch nothing of theirs, lest you be consumed in all their sins.' " The people obeyed, for a sense of approaching judgment rested on all. The chief rebels saw themselves abandoned by those whom they had deceived, but they stood their ground with their families, defying the divine warning.

Moses now declared in the hearing of the congregation, " 'By this you shall know that the LORD has sent me to do all these works, for I have not done them of my own will. If these men die naturally like all men, . . . then the LORD has not sent me. But if the LORD creates a new thing, and the earth opens its mouth and swallows them up with all that belongs to them, and they go down alive into the pit, then you will understand that these men have rejected the LORD.' "

As he finished speaking, the solid earth split open and the rebels went down alive into the pit, with all their goods, and "they perished from among the congregation." The people fled, self-condemned as partakers in the sin.

But the judgments were not ended. Fire flashing from the cloud consumed the two hundred fifty princes who had offered incense. These men had not been destroyed with the chief conspirators. They were permitted to see their end and to have opportunity to repent. But their sympathies were with the rebels, and they shared their fate.

The entire congregation shared in their guilt, for to a greater or lesser degree, all had sympathized with them. Yet the people who had permitted themselves to be deceived were still granted space to repent.

Jesus, the Angel who went before the Hebrews, was working to save them from destruction. The judgment of God had come very near and appealed to them to repent. Now, if they would respond to God's leading, they could be saved. But their rebellion was not cured. That night they returned to their tents terrified, but not repentant.

Korah had flattered them until they really believed themselves to be a very good people, wronged and abused by Moses. They had foolishly cherished the hope that a new order of things was about to be established in which praise would substitute for reproof and ease for anxiety and conflict. The men who had died had spoken flattering words and professed great interest and love for them, and the people concluded that somehow Moses had been the cause of their destruction.

The Israelites had proposed putting both Moses and Aaron to death. Yet they did not spend that night of probation in repentance and confession but in devising some way to resist the evidence that showed them to be the greatest of sinners. They still cherished hatred of the men God had appointed and braced themselves to resist their authority.

"On the next day all the congregation of the children of Israel murmured against Moses and Aaron, saying, 'You have killed the people of the LORD.' " And they were about to move violently against their faithful, self-sacrificing leaders.

Moses' Love for Erring Israel

Divine glory appeared in the cloud above the tabernacle, and a voice spoke to Moses and Aaron, " 'Get away from among this congregation, that I may consume them in a moment.' "

In this fearful crisis Moses lingered, showing a true shepherd's interest for the flock of his care. He pleaded that God might not completely destroy the people of His choice.

But the agent of wrath had gone out; the plague was doing its work of death. By his brother's direction, Aaron took a censer and hurried into the middle of the congregation to "make atonement for them." "And he stood between the dead and the living." The plague was stopped, but not until fourteen thousand of Israel lay dead.

Now the people were compelled to believe the unwelcome truth that they were to die in the wilderness. " 'Surely we die,' " they exclaimed, " 'we perish, we all perish!' " They confessed that they had sinned in rebelling against their leaders and that Korah and his company had experienced the just judgment of God.

Don't the same evils still exist that lay at the foundation of Korah's ruin? Pride and ambition are widespread, opening the door to envy and struggles for supremacy. People are alienated from God and unconsciously drawn into the ranks of Satan. Like Korah and his companions, many are thinking, planning, and working so eagerly to exalt themselves that they are ready to twist the truth, lying about and misrepresenting the Lord's servants. By persistently repeating falsehood, they finally come to believe it to be truth.

The Hebrews were not willing to submit to the Lord's directions and restrictions. They were unwilling to receive correction. This was the secret of their complaints against Moses. All through the history of the church, God's servants have had to meet the same spirit.

Rejection of light darkens the mind and hardens the heart, making it easier to take the next step in sin, to reject even clearer light, until habits of wrongdoing finally become set. The person who faithfully preaches God's word and condemns sin is too often repaid with hatred. Soothing their consciences with lies, the jealous and resentful spread discord in the church and weaken the hands of those who want to build it up.

The envious and faultfinding have misrepresented every advance made by those whom God has called to lead His work. It was this way in the time of Luther, of the Wesleys, and other reformers. So it is today.

Korah and his companions rejected light until they became so blinded that the most striking manifestations of power were not sufficient to convince them; they attributed them all to human or satanic sources. The people did the same thing. Despite the most convincing evidence of God's displeasure, they dared to attribute His judgments to Satan, declaring that Moses and Aaron had caused the death of good and holy men. They committed the sin against the Holy Spirit. " 'Anyone who speaks a word against the Son of Man,' " said Christ, " 'it will be forgiven him; but whoever speaks against the Holy Spirit, it will not be forgiven him.' " Matthew 12:32. It is through the Holy Spirit that God communicates with us; and those who deliberately reject this agency as satanic have cut off the channel of communication between themselves and Heaven.

If we finally reject the Spirit's work, there is no more that God can do for us. We have cut ourselves off from God, and sin has no remedy to cure itself. " 'Let him alone' " (Hosea 4:17) is the divine command. Then "there no longer remains a sacrifice for sins, but a certain fearful expectation of judgment, and fiery indignation which will devour the adversaries." Hebrews 10:26, 27.

Forty Years of Wandering in the Wilderness

For nearly forty years the people of Israel were lost to view in the vast, out-of-the-way desert. In the rebellion at Kadesh they had rejected God, and for the time God had rejected them. Since they had proved unfaithful to His covenant, they were not to receive the sign of the covenant, the rite of circumcision. Their desire to return to the land of slavery had shown them to be unworthy of freedom; and the Passover, instituted to commemorate deliverance from slavery, was not to be observed.

Yet the tabernacle service continued, testifying that God had not completely forsaken His people. And His divine care still supplied their wants. " 'The LORD your God . . . knows your trudging through this great wilderness. These forty years the LORD your God has been with you; you have lacked nothing.' " Deuteronomy 2:7. God cared for Israel even during these years of banishment: " 'You also gave Your good Spirit to instruct them. . . . In the wilderness . . . their clothes did not wear out and their feet did not swell.' " Nehemiah 9:20, 21.

The wilderness was to provide a discipline for the rising generation as they prepared to enter the Promised Land. Moses declared, " 'As a man chastens his son, so the LORD your God chastens you,' " " 'to humble you and test you, to know what was in your heart, whether you would keep His commandments or not. So He . . . allowed you to hunger, and fed you with manna which you did not know nor did your fathers know, that He might make you know that man shall not live by bread alone; but man lives by every word that proceeds from the mouth of the LORD.' " Deuteronomy 8:5, 2, 3.

"In all their affliction He was afflicted, and the Angel of His Presence saved them; in His love and in His pity He redeemed them; and He bore them and carried them all the days of old." Isaiah 63:9.

The revolt of Korah had resulted in the death of fourteen thousand of Israel. And isolated cases of rebellion showed the same spirit of contempt for divine authority.

On one occasion one of the mixed multitude that had come up with Israel from Egypt left his own part of the camp and entered that of the Israelites, claiming the right to pitch his tent there. A quarrel developed between him and an Israelite, and the matter was referred to the judges. They decided against the offender.

Enraged at this decision, he cursed the judge and blasphemed the name of God. He was immediately brought before Moses. The man was placed under guard until the will of God could be known. God Himself pronounced sentence. By divine direction the blasphemer was conducted outside the camp and stoned to death. Those who had been witnesses to the sin placed their hands upon his head, thus solemnly testifying to the truth of the charge against him. Then they threw the first stones, and the people who stood by then joined in executing the sentence. [See Leviticus 24:14; Deuteronomy 17:7.]

Should Sabbath Breakers Be Stoned?

If this man's sin had been allowed to go unpunished, others would have been encouraged in evil, and as a result, many lives would eventually have been sacrificed.

The mixed multitude that came up with the Israelites from Egypt claimed to worship the true God and to have renounced idolatry, but they were more or less corrupted with idolatry and irreverence. They seeded the camp with idolatrous practices and grumblings against God.

Soon someone violated the Sabbath. The Lord's announcement that He would disinherit Israel had awakened a spirit of rebellion. One of the people, angry at being excluded from Canaan and determined to show his defiance of God's law, dared to transgress the fourth commandment openly by going out to gather sticks on the Sabbath. During the stay in the wilderness, building fires on the seventh day had been prohibited. The prohibition was not to continue in the land of Canaan, but in the wilderness fire was not needed for warmth. This was a willful and deliberate violation of the fourth commandment—a sin of presumption.

Moses brought the case before the Lord, and the direction was given, " 'The man must surely be put to death; all the congregation shall stone him with stones outside the camp.' " Numbers 15:35. The sins of blasphemy and willful Sabbath breaking received the same punishment, since they were equally an expression of contempt for God's authority.

Many who reject the Sabbath as Jewish urge that, if it is to be kept, the penalty of death must be inflicted for its violation. But blasphemy received the same punishment as Sabbath breaking. Though God may not now punish the transgression of His law with earthly penalties, yet in the final judgment death is the fate of those who violate His sacred precepts.

During the entire forty years in the wilderness, the people were reminded of the Sabbath every week by the miracle of the manna. Yet God declares through His prophet, " 'They greatly defiled My Sabbaths.' " Ezekiel 20:13-24. And this is listed among the reasons for excluding the first generation from the Promised Land.

When their period of time in the desert ended, "the people stayed in Kadesh." Numbers 20:1. Here Miriam died and was buried. From that scene of rejoicing on the shores of the Red Sea to the wilderness grave that ended a lifelong wandering—such had been the fate of millions who had come out of Egypt with high hopes. Sin had dashed the cup of blessing from their lips. Would the next generation learn the lesson?

Moses Fails on the Border of Canaan*

The living stream that refreshed Israel in the desert first flowed from the rock that Moses struck in Horeb. During all their wanderings, wherever the need existed, a miracle made water gush out beside their encampment.

It was Christ who caused the refreshing stream to flow for Israel. "They drank of that spiritual Rock that followed them, and that Rock was Christ." 1 Corinthians 10:4. He was the source of all physical as well as spiritual blessings. "They did not thirst when He led them through the deserts; He caused the waters to flow from the rock for them; He also split the rock, and the waters gushed out." "It ran in the dry places like a river." Isaiah 48:21; Psalm 105:41.

As the life-giving waters flowed from the smitten rock, so from Christ, "smitten by God," "wounded for our transgressions," "bruised for our iniquities" (Isaiah 53:4, 5), the stream of salvation flows for a lost race. As the rock had been struck once, so Christ was to be "offered once to bear the sins of many." Hebrews 9:28. Our Savior was not to be sacrificed a second time. It is only necessary for those who seek the blessings of His grace to ask in the name of Jesus; then the life-giving blood will flow out afresh, symbolized by the flowing water for Israel.

Just before the Hebrews reached Kadesh, the living stream that for many years had gushed out beside their encampment ceased. The Lord would test whether they would trust His leading or imitate the unbelief of their ancestors.

They were now in sight of the hills of Canaan, only a short distance from Edom. Through Edom ran the appointed route to Canaan. God had directed Moses, " 'Command the people, saying, "You are about to pass through the territory of your brethren, the descendants of Esau, . . . and they will be afraid of you. . . . You shall buy food from them with money, that you may eat; and you shall also buy water from them with money, that you may drink." ' " Deuteronomy 2:4-6.

These directions should have been enough to explain why their supply of water had been cut off; they were about to pass through a

---

* This chapter is based on Numbers 20:1-13.

well-watered, fertile country, in a direct route to the land of Canaan. When the miraculous flow of water ceased, this should have been a cause to rejoice, a sign that the wilderness wandering was ended. But the people seemed to have given up all hope that God would bring them into Canaan, and they clamored for the blessings of the wilderness.

The water stopped before they reached Edom. They had opportunity for a little while to walk by faith instead of sight. But the first test developed the same spirit shown by their forefathers. They forgot the hand that for so many years had supplied their wants. Instead of turning to God for help, they complained in desperation, exclaiming, " 'If only we had died when our brethren died before the LORD!' " (that is, in the rebellion of Korah).

Moses and Aaron, the leaders, went to the door of the tabernacle and fell on their faces. Moses was directed, " 'Take the rod; you and your brother Aaron gather the assembly together. Speak to the rock before their eyes, and it will yield its water; thus you shall bring water for them out of the rock.' "

The two brothers were now old men. They had long put up with the rebellion of Israel. But now, finally Moses lost patience. " 'Hear now, you rebels!' " he cried. " 'Must we bring water for you out of this rock?' " Instead of merely speaking to the rock, as God had commanded him, he struck it twice with the rod.

The water gushed out abundant-ly, but a great wrong had been done. Moses had spoken from irritated feelings. " 'Hear now, you rebels,' " he said. This accusation was true, but even truth is not to be spoken in passion or impatience. When he took it on himself to accuse them, he grieved the Spirit of God. His lack of self-control was evident. This gave the people occasion to question whether his past course had been under the direction of God. They now found the excuse they wanted for rejecting the reproofs God had sent through His servant.

Moses Distrusted God

Moses showed distrust of God. "Shall we bring water?" he questioned, as if the Lord would not do what He promised. " 'You did not believe Me,' " the Lord declared to the two brothers, " 'to hallow Me in the eyes of the children of Israel.' " When the water failed, their own faith in God's promise had been shaken by the rebellion of the people. The first generation had been condemned to die in the wilderness because of their unbelief. Would these also fail?

Exhausted and disheartened, Moses and Aaron had made no effort to oppose the current of popular feeling. They might have set the matter before the people in such a light as to enable them to bear this test. They might have quelled the complaining before asking God to do the work for them. What a series of evil events might have been prevented!

The rock, a symbol of Christ, had been struck once, as Christ was to be offered once. Now, Moses needed only to speak to the rock, as we have only to ask for blessings in the name of Jesus. By striking the rock a second time, Moses destroyed the significance of this beautiful symbol of Christ. More than this, Moses and Aaron assumed power that belongs only to God. The leaders of Israel should have used the occasion to impress the people with reverence for God and to strengthen their faith in His power and goodness. When they angrily cried, " 'Must *we* bring water for you out of this rock?' " they put themselves in God's place, as though the power lay within themselves. Moses had lost sight of his Almighty Helper and, left to himself, had marred his record by human weakness. The man who might have stood firm and unselfish to the close of his work had been overcome at last.

This time God did not pronounce judgments on those who had so provoked Moses and Aaron; all the reproof fell on the leaders. Moses and Aaron had felt themselves wronged, losing sight of the fact that the complaining was not against them but against God. Looking to themselves, they unconsciously fell into sin and failed to lead the people to see their guilt before God.

"The LORD spoke to Moses and Aaron, 'Because you did not believe Me, to hallow Me in the eyes of the children of Israel, therefore you shall not bring this congregation into the land which I have given them.' " They must die before the crossing of the Jordan. They had not sinned willfully or deliberately; they had been overcome by a sudden temptation, and their repentance was immediate and heartfelt. The Lord accepted their repentance, but because of the harm their sin might do among the people, He could not cancel its punishment.

Moses told the people that because he had failed to give the glory to God, he could not lead them into the Promised Land. He asked them to notice the severe punishment administered to him, and then consider how God must regard their complaints in blaming a mere man for the judgments that they had brought on themselves. He told them how he had pleaded with God to cancel the sentence and had been refused.

Throughout their journeyings as they had complained of the difficulties in the way, Moses had told them, "Your murmurings are against God. It is not I, but God, who has worked to deliver you." But his hasty words, " 'Shall *we* bring water?' " were a virtual admission of their charge. His error would thus confirm them in their unbelief and justify their complaints. The Lord would remove this impression from their minds forever by forbidding Moses to enter the Promised Land. Here was unmistakable evidence that their leader was not Moses but the mighty Angel of whom the Lord had said, " 'Behold, I send an Angel before you to keep you in the way and to bring you into the place which I have prepared. Beware of Him and obey His voice; . . . for My name is in Him.' " Exodus 23:20, 21.

Why the Sin of Moses and Aaron Must Be Punished

" 'The LORD was angry with me on your account,' " said Moses. The whole congregation knew about the transgression. If God had passed it by lightly, the people would have thought that a leader's impatience under great provocation might be excused. But when Moses and Aaron were not to enter Canaan because of that one sin, the people knew that God plays no favorites.

People of all future time must see the God of heaven as impartial, one who never justifies sin. God's goodness and love prompt Him to deal with sin as an evil that is fatal to the peace and happiness of the universe.

God had forgiven the people for greater transgressions, but He could not deal with sin in the leaders the same way He did in those who were led. He had honored Moses above every other person on earth. The fact that he had been blessed with such great light and knowledge made his sin more serious. Past faithfulness will not atone for one wrong act. Greater light and privileges granted to someone only make failure less excusable and the resulting punishment heavier.

Moses' sin was a common one. The psalmist says that "he spoke rashly with his lips." Psalm 106:33. To human judgment this may seem a small thing, but if God dealt so severely with this sin in His most faithful and honored servant, He will not excuse it in others. The spirit of self-exaltation, the inclination to condemn our fellow believers, is displeasing to God. The more important one's position, the greater the need to cultivate patience and humility.

If those in positions of responsibility take to themselves the glory that is due to God, Satan has gained a victory. Every impulse of our nature and tendency of the heart needs to be under the control of the Spirit of God moment by moment. Therefore however great our light, however much we may enjoy divine favor, we should ever walk humbly before the Lord, pleading in faith that God will control every impulse.

The burdens placed on Moses were very great. Few people will ever be as severely tested as he was. Yet this did not excuse his sin. No matter how great the pressure brought on the soul, transgression is our own act. It is not in the power of earth or hell to compel anyone to do evil. No matter how severe or unexpected the temptation, God has provided help for us, and in His strength we may conquer.

Why the Long Journey Around Edom?*

Israel's encampment at Kadesh was only a short distance from the borders of Edom, and both Moses and the people greatly desired to follow the route through this country to the Promised Land. So they sent a message to the Edomite king:

" 'Thus says your brother Israel: . . . "here we are in Kadesh, a city on the edge of your border. Please let us pass through your country. We will not pass through fields or vineyards, nor will we drink water from wells; we will go along the King's Highway; we will not turn aside to the right hand or to the left until we have passed through your territory." ' "

To this courteous request, the Edomite king returned a threatening refusal: " 'You shall not pass through my land, lest I come out against you with the sword.' "

The leaders of Israel sent a second appeal to the king, with the promise, " 'We will go by the Highway, and if I or my livestock drink any of your water, then I will pay for it; let me only pass through on foot, nothing more.' "

" 'You shall not pass through,' " was the answer. Armed bands of Edomites were already posted at the difficult passes, and the Hebrews were forbidden to use force. They must make the long journey around the land of Edom.

If the people had trusted in God, the Captain of the Lord's army would have led them through Edom. The inhabitants of the land, instead of reacting with hostility, would have shown them favor. But the Israelites did not act promptly on God's word, and the golden opportunity passed. When they were finally ready to present their request to the king, it was refused. Ever since they left Egypt, Satan had been throwing hindrances in their way so that they might not inherit Canaan. And by their own unbelief they had repeatedly opened the door for him.

When God tells His children to go forward, Satan tempts them to displease the Lord by hesitation and delay. He tries to stir up strife, complaining, or unbelief and thus deprive them of the blessings God wants to give. God's servants should be minutemen. Any delay on their part gives time for Satan to work to defeat them.

---

* This chapter is based on Numbers 20:14-29; 21:1-9.

The Edomites were descendants of Abraham and Isaac. For the sake of these two servants of His, God had given them Mount Seir for a possession. They were not to be disturbed unless by their sins they placed themselves beyond His mercy. The Hebrews were to utterly destroy the inhabitants of Canaan, who had filled up the measure of their iniquity; but the Edomites still could repent and were to be dealt with mercifully. God shows compassion before He inflicts judgments.

The Israelites were forbidden ever to take revenge for the insult given them in refusing to let them pass through the land. They must not expect to possess any part of the land of Edom. God had promised them a large inheritance, but they were not to feel that they alone had rights in the earth; they were not to seek to crowd out all others. They were to beware of doing injustice to the Edomites. They were to trade with them, promptly paying for all they received. As an encouragement to trust in God and obey His word, they were reminded, " 'The Lord your God has blessed you . . . ; you have lacked nothing.' " Deuteronomy 2:7. Their God was rich in resources. They should demonstrate the principle, "You shall love your neighbor as yourself."

If they had passed through Edom as God had intended, the passage would have proved a blessing to the Edomites. They would have become acquainted with God's people and His worship and would have seen how the God of Jacob prospered those who loved and feared Him. But the unbelief of Israel had prevented all this. They must cross the desert again and quench their thirst from the miraculous spring that they would no longer have needed if they had only trusted in Him.

Aaron Dies in Moses' Arms

So the multitude of Israel again made their way over the sterile wasteland that seemed even more dreary after a glimpse of the green spots among the hills and valleys of Edom. From the mountain range overlooking this gloomy desert rises Mount Hor, whose summit was to be the place of Aaron's death and burial. When the Israelites came to this mountain, God commanded Moses:

" 'Take Aaron and Eleazar his son, and bring them up to Mount Hor; and strip Aaron of his garments and put them on Eleazar his son; for Aaron shall be gathered to his people and die there.' " Together these two old men and the younger one climbed up the mountain. The heads of Moses and Aaron were white. Their long and eventful lives had included the deepest trials and the greatest honors that had ever come to anyone. All their powers had been developed, exalted, and dignified by communication with the Infinite One. Their faces gave evidence of great intellectual power, firmness and nobility of purpose, and strong affections.

Many years together they had met unnumbered dangers, but the time had come when they must be separated. They moved on very slowly, for every moment in each other's society was precious. The ascent was steep and exhausting, and as they often paused to rest, they talked together of the past and the future. Before them was spread out the scene of their desert wanderings. In the plain below were encamped the vast hosts of Israel, for whom these chosen men had spent the best part of their lives and made great sacrifices. Somewhere beyond the mountains of Edom was the path leading to the Promised Land, that land whose blessings Moses and Aaron were not to enjoy. A solemn sadness rested on their faces as they remembered what had kept them from entering the land promised to their fathers.

Aaron's work for Israel was done. Forty years before, at the age of eighty-three, God had called him to unite with Moses in his challenging mission. He had held up the great leader's hands when the Hebrew army gave battle to Amalek. He had been privileged to ascend Mount Sinai, to behold the divine glory. The Lord had honored him with the sacred consecration of high priest and had sustained him in that holy office by terrible displays of judgment in the destruction of Korah and his followers. When his two sons were killed for disregarding God's express command, he did not rebel or even complain.

Yet the record of his noble life had been marred when he yielded to the clamors of the people and made the golden calf at Sinai and again when he united with Miriam in criticizing Moses. And he, with Moses, offended the Lord at Kadesh by disobeying the command to speak to the rock that it might give forth water.

Aaron carried the names of Israel on his breast. He communicated to the people the will of God. He entered the Most Holy Place on the Day of Atonement, "not without blood," as a mediator for all Israel. The exalted nature of that sacred office as representative of our great High Priest made Aaron's sin at Kadesh very great.

With deep sorrow Moses removed from Aaron the holy garments and placed them on Eleazar, his successor by divine decree. For his sin at Kadesh, Aaron was denied the privilege of officiating as God's high priest in Canaan—of offering the first sacrifice in the beautiful land. Moses was to continue leading the people to the very borders of Canaan, but he was not to enter it. If these servants of God had endured the test at Kadesh without complaint, how different their future would have been! A wrong act can never be undone. Even the work of a lifetime may not recover what has been lost in a single moment of temptation or thoughtlessness.

As the people looked around in their vast congregation, they saw that nearly all the adults who left Egypt had perished in the wilderness. With foreboding of evil they remembered the sentence pronounced against Moses and Aaron. Some were aware of the purpose of that mysterious journey to the summit of Mount Hor, and their concern was heightened by bitter memories and self-accusations.

Lessons From the Death of Aaron

Moses and Eleazar were at last seen slowly coming down the mountainside. The priestly garments were upon Eleazar, showing that he had succeeded his father in the sacred office. As the people gathered about, Moses told them that Aaron had died in his arms on Mount Hor and that they had buried him there. The congregation broke into mourning and lamentation. "All the house of Israel mourned for Aaron thirty days."

The Scriptures give only the simple record, "There Aaron died, and there he was buried." Deuteronomy 10:6 KJV. In striking contrast, in modern times the funeral services of a person of high position are often turned into opportunities for extravagant display. When Aaron died, there were only two of his nearest friends to attend his burial. That lonely grave was forever hidden from the sight of Israel. God is not honored in the great display and extravagant expense incurred in returning bodies to the dust.

The death of Aaron forcibly reminded Moses that his own end was near. He deeply felt the loss of the one who for so many years had shared his joys and sorrows. Moses must now work alone, but he knew God was his friend, and he leaned more heavily on Him.

Soon after leaving Mount Hor the Israelites suffered defeat in a battle with Arad, one of the Canaanite kings. But as they asked God for help, divine aid was granted, and their enemies were completely destroyed. But instead of inspiring gratitude, this victory made the people boastful and self-confident.

They continued their journey toward the south through a hot valley, with no shade or vegetation. They suffered fatigue and thirst. Again they failed to endure the test of faith and patience. By dwelling on the dark side they separated themselves farther from God. They lost sight of the fact that if they had not complained when the water ceased at Kadesh, they would have been spared the journey around Edom. They flattered themselves that if God and Moses had not interfered, they might now have been in possession of the Promised Land. After making their situation much harder than God intended, they harbored bitter thoughts concerning His dealings with them, finally becoming discontented with everything. Egypt looked more desirable than liberty and the land to which God was leading them!

What Happens in Unbelief

"And the people spoke against God and against Moses: 'Why have you brought us up out of Egypt to die in the wilderness? For there is no food and no water, and our soul loathes this worthless bread.' "

Moses faithfully set before the people their great sin. God's power alone had preserved them in " 'that great and terrible wilderness, in which were fiery serpents and scorpions and thirsty land where there was no water.' " Deuteronomy 8:15. In all the way they had found water, bread from heaven, and peace and safety under the shadowy cloud by day and the pillar of fire by night. Angels had cared for them as they climbed rocky heights or threaded the rugged paths of the wilderness. There was not a feeble one in all their ranks. Their feet had not swollen in their long journeys, nor had their clothes worn out. God had subdued before them the fierce beasts of prey and the poisonous reptiles of the forest and desert.

God's Protecting Hand Removed

Shielded by divine power, they had not realized the countless dangers that surrounded them. In their unbelief they expected death, and now the Lord permitted death to come on them. The poisonous serpents that infested the wilderness were called fiery serpents because their sting caused violent inflammation and speedy death. As the protecting hand of God was removed, great numbers of the people were attacked by these venomous creatures.

In almost every tent were the dying or the dead. Often the silence of night was broken by piercing cries that told of fresh victims. All were busy caring for sufferers or trying to protect those not yet stricken. When compared with their present suffering, the former difficulties and trials of the people seemed unworthy of a thought.

The people now came to Moses with confessions and pleadings. " 'We have sinned,' " they said, " 'for we have spoken against the LORD and against you.' " Only a short time before, they had accused him of being the cause of all their distress and afflictions. But as soon as real trouble came, they ran to him as the only one who could intercede with God for them. " 'Pray to the LORD that He take away the serpents from us.' "

God commanded Moses to make a serpent of bronze and to elevate it among the people. All who had been bitten were to look to it and find relief. The joyful news went out that all who had been bitten might look at the bronze serpent and live. Many had already died, and when Moses raised the serpent on the pole, some would not believe that merely looking at that metallic image could heal them; these died in their unbelief.

Yet many had faith in the provision God had made. Fathers, mothers, brothers, and sisters were occupied in helping suffering, dying friends to fix their listless eyes on the serpent. Though faint and dying, if they could only once look, they were healed.

The Bronze Serpent a Symbol of the Savior

The lifting up of the bronze serpent was to teach Israel an important lesson. They could not save themselves from the poison in their wounds; God alone was able to heal. Yet they were required to show their faith in the provision He had made. They must look in order to live. By looking on the serpent they showed their faith. They knew that there was no virtue in the serpent itself, but it was a symbol of Christ.

Before this, many had brought offerings to God and felt that doing so made ample atonement for their sins. The Lord wanted to teach them that their sacrifices had no more power than the serpent of bronze but were to lead their minds to Christ, the great sin offering.

" 'As Moses lifted up the serpent in the wilderness,' " even so was the Son of man " 'lifted up, that whoever believes in Him should not perish but have eternal life.' " John 3:14, 15. All who have lived on earth have felt the deadly sting of "that serpent of old, called the Devil and Satan." Revelation 12:9. The fatal effects of sin can be removed only by the provision that God has made. The Israelites saved their lives because they believed God's word and trusted in the means provided for their recovery. So the sinner may look to Christ and live, receiving pardon through faith in the atoning sacrifice. Christ has power and virtue to heal the repenting sinner.

While sinners cannot save themselves, they still have something to do to secure salvation. " 'The one who comes to Me,' " says Christ, " 'I will by no means cast out.' " John 6:37. We must *come* to Him; and when we repent we must believe that He accepts and pardons us. Faith is the gift of God, but the power to exercise it is ours. Faith is the hand by which the sinner takes hold of the divine offers of grace and mercy.

Many have clung to the idea that they could do something to make themselves worthy. They have not looked away from self, believing that Jesus is an all-sufficient Savior. We must not think that our own merits will save us. Christ is our only hope of salvation.

When we see our sinfulness, we should not fear that we have no Savior or that He has no thoughts of mercy toward us. At this very time He is inviting us to come to Him and be saved.

Many of the Israelites saw no help in the remedy that Heaven had appointed. They knew that without divine aid their own fate was certain, but they continued to bemoan their sure death until their eyes were glazed. They could have had instant healing. As we look at our helpless condition without Christ, we are not to yield to discouragement but to rely on the merits of a crucified and risen Savior. Look and live. Jesus will save all who come to Him. Not one who trusts in His merits will be left to perish.

Many wander in the mazes of philosophy in search of reasons they will never find, while they reject the evidence that God has been pleased to give. God gives sufficient evidence on which to base faith; and if this evidence is not accepted, the mind is left in darkness. If those who were bitten by the serpents had stopped to doubt and question before they consented to look, they would have perished. It is our duty to look, and the look of faith will give life.

The Conquest of Bashan*

After passing south of Edom, the Israelites turned northward toward the Promised Land. Their route now lay over a vast, high plain, swept by cool, fresh breezes, a welcome change from the parched valley. They pressed forward, happy and hopeful. God had commanded, " 'Do not harass Moab, nor contend with them in battle, for I will not give you any of their land as a possession, because I have given Ar to the descendants of Lot.' " The same was repeated concerning the Ammonites, also descendants of Lot.

The people of Israel soon reached the country of the Amorites. This strong, warlike people had crossed the Jordan, made war on the Moabites, and gained some of their territory. The route to the Jordan lay directly through this territory, and Moses sent a friendly message to Sihon, the Amorite king: " 'Let me pass through your land. . . . You shall sell me food for money, that I may eat, and give me water for money, that I may drink; only let me pass through on foot.' "

The answer was a decided refusal, and all the hosts of the Amorites were summoned to oppose the invaders. This formidable army struck terror to the Israelites. In skill for warfare, their enemies had the advantage. To all human appearance, the Amorites would make a speedy end of Israel.

But Moses kept his eyes on the cloudy pillar. This evidence of God's presence was still with them. At the same time he directed them to do all that human power could do in preparing for war. Their enemies were confident that they would blot out the Israelites from the land. But from the Owner of all lands the message had gone out to Israel: " 'Rise, take your journey, and cross over the River Arnon. Look, I have given into your hand Sihon the Amorite, king of Heshbon, and his land. Begin to possess it, and engage him in battle. This day I will begin to put the dread and fear of you upon the nations under the whole heaven, who shall hear the report of you, and shall tremble and be in anguish because of you.' "

*This chapter is based on Deuteronomy 2; 3:1-11.

How God Revealed His Love to Wicked Nations

These nations on the borders of Canaan would have been spared if they had not stood to oppose Israel in defiance of God's word. The Lord gave Abraham the promise, " 'In the fourth generation they shall return here, for the iniquity of the Amorites is not yet complete.' " Genesis 15:16. God spared them for four hundred years to give unmistakable evidence that He was the only true God. All His wonders in bringing Israel from Egypt were familiar to them. They might have known the truth, but they rejected the light and clung to their idols.

When the Lord brought His people to the borders of Canaan a second time, those heathen nations were granted additional evidence of His power. They saw that God was with Israel in the victory over King Arad and the Canaanites and in the miracle to save those dying from the sting of the serpents. In all their journeys and encampments the Israelites had done no harm to the people or their possessions. On reaching the border of the Amorites, Israel had asked permission only to travel directly through the country, promising to observe the same rules that had governed their relations with other nations. When the Amorite king refused and defiantly gathered his armies for battle, their cup of iniquity was full, and God would now exercise His power to overthrow them.

The Israelites crossed the river Arnon and advanced against the foe.

An engagement took place, and the armies of Israel were victorious. Soon they were in possession of the Amorite country. The Captain of the Lord's host defeated the enemies of His people. He would have done the same thirty-eight years before, if Israel had trusted in Him.

The army of Israel eagerly pressed forward and soon reached a country that might well test their courage and faith in God. Before them lay the powerful kingdom of Bashan, crowded with great stone cities that to this day excite the wonder of the world—" 'sixty cities . . . with high walls, gates, and bars, besides a great many rural towns.' " The houses were constructed of huge black stones, so large as to make the buildings unconquerable by any force brought against them. It was a country filled with wild caverns and rocky strongholds. The inhabitants, descendants from a giant race, were of impressive size and strength and known for such violence and cruelty as to be the terror of all surrounding nations. Og, the king, was remarkable for size even in a nation of giants.

But the cloudy pillar moved forward, and the Hebrew hosts advanced to Edrei, where the giant king waited for them. Og had skillfully chosen the place of battle. The city of Edrei stood on the border of a high, broad flatland rising abruptly from the plain and covered with jagged rocks. It could be approached only by narrow pathways, steep and difficult to navigate. In case of defeat, his forces could find refuge in that wilderness of rocks where it would be impossible for strangers to follow.

Moses Trusted God

Confident of success, the king came out with an immense army on the open plain. When the Hebrews looked at that giant of giants towering above the soldiers of his army, when they saw the seemingly invincible fortress with unseen thousands entrenched behind it, the hearts of many quaked with fear. But Moses was calm and firm; the Lord had said concerning the king of Bashan, " 'Do not fear him, for I have delivered him and all his people and his land into your hand; you shall do to him as you did to Sihon king of the Amorites.' "

No mighty giants, walled cities, armed hosts, nor rocky fortresses could stand before the Captain of the Lord's host. The Lord led the army, and the Lord conquered in behalf of Israel. The giant king and his army were destroyed, and the Israelites soon took possession of the whole country. Thus that strange people who had given themselves up to abominable idolatry were blotted from the earth.

Israel's Fatal Mistake

Many recalled the events that nearly forty years before had doomed Israel to long desert wandering. The report of the spies concerning the Promised Land was correct in many respects. The cities were walled and very great and inhabited by giants. But now they could see the fatal mistake of the previous generation in distrusting the power of God. This had prevented them from entering the beautiful land at once.

God had promised His people that if they would obey His voice He would go ahead of them and fight for them. He would drive out the inhabitants of the land. But now Israel must advance against alert and powerful foes and do battle with well-trained armies that had been preparing to resist.

The earlier generation had failed dramatically. But the test was more severe now than when God had commanded Israel to go forward. The difficulties had greatly increased since they refused to advance when told to do so.

God still tests His people. And if they fail He brings them again to the same point, and the second time the test will be more severe than the first.

The mighty God of Israel is our God. In Him we may trust, and if we obey His requirements He will work for us as He did for His ancient people. The way will sometimes be so blocked by obstacles, apparently insurmountable, as to dishearten those who will yield to discouragement; but God is saying, Go forward. The difficulties that fill your soul with dread will disappear as you move forward in the path of obedience, humbly trusting in God.

Balaam Tries to Curse Israel*

Preparing to invade Canaan immediately, the Israelites encamped beside the Jordan above its entrance into the Dead Sea, just opposite the plain of Jericho, on the borders of Moab. The Moabites had not been harassed by Israel, yet they had watched with troubled uneasiness all that had taken place in the surrounding countries. The Amorites, who had forced them to retreat, had been conquered by the Hebrews. Israel now possessed the territory the Amorites had taken from Moab. The armies of Bashan had fallen before the mysterious power cloaked in the cloudy pillar, and the Hebrews occupied the giant strongholds.

The Moabites dared not risk launching an attack, but as Pharaoh had done, they determined to enlist sorcery to counteract the work of God. The people of Moab had close connections with the Midianites, and Balak, the king of Moab, secured their cooperation against Israel by the message, " 'Now this company will lick up all that is around us, as an ox licks up the grass of the field.' " Balaam of Mesopotamia was reported to possess supernatural powers, and his fame had reached Moab. So messengers were sent to enlist his divinations and enchantments against Israel.

The ambassadors set out at once on their long journey. When they found Balaam they delivered the message of their king: " 'Look, a people has come from Egypt. See, they cover the face of the earth, and are settling next to me! Therefore please come at once, curse this people for me, for they are too mighty for me. Perhaps I shall be able to defeat them and drive them out of the land, for I know that he whom you bless is blessed, and he whom you curse is cursed.' "

Balaam was once a prophet of God. But he had backslidden and given himself up to covetousness. When the messengers announced their errand, he well knew that it was his duty to refuse the rewards of Balak and send the ambassadors away. But he took a chance on dallying with temptation and urged the messengers to stay that night, declaring that he could give no answer till he had asked counsel of the

---

* This chapter is based on Numbers 22 to 24.

Lord. Balaam knew that his curse could not harm Israel, but his pride was flattered by the words, " 'He whom you bless is blessed, and he whom you curse is cursed.' " The bribe of costly gifts inflamed his covetousness, and while he professed to obey the will of God, he tried to comply with the desires of Balak.

In the night the angel of God came to Balaam with the message, " 'You shall not go with them; you shall not curse the people, for they are blessed.' "

How One Sin Opened the Door to Satan's Control

In the morning, Balaam sent the messengers away but did not tell them what the Lord had said. Angry that his visions of wealth and honor had been dispelled, he exclaimed, " 'Go back to your land, for the LORD has refused to give me permission to go with you.' "

Balaam "loved the wages of unrighteousness." 2 Peter 2:15. The sin of covetousness had destroyed his integrity; through this one fault Satan gained entire control of him. The tempter constantly presents worldly gain and honor to lure people from the service of God. Thus many are persuaded to leave the path of strict integrity. One wrong step makes the next easier, and they become more and more reckless. They will do the most terrible things once they have given themselves to the control of greed and desire for power. Many flatter themselves that they can lay aside strict uprightness for a while

and change their course when they please. They are entangling themselves in Satan's trap, and seldom do they escape.

When the messengers told Balak of the prophet's refusal, they gave no hint that God had forbidden him. Supposing that Balaam's delay was to obtain a richer reward, the king sent princes more numerous and more honorable than the first, with authority to accept any terms Balaam might demand. Balak's urgent message was, " 'Please, let nothing hinder you from coming to me. for I will certainly honor you greatly, and I will do whatever you say to me. Therefore please come, curse this people for me.' "

In response, Balaam professed great high-mindedness and integrity—no amount of gold and silver could persuade him to go contrary to the will of God. But he longed to comply with the king's request. Although God had already made His will known to him, he urged the messengers to stay so that he could further inquire of God.

In the night, the Lord appeared to Balaam and said, " 'If the men come to call you, rise and go with them; but only the word which I speak to you—that you shall do.' " To that extent the Lord would permit Balaam to follow his own will, because he was determined upon it. He chose his own course and then tried to get the approval of the Lord.

Thousands today are following a similar course. Their duty is plainly set before them in the Bible or clearly indicated by circumstances and reason. But because these evidences are contrary to what they want, they set them aside and apparently go to God to learn their duty. They pray long and earnestly for light. But God will not be trifled with. He often permits such persons to follow their own desires and suffer the result. " 'My people would not heed My voice. . . . So I gave them over to their own stubborn heart, to walk in their own counsels.' " Psalm 81:11, 12. One who clearly sees a duty should not go to God with the prayer to be excused from performing it.

A Donkey "Sees" More Than a Prophet

Annoyed at Balaam's delay and expecting another refusal, the messengers from Moab set out on their homeward journey without further consultation. Every excuse for complying with Balak's request had now been removed. But Balaam was determined to get the reward. Taking the donkey he usually rode, he set out and pressed eagerly forward, impatient to gain the coveted reward.

But "the Angel of the LORD took His stand in the way as an adversary against him." Balaam did not see the divine messenger, but the animal did and turned aside from the highway into a field. With cruel blows, Balaam brought the beast back into the path. But again, in a narrow place shut in by walls, the angel appeared. The donkey, trying to avoid the menacing figure, crushed her master's foot against the wall. Balaam did not

know that God was obstructing his path. He became exasperated, and beating his mount unmercifully, forced it to proceed.

Again, "in a narrow place where there was no way to turn either to the right hand or to the left," the angel appeared, and the poor donkey, trembling with terror, fell to the earth under its rider. Balaam's rage was limitless, and with his staff he struck the animal more cruelly than before. God now opened its mouth, and by "a dumb donkey speaking with a man's voice" He "restrained the madness of the prophet." 2 Peter 2:16. " 'What have I done to you,' " it said, " 'that you have struck me these three times?' "

Furious, Balaam answered the beast as he would have spoken to an intelligent being: " 'Because you have abused me. I wish there were a sword in my hand, for now I would kill you!' "

The eyes of Balaam were now opened, and he saw the angel of God standing with drawn sword ready to kill him. In terror "he bowed his head and fell flat on his face." The angel said, " 'Behold, I have come out to stand against you, because your way is perverse before Me. The donkey saw me and turned aside from Me these three times. If she had not turned aside from Me, surely I would also have killed you by now, and let her live.' "

Balaam owed his life to the poor animal he had treated so cruelly. The man who claimed to be a prophet of the Lord was so blinded by greed and ambition that he could not discern the angel of God visible to his beast. "The god of this world hath blinded the minds of them which believe not." 2 Corinthians 4:4, KJV. How many rush on in forbidden paths, transgressing the divine law, and cannot tell that God and His angels are against them! Like Balaam they are angry at those who would prevent their ruin.

"A righteous man regards the life of his animal, but the tender mercies of the wicked are cruel." Proverbs 12:10. Few realize as they should the sinfulness of abusing animals or leaving them to suffer from neglect. Animals were created to serve us, but we have no right to cause them pain by harsh treatment.

Those who will abuse an animal because it is in their power are both cowards and tyrants. Many do not realize that their cruelty will ever be known, because the poor unspeaking animal cannot reveal it. But if the eyes of these people could be opened, they would see an angel of God standing as a witness to testify against them in the courts above. A day is coming when judgment will be pronounced against those who abuse God's creatures.

Balaam Prevented From Cursing Israel

When he saw the messenger of God, Balaam exclaimed in terror, " 'I have sinned, for I did not know that You stood in the way against me. Now therefore, if it displeases You, I will turn back.' " The Lord allowed him to proceed on his journey, but divine power would control his words. God would give Moab evidence that the Hebrews were under the guardianship of Heaven, and He did this when He showed them how powerless Balaam was to utter a curse against them.

The king of Moab, informed of Balaam's approach, went out to meet him. When he expressed astonishment at Balaam's delay in view of the rich rewards awaiting him, the prophet answered, " 'Have I any power at all to say anything? The word that God puts in my mouth, that I must speak.' " Balaam greatly regretted this restriction; he feared that his intentions could not be carried out.

The king, with the chief dignitaries of the kingdom, escorted Balaam to "the high places of Baal," where he could see the Hebrew camp. How little the Israelites knew of what was taking place so near them! How little they knew of the care of God, extended over them day and night!

Balaam had some knowledge of the sacrificial offerings of the Hebrews, and he hoped that by making more impressive sacrifices he could ensure the success of his sinful projects. Seven altars were erected, and he offered a sacrifice on each. He then withdrew to a "desolate height" to meet with God.

With the nobles and princes of Moab, the king stood beside the sacrifice, watching for the return of the prophet. He came at last, and the people waited for the words that would paralyze forever that strange power exerted in behalf of the hated Israelites. Balaam said:

"Balak the king of Moab
   has brought me from Aram,
From the mountains of the east.
'Come, curse Jacob for me,
And come, denounce Israel!'

"How shall I curse
   whom God has not cursed? . . .

"Who can count the dust of Jacob,
Or number one-fourth of Israel?
Let me die the death of the righteous,
And let my end be like his!"
   Numbers 23:7-10

As Balaam looked on Israel's encampment, he was astonished at the evidence of their prosperity. He had been told they were a rude, disorganized multitude, infesting the country in roving bands, a pest and terror to surrounding nations. But what he saw was just the opposite of all this. He saw the vast extent and perfect arrangement of their camp, everything bearing the marks of discipline and order. He was shown the favor with which God regarded Israel and their distinctive character as His chosen people. They were not to stand on a level with other nations but to be exalted above them all. They were to be "a people dwelling alone, not reckoning itself among the nations." How strikingly was this prophecy fulfilled in the subsequent history of Israel! Through all the years, they have remained a distinct people.

Balaam Sees God's Favor on Israel

Balaam saw the increase and prosperity of the true Israel of God to the close of time, the special favor of the Most High on those who love and fear Him. He saw them supported by His arm as they entered the dark valley of the shadow of death. And he witnessed them coming out of their graves, crowned with glory, honor, and immortality. He viewed the redeemed rejoicing in the unfading glories of the earth made new. As he saw the crown of glory on every brow and their endless life of happiness, he uttered the solemn prayer, " 'Let me die the death of the righteousness, and let my end be like his!' "

If Balaam had been in the habit of accepting the light God had given, he would have severed all connection with Moab immediately. He would have returned to God with deep repentance. But Balaam loved the wages of unrighteousness.

Balak had expected a curse that would fall like a withering blight on Israel, and he passionately exclaimed, " 'What have you done to me? I took you to curse my enemies, and look, you have blessed them bountifully!' " Balaam professed to have spoken from a conscientious regard for the will of God the words that had been forced from his lips by divine power. " 'Must I not take heed to speak what the LORD has put in my mouth?' "

Balak Tries Again

Balak decided that the impressive spectacle presented by the vast encampment of the Hebrews had so frightened Balaam that he did not dare to practice his magic arts against them. The king determined to take the prophet to some point where he could see only a small part of the camp. Again seven altars were built, and the same offerings were placed on them as at the first. The king and his princes stayed by the sacrifices, while Balaam stepped away to meet with God. Again the prophet was entrusted with a divine message, which he was powerless to change or withhold.

When he appeared, Balak asked him, " 'What has the Lord spoken?' " The answer struck terror to the heart of king and princes:

"God is not a man, that He should
   lie, . . .
Behold, I have received
   a command to bless;
He has blessed, and I cannot reverse
   it.

"He has not observed iniquity in
   Jacob,
Nor has He seen wickedness in Israel.
The Lord his God is with him,
And the shout of a King
   is among them."

The great magician had tried his power of enchantment, but while Israel was under the divine protection, no people or nation, aided by all the power of Satan, would be able to prevail against them. All the world should wonder at the marvelous work of God for His people— that a man should be so controlled by divine power as to utter, instead of curses, rich and precious promises in sublime poetry. In future times when Satan inspired evildoers to misrepresent and destroy God's people, this occurrence would strengthen their courage and faith in God.

The king of Moab, disheartened and distressed, exclaimed, " 'Neither curse them at all, nor bless them at all!' " Yet he determined to try again. He now took Balaam to Mount Peor, where there was a temple devoted to the immoral worship of Baal. Here they offered the same number of sacrifices. But Balaam did not even pretend to work his sorcery. He looked out over the tents of Israel, and the divine message came from his lips:

"How lovely are your tents, O Ja-
   cob!
Your dwellings, O Israel!
Like valleys that stretch out,
Like gardens by the riverside, . . .

"His king shall be higher than Agag,
And his kingdom shall be exalted. . . .

"Blessed is he who blesses you,
And cursed is he who curses you."

Balaam prophesied that Israel's king would be greater than Agag. This was the name given to the kings of the Amalekites, who were at this time a very powerful nation. But Israel, if true to God, would conquer all her enemies. The King of Israel was the Son of God; His throne was one day to be established in the earth and His power to be exalted above all earthly kingdoms.

Balaam Loses All He Tried to Gain

Balak was overwhelmed with disappointed hope, fear, and rage. He was angry that Balaam could have given him the least encouragement to expect a favorable response. He looked with scorn on the prophet's compromising, deceptive course, and exclaimed fiercely, " 'Now therefore, flee to your place. I said I would greatly honor you, but in fact, the LORD has kept you back from honor.' " The answer was that the king had been forewarned that Balaam could speak only the message given him from God.

Before returning to his people, Balaam uttered a beautiful prophecy of the world's Redeemer and the final destruction of the enemies of God:

"I see Him, but not now;
I behold Him, but not near;
A Star shall come out of Jacob;
A Scepter shall rise out of Israel,
And batter the brow of Moab,
And destroy all the sons of tumult."

He closed by predicting the complete destruction of Moab and Edom, of Amalek and the Kenites, thus leaving the Moabite king with no ray of hope.

Disappointed in his hopes for wealth and promotion, and conscious that he had brought on himself the displeasure of God, Balaam returned from his self-chosen mission. The controlling power of the Spirit of God left him, and his covetousness took over. He was ready to resort to any means to gain the reward promised by Balak. Balaam knew that the prosperity of Israel depended on their obedience to God. There was no way to cause their overthrow except by leading them into sin.

He immediately returned to Moab and laid his plans before the king— to separate the children of Israel from God by enticing them into idolatry. If they could be led to engage in the sensually unbridled worship of Baal and Ashtaroth, their omnipotent Protector would become their enemy, and they would fall prey to the fierce, warlike nations around them. The king readily accepted this plan, and Balaam remained to assist in putting it into effect.

Balaam witnessed the success of his satanic scheme. He saw the curse of God imposed on His people and thousands falling under His judgments. But the divine justice that punished sin in Israel did not permit the tempters to escape. In the war of Israel against the Midianites, Balaam was killed. He had felt a premonition that his end was near when he exclaimed, " 'Let me die the death of the righteous, and let my end be like his!' " But he had not chosen to live the life of the righteous; he died with the enemies of God.

The fate of Balaam was similar to that of Judas. Both men tried to unite the service of God with greed for riches and met with notable failure. Balaam acknowledged the true God; Judas believed in Jesus. Balaam hoped to make the service of Jehovah the steppingstone to wealth and worldly honor; Judas expected by his connection with Christ to secure riches and promotion in the worldly kingdom that he believed the Messiah was about to set up. Both Balaam and Judas received great light, but a single cherished sin poisoned the entire character and caused their destruction.

Little by little, one cherished sin will debase the character. The indulgence of one evil habit breaks down the defenses of the soul and opens the way for Satan to lead us astray. The only safe course is to pray, as David did, "Uphold my steps in Your paths, that my footsteps may not slip." Psalm 17:5.

How Balaam Led Israel Into Sin *

With renewed faith in God the victorious armies of Israel returned from Bashan and were confident of conquering Canaan immediately. Only the river Jordan lay between them and the Promised Land. Just across the river was a rich plain watered with streams and shaded by fruitful palm trees. On the western border rose the towers and palaces of Jericho, "the city of palm trees."

On the eastern side of Jordan was a plain several miles wide and extending some distance along the river. This sheltered valley had a tropical climate. Here the Israelites encamped and found an agreeable resting place in the acacia groves.

But amid these attractive surroundings they were to encounter an evil more deadly than hosts of armed men or wild beasts of the wilderness. That country, rich in natural advantages, had been defiled by its inhabitants. In the public worship of Baal, the most degrading scenes were enacted. On every side were places noted for idolatry and sexual immorality. Even the names suggested corruption.

The Israelites' minds became familiar with the degrading thoughts constantly suggested. Their life of ease produced its demoralizing effect, and almost unconsciously they were departing from God into a condition where they would fall prey to temptation.

During the time of their encampment beside Jordan, Moses was preparing for the occupation of Canaan. The great leader was fully employed in this work. But this time of suspense was most trying to the people. Before many weeks had elapsed, their history was marred by frightful departures from virtue and integrity.

Midianite women began quietly entering the camp. These women planned to seduce the Hebrews into violating the law of God and to lead them into idolatry. They studiously concealed these motives under the cloak of friendship.

At Balaam's suggestion, the king of Moab declared a grand festival in honor of their gods. It was secretly arranged that Balaam should persuade the Israelites to attend. They regarded him as a prophet of God, and he had little difficulty accom-

---

* This chapter is based on Numbers 25.

plishing his aim. Great numbers of the people joined him in witnessing the festivities. Drawn in with music and dancing, and allured by the beauty of women dedicated to the heathen worship, they cast off their loyalty to Jehovah. Wine clouded their senses and broke down the barriers of self-control. Having defiled their consciences by indecent acts, they were persuaded to bow down to idols. They offered sacrifices on heathen altars and participated in degrading rites.

The poison spread like a deadly infection through the camp of Israel. Those who would have conquered in battle were overcome by the wiles of women. The people seemed to have lost their judgment. The rulers and leading men were among the first to transgress, and so many of the people were guilty that the apostasy became national. "Israel was joined to Baal of Peor." When Moses became aware of the evil, not only were the Israelites participating in the sensuous worship at Mount Peor, but the heathen rites were carried on in the camp of Israel. The aged leader was filled with indignation, and the wrath of God was kindled.

Their evil practices did to Israel what all the hocus-pocus of Balaam could not do—they separated them from God. A terrible plague broke out in the camp, in which tens of thousands died. God commanded that the leaders in apostasy be put to death, and this order was promptly obeyed. Then their bodies were hung up in the sight of all Israel so that the congregation, seeing the leaders so severely dealt with, might have a deep sense of God's abhorrence of their sin. All felt that the punishment was just, and with tears and humiliation the people confessed their sin.

While they were weeping before God at the door of the tabernacle, Zimri, one of the nobles of Israel, came boldly into the camp accompanied by a Midianite harlot, whom he escorted to his tent. Never was vice bolder or more stubborn. Zimri declared his "sin as Sodom" (Isaiah 3:9) and gloried in his shame.

The priests and leaders had bowed low in grief and humiliation, pleading with the Lord to spare His people, when this prince in Israel flaunted his sin in the sight of the congregation, as if to defy the vengeance of God and mock the judges of the nation. Phinehas, the son of Eleazar the high priest, got up, and seizing a javelin "went after the man of Israel into the tent" and killed them both. Thus the plague was stopped. The priest who had executed the divine judgment was honored before all Israel.

Phinehas Made an Atonement for Israel

Phinehas " 'has turned back My wrath from the children of Israel,' " was the divine message. " 'He was zealous for his God, and made atonement for the children of Israel.' "

The judgments inflicted on Israel destroyed the survivors of that vast company from nearly forty years before who had incurred the sentence, " 'They shall surely die in the wilderness.' " During their encampment on the plains of Jordan, "of those who were numbered by Moses and Aaron the priest when they numbered the children of Israel in the Wilderness of Sinai . . . there was not left a man of them, except Caleb the son of Jephunneh and Joshua the son of Nun." Numbers 26:64, 65.

God had sent judgments on Israel for yielding to the seductions of the Midianites, but the tempters were not to escape the wrath of divine justice. " 'Take vengeance for the children of Israel on the Midianites' " was the command of God to Moses; " 'afterward you shall be gathered to your people.' " One thousand men were chosen from each of the tribes and sent out under the leadership of Phinehas. "And they warred against the Midianites, just as the LORD commanded Moses, and they killed . . . the five kings of Midian. Balaam the son of Beor they also killed with the sword." Numbers 31:1-8.

Such was the end of those who plotted evil against God's people. When people "gather together against the life of the righteous," the Lord will bring upon them "their own iniquity, and shall cut them off in their own wickedness." Psalm 94:21, 23.

Strong Men Conquered by Women

When the Hebrews transgressed God's law through yielding to temptation, their defense left them. When the people of God are faithful to His commandments, " 'there is no sorcery against Jacob, nor is there any divination against Israel.' " Numbers 23:23. Hence all the wily arts of Satan are exerted to seduce them into sin. If those who claim to be the custodians of God's law transgress its precepts, they will be unable to stand before their enemies.

The Israelites who could not be overcome by warfare or the sorcery of Midian fell victim to her harlots. Such is the power that a woman, enlisted in the service of Satan, has exerted to destroy souls. "She has cast down many wounded, and all who were slain by her were strong men." Proverbs 7:26. Joseph was tempted in this way. This is also why Samson betrayed his strength into the hands of the Philistines. Here David stumbled. And Solomon, the wisest of kings, became a slave of passion and sacrificed his integrity to the same bewitching power.

Satan has studied with fiendish intensity for thousands of years, and through successive generations he has worked to overthrow princes in Israel by the same temptations that were so successful at Baal Peor. As we approach the close of time, on the borders of the heavenly Canaan, Satan will intensify his efforts to prevent the people of God from entering the beautiful land. He will prepare his temptations for those in holy office; if he can lead them to pollute their souls, he can destroy many through them. By worldly friendships, the charms of beauty, pleasure-seeking, merry-making, feasting, or liquor, he tempts people to violate the seventh commandment.

Those who will dishonor God's

image and defile His temple in their own bodies will not draw back from any dishonor to God that will gratify the desire of their depraved hearts. It is impossible for slaves of passion to realize the sacred obligation of the law of God, to appreciate the atonement, or to place a right value on the soul. Goodness, purity, truth, reverence for God, and love for sacred things—all are burned up in the fires of lust. The heart becomes a blackened and desolate waste. Beings formed in the image of God are dragged down to a level with the animals.

Dangers of Ungodly Associates

By leading the followers of Christ to associate with the ungodly and unite in their amusements, Satan is most successful in drawing them into sin. God requires of His people now as much difference from the world in customs, habits, and principles as He required of Israel anciently. The warnings He gave the Hebrews against blending in with the heathen were not more explicit than are those forbidding Christians to conform to the spirit and customs of the ungodly. We cannot be too firm in shunning the company of those who exert an influence to lead us away from God. While we pray "Lead us not into temptation," we are to shun temptation as far as possible.

When the Israelites were in ease and security they were drawn into sin. Ease and self-indulgence left the fortress of the heart unguarded, and debasing thoughts found entrance. Traitors within the walls overthrew the strongholds of principle and betrayed Israel into the power of Satan. This is how Satan seeks to ruin people. A long preparatory process, unknown to the world, goes on in the heart before the Christian commits open sin. The mind does not come down all at once from purity and holiness to depravity, corruption, and crime. By indulging impure thoughts, sin once hated will become pleasant.

We cannot walk the streets of our cities without seeing startling advertisements of crime to be presented in some novel or to be acted at some theater. The course pursued by the immoral and corrupt is kept before the people in magazines, and everything that can stir up passion is brought before them in exciting stories. They hear so much of debasing crime that the conscience becomes hardened, and they dwell on these things with greedy interest.

Many amusements popular with those who claim to be Christians lead to the same results as did those of the heathen. Through the drama Satan has worked for ages to excite passion and glorify vice. Satan employs the opera, the dance, the card table to open the door to sensual indulgence. In every gathering for pleasure where pride is fostered or appetite indulged, where one is led to forget God and lose sight of eternal interests, there Satan is binding his chains around that person.

How to Overcome Temptation

The heart must be renewed by divine grace. Whoever tries to build up a virtuous character independent of the grace of Christ is building a house on shifting sand. In the fierce storms of temptation it will surely come crashing down. David's prayer should be the cry of every person: "Create in me a clean heart, O God, and renew a steadfast spirit within me." Psalm 51:10.

Yet we have a work to do to resist temptation. Those who would not fall prey to Satan's schemes must guard well the avenues of the soul; avoid reading, seeing, or hearing anything that will suggest impure thoughts. This will require earnest prayer and constant watchfulness. The abiding influence of the Holy Spirit will attract the mind upward to think on pure and holy things. "How can a young man cleanse his way? By taking heed according to Your word." "Your word," says the psalmist, "I have hidden in my heart, that I might not sin against You." Psalm 119:9, 11.

Israel's sin at Beth Peor brought the judgments of God on the nation. The same sins may not be punished as speedily now, but nature has set terrible penalties, penalties that will come upon every transgressor sooner or later. These sins more than any other have caused the fearful physical and moral decline of our race and the weight of disease and misery with which the world is cursed. People may succeed in hiding their sin from others, but they will reap the result in suffering, disease, or death. And beyond this life stands the judgment. "Those who practice such things will not inherit the kingdom of God" but will have their part with Satan and the evil angels in that "lake of fire" which "is the second death." Galatians 5:21; Revelation 20:14.

God Teaches His Law to a New Generation*

The Lord announced to Moses that the time had come to possess Canaan. As the aged prophet stood upon the heights overlooking the Promised Land, with deep earnestness he pleaded, " 'O Lord GOD, You have begun to show Your servant Your greatness and Your mighty hand, for what god is there in heaven or on earth who can do anything like Your works and Your mighty deeds? I pray, let me cross over and see the good land beyond the Jordan, those pleasant mountains, and Lebanon.' "

The answer was, " ' "Speak no more to Me of this matter. Go up to the top of Pisgah, and lift your eyes toward the west, the north, the south, and the east; behold it with your eyes, for you shall not cross over this Jordan." ' "

Without a complaint Moses submitted to the decree of God. And now his great concern was for Israel. From a full heart he poured forth the prayer, " 'Let the LORD, the God of the spirits of all flesh, set a man over the congregation, who may . . . bring them in, that the congregation of the LORD may not be like sheep which have no shepherd.' " Numbers 27:16, 17.

The answer came, " 'Take Joshua the son of Nun with you, a man in whom is the Spirit, and lay your hand on him; set him before Eleazar the priest and before all the congregation, and inaugurate him in their sight. And you shall give some of your authority to him, that all the congregation of the children of Israel may be obedient.' " Verses 18-20.

Joshua, a man of wisdom, ability, and faith, was chosen to succeed Moses. He was solemnly set apart as the leader of Israel. The words of the Lord concerning Joshua came through Moses to the congregation, " 'At his word they shall go out, and at his word they shall come in, both he and all the children of Israel with him, all the congregation.' " Verse 21.

Moses stood before the people to give his last warnings and admonitions, his face shining with a holy light. His hair was white with age, but he stood straight and his eye was clear and undimmed. With deep feeling he portrayed the love and mercy of their Almighty Protector.

---

* This chapter is based on Deuteronomy 3 to 6; 28.

" 'Ask from one end of heaven to the other, whether any great thing like this has happened, or anything like it has been heard. Did any people ever hear the voice of God speaking out of the midst of the fire, as you have heard, and live? Or did God ever try to go and take for Himself a nation from the midst of another nation, by trials, by signs, by wonders, by war, by a mighty hand and an outstretched arm, and by great terrors, according to all that the LORD your God did for you in Egypt before your eyes?' "

" 'Because the LORD loves you, and because He would keep the oath which He swore to your fathers, the LORD has brought you out with a mighty hand, and redeemed you from the house of bondage, from the hand of Pharaoh king of Egypt. Therefore know that the LORD your God, He is God, the faithful God who keeps covenant and mercy for a thousand generations with those who love Him and keep His commandments.' " Deuteronomy 7:8, 9.

The people of Israel had often felt impatient and rebellious because of their long wandering in the wilderness, but this delay in possessing Canaan was not God's fault. He was more grieved than they because He could not bring them into the Promised Land immediately and display His mighty power before all nations. With their distrust of God, they had not been prepared to enter Canaan. If their fathers had yielded in faith to the direction of God, walking in His instruction, they would long before have been settled in Canaan, a prosperous, holy, happy people. Their delay dishonored God and detracted from His glory in the sight of surrounding nations.

Moses said, " 'Surely I have taught you statutes and judgments, just as the LORD my God commanded me, that you should act according to them in the land which you go to possess. Therefore be careful to observe them; for this is your wisdom and your understanding in the sight of the peoples who will hear all these statutes, and say, "Surely this great nation is a wise and understanding people." ' "

And he challenged the Hebrew multitude: " 'What great nation is there that has such statutes and righteous judgments as are in all this law which I set before you this day?' " The laws that God gave His ancient people were wiser, better, and more humane than those of the most civilized nations of the earth. God's law bears the stamp of the divine.

How must these words have moved the hearts of Israel as they remembered that Moses, who so glowingly pictured the blessings of the beautiful land, had been, through their sin, shut out from sharing the inheritance of his people:

" 'The land which you cross over to possess is a land of hills and valleys, which drinks water from the rain of heaven;' " " 'a land of brooks of water, of fountains and springs, that flow out of valleys and hills; a land of wheat and barley, of vines and fig trees and pomegranates, a land of olive oil and honey; a land in which you will eat bread without scarcity, in which you will lack nothing; a land whose stones are iron and out of whose hills you can dig copper' "; " 'a land for which the LORD your God cares; the eyes of the LORD your God are always on it, from the beginning of the year to the very end of the year.' " Deuteronomy 11:11; 8:7-9; 11:12.

" 'So it shall be, when the LORD your God brings you into the land of which He swore to your fathers, to Abraham, Isaac, and Jacob, to give you large and beautiful cities which you did not build, houses full of all good things, which you did not fill, hewn-out wells which you did not dig, vineyards and olive trees which you did not plant—when you have eaten and are full—then beware, lest you forget the LORD.' " " 'Take heed to yourselves, lest you forget the covenant of the LORD your God. . . . For the LORD your God is a consuming fire, a jealous God.' " If they would do evil in the sight of the Lord, then, said Moses, " 'You will soon utterly perish from the land which you cross over the Jordan to possess.' "

Moses completed the work of writing all the laws, statutes, and judgments that God had given him and the regulations concerning the sacrificial system. The book containing these was placed for safekeeping in the side of the ark.

Blessings Conditional

Still the great leader was filled with fear that the people would stray from God. In a lofty and thrilling address he set before them the blessings that would be theirs on condition of obedience, and the curses that would follow transgression:

" 'If you diligently obey the voice of the LORD your God, to observe carefully all His commandments which I command you today,' " " 'blessed shall you be in the city, and blessed shall you be in the country,' " in " 'the fruit of your body, the produce of your ground and the increase of your herds. . . . Blessed shall be your basket and your kneading bowl. . . . The LORD will cause your enemies who rise against you to be defeated before your face. . . . The LORD will command the blessing on you in your storehouses and in all to which you set your hand.' "

" 'But it shall come to pass, if you do not . . . observe carefully all His commandments and His statutes which I command you today, that all these curses will come upon you,' " " 'and you shall become an astonishment, a proverb, and a byword among all nations where the LORD will drive you.' " " 'Then the LORD will scatter you among all peoples, from one end of the earth to the other. . . . And among those nations you shall find no rest, nor shall the sole of your foot have a resting place; but there the LORD will give you a trembling heart, failing eyes, and anguish of soul. Your life shall hang in doubt before you; you shall fear day and night, and have no assurance of life. In the morning you shall say, "Oh, that it were evening!" And at evening you shall say, "Oh, that it were morning!" ' "

By the Spirit of Inspiration, looking far down the ages, Moses pictured the terrible scenes of Israel's final overthrow as a nation and the destruction of Jerusalem by the armies of Rome. The horrible sufferings of the people centuries later during the siege of Jerusalem under Titus were vividly portrayed: " 'They shall besiege you at all your gates until your high and fortified walls, in which you trust, come down throughout all your land. . . . You shall eat the fruit of your own body, the flesh of your sons and your daughters . . . in the siege and desperate straits in which your enemy shall distress you.' " " 'The tender and delicate woman among you, who would not venture to set the sole of her foot on the ground because of her delicateness and sensitivity, will refuse to the husband of her bosom . . . her children whom she bears; for she will eat them secretly for lack of all things in the siege and desperate straits in which your enemy shall distress you at all your gates.' "

Moses closed with these impressive words: " 'I call heaven and earth as witnesses today against you, that I have set before you life and death, blessing and cursing; therefore choose life, that both you and your descendants may live; that you may

love the LORD your God, that you may obey His voice, and that you may cling to Him, for He is your life and the length of your days; and that you may dwell in the land which the LORD swore to your fathers, to Abraham, Isaac, and Jacob, to give them.' " Deuteronomy 30:19, 20.

To impress these truths more deeply on all minds, the great leader put them into sacred verse. The people were to commit this poetic history to memory and teach it to their children and grandchildren, so that it would never be forgotten.

In the future, when their children would ask, " 'What is the meaning of the testimonies, the statutes, and the judgments which the LORD our God has commanded you?' " then the parents were to repeat the history of God's gracious dealings with them— how the Lord had acted to deliver them so that they might obey His law: " 'The LORD commanded us to observe all these statutes, to fear the LORD our God, for our good always, that He might preserve us alive, as it is this day. Then it will be righteousness for us, if we are careful to observe all these commandments before the LORD our God, as He has commanded us.' "

The Death of Moses*

In all God's dealings with His people, mingled with His love and mercy is the most striking evidence of His strict and impartial justice. The great Ruler of nations had declared that Moses was not to lead Israel into the beautiful land, and the earnest pleading of God's servant could not reverse His sentence. Yet Moses had faithfully tried to prepare the congregation to enter the promised inheritance. At God's command, Moses and Joshua went to the tabernacle, while the pillar of cloud came and stood over the door. Here the people were solemnly committed to the care of Joshua. The work of Moses as leader of Israel was ended.

Still he forgot himself in his interest for his people. In the presence of the multitude, Moses addressed these words of holy cheer to his successor in the name of God: " 'Be strong and of good courage; for you shall bring the children of Israel into the land of which I swore to them, and I will be with you.' " He then turned to the elders and officers of the people, giving them a solemn command to obey faithfully the instructions he had given them from God.

As the people gazed on the old man so soon to be taken from them, they recalled with new appreciation his fatherly tenderness, his wise counsels, and his untiring labors. They remembered bitterly that their own misbehavior had provoked Moses to the sin for which he must die.

God wanted them not to make the life of their future leader as difficult as they had made the life of Moses. God speaks to His people by giving them blessings, and when they do not appreciate these, He speaks to them by removing the blessings.

That very day the command came to Moses, " 'Go up . . . Mount Nebo . . . ; view the land of Canaan, which I give to the children of Israel as a possession; and die on the mountain which you ascend, and be gathered to your people.' " Moses was now to leave on a new and mysterious errand. He must go out to resign his life into the hands of his Creator. He knew that he was to die alone; no earthly friend would be permitted to minister to him in his last hours. There was a mystery and awfulness about the scene from

---

* This chapter is based on Deuteronomy 31 to 34.

which his heart drew back. The severest trial was to be separated from the people with whom his life had been united for so long. But with unquestioning faith he committed himself and his people to God's love and mercy.

Moses' Last Blessing

For the last time Moses stood in the assembly of his people. Again the Spirit of God rested on him, and in grand and touching language he pronounced a blessing on each of the tribes, closing with a special blessing on them all:

"The eternal God is your refuge,
And underneath are the everlasting
    arms. . . .
Then Israel shall dwell in safety,
The fountain of Jacob alone,
In a land of grain and new wine;
His Heavens shall also drop dew.
Happy are you, O Israel!
Who is like you,
    a people saved by the LORD,
The shield of your help."
Deuteronomy 33:27-29

Moses turned from the congregation, and in silence and alone made his way up "Mount Nebo, to the top of Pisgah." On that lonely height he stood and gazed with undimmed eyes on the scene spread out before him.

Far away to the west lay the blue waters of the Mediterranean Sea. In the north Mount Hermon stood out against the sky. To the east was the high plain of Moab. And beyond lay Bashan, the scene of Israel's tri-umph. To the south stretched the desert, where they had wandered so long.

Alone, Moses reviewed his life of hardships since he turned from courtly honors and from a prospective kingdom in Egypt to stake his future with God's chosen people. He called to mind those long years in the desert with Jethro's flocks, the Angel's appearance at the burning bush, and his call to deliver Israel. Again he could see the mighty miracles of God's power displayed on behalf of the chosen people and His long-suffering mercy during the years of their wandering and rebellion. Of all the adults in the vast army that left Egypt, only two had been found so faithful that they could enter the Promised Land. His life of trial and sacrifice seemed to have been almost in vain.

Yet he knew that God had given him his mission and work. When first called to lead Israel from bondage, he shrank from the responsibility, but he had not refused the burden. Even when the Lord had proposed to release him and destroy rebellious Israel, Moses could not consent. He had received special evidences of God's favor; he had obtained a rich experience in the fellowship of God's love during the stay in the wilderness. He felt he had made a wise decision in choosing to bear affliction with the people of God rather than to enjoy the pleasures of sin for a season.

As he looked back on his experience, one wrong act spoiled the record. If that transgression could be blotted out, he felt that he would be ready to die. He was assured that repentance and faith in the promised Sacrifice were all that God required, and again Moses confessed his sin and asked earnestly for pardon in the name of Jesus.

Now a panoramic view of the Land of Promise was presented to him, not faint and uncertain in the dim distance but standing clear, distinct, and beautiful to his delighted vision. In this scene he saw it not as it then appeared but as it would become with God's blessing. There were mountains clothed with cedars, hills gray with olives and fragrant with the scent of the vine, wide green plains bright with flowers and rich in fruitfulness, palm trees, waving fields of wheat and barley, sunny valleys musical with the ripple of brooks and the song of birds, beautiful cities and lovely gardens, lakes rich in "the abundance of the seas," grazing flocks on the hillsides, and even amid the rocks the wild bees' hoarded treasures. It was truly such a land as Moses, inspired by the Spirit of God, had described to Israel.

Moses Previews Israel's History

Moses saw the chosen people in Canaan, each of the tribes in its own territory. He had a view of their history—the long, sad story of their apostasy and its punishment. He saw them dispersed among the nations, the glory departed from Israel, her beautiful city in ruins, and her people captives in strange lands. He saw them restored to the land of their heritage, and at last brought under the dominion of Rome.

He was permitted to behold the first advent of our Savior. He saw Jesus as a baby in Bethlehem. He heard the voices of the angel choir break forth in the glad song of praise to God and peace on earth. In the night sky he saw the star guiding the Wise Men of the east to Jesus, and a great light flooded his mind as he recalled those prophetic words, " 'A Star shall come out of Jacob; a Scepter shall rise out of Israel.' " Numbers 24:17. He witnessed Christ's humble life in Nazareth, His ministry of love and sympathy and healing. He saw Him rejected by a proud, unbelieving nation. Amazed, he listened to their boastful exaltation of the law of God, while they despised and rejected Him by whom the law was given. He saw Jesus on the Mount of Olives as with tears He said Goodbye to the city of His love.

As Moses watched the final rejection of that people for whom he had worked, prayed, and sacrificed, for whom he had been willing to have his own name blotted from the book of life, as he listened to those fearful words, " 'See! Your house is left to you desolate' " (Matthew 23:38), his heart was torn with anguish. Bitter tears fell from his eyes in sympathy with the sorrow of the Son of God.

Moses Sees the Crucifixion and the Earth Made New

He followed the Savior to Gethsemane and saw the agony in the garden, the betrayal, the mockery and scourging, the crucifixion. Moses saw that as he had lifted up the bronze serpent in the wilderness, so the Son of God must be lifted up, so " 'that whoever believes in Him should not perish but have eternal life.' " John 3:15. Grief, indignation, and horror filled the heart of Moses as he viewed the hypocrisy and satanic hatred of the Jewish nation directed against their Redeemer.

He heard Christ's agonizing cry, " 'My God, my God, why have You forsaken me?' " Mark 15:34. He saw Him lying in Joseph's new tomb. The darkness of hopeless despair seemed to enshroud the world. But he looked again and saw Him a conqueror ascending to heaven, escorted by adoring angels and leading a multitude of captives rescued from the grave.

Moses watched the disciples of Jesus as they went out to carry His gospel to the world. Though Israel "according to the flesh" had failed to be the light of the world, though they had forfeited their blessings as His chosen people, yet God had not cast off the children of Abraham. All who through Christ would become the children of faith were to be counted as Abraham's descendants, inheritors of the covenant promises. Like Abraham they were called to make known to the world the law of God and the gospel of His Son. Moses saw the light of the gospel shining through the disciples of Jesus and thousands from the lands of the Gentiles accepting the faith. He rejoiced in the increase and prosperity of Israel.

And now another scene passed before him. He had been shown how Satan would lead the Jews to reject Christ while they professed to honor His Father's law. He now saw the world under a similar deception, claiming to accept Christ while rejecting God's law. He had heard from the priests and elders the frenzied cry, "Away with Him!" "Crucify Him, crucify Him!" And now he heard from professedly Christian teachers the cry, "Away with the law!"

He saw the Sabbath trampled underfoot and a substitute day of worship established in its place. Moses was filled with astonishment and horror. How could those who believed in Christ set aside the law that is the foundation of His government in heaven and earth? With joy Moses saw the law of God still honored and exalted by a faithful few. He saw the last great struggle of earthly powers to destroy those who keep God's law. He heard God's covenant of peace with those who have kept His law, as He speaks from His holy habitation. He saw the second coming of Christ in glory, the righteous dead raised to immortal life, and the living saints translated without seeing death and together ascending with songs of gladness to the City of God.

Still another scene opens to his view—the earth freed from the curse, lovelier than the fair Land of Promise so recently spread out before him. No sin is there, and death cannot enter. With joy unspeakable Moses looks on the scene, a more glorious deliverance than his brightest hopes have ever pictured. With their earthly wanderings forever past, the Israel of God have at last entered the beautiful land.

Again the vision faded, and his eyes rested on the land of Canaan in the distance. Then, like a tired warrior, he lay down to rest. "So Moses the servant of the LORD died there in the land of Moab, according to the word of the LORD. And He buried him in a valley in the land of Moab, opposite Beth Peor; but no one knows his grave." If they had known the place of his burial, many would have been in danger of committing idolatry over his dead body. For this reason the site was kept secret. Angels of God buried the body of His faithful servant and watched over the lonely grave.

But he was not long to remain in the tomb. Christ Himself, with the angels who had buried Moses, came down from heaven to call forth the sleeping saint. Satan had rejoiced at his success in causing Moses to sin and thus come under the dominion of death. The great adversary declared that the divine sentence, " 'Dust you are, and to dust you shall return' " (Genesis 3:19), gave him possession of the dead. The power of the grave had never been broken, and he claimed all who were in the tomb as his captives, never to be released.

As the Prince of life and the shining ones approached the grave, Satan was alarmed for his supremacy. He stood to dispute an invasion of the territory that he claimed as his own. He declared that even Moses was not able to keep the law of God. He had taken to himself the glory due to Jehovah, the very sin that had caused Satan to be banished from heaven, and by transgression he had come under the dominion of Satan. The traitor-in-chief repeated the original charges he had made, that God was unjust toward him.

Christ might have reminded him of the cruel work that his deceptions had brought about in heaven, causing the ruin of a vast number of its inhabitants. He might have pointed to the falsehoods told in Eden that had led to Adam's sin and brought death on the human race. He might have reminded Satan that it was his own work in tempting Israel to complain and rebel that had worn down the longsuffering patience of their leader and in an unguarded moment had surprised him into the sin for which he had fallen under death. But Christ referred all to His Father, saying, " 'The Lord rebuke you!' " Jude 9. The Savior entered into no dispute with His adversary, but then and there began His work of breaking Satan's power and bringing the dead to life. Here was evidence of Jesus' supremacy. Satan was deprived of his prey; the righteous dead would live again. Moses came out from the tomb glorified, and he ascended with his Deliverer to the City of God.

God shut Moses out of Canaan to teach a lesson that we should never forget—that He requires exact obedience and that all should beware of taking to themselves the glory due their Maker. He could not grant the prayer of Moses that he share the inheritance of Israel, but He did not forget or forsake His servant. On the top of Pisgah, God called Moses to an inheritance infinitely more glorious than the earthly Canaan.

On the mount of transfiguration Moses was present with Elijah, who had been translated. And thus the prayer of Moses was at last fulfilled. He stood on "the pleasant mountain," within the heritage of his people, bearing witness to Him in whom all the promises to Israel centered. This is the last scene revealed to mortal vision in the history of that man so highly honored by Heaven.

Crossing the Jordan*

Not until their departed leader was taken from them did the Israelites fully realize the value of his wise counsels, his parental tenderness, and his unswerving faith.

Moses was dead, but his influence would live on. After the sun has sunk behind the hills, its glow still lights up the mountain peaks; so the works of the holy and the good shed light on the world long after those who performed these deeds have passed away. "The righteous will be in everlasting remembrance." Psalm 112:6.

While the people were filled with grief at their great loss, they were not left alone. The pillar of cloud rested over the tabernacle by day and the pillar of fire by night. God was willing still to be their guide and helper if they would walk in the way of His commandments.

Joshua was now the recognized leader of Israel. Courageous, persistent, unmindful of self, and above all, inspired by a living faith in God—this was the kind of man God chose to lead the armies of Israel. He had acted as prime minister to Moses, and by his quiet, sincere faithfulness, his firmness when others wavered, his determination to maintain the truth in the midst of danger, he had shown his fitness to succeed Moses.

Joshua looked to the work before him with great anxiety, but the assurance of God removed his fears: " 'As I was with Moses, so I will be with you: I will not leave you nor forsake you. . . . To this people you shall divide as an inheritance the land which I swore to their fathers to give them.' "
" 'Every place that the sole of your foot will tread upon I have given you.' "
" 'Only be strong and very courageous, that you may observe to do according to all the law which Moses My servant commanded. . . . This Book of the Law shall not depart from your mouth, but you shall meditate in it day and night.' " " 'Do not turn from it to the right hand or to the left. . . . For then you will make your way prosperous, and then you will have good success.' "

" 'Arise' " had been the first message of God to Joshua, " 'go over this Jordan, you and all this people, to the land which I am giving to them.' " Joshua knew that whatever God would command, He would make a way for His people to perform. In this

_____

* This chapter is based on Joshua 1 to 5:12.

faith the courageous leader at once began preparations for an advance.

Just across from the Israelites' camp was the strongly fortified city of Jericho, the key to the whole country. It would present a major obstacle to Israel. So, Joshua sent two young men as spies to learn something about its population, resources, and strength of fortifications. The inhabitants of the city, terrified and suspicious, were on the alert, and the messengers were in great danger. But they were preserved by Rahab, a woman of Jericho, at the risk of her own life. In return for her kindness, they promised her protection when the city would be taken.

People of Jericho Already Terrified

The spies returned with the report, " 'Truly the LORD has delivered all the land into our hands, for indeed all the inhabitants of the country are fainthearted because of us.' " In Jericho they had been told, " 'We have heard how the LORD dried up the water of the Red Sea for you when you came out of Egypt, and what you did to the two kings of the Amorites who were on the other side of the Jordan, Sihon and Og, whom you utterly destroyed. And as soon as we heard these things, our hearts melted; neither did there remain any more courage in anyone because of you, for the LORD your God, He is God in heaven above and on earth beneath.' "

Orders were now issued to prepare to advance. The people were to take a three-day supply of food, and the army was to be prepared for battle. Leaving their encampment, the host went down to the edge of the Jordan. All knew that without divine aid they could not hope to cross the river. At this time of year the melting snows of the mountains had raised the Jordan so that the river overflowed, making it impossible to ford. It was God's will that the crossing of Jordan should be miraculous.

By divine direction, Joshua commanded the people to put away their sins and free themselves from all outward impurity, " 'for tomorrow,' " he said, " 'the LORD will do wonders among you.' " The "ark of the covenant" was to lead the way, carried toward the river by the priests from its place in the center of the camp. " 'By this you shall know that the living God is among you, and that He will without fail drive out from before you the Canaanites. . . . Behold, the ark of the covenant of the Lord of all the earth is crossing over before you into the Jordan.' "

At the appointed time the onward movement began, with the ark leading, carried on the shoulders of the priests. A vacant space of more than half a mile separated the ark from the people. All watched with deep interest as the priests advanced down the bank of the Jordan. They saw the sacred ark move steadily toward the surging stream till the feet of the bearers went into the waters. Then suddenly the tide above was swept back, while the current below flowed on, and the bed of the river was exposed.

The priests advanced to the middle of the channel and stood there while the entire mass of people descended and crossed to the farther side. The power that held back the waters of Jordan was the same that had opened the Red Sea to the previous generation forty years before. When the people had all passed over, the ark itself was carried to the western shore. No sooner had "the soles of the priests' feet touched the dry land" than the imprisoned waters rushed down, an overpowering flood, in the natural channel of the stream.

While the priests bearing the ark were still in the middle of the Jordan, twelve men, one from each tribe, each took a stone from the riverbed where the priests were standing and carried them over to the western side. These stones were to be set up as a monument in the first camping place beyond the river, as Joshua said, " 'that all the peoples of the earth may know the hand of the LORD, that it is mighty, that you may fear the LORD your God forever.' "

This miracle assured Israel of God's continued presence and protection, demonstrating that He would work for them through Joshua as He had through Moses. The Lord had declared to Joshua before the crossing, " 'This day I will begin to exalt you in the sight of all Israel, that they may know that, as I was with Moses, so I will be with you.' "

When the news that God had held back the waters of Jordan for the children of Israel reached the kings of the Amorites and Canaanites, their hearts melted with fear. To the Canaanites, to all Israel, and to Joshua himself, unmistakable evidence had been given that the living God, the King of heaven and earth, was among His people. He would not fail them nor forsake them.

A short distance from Jordan the Hebrews made their first camp in Canaan. The suspension of the Passover and the rite of circumcision had been an evidence of the Lord's displeasure because of their desire to return to the land of bondage and their breaking of the covenant. Now, however, the years of rejection had ended. The sign of the covenant was restored. The rite of circumcision was performed on those who had been born in the wilderness. And the Lord declared to Joshua, " 'This day I have rolled away the reproach of Egypt from you.' "

Heathen nations had ridiculed the Lord and His people because the Hebrews had failed to take possession of Canaan soon after leaving Egypt. Their enemies had triumphed because Israel had wandered so long in the wilderness, and they had mockingly declared that the God of the Hebrews was not able to bring them into the Promised Land. The Lord had now unmistakably shown His power and favor by opening the Jordan before His people, and their enemies could no longer deride them.

They celebrated the Passover, and "the manna ceased on the day after they had eaten the produce of the land; and the children of Israel no longer had manna, but they ate the food of the land of Canaan." The long years of their desert wanderings were over. The feet of Israel were at last treading the Promised Land.

The Miraculous Fall of Jericho *

The Hebrews had entered Canaan but they had not conquered it. It was inhabited by a powerful race that stood ready to oppose the invasion of their territory. Their horses and iron battle chariots, their knowledge of the country, and their training in war would give them great advantage. Further, the country was guarded by " 'cities great and fortified up to heaven.' " Deuteronomy 9:1. In the coming conflict the Israelites could hope for success only in the assurance of a strength not their own.

The large and wealthy city of Jericho lay just a short distance from their camp at Gilgal. Behind its massive fortifications, this proud city defied the God of Israel. Jericho was especially devoted to Ashtaroth, the goddess of the moon. Here centered all the most vile and degrading aspects of the Canaanite religion. With the fearful results of their sin at Beth Peor fresh on their minds, the people of Israel could look upon this heathen city only with disgust and horror.

Joshua saw taking Jericho as the first step in the conquest of Canaan. Withdrawing from the camp to meditate and pray, he saw an impressive armed warrior "with His sword drawn in His hand." To Joshua's challenge, " 'Are You for us or for our adversaries?' " the answer was given, " 'As Commander of the army of the LORD I have now come.' " The mysterious stranger was Christ, the Exalted One. Awe-struck, Joshua fell on his face and worshiped. Then he heard the assurance, " 'I have given Jericho into your hand, its king, and the mighty men of valor,' " and he received instruction for capturing the city.

In obedience to the divine command, Joshua marshaled the armies of Israel. No assault was to be made. They were simply to walk around the city, carrying the ark of God and blowing trumpets. The ark of God, surrounded by a halo of divine glory, was carried by priests dressed in the special clothing of their sacred office. The army of Israel followed. Such was the procession that circled the doomed city.

No sound was heard but the tread of that mighty host and the solemn blast of the trumpets, echoing among

* This chapter is based on Joshua 5:13-15; 6; 7.

the hills and resounding through the streets of Jericho.

Amazed and alarmed, the watchmen of the city reported to those in authority. When they saw that mighty assembly marching around their city once each day, with the sacred ark and the attendant priests, the mystery of the scene struck terror to the hearts of priest and people. They inspected their strong defenses again, feeling certain they could successfully resist the most powerful attack. Many ridiculed the thought that any harm would come to them through these odd demonstrations. Others were awed as they watched the procession each day. They remembered that the Red Sea had once parted before this people and that a passage had just been opened for them through the river Jordan.

God's Simple Method of Conquering Jericho

For six days Israel made the circuit of the city. The seventh day came, and with the first dawn of light, Joshua marshaled the armies of the Lord. Now they were to march seven times around Jericho, and at a mighty blast from the trumpets they were to shout with a loud voice, for God had given them the city.

The vast army marched solemnly around the walls. All was silent, except the steady tread of many feet. The watchers on the walls looked on with rising fear as the first circuit ended, and there followed a second, then a third, a fourth, a fifth, a sixth. What could be the purpose of these mysterious movements?

They did not have long to wait. As the seventh circuit was completed, the long procession stopped. The trumpets, which for a time had been silent, now broke forth in a blast that shook the very earth. The walls of solid stone, with their massive towers and defenses, tottered and heaved from their foundations, and fell to the earth with a crash. The inhabitants of Jericho were paralyzed with terror, and the armies of Israel marched in and took the city.

The Israelites had not gained the victory by their own power; and as firstfruits of the land, the city and all it contained were to be devoted as a sacrifice to God. In the conquest of Canaan the Israelites were not to fight for themselves, not to seek for riches or self-exaltation, but for the glory of Jehovah their king. The command had been given, " 'Keep yourselves from the accursed things, lest you become accursed . . . and make the camp of Israel a curse, and trouble it.' "

All the inhabitants, with every living thing, were killed. Only faithful Rahab with her household was spared in fulfillment of the spies' promise. The city palaces and temples, its magnificent dwellings with all their luxurious furnishings, the rich draperies and the costly garments, were burned. Whatever could not be destroyed by fire, " 'the silver and gold, and vessels of bronze and iron,' " was to be devoted to the service of the tabernacle. Jericho was never to be rebuilt as a stronghold; judgments were threatened on anyone who would presume to restore the walls that divine power had thrown down.

The utter destruction of the people of Jericho was a fulfillment of commands previously given concerning the inhabitants of Canaan: " 'You shall conquer them and utterly destroy them.' " " 'Of the cities of these peoples, . . . you shall let nothing that breathes remain alive.' " Deuteronomy 7:2; 20:16.

To many these commands seem contrary to the spirit of love and mercy commanded in other portions of the Bible. But they were actually the instructions of infinite wisdom and goodness. God was about to establish Israel in Canaan. They were not only to be inheritors of the true religion, they were to spread its principles throughout the world. The Canaanites had abandoned themselves to debasing heathenism, and it was necessary that the country be cleared of anything that would surely prevent God's gracious purposes from being fulfilled.

The inhabitants had been given plenty of opportunity to repent. Forty years before, the judgments on Egypt had testified to the power of the God of Israel. The defeat of Midian, of Gilead and Bashan, had further shown that He was above all gods. His hatred of impurity had been demonstrated in the judgments on Israel for taking part in the abominable rites of Baal Peor. The inhabitants of Jericho knew of all these events. Though they refused to obey it, many shared Rahab's conviction that the God of Israel " 'is God in heaven above and on earth beneath.' " Like the people

before the Flood, the Canaanites lived only to blaspheme Heaven and defile the earth. Both love and justice demanded that these rebels against God and foes of humanity be destroyed.

"By faith the walls of Jericho fell down." Hebrews 11:30. The Commander of the Lord's host communicated only with Joshua, not to all the congregation. It rested with them to believe or doubt the words of Joshua. *They* could not see the army of angels who attended them under the leadership of the Son of God. They might have reasoned: "How ridiculous, marching daily around the walls of the city, blowing trumpets of rams' horns. This can have no effect on those towering fortifications." But God wanted to impress on their minds that their strength was not in human wisdom or might but only in the God of their salvation. God will do great things for those who trust Him. If they will place their entire confidence in Him and faithfully obey Him, He will help His believing children in every emergency.

Why Israel Was Defeated at Ai

Soon after the fall of Jericho, Joshua prepared to attack Ai, a small town among the hills a few miles west of the Jordan Valley. Spies brought the report that the inhabitants were few, and only a small force would be needed to overthrow it.

The great victory that God had given them had made the Israelites self-confident. They failed to realize that divine help alone could give them success. Even Joshua laid his plans for the conquest of Ai without seeking counsel from God.

The Israelites had begun to look on their foes with contempt. They expected an easy victory and thought three thousand men were enough to take the place. These marched almost to the city's gate, only to meet determined resistence. Panic-stricken at how many and well-prepared their enemies were, they fled in confusion down the steep slope. The Canaanites "chased them from before the gate . . . and struck them down on the descent." Though the loss was small in numbers—thirty-six men killed—the defeat was disheartening. "The hearts of the people melted and became like water."

Joshua looked on their defeat as an expression of God's displeasure. In distress and concern he "tore his clothes, and fell to the earth on his face before the ark of the Lord until evening, both he and the elders of Israel; and they put dust on their heads."

" 'Alas, Lord GOD,' " he cried, " 'why have You brought this people over the Jordan at all—to deliver us into the hand of the Amorites, to destroy us? . . . O Lord, what shall I say when Israel turns its back before its enemies? For the Canaanites and all the inhabitants of the land will hear of it, and surround us, and cut off our name from the earth. Then what will You do for Your great name?' "

The answer was, " 'Get up! Why do you lie thus on your face? Israel has . . . transgressed My covenant which I commanded them.' " It was a time for prompt and decided action,

not for despair and wailing. There was secret sin in the camp, and it must be searched out and put away. " 'Neither will I be with you anymore, unless you destroy the accursed from among you.' "

One Family's Sin Brings Defeat to All Israel

One of those appointed to execute God's judgments had disregarded His command. And the nation was held accountable for the transgressor's guilt: " 'They have even taken some of the accursed things, and have stolen and deceived.' " They were to cast lots to detect the guilty. This took a little time and left the matter in doubt so that the people might feel their responsibility and be led to search their hearts and humble themselves before God.

Early in the morning, Joshua gathered the people together, and the solemn and impressive ceremony began. Step by step the investigation went on. Closer and closer came the fearful test. First the tribe, then the family, then the household, then the man was selected, and the finger of God pointed out Achan the son of Carmi, of the tribe of Judah, as the troubler of Israel.

After Joshua solemnly commanded Achan to admit the truth, the wretched man made full confession of his crime: " 'Indeed I have sinned against the LORD God of Israel. . . . When I saw among the spoils a beautiful Babylonian garment, two hundred shekels of silver, and a wedge of gold weighing fifty shekels, I coveted them and took them. And there they are, hidden in the earth in the midst of my tent.' " Messengers removed the earth at the place specified, and "there it was, hidden in his tent, with the silver under it. And they . . . brought them to Joshua . . . and laid them out before the LORD."

" 'Why have you troubled us?' " demanded Joshua. " 'The LORD will trouble you this day.' " Because the people had been held responsible for Achan's sin and had suffered from its consequences, they were to take part in its punishment. "All Israel stoned him with stones." In the book of Chronicles his memorial is written—"Achar, the troubler of Israel." 1 Chronicles 2:7.

Achan committed his sin in defiance of direct, solemn warnings and mighty displays of God's power. The fact that divine power alone had given victory to Israel, that they had not taken Jericho by their own strength, gave solemn weight to the command forbidding them to partake of the spoils. God had overthown this stronghold, and the city with all that it contained was to be devoted to Him alone.

Achan Refuses to Repent

Of the millions of Israel there was only one man who had dared to transgress the command of God. Achan's covetousness was awakened by that costly robe from Shinar; even when it had brought him face to face with death he called it "a *beautiful* Babylonian garment." And he took the gold and silver devoted to the treasury of the Lord; he robbed God of the firstfruits of the land of Ca-

naan. Rarely is violation of the tenth commandment even rebuked. The enormity of this sin, and its terrible results, are the lessons of Achan's history.

Achan had cherished greed for wealth until it became a habit, binding him in chains almost impossible to break. He would have been filled with horror at the thought of bringing disaster on Israel; but his perceptions were deadened by sin, and when temptation came, he fell an easy victim.

We are as directly forbidden to covet as Achan was to take the spoils of Jericho. We are warned, " 'You cannot serve God and mammon.' " " 'Take heed and beware of covetousness.' " "Let it not even be named among you." Matthew 6:24; Luke 12:15; Ephesians 5:3. We have as examples the fearful doom of Achan, of Judas, of Ananias and Sapphira. Back of all these we have Lucifer. Yet, despite all these warnings, covetousness is widespread.

Everywhere its slimy track is seen. It creates strife in families; it excites envy and hatred in the poor against the rich; it prompts the rich to grind down the poor. And this evil exists not just in the world but in the church. How common even here to find selfishness, greed, neglect of charities, and robbery of God "in tithes and offerings." Many a churchgoer comes regularly to communion service, while among his possessions are hidden unlawful gains, things that God has cursed. For a "beautiful Babylonian garment" multitudes sacrifice their hope of heaven. The cries of the suffering and poor go unheeded; the gospel light is hindered in its course; practices contradict the Christian profession; yet the covetous so-called Christian continues to heap up treasures. " 'Will a man rob God? Yet you have robbed Me' " (Malachi 3:8), says the Lord.

The Difference Between Genuine and Forced Confessions

For one person's sin the displeasure of God will rest on His church till the transgression is found and put away. The influence the church should fear the most is not that of open opposers, infidels, and blasphemers but of inconsistent ones that keep back the blessing of the God of Israel and bring weakness on His people. With deep repentance and searching of heart, let each seek to discover the hidden sins that shut out God's presence.

Achan had seen the armies of Israel return from Ai defeated and disheartened, yet he did not come forward and confess his sin. He had seen Joshua and the elders bowed to the earth in grief too great for words. But he still kept silence. He had listened to the announcement that a great crime had been committed and had even heard its nature stated clearly. But his lips were sealed. His heart filled with terror as he saw his tribe pointed out, then his family and his household! But still he did not confess until the finger of God was placed on him. Then, when he could no longer hide his sin, he admitted the truth.

There is a vast difference between admitting facts after they have been proved and confessing sins known only to ourselves and to God. Achan's confession only served to show that his punishment was just. He had no genuine repentance, no sorrow for sin, no change of purpose, no abhorrence of evil.

Similarly, the guilty will make their confessions when they stand before the judgment bar of God, after every case has been decided for life or death. An acknowledgment of sin will be forced from each of the lost by an awful sense of condemnation and a fearful looking for of judgment. But such confessions cannot save the sinner.

When the records of heaven are opened, the Judge will not declare to the sinner his guilt but will cast one penetrating, convicting glance, and every deed, every transaction of life, will be vividly impressed on the memory of the wrongdoer. The sins long hidden from human eyes will then be proclaimed to the whole world.

The Blessings and the Curses[*]

After the execution of the sentence on Achan, Joshua was commanded to gather all the men of war and again advance against Ai. The power of God was with His people, and in short order they captured the city.

The people were eager to settle in Canaan; they had no homes or lands yet for their families, and to get these they must drive out the Canaanites. But a higher duty demanded their first attention. They must renew their covenant of loyalty to God.

Moses' last instructions had included directions to hold a special service on Mounts Ebal and Gerizim at Shechem, to recognize the law of God. So, in obedience, the men, "the women, the little ones, and the strangers who were living among them" left Gilgal and marched through the country of their enemies to the valley of Shechem, near the center of the land. Though they were surrounded by unconquered enemies, "the terror of God was upon the cities that were all around them" (Genesis 35:5), and the Hebrews were not attacked or threatened.

Here both Abraham and Jacob had pitched their tents. Here Jacob bought the field in which the tribes were to bury the body of Joseph. Here also was the well that Jacob had dug.

The spot chosen was well fit to be the theater to enact this impressive scene. The lovely valley, its green fields dotted with olive groves, watered with brooks from living fountains, and hemmed with wild flowers, spread out invitingly between the barren hills. Ebal and Gerizim, on opposite sides of the valley, nearly approach each other, their lower spurs seeming to form a natural pulpit. Every word spoken on one was distinctly audible on the other. The mountainsides, receding, afforded space for a vast assembly.

A monument of great stones was set up on Mount Ebal. On these stones, previously prepared by a covering of plaster, Joshua inscribed the law—not only the ten precepts spoken from Sinai and engraved on tables of stone but the law communicated to Moses and written in a book. Beside this monument he

---

* This chapter is based on Joshua 8.

built an altar of unhewn stone and on it offered sacrifices to the Lord. Because of their transgressions of God's law, Israel justly deserved His wrath, and they would have felt it immediately if not for the atonement of Christ, represented by the altar of sacrifice.

Six tribes were stationed on Mount Gerizim, the others on Ebal, and the priests with the ark occupied the valley between. In the presence of this vast assembly, Joshua read the blessings that follow obedience to God's law. All the tribes on Gerizim responded, "Amen." He then read the curses, and the tribes on Ebal likewise gave their agreement, thousands upon thousands of voices uniting in the solemn response. Following this came the reading of the law of God, together with the statutes and judgments that Moses had delivered.

At Sinai Israel had received the law from the mouth of God, and its sacred precepts, written by His own hand, were preserved in the ark. Now it had been written again, where all could read for themselves the conditions of the covenant that was to prevail while they possessed Canaan. It had not been many weeks since Moses gave the whole book of Deuteronomy in speeches to the people, yet now Joshua read the law again.

Not only the men of Israel, but all the women and the little ones listened to the reading of the law, for it was important that they also should know and do their duty. Moses commanded: " 'At the end of every seven years, . . . when all Israel comes to appear before the LORD your God in the place which He chooses, you shall read this law before all Israel in their hearing. Gather the people together, men and women and little ones, and the stranger who is within your gates, that they may hear and that they may learn to fear the LORD your God and carefully observe all the words of this law, and that their children, who have not known it, may hear and learn to fear the LORD your God as long as you live in the land which you cross the Jordan to possess.' " Deuteronomy 31:10-13.

Why We Must Diligently Study God's Word

Satan is always at work trying to pervert what God has spoken, to darken the understanding and lead people into sin. God is constantly seeking to draw them close under His protection, so that Satan may not use his deceptive power on them. God has stooped low to speak to them with His own voice, to write with His own hand the living law committed to humanity as a perfect guide. Because Satan is so ready to turn the affections from the Lord's promises and requirements, great diligence is needed to anchor them firmly in the mind.

The facts and lessons of Bible history should be presented in simple language, adapted to the understanding of the young. Parents can interest their children in the variety of knowledge found in the sacred pages. But they must be interested themselves. Those who want their children to love and reverence God must talk of His goodness, His majesty, and His power, as revealed in His Word and in the works of creation.

Every chapter and every verse of the Bible is a communication from God to us. If studied and obeyed, it would lead God's people, as the Israelites were led, by the pillar of cloud by day and the pillar of fire by night.

A Canaanite Tribe Deceives Israel*

From Shechem the Israelites returned to their camp at Gilgal. Here a strange delegation visited them, claiming that they had come from a distant country. This seemed to be confirmed by the way they looked. Their clothing was old and worn, their sandals patched, their food moldy, and the skins that they used for wine bottles were torn and patched, as if hastily repaired on the journey.

In their "far off" home—professedly a long way from Palestine—they had heard of the wonders that God had performed and had been sent to make a treaty with Israel. The Hebrews had been specially warned against entering into any treaty with the idolaters of Canaan, and a doubt arose in the minds of the leaders about the truth of the strangers' words.

" 'Perhaps you dwell among us,' " they said. To this the ambassadors replied, " 'We are your servants.' " But when Joshua directly demanded of them, " 'Who are you, and where do you come from?' " they added, " 'This bread of ours we took hot for our provision from our houses on the day we departed to come to you. But now look, it is dry and moldy.

And these wineskins which we filled were new, and see, they are torn; and these our garments and our sandals have become old because of the very long journey.' "

The Hebrews "did not ask counsel of the LORD. So Joshua made peace with them, and made a covenant with them to let them live, and the rulers of the congregation swore to them." So the treaty was ratified. Three days afterward Israel discovered the truth. "They heard that they were their neighbors who dwelt near them." The Gibeonites had resorted to trickery to preserve their lives.

The Israelites became more indignant when, after three days' journey, they reached the cities of the Gibeonites near the center of the land. But the princes refused to break the treaty, though it was secured by fraud, because they had "sworn to them by the LORD God of Israel." "The children of Israel did not attack them." The Gibeonites had pledged themselves to renounce idolatry and accept the worship of Jehovah, and preserving their lives was not a violation of God's command to destroy the idolatrous Canaanites.

---

* This chapter is based on Joshua 9 and 10.

Though the oath had been secured by deception, it was not to be disregarded. No consideration of gain, of revenge, or self-interest can in any way affect the binding nature of an oath or pledge. He that "may ascend into the hill of the LORD," and "stand in His holy place," is "he who swears to his own hurt and does not change." Psalm 24:3; 15:4.

How the Gibeonites Made Themselves Slaves

The Gibeonites were permitted to live but were attached to the sanctuary as slaves to perform menial services. "That day Joshua made them woodcutters and water carriers for the congregation and for the altar of the LORD." These conditions they gratefully accepted, glad to purchase life on any terms. " 'Here we are, in your hands,' " they said to Joshua; " 'do with us as it seems good and right to do to us.' "

Gibeon, the most important of their towns, "was a great city, like one of the royal cities, . . . and all its men were mighty." It is a striking evidence of the terror with which the Israelites had inspired the inhabitants of Canaan, that the people of a powerful city would resort to such a humiliating means to save their lives.

But the Gibeonites would have been better off if they had dealt honestly with Israel. Their deception brought them only disgrace and slavery. God had made provision that all who would renounce heathenism and connect with Israel would share the blessings of the covenant. With few exceptions such people were to enjoy equal favors and privileges with Israel.

The Gibeonites could have been received on these terms. It was no minor humiliation to those citizens of a royal city, of which "all its men were mighty," to be made woodcutters and water carriers. Thus through all their generations, their servile condition would testify that God hates falsehood.

Joshua's Long Day

The submission of Gibeon filled the kings of Canaan with dismay. They took immediate steps for revenge on those who had made peace with the invaders. Five of the Canaanite kings allied themselves against Gibeon. The Gibeonites were unprepared for defense and sent a message to Joshua at Gilgal: " 'Do not forsake your servants; come up to us quickly, save us and help us, for all the kings of the Amorites who dwell in the mountains have gathered together against us.' " The danger threatened not only the people of Gibeon but also Israel. This city controlled the passes to central and southern Palestine, and Israel must hold it in order to conquer the country.

The besieged Gibeonites had feared that Joshua would reject their appeal because of the fraud that they had practiced. But since they had submitted to Israel and had accepted the worship of God, he felt obligated to protect them. And the Lord encouraged him. " 'Do not fear them,' " was the divine message, " 'for I have delivered them into your hand; not a man of them shall stand before you.' " "So Joshua ascended from

Gilgal, he and all the people of war with him, and all the mighty men of valor."

Scarcely had the allied princes mustered their armies around the city when Joshua was upon them. The immense host fled from the Hebrews up the mountain pass to Beth Horon, and from the top they rushed down the steep descent on the other side. Here a fierce hailstorm burst upon them. "The LORD cast down large hailstones from heaven. . . . There were more who died from the hailstones than the children of Israel killed with the sword."

While the Amorites were fleeing in panic, Joshua looked down from the ridge above and saw that the day would be too short to accomplish his work. If not fully defeated, their enemies would renew the struggle. "Then Joshua spoke to the LORD . . . , and he said in the sight of Israel: 'Sun, stand still over Gibeon; and Moon, in the Valley of Aijalon.' So the sun stood still, and the moon stopped, till the people had revenge upon their enemies. . . . The sun stood still in the midst of heaven, and did not hasten to go down for about a whole day."

Before evening fell, God's promise to Joshua had been fulfilled. The enemy had been given into his hand. The events of that day would long remain in the memory of Israel. "There has been no day like that, before it or after it, that the LORD heeded the voice of a man; for the LORD fought for Israel." "The sun and moon stood still in their habitation; at the light of Your arrows they went, at the shining of Your glittering spear. You marched through the land in indignation; You trampled the nations in anger. You went forth for the salvation of Your people." Habakkuk 3:11-13.

Joshua had received the promise that God would overthrow these enemies of Israel, yet he put forth an effort as earnest as though success depended on the armies of Israel alone. He did all that human energy could do, and then he called out in faith for divine aid. The secret of success is the union of divine power with human effort. The man who commanded, " 'Sun, stand still over Gibeon; and Moon, in the Valley of Aijalon,' " is the man who lay flat on the earth for hours in prayer at Gilgal. People of prayer are people of power.

This mighty miracle testifies that the creation is under the control of the Creator. In this miracle, all who exalt nature above the God of nature stand rebuked.

At His own will God gathers the forces of nature to overthrow the might of His enemies—"fire and hail, snow and clouds; stormy wind, fulfilling His word." Psalm 148:8. We are told of a greater battle to take place in the closing scenes of earth's history, when "the LORD has opened His armory, and has brought out the weapons of His indignation." Jeremiah 50:25.

John the revelator describes the destruction that is to take place when the "loud voice . . . out of the temple of heaven" announces, " 'It is done!' " He says, "Great hail from heaven fell upon men, every hailstone about the weight of a talent." Revelation 16:17, 21.

Home
at Last*

The victory at Beth Horon was speedily followed by the conquest of southern Canaan. "Joshua conquered all the land: the mountain country and the South and the lowland. . . . All these kings and their land Joshua took at one time, because the LORD God of Israel fought for Israel."

The tribes of northern Palestine, terrified at the success of Israel's armies, now entered into a league against them. "So they went out, they and all their armies with them." This army was much larger than any that the Israelites had encountered before in Canaan—"as many people as the sand that is on the seashore in multitude, with very many horses and chariots. And when all these kings had met together, they came and camped together at the waters of Merom to fight against Israel."

Again Joshua received a message of encouragement: " 'Do not be afraid because of them, for tomorrow about this time will I deliver all of them slain before Israel.' "

Near Lake Merom he attacked the camp of the allies, and "the LORD delivered them into the hand of Israel, who defeated them and chased them . . . until they left none of them remaining." At the command of God the chariots were burned and the horses lamed, thus making them unfit for battle. The Israelites were not to put their trust in chariots or horses, but in "the name of the LORD their God."

One by one the cities were taken, and Hazor, the stronghold of the confederacy, was burned. The war continued for several years, but at its close Joshua was master of Canaan. "Then the land rested from war."

The power of the Canaanites had been broken, but they had not been fully driven out. However, Joshua was not to continue the war. The whole land, both the parts already conquered and what was still not subdued, was to be apportioned among the tribes. Each tribe then had the duty to fully subdue its own inheritance. If the people proved faithful to God, He would drive out their enemies from before them.

The location for each tribe was determined by lot. Moses himself

---

* This chapter is based on Joshua 10:40-43; 11; 14 to 22.

had set the borders of the country as it was to be divided among the tribes, and he had appointed a prince from each tribe to attend to the distribution. Forty-eight cities in various parts of the country were assigned the Levites as their inheritance.

Caleb Asks for the Most Difficult Place

Caleb and Joshua were the only ones among the original twelve spies who had brought a good report of the Land of Promise, encouraging the people to go up and possess it in the name of the Lord. Caleb now reminded Joshua of the promise then made, as the reward of his faithfulness: " 'Surely the land where your foot has trodden shall be your inheritance and your children's forever, because you have wholly followed the Lord.' " He therefore requested that Hebron be given him as a homestead. Here had been the home of Abraham, Isaac, and Jacob, and here, in the cave of Machpelah, they were buried.

Hebron was the headquarters of the dreaded Anakim, whose impressive appearance had terrified the spies and destroyed the courage of all Israel. This was the place that Caleb, trusting in the strength of God, chose for his inheritance.

" 'Behold, the Lord has kept me alive,' " he said, " 'these forty-five years, ever since the Lord spoke this word to Moses . . . ; and now, here I am this day, eighty-five years old. As yet I am as strong this day as on the day that Moses sent me; just as my strength was then, so now is my strength for war, both for going out and for coming in. Now therefore, give me this mountain of which the Lord spoke in that day; for you heard in that day how the Anakim were there, and that the cities were great and fortified. It may be that the Lord will be with me, and I shall be able to drive them out as the Lord said.' "

His claim was immediately granted. "Joshua blessed him, and gave Hebron to Caleb the son of Jephunneh as an inheritance," "because he wholly followed the Lord God of Israel." Caleb had believed God's promise that He would put His people in possession of Canaan. He had endured the long wandering in the wilderness, sharing the disappointments and burdens of the guilty. Yet he made no complaint but exalted the mercy of God that preserved him in the wilderness when his brethren were claimed by death. He did not ask for a land already conquered but the place that, more than all others, the spies had thought impossible to subdue. The brave old warrior wanted to give the people an example that would honor God and encourage the tribes to subdue the land that the earlier generation had considered unconquerable.

Trusting in God to be with him, he "drove out the three sons of Anak." Then, having secured the land for himself and his household, he did not settle down to enjoy his inheritance but pushed on to further conquests for the benefit of the nation and the glory of God.

The cowards and rebels had perished in the wilderness, but the righteous spies ate of the grapes of Eshcol.* The unbelieving had seen their fears fulfilled. They had declared it impossible to inherit Canaan, and they did not possess it. But those who trusted in the strength of their Almighty Helper entered the beautiful land. Through faith the ancient worthies "subdued kingdoms, . . . escaped the edge of the sword, out of weakness were made strong, became valiant in battle, turned to flight the armies of the aliens." "This is the victory that has overcome the world—our faith." Hebrews 11:33, 34; 1 John 5:4.

Another claim revealed a spirit widely different from Caleb's. The children of Joseph, the tribe of Ephraim with the half tribe of Manasseh, demanded a double portion of territory. The portion designated for them was the richest in the land, including the fertile plain of Sharon; but many of the principal towns in the valley were still held by the Canaanites, and the tribes didn't want the toil and danger of conquering their inheritance, and desired an additional portion in territory already subdued. The tribe of Ephraim was one of the largest in Israel, as well as the one to which Joshua himself belonged. " 'Why have you given us only one lot and one share to inherit,' " they said, " 'since we are a great people?' "

But the inflexible leader's answer was, " 'If you are a great people, then go up to the forest country and clear a place for yourself there in the land of the Perizzites and the giants, since the mountains of Ephraim are too confined for you.' "

Their reply showed the real cause of complaint. They lacked faith and courage to drive out the Canaanites. " 'The mountain country is not enough for us,' " they said, " 'and all the Canaanites who dwell in the land of the valley have chariots of iron.' "

If the Ephraimites had possessed the courage and faith of Caleb, no enemy could have stood before them. Joshua firmly confronted their desire to shun hardship and danger: " 'You are a great people and have great power,' " he said; " 'you shall drive out the Canaanites, though they have iron chariots and are strong.' " With the help of God they need not fear the chariots of iron.

Now the tabernacle was to be taken from Gilgal to its permanent location, Shiloh, a little town in Ephraim near the center of the land, and easy for all the tribes to access. Here a portion of the country had been thoroughly subdued, so that worshipers would not be attacked. "Now the whole congregation of the children of Israel assembled together at Shiloh, and set up the tabernacle of meeting there."

The ark remained at Shiloh for three hundred years until, because of

---

*Eshcol was the place where, forty years before, the spies had cut a cluster of grapes that they carried on a pole between two men. See Numbers 13:23.

the sins of Eli's house, it was captured by the Philistines.

Shiloh Becomes a Warning

The sanctuary service was finally transferred to the temple at Jerusalem, and Shiloh fell into ruins. Long afterward God used Shiloh's fate as a warning to Jerusalem. " 'Go now to My place which was in Shiloh,' " the Lord declared by Jeremiah, " 'where I set My name at the first, and see what I did to it because of the wickedness of My people Israel. . . . Therefore I will do to this house which is called by My name, in which you trust, and to this place which I gave to you and your fathers, as I have done to Shiloh.' " Jeremiah 7:12, 14.

"When they had made an end of dividing the land," Joshua presented his claim. He asked for no extensive province, but only a single city, Timnath-serah, "the portion that remains." The conqueror, instead of being the first to take the spoils of conquest for himself, waited to make his claim until the humblest of his people had been served.

Cities of Refuge

Six cities assigned to the Levites were appointed as cities of refuge, " 'that the manslayer who kills any person accidentally may flee there. They shall be cities of refuge . . . , that the manslayer may not die until he stands before the congregation in judgment.' " Numbers 35:11, 12. This merciful provision was necessary because responsibility to punish the murderer fell to the nearest rela-

tive or the next heir of the one killed. In cases where guilt was clearly evident, it was not necessary to wait for a trial by magistrates. The avenger might pursue the criminal and put him to death wherever he could be found. The Lord did not abolish this custom but made provision to ensure the safety of those who took life unintentionally.

The cities of refuge could be reached within half a day from every part of the land. The roads leading to them were always kept in good repair. Signposts were erected bearing the word *Refuge* in plain, bold characters, so that the fleeing one might not be delayed for a moment. Any person—Hebrew, stranger, or temporary resident—might use this provision. The killer was to be tried fairly by proper authorities, and only when found innocent of intentional murder was the fugitive protected in the city of refuge. The guilty were given up to the avenger. When the high priest died, however, all who had taken shelter in the cities of refuge were free to return home.

In a trial for murder, the accused was not to be condemned on the testimony of one witness, even though circumstantial evidence of guilt might be strong. " 'Whoever kills a person, the murderer shall be put to death on the testimony of witnesses; but one witness is not sufficient testimony against a person for the death penalty.' " Numbers 35:30. It was Christ who gave Moses these directions for Israel, and when He was personally on earth the Great Teacher repeated the lesson that one person's testimony is not to acquit or condemn. One person's opinions are not to settle disputed questions. " 'By the mouth of two or three witnesses every word may be established.' " Matthew 18:16.

No atonement or ransom could rescue a person proved guilty of murder. " 'You shall take no ransom for the life of a murderer who is guilty of death, but he shall be surely put to death.' " " 'No atonement can be made for the land, for the blood that is shed on it, except by the blood of him who shed it.' " Numbers 35:31, 33. The safety and purity of the nation demanded that the sin of murder be severely punished.

The cities of refuge were a symbol of the refuge provided in Christ. By shedding His own blood the Savior has provided a sure retreat for the transgressors of God's law. They may flee there for safety from the second death. No power can take out of His hands the souls who go to Him for pardon.

A person who fled to the city of refuge could not afford delay. There was no time to say Goodbye to loved ones. Fatigue was forgotten, difficulties were ignored. The fugitive dared not slow down until safely within the city.

As lingering and carelessness might rob fugitives of their only chance for life, so delays and indifference may result in the ruin of the soul. Satan, the great adversary, is pursuing every transgressor of God's holy law, and all who do not earnestly seek shelter in the eternal refuge will become a prey to the destroyer.

The prisoner who went outside the city of refuge at any time was fair game for the avenger of blood. So today, it is not enough that sinners *believe* in Christ for pardon of sin; by faith and obedience, they must *abide* in Him.

Civil War Avoided

Two tribes, Gad and Reuben, with half the tribe of Manasseh, had received their inheritance before crossing the Jordan. The wide upland plains and rich forests of Gilead and Bashan had attractions that could not be found in Canaan itself. The two and a half tribes, desiring to settle here, had pledged to supply their quota of armed men to go with their brethren across the Jordan and share their battles until they also would enter upon their inheritance. When the ten tribes entered Canaan, forty thousand of "the men of Reuben, the men of Gad, and half the tribe of Manasseh . . . prepared for war crossed over before the LORD for battle, to the plains of Jericho." Joshua 4:12, 13. For years they fought bravely by the side of their brethren. As they had united with them in the conflicts, so they shared the spoils. They returned " 'with much riches . . . , with very much livestock, with silver, with gold, with bronze, with iron, and with very much clothing,' " all of which they were to share with those who had remained with the families and flocks.

With a burdened heart Joshua watched them leave, knowing how strong the temptations would be in their isolated and wandering life to fall into the customs of the heathen tribes that lived on their borders.

While Joshua and other leaders were still troubled with anxious forebodings, strange news reached them. Beside the Jordan, the two and a half tribes had erected a great altar similar to the altar of burnt offering at Shiloh. On pain of death, the law of God prohibited the establishment of any other worship than the one at the sanctuary; it would lead the people away from the true faith.

It was decided to send a delegation to get an explanation of their conduct from the two and a half tribes. Ten princes were chosen, one from each tribe. Their leader was Phinehas, who had distinguished himself by his zeal in the matter of Peor.

Taking it for granted that their brethren were guilty, the ambassadors met them with sharp rebuke. They told them to remember how judgments had come on Israel for joining themselves to Baal Peor. Phinehas told the Gadites and Reubenites that if they were unwilling to live in that land without an altar for sacrifice, they would be welcome to share in the possessions and privileges of the tribes on the other side.

In reply, the accused explained that their altar was not intended for sacrifice but simply as a witness that, although separated by the river, they were of the same faith as their relatives in Canaan. They had feared that in future years their children might be excluded as having no part in Israel. This altar, patterned after the altar of the Lord at Shiloh, would be a witness that its builders were also worshipers of the living God.

With great joy the ambassadors accepted this explanation, and the people united in rejoicing and praise to God.

The tribes of Gad and Reuben now placed an inscription on their altar pointing out the purpose for which it was erected. They said, " 'It is a witness between us that the LORD is God.' " In this way they tried to prevent future misunderstanding and remove a possible cause of temptation.

How to Avoid Useless Strife

Often difficulties arise from a simple misunderstanding, and without courtesy and restraint serious results may follow. The ten tribes decided to act promptly and earnestly; but instead of courteously asking about the facts in the case, they met their brethren with scolding and condemnation. If the people of Gad and Reuben had retorted in the same spirit, war would have been the result. It is important not to be lax in dealing with sin; it is equally important to shun harsh judgment and groundless suspicion.

No one was ever reclaimed from a wrong position by scolding and blame, but these things have driven many further from the right path to harden their hearts against conviction. A self-controlled, courteous approach may save the erring.

While honestly seeking to promote the cause of true religion, the Reubenites were misjudged and severely reprimanded; yet they listened with courtesy and patience to the accusations before attempting to make their defense and then fully explained their motives and showed their innocence.

Even under false accusation, those in the right can afford to be calm and considerate. God knows the truth about everything that people misunderstand and misinterpret, and we can safely leave our case in His hands. He will defend the cause of those who put their trust in Him.

Just before His crucifixion, Christ prayed that His disciples might be one as He is one with the Father, that the world might believe that God had sent Him. This touching prayer reaches down the ages, even to our day. While we are not to sacrifice one principle of truth, it should be our constant aim to reach this state of unity. Jesus said, " 'By this all will know that you are My disciples, if you have love for one another.' " John 13:35.

The Last Words of Joshua*

When the wars and conquest ended, Joshua had withdrawn to the peaceful seclusion of his home at Timnath Serah. "Now it came to pass, a long time after the LORD had given rest to Israel from all their enemies round about, that Joshua . . . called for all Israel, for their elders, for their heads, for their judges, and for their officers."

As Joshua felt the effects of old age coming on him and realized that his work must soon close, he was deeply concerned for the future of his people. " 'You have seen,' " he said, " 'all that the LORD your God has done to all these nations because of you, for the LORD your God is He who has fought for you.' " Although the Canaanites had been subdued, they still possessed quite a bit of the land promised to Israel, and Joshua urged his people not to forget the Lord's command to drive out these idolatrous nations.

The tribes had all gone to their homes, the army had disbanded, and renewing the war looked like a difficult and doubtful undertaking. But Joshua declared: " 'The LORD your God will expel them from before you and drive them out of your sight. So you shall possess their land, as the LORD your God has promised you. Therefore be very courageous to keep and to do all that is written in the Book of the Law of Moses, lest you turn aside from it to the right hand or to the left.' "

God had faithfully fulfilled His promises to them. " 'You know in all your hearts and in all your souls,' " he said, " 'that not one thing has failed of all the good things which the LORD your God spoke concerning you. All have come to pass for you, and not one word of them has failed.' "

As the Lord had fulfilled His promises, so He would fulfill His threatenings. " 'It shall come to pass, that as all the good things have come upon you which the LORD your God promised you, so the LORD will bring upon you all harmful things. . . . When you have transgressed the covenant of the LORD . . . , then the anger of the LORD will burn against you, and you shall perish quickly from the good land which He has given you.' "

In all His dealings with His creatures, God has upheld the principles

---

This chapter is based on Joshua 23 and 24.

of righteousness by revealing sin in its true character—by demonstrating that its sure result is misery and death. Unconditional pardon for sin never has been offered, and it never will be. Such pardon would fill the unfallen universe with dismay. God has faithfully pointed out the results of sin, and if these warnings were not true, how could we be sure that His promises would be fulfilled?

Before the death of Joshua the leaders and representatives of the tribes again assembled at Shechem. No spot in all the land possessed so many sacred associations. Here were the mountains Ebal and Gerizim, the silent witnesses of those vows that now they had assembled to renew in the presence of their dying leader. God had given them a land for which they did not labor, cities that they had not built, and vineyards and oliveyards that they had not planted. Joshua reviewed the history of Israel once more, recounting the wonderful works of God so that all might have a sense of His love and mercy and might serve Him "in sincerity and in truth."

By Joshua's order the ark had been brought from Shiloh. This symbol of God's presence would deepen the impression he wished to make upon the people. After presenting the goodness of God toward Israel, he called for them to choose whom they would serve. To some extent they were still worshiping idols secretly, and Joshua tried now to bring them to a decision to banish this sin from Israel. " 'If it seems evil to you to serve the LORD,' " he said, " 'choose for yourselves this day whom you will serve.' " Joshua wanted to lead them to serve God not by compulsion but willingly. To serve Him merely from hope of reward or fear of punishment was unacceptable. Open apostasy would not be more offensive to God than hypocrisy and mere formal worship.

The Importance of Right Choice

The aged leader urged the people to consider what he had set before them. If it seemed evil to serve the Lord, the source of power, the fountain of blessing, let them that day choose whom they would serve—" 'the gods which your fathers served,' " from whom Abraham was called out, " 'or the gods of the Amorites, in whose land you dwell.' "

These last words were a sharp rebuke to Israel. The gods of the Amorites had not been able to protect their worshipers. Because of their debasing sins, that wicked nation had been destroyed, and the good land that they once possessed had been given to God's people. How foolish for Israel to choose the gods for whose worship the Amorites had been destroyed!

" 'As for me and my house,' " said Joshua, " 'we will serve the LORD.' " The people felt the same holy zeal that inspired the leader's heart, and they gave the unhesitating response, " 'Far be it from us that we should forsake the LORD, to serve other gods.' "

But before they could make any permanent reformation, they must feel their complete inability in themselves to obey God. While they trusted their own righteousness, it was impossible for them to obtain pardon; they could not meet the claims of God's perfect law, and it was hopeless for them to pledge themselves to serve God. Only by faith in Christ could they secure pardon of sin and receive strength to obey God's law. They must trust totally in the merits of the promised Savior.

With deep earnestness they once more stated their pledge of loyalty:

" 'The LORD our God we will serve, and His voice we will obey!' "

"So Joshua made a covenant with the people that day, and made for them a statute and an ordinance in Shechem. . . . So Joshua let the people depart, each to his own inheritance."

His work was done. He had "wholly followed the LORD." The noblest testimony to his character as a leader is the history of the generation that had come under the influence of his work: "Israel served the LORD all the days of Joshua, and all the days of the elders who outlived Joshua."

The Blessing of Tithes and Offerings

In the Hebrew system one tenth of the people's income was set apart to support the public worship of God. " 'All the tithe . . . is the LORD's. It is holy to the LORD.' " Leviticus 27:30.

But the tithing system did not originate with the Hebrews. From earliest times the LORD claimed a tithe as His. Abraham paid tithes to Melchizedek, priest of God. Genesis 14:20. Jacob promised the LORD, " 'Of all that You give me I will surely give a tenth to You.' " Genesis 28:22. God is the source of every blessing to His creatures, and to Him our gratitude is due.

The LORD declares, " 'The silver is Mine, and the gold is Mine.' " Haggai 2:8. It is God who gives us power to get wealth. To acknowledge that all things came from Him, the LORD directed that we should return a portion of His abundance to Him.

"The tithe . . . is the LORD's." The form of expression is the same as in the Sabbath law: "The seventh day is the Sabbath of the LORD your God." Exodus 20:10. God reserved a specified portion of our time and our means, and we cannot, without guilt, use either for our own interests.

The tithe was to be devoted exclusively to the Levites who had been set apart for the service of the sanctuary. In no way, however, was this the limit of the contributions for religious purposes. The tabernacle, like the temple later, was built entirely by freewill offerings; and to provide for necessary repairs and other expenses, Moses directed that periodically each person should contribute a half shekel for "the service of the tabernacle." See Exodus 30:12-16. From time to time, people brought sin offerings and thank offerings to God. And liberal provision was made for the poor.

The people were constantly reminded that God was the true owner of their fields, their flocks, and their herds. He sent them sunshine and rain for their seedtime and harvest, and He made them managers of His goods.

As the Israelites gathered at the tabernacle, laden with the firstfruits of field and orchard and vineyard, they made a public acknowledgment of God's goodness. When the priest accepted the gift, the offerer said, " 'My father was a Syrian, about to perish,' " and he described the stay in Egypt and the affliction from which God had delivered Israel. " 'He has brought us to this place and has given us this land, "a land flowing with milk and honey;" and now, behold, I have brought the firstfruits of the land which You, O LORD, have given me.' " Deuteronomy 26:5, 9, 10.

The Secret of Prosperity

Says Solomon, the wise man, "There is one who scatters, yet increases more; and there is one who withholds more than is right, but it leads to poverty." Proverbs 11:24. The apostle Paul teaches the same lesson in the New Testament: "He who sows sparingly will also reap sparingly, and he who sows bountifully will also reap bountifully. . . . God is able to make all grace abound toward you, that you, always having all sufficiency in all things, have an abundance for every good work." 2 Corinthians 9:6-8.

God intended that Israel would be light bearers to all the earth. The LORD has decreed that the spread of light and truth in the earth shall depend on the witness and offerings of those who have received the heavenly gift. He could have made angels the ambassadors of His truth, but in His love and wisdom He called men and women to become colaborers with Himself, by choosing them to do this work.

In the days of Israel the tithe and freewill offerings were needed to maintain the divine service. Should the people of God in this age give less? Christ laid down the principle that our offerings to God should be in proportion to the light and privileges that are ours. " 'Everyone to whom much is given, from him much will be required.' " Luke 12:48. " 'Freely you have received, freely give.' " Matthew 10:8. Since we have before us the unparalleled sacrifice of the glorious Son of God, shouldn't our gratitude find expression in more generous gifts?

The work of the gospel, as it widens, requires greater financial support to sustain it than was called for anciently. This makes the law of tithes and offerings even more crucial today. If God's people were to sustain His cause liberally by voluntary gifts, He would be honored and many more souls would be won to Christ.

The plan of Moses to raise means for the building of the tabernacle was highly successful. He made no grand feast. He did not invite the people to scenes of laughter, dancing, and amusement. Neither did he hold lotteries. The Lord directed Moses to accept gifts from everyone who gave willingly, from the heart. And the offerings came in such great amounts that Moses told the people to stop giving, for they had given more than could be used.

God has made us His managers. The Lord says, " 'Those who honor Me I will honor.' " 1 Samuel 2:30. "God loves a cheerful giver" (2 Corinthians 9:7), and when His people bring their gifts and offerings to Him with grateful hearts, "not grudgingly or of necessity," His blessing will be with them, as He has promised.

God's Care for the Poor

To promote bringing the people together for religious service, as well as to provide for the poor, God required a second tithe of all the increase. Concerning the first tithe, the Lord declared, " 'I have given the children of Levi *all the tithes* in Israel.' " Numbers 18:21. The second tithe, for two years they were to bring to the place where the sanctuary was established. After presenting a thank offering to God and a portion to the priest, the offerers were to use the remainder for a religious feast in which the Levite, the stranger, the fatherless, and the widow should participate.

Every third year this second tithe was to be used at home, in entertaining the Levite and the poor. This tithe would provide a fund for charity and hospitality.

And further provision was made for the poor. After recognition of God's claims, nothing distinguishes the laws given by Moses more than the liberal, tender, and hospitable spirit that they embody toward the poor. Although God had promised to bless His people, He declared that there would always be poor in the land. Then, as now, people could experience misfortune, sickness, and loss of property; yet as long as they followed God's instruction, there were no beggars among them nor any who suffered for lack of food.

The law of God gave the poor a right to a certain portion of the soil's produce. A hungry person was free to go to a neighbor's field, orchard, or vineyard to obtain food.

All the gleanings of harvest field, orchard, and vineyard belonged to the poor. " 'When you reap your harvest in your field,' " said Moses, " 'and forget a sheaf in the field, you shall not go back to get it. . . . When you beat your olive trees, you shall not go over the boughs again. . . . When you gather the grapes of your vineyard, you shall not glean it afterward; it shall be for the stranger, the fatherless, and the widow. And you shall remember that you were a slave in the land of Egypt.' " Deuteronomy 24:19-22. Also see Leviticus 19:9, 10.

God's Mercy to Poor People

Every seventh year special provision was made for the poor. At planting time, which followed the harvest, the people were not to sow; they were not to tend the vineyard in the spring; and they must not expect either harvest or vintage. The yield of this year was to be free for the stranger, the fatherless, and the widow, and even for the creatures of the field. Exodus 23:10, 11; Leviticus 25:5.

But if the land ordinarily produced only enough to meet the needs of the people, how were they to survive during the year when they gathered no crops? The promise of God made ample provision: " 'I will command My blessing on you in the sixth year,' " He said, " 'and it will bring forth produce enough for three years. And you shall sow in the eighth year, and eat old produce until the ninth year; until its produce comes in, you shall eat of the old harvest.' " Leviticus 25:21, 22.

The sabbatical year was to be a benefit to both land and people. The soil, lying unworked for one season, afterward would produce more plentifully. The people were released from the pressing field labor. All enjoyed greater leisure, opportunity for restoring their physical powers, more time for meditation and studying the teachings of the Lord, and for instructing their households.

In the sabbatical year the Hebrew slaves were to be given their liberty. " 'When you send him away free from you, you shall not let him go away empty-handed; you shall supply him liberally from your flock, from your threshing floor, and from your winepress. From what the LORD has blessed you with, you shall give to him.' " Deuteronomy 15:13, 14.

The wages of a laborer were to be paid promptly. " 'Each day you shall give him his wages, and not let the sun go down on it, for he is poor and has set his heart on it.' " Deuteronomy 24:15.

Special directions also were given about how to treat runaway slaves: " 'You shall not give back to his master the slave who has escaped from his master to you. He may dwell with you in your midst, . . . where it seems best to him; you shall not oppress him.' " Deuteronomy 23:15, 16.

To the poor, the seventh year was a year of release from debt. The Hebrews were to lend money without interest to their needy brethren. To take usury from the poor was expressly forbidden: " 'If one of your brethren becomes poor, and falls into poverty among you, then you shall help him, like a stranger or a sojourner, that he may live with you. Take no usury or interest from him; but fear your God, that your brother may live with you. You shall not lend him your money for usury, nor lend him your food at a profit.' " Leviticus 25:35-37. If the debt remained unpaid until the year of release, the principal itself could not be recovered. " 'If there is among you a poor man of your brethren, . . . you shall not harden your heart nor shut your hand from your poor brother. . . . Beware lest there be a wicked thought in your heart, saying, "The seventh year, the year of release, is at hand," and your eye be evil against your poor brother and you give him nothing, and he cry out to the LORD against you, and it become sin among you.' " " 'The poor will never cease from the land; therefore I command you, saying, "You shall open your hand wide to your brother, to your poor and your needy, in your land," ' " " ' "and willingly lend him sufficient for his need, whatever he needs." ' " Deuteronomy 15:7-9, 11, 8.

None need fear that their liberality would bring them to poverty. " 'You shall lend to many nations,' " God said, " 'but you shall not borrow; you shall reign over many nations, but they shall not reign over you.' " Deuteronomy 15:6.

Preventing Extremes of Wealth or Poverty

After "seven times seven years" came the great year of release—the Jubilee. " 'Then you shall cause the trumpet of the Jubilee to sound . . . throughout all your land. And you shall consecrate the fiftieth year, and proclaim liberty throughout all the land to all its inhabitants . . . and each of you shall return to his family.' " Leviticus 25:9, 10.

"On the tenth day of the seventh month; on the Day of Atonement," the trumpet of Jubilee was sounded, calling all the children of Jacob to welcome the year of release.

As in the sabbatical year, the land was not to be sown or reaped, and all that it produced was to be considered the rightful property of the poor. Hebrew slaves who did not receive their liberty in the sabbatical year were now set free.

But what especially distinguished the year of Jubilee was the return of all landed property to the family of the original possessor. No one was at liberty to trade his estate. Neither was he to sell his land unless poverty forced him to do so. Whenever he or any of his relatives might desire to redeem it, the purchaser must not refuse to sell it. If unredeemed, it would go back to its possessor or his heirs in the Year of Jubilee.

The Lord declared to Israel: " 'The land shall not be sold permanently, for the land is Mine; for you are strangers and sojourners with Me.' " Leviticus 25:23. God was the rightful owner, the original land holder. It was to be impressed on everyone that the poor and unfortunate have as much right to a place in God's world as the wealthy.

Our merciful Creator made provisions such as these to lessen suffering, to bring some ray of hope, to flash some gleam of sunshine into the life of the destitute and distressed.

Great evils result from the continued accumulation of wealth by one class and the poverty of another. The sense of this inequality would arouse the passions of the poorer class. There would be a feeling of despair and desperation that would tend to demoralize society and open the door to crimes of every kind. The regulations that God established were to promote social equality. The sabbatical year and the Jubilee would set right in a great measure the things that had gone wrong in the social and political order of the nation.

These regulations, designed to bless the rich no less than the poor, would restrain greed and cultivate a noble spirit of kindness. By encouraging goodwill between all classes, they would promote stability of government.

We are all woven together in the great web of humanity. Whatever we can do to benefit others will reflect in blessing on ourselves. The law of mutual dependence runs through all classes of society. The poor are not more dependent on the rich than are the rich on the poor. While the one class ask a share in the blessings God has bestowed on their wealthier neighbors, the other need the faithful service, the strength of brain and bone and muscle, that are the resources of the poor.

God's Plan Would Solve Social and Economic Problems Today

Many enthusiastically urge that all people should share equally in earthly blessings. But this was not the intent of the Creator. A diversity of condition is one of the means by which God designs to develop character. He wants those who have worldly possessions to regard themselves as managers of His goods, entrusted to them to use for the benefit of the needy.

Christ has said that we will always have the poor with us. The heart of our Redeemer sympathizes with the lowliest of His earthly children. He tells us that they are His representatives on earth, placed among us to awaken in our hearts the love He feels toward the suffering and oppressed. He regards an act of cruelty or neglect toward them as done to Him.

If the law God gave for the benefit of the poor had continued to be followed, how different would be the condition of the world today, morally, spiritually, and economically! Such widespread poverty as now is seen in many lands would not exist.

The principles that God has laid down would prevent the terrible evils that result from the oppression of the poor by the rich and the suspicion and hatred of the rich by the poor. While these principles might keep a person from amassing great wealth, they would prevent the ignorance and destitution of tens of thousands whose poorly-paid servitude is what it takes to build up these colossal fortunes. They would bring a peaceful solution to problems that now threaten the world with lawlessness and bloodshed.

Annual Feasts
of Rejoicing*

The people of Israel were surrounded by fierce, warlike tribes, eager to seize their lands; yet three times every year all the people who could make the journey were directed to leave their homes and travel to the place of assembly near the center of the land. What was to keep their enemies from sweeping down on those unprotected households to destroy them with fire and sword? What was to prevent an invasion that would bring Israel into captivity?

God had promised to be the protector of His people. " 'I will cast out the nations before you and enlarge your borders; neither will any man covet your land when you go up to appear before the LORD your God three times in the year.' " Exodus 34:24.

The first of these festivals, the Passover, occurred in Abib, the first month of the Jewish year, corresponding to the last of March and the beginning of April. The cold of winter was past, the latter rains had ended, and all nature rejoiced in the freshness and beauty of springtime. The grass was green on the hills and valleys, and wild flowers everywhere

brightened the fields. The moon, now approaching full, made the evening delightful.

Throughout the land, groups of pilgrims were making their way toward Jerusalem. The shepherds, the herdsmen, fishers from the Sea of Galilee, farmers from their fields, and sons of the prophets from the sacred schools—all turned their steps toward the place where God's presence was revealed. Many went on foot. The caravans often became very large before reaching the Holy City.

Nature's gladness awakened joy in the hearts of Israel. The people chanted the grand Hebrew psalms, exalting the glory and majesty of Jehovah. At the sound of the signal trumpet, with the music of cymbals, the chorus of thanksgiving arose, swelled by hundreds of voices:

I was glad when they said to me,
"Let us go into the house of the
    LORD."
Psalm 122:1

As they saw around them hills where the heathen had long kindled

---

* This chapter is based on Leviticus 23.

their altar fires, the children of Israel sang:

I will lift up my eyes to the hills—
From whence comes my help?
My help comes from the LORD,
Who made heaven and earth.
Psalm 121:1, 2

Cresting the hills and coming in view of the Holy City, they looked with reverent awe on the throngs of worshipers making their way to the temple. As they heard the trumpets of the Levites announcing the sacred service, they caught the inspiration of the hour, and sang:

Great is the LORD, and greatly to be praised
In the city of our God,
In His holy mountain.
Beautiful in elevation,
The joy of the whole earth,
Is Mount Zion on the sides of the north,
The city of the great King.
Psalm 48:1, 2

Open to me the gates of righteousness;
I will go through them,
And I will praise the LORD.
Psalm 118:19

All the homes in Jerusalem were thrown open to the pilgrims, and rooms were furnished free. But this was not enough, and tents were pitched in every available space in the city and on the surrounding hills.

On the fourteenth day of the month, at evening, the Passover was celebrated. Its solemn, impressive ceremonies commemorated deliverance from bondage in Egypt and pointed forward to the sacrifice that would deliver from the bondage of sin. When the Savior gave His life on Calvary, the significance of the Passover ended, and the ordinance of the Lord's Supper was begun as a memorial of the same event that the Passover had symbolized in advance.

Meaning of the Festivals

The Passover was followed by the seven days' Feast of Unleavened Bread. On the second day of the feast, the firstfruits of the year's harvest were presented before God. The priest waved a sheaf of grain before the altar of God to acknowledge that everything was His. The harvest was not to be gathered until this ceremony had been performed.

Fifty days after the offering of firstfruits came Pentecost, the feast of harvest. As an expression of gratitude for grain, two loaves baked with yeast were presented before God. Pentecost occupied only one day.

In the seventh month came the Feast of Tabernacles, or ingathering. This feast acknowledged God's rich blessings in the products of orchard, olive grove, and vineyard. It was the crowning festival-gathering of the year. The harvest had been gathered into the granaries; the fruits, oil, and wine had been stored; and now the people came with their tributes of thanksgiving to God.

This feast was an occasion of rejoicing. It took place just after the great Day of Atonement, when the people had received assurance that their sins would be remembered no more. At peace with God, with the work of the harvest ended and the toils of the new year not yet begun, the people could give themselves fully to the sacred, joyous experiences of the hour. As far as possible, all the household were to attend the feasts, and the servants, the Levites, the stranger, and the poor were made welcome to their hospitality.

Like the Passover, the Feast of Tabernacles commemorated past events. In memory of their pilgrim life in the wilderness, the people were to leave their homes and dwell in booths, or arbors, formed from the green branches "of beautiful trees, branches of palm trees, the boughs of leafy trees, and willows of the brook." Leviticus 23:40.

At these yearly gatherings the hearts of old and young would be encouraged in God's service. As the people from different parts of the land associated together, the ties that bound them to God and to one another would strengthen. Just as Israel celebrated the deliverance God had performed for their ancestors and how He miraculously preserved them during their journeyings from Egypt, so we should gratefully call to mind the ways He has devised for bringing us out from darkness into the precious light of His grace and truth.

Those who lived long distances from the tabernacle must have spent more than a month of every year in attending the annual feasts. This example of devotion should help us grasp the importance of religious worship, the need for making our selfish, worldly interests secondary to those that are spiritual and eternal. We experience a loss when we neglect coming together to encourage one another in the service of God. All of us are children of one Father, dependent on one another for happiness. Properly cultivating the social elements of our nature brings us into sympathy with others and gives us happiness.

The Feast of Tabernacles not only pointed back to the time spent in the wilderness but forward to the great day of final ingathering. The Lord will send His reapers to gather the weeds in bundles for the fire and to gather the wheat into His storehouse. At that time the wicked will be destroyed. They will become "as though they had never been." Obadiah 16. And every voice in the whole universe will unite in joyful praise to God.

When the ransomed of the Lord are safely gathered into the heavenly Canaan, forever delivered from slavery to sin, they will "rejoice with joy inexpressible and full of glory." 1 Peter 1:8. Then Christ's great work of atonement will have been completed and their sins forever blotted out.

And the ransomed of the LORD shall
    return,
And come to Zion with singing,
With everlasting joy on their
    heads. . . .
And sorrow and sighing shall flee
    away.
Isaiah 35:10

The Judges, Deliverers of Israel*

Satisfied with the territory already gained, the tribes lost their zeal and discontinued the war. "When Israel was strong, ... they put the Canaanites under tribute, but did not completely drive them out." Judges 1:28.

On His part, the Lord had faithfully fulfilled the promises He made to Israel. It only remained for them to complete the work of driving out the inhabitants of the land. But they failed to do this. By making treaties with the Canaanites they violated the command of God and failed to fulfill the condition on which He had promised them possession of Canaan.

At Sinai God had warned them against idolatry. " 'You shall not bow down to their gods, nor serve them, nor do according to their works; but you shall utterly overthrow them and completely break down their sacred pillars.' " As long as they remained obedient, God would subdue their enemies: " 'I will send My fear before you, I will cause confusion among all the people to whom you come. . . . And I will send hornets before you, which shall drive out the Hivite, the

Canaanite, and the Hittite from before you. I will not drive them out from before you in one year, lest the land become desolate and the beast of the field become too numerous for you. Little by little I will drive them out from before you, until you have increased, and you inherit the land. . . . You shall make no covenant with them, nor with their gods. They shall not dwell in your land, lest they make you sin against Me. For if you serve their gods, it will surely be a snare to you.' " Exodus 23:24, 27-33.

God had placed His people in Canaan to hold back the tide of moral evil, so that it would not flood the world. God would give nations greater and more powerful than the Canaanites into their hands. " 'You will dispossess greater and mightier nations than yourselves. . . . From the wilderness and Lebanon, from the river, the River Euphrates, even to the Western Sea, shall be your territory.' " Deuteronomy 11:23, 24.

But they chose ease and self-indulgence. They let their opportunities slip away for completing the conquest of the land. And for many

---

* This chapter is based on Judges 6 to 8; 10.

generations they were afflicted by the survivors of these idolatrous peoples, that were as "irritants" in their eyes and "thorns" in their sides. Numbers 33:55.

The Israelites "mingled with the Gentiles and learned their works." They intermarried with the Canaanites, and idolatry spread like a plague throughout the land. "They even sacrificed their sons and their daughters to demons. . . . And the land was polluted with blood." "Therefore the wrath of the LORD was kindled against His people, so that He abhorred His own inheritance." Psalm 106:35-40.

Until the generation that had received instruction from Joshua died out, idolatry made little headway, but the parents prepared the way for the apostasy of their children. The simple habits of the Hebrews had secured them physical health, but association with the heathen led to indulgence of appetite and passion, which gradually weakened the mental and moral powers. By their sins the Israelites were separated from God, and they could no longer overcome their enemies. Thus they came into subjection to the very nations that they might have subdued.

"They forsook the LORD God of their fathers, who had brought them out of the land of Egypt." "They provoked Him to anger with their high places, and moved Him to jealousy with their carved images." Therefore the Lord "forsook the tabernacle of Shiloh, the tent which He had placed among men, and delivered His strength into captivity, and His glory

into the enemy's hand." Judges 2:12; Psalm 78:58, 60, 61.

Yet He did not utterly forsake His people. There was always a remnant who were true to Jehovah, and from time to time the Lord raised up faithful and valiant men to put down idolatry and deliver the Israelites from their enemies. But when the deliverer died and the people were released from his authority, they would gradually return to their idols. Thus the story of backsliding and chastisement, of confession and deliverance, was repeated again and again.

The Sad Story of Continual Backsliding

The king of Mesopotamia, the king of Moab, after them the Philistines and the Canaanites of Hazor led by Sisera, in turn became oppressors of Israel. Othniel, Shamgar, Ehud, Deborah, and Barak were raised up as deliverers of their people. But again "the children of Israel did evil in the sight of the LORD. So the LORD delivered them into the hand of Midian."

The Midianites had been nearly destroyed by Israel in the days of Moses, but they had since become numerous and powerful. They thirsted for revenge, and now that the protecting hand of God was withdrawn from Israel, the opportunity had come. The whole land suffered from their ravages. Like a plague of locusts they spread over the country. They came as soon as the harvests began to ripen and stayed until the last fruits had been gathered. They stripped the fields of their increase and robbed and mistreated the inhabitants. The Israelites living in the open country were forced to seek safety in fortresses or even find shelter in caves among the mountains. For seven years this oppression continued. Then, as the people in their distress confessed their sins, God again raised up a helper for them.

The divine call came to Gideon to deliver his people. At the time he was threshing wheat. Not daring to beat it out on the ordinary threshing floor, he had gone to a spot near the winepress. The season of ripe grapes was still far off, and no one yet took much notice of the vineyards. As Gideon worked in secrecy, he sadly thought about the condition of Israel and how to break the oppressor's yoke.

How the Lord Called Gideon

Suddenly the "Angel of the Lord" appeared and spoke to him with the words, " 'The Lord is with you, you mighty man of valor.' "

" 'O my lord,' " was his answer, " 'if the Lord is with us, why then has all this happened to us? And where are all His miracles which our fathers told us about? . . . The Lord has forsaken us and delivered us into the hands of the Midianites.' "

The Messenger of heaven replied, " 'Go in this might of yours, and you shall save Israel from the hand of the Midianites. Have I not sent you?' "

Gideon wanted some sign that the one now addressing him was the Covenant Angel, who had performed mighty deeds for Israel in times past.

Hurrying to his tent, from his few supplies he prepared a kid and unleavened bread, which he brought out and set before Him. But the Angel told him, " 'Take the meat and the unleavened bread and lay them on this rock, and pour out the broth.' " Gideon did so, and then the sign he desired was given: with the staff in His hand, the Angel touched the meat and the unleavened bread, and a flame bursting from the rock consumed the sacrifice. Then the Angel vanished.

Gideon's father, Joash, who shared in the apostasy of his countrymen, had built a large altar to Baal at Ophrah. The Lord commanded Gideon to destroy this altar and to set up an altar to Jehovah over the rock where the offering had been consumed, and there present a sacrifice to the Lord. The work of offering sacrifices had been committed to the priests and restricted to the altar at Shiloh, but He who had established the ritual service had power to change its requirements. Gideon must declare war on idolatry before going out to battle with the enemies of his people.

Gideon performed the work in secret, accomplishing everything in one night with the aid of his servants. Great was the rage of the men of Ophrah when they came next morning to offer their worship to Baal. Joash, who had been told of the Angel's visit, stood in defense of his son. " 'Would you plead for Baal? Would you save him? Let the one who will plead for him be put to death by morning!' " If Baal could not defend his own altar, how could he be trusted to protect his worshipers?

All thoughts of harming Gideon were dismissed. When he sounded the trumpet of war, the men of Ophrah were among the first to gather to his cause. Messengers were sent to his own tribe of Manasseh, and also to Asher, Zebulun, and Naphtali, and all answered the call.

How Could Gideon Be Sure?

Gideon prayed, " 'If You will save Israel by my hand as You have said— look, I shall put a fleece of wool on the threshing floor; if there is dew on the fleece only, and it is dry on all the ground, then I shall know that You will save Israel by my hand, as You have said.' " In the morning the fleece was wet, while the ground was dry. But now a doubt arose, since wool naturally absorbs moisture when there is any in the air; the test might not be decisive. So he asked that the sign be reversed. His request was granted.

Encouraged, Gideon led his forces out to battle the invaders. "All the Midianites and Amalekites, the people of the East, gathered together; and they crossed over and encamped in the Valley of Jezreel." The entire force under Gideon's command numbered only thirty-two thousand men. But with the vast army of the enemy spread out before him, the word of the Lord came: " 'The people who are with you are too many for Me to give the Midianites into their hands, lest Israel claim glory for itself against Me, saying, "My own

hand has saved me." Now therefore, proclaim in the hearing of the people, saying, "Whoever is fearful and afraid, let him turn and depart at once from Mount Gilead." ' " Those unwilling to face danger and hardship would add no strength to the armies of Israel.

Gideon was astonished at the declaration that his army was too large. But the Lord saw the pride and unbelief in the hearts of His people. Stirred by the appeals of Gideon, they had promptly enlisted; but many were filled with fear when they saw the huge army of Midian. Yet, if Israel had triumphed, those very ones would have taken glory to themselves instead of crediting the victory to God.

Only Three Hundred Left

Gideon obeyed the Lord's direction, and with a heavy heart he saw more than two-thirds of his force depart for their homes. Again the word of the Lord came to him: " 'The people are still too many; bring them down to the water, and I will test them for you there. Then it will be, that of whom I say to you, "This one shall go with you," the same shall go with you; and of whomever I say to you, "This one shall not go with you," the same shall not go.' "

The people were led down to the waterside, expecting to make an immediate advance against the enemy. A few quickly took a little water in the hand and sucked it up as they went on; but nearly all bowed on their knees and leisurely drank from the surface of the stream. Those who took the water in their hands were just three hundred out of ten thousand. These were selected; all the rest were permitted to return to their homes.

Those who were intent on supplying their own wants in time of peril were not to be trusted in an emergency. The three hundred chosen men not only possessed courage and self-control, they were men of faith. They had not defiled themselves with idolatry. God could direct them, and through them He could work deliverance for Israel. God is honored not so much by great numbers as by the character of those who serve Him.

The Israelites were stationed on the brow of a hill overlooking the valley where the invaders lay encamped "as numerous as locusts; and their camels were without number, as the sand by the seashore in multitude." Gideon trembled as he thought of the conflict to come in the morning. But the Lord told him to go down to the camp of the Midianites. He would hear something there for his encouragement.

Waiting in the darkness and silence, he heard a soldier telling a dream to his companion: " 'To my surprise, a loaf of barley bread tumbled into the camp of Midian; it came to a tent and struck it so that it fell and overturned, and the tent collapsed.' " The other answered in words that stirred the heart of that unseen listener: " 'This is nothing else but the sword of Gideon the son of Joash, a man of Israel; for into his

hand God has delivered Midian and the whole camp.' "

Gideon recognized the voice of God speaking through those Midianite strangers. Returning to the few men under his command, he said, " 'Arise, for the LORD has delivered the camp of Midian into your hand.' "

God's Simple Battle Plan

By divine direction a plan of attack was suggested. The three hundred men were divided into three companies. Every man was given a trumpet and a torch that was concealed in a clay pitcher. The men were stationed to approach the Midianite camp from different directions. In the dead of night, at a signal from Gideon's war horn, the three companies sounded their trumpets. Then, breaking their pitchers and waving the blazing torches, they rushed toward the enemy with the terrible war cry, " 'The sword of the LORD and of Gideon!' "

The sleeping army was suddenly aroused. On every side the soldiers saw the light of flaming torches. In every direction they heard the sound of trumpets with the cry of the attackers. Believing themselves at the mercy of an overwhelming force, the Midianites were panic-stricken. With wild cries of alarm they fled in panic, and mistaking their own companions for enemies, they killed one another.

As news of the victory spread, thousands of the Israelites who had been dismissed to their homes returned and joined in chasing their fleeing enemies. Gideon sent messengers to the tribe of Ephraim, rousing them to intercept the escaping soldiers at the southern fords. Meanwhile, with his three hundred, "exhausted but still in pursuit," Gideon crossed the stream close behind those who had already reached the farther side. Gideon overtook Zebah and Zalmunna, the two princes who escaped with fifteen thousand men; he scattered their force completely and captured and killed the leaders.

One hundred twenty thousand of the invaders died. The power of the Midianites was broken. They were never again able to make war on Israel. No words can describe the terror of the surrounding nations when they learned what simple means had succeeded against the power of a bold, warlike people.

The leader God chose to overthrow the Midianites was not a ruler, a priest, or a Levite. He thought of himself as the least in his father's house. But he was distrustful of self and was willing to follow the guidance of the Lord. God selects those whom He can best use. "Before honor is humility." Proverbs 15:33. He will make them strong by joining their weakness to His might and wise by connecting their ignorance with His wisdom.

Few can be trusted with any large amount of responsibility or success without becoming forgetful of their dependence on God. This is why, in choosing instruments for His work, the Lord passes by those whom the world honors as great, talented, and brilliant. They are proud and feel qualified to act without counsel from God.

Trust in God and obedience to His will are as essential in spiritual warfare as they were to Gideon and Joshua in their battles with the Canaanites. God is just as willing to work with the efforts of His people now and to accomplish great things through weak instruments. God is "able to do exceedingly abundantly above all that we ask or think." Ephesians 3:20.

When the men of Israel had rallied to Gideon's call against the Midianites, the tribe of Ephraim had remained behind. Gideon sent them no special appeal, and they took this as an excuse not to join their brethren. But when news of Israel's triumph reached them, the Ephraimites were envious because they had not shared it.

After the spectacular defeat of the Midianites, they followed up the battle and helped complete the victory. Nevertheless, they were jealous and angry, as though Gideon had been following His own will and judgment. They did not discern God's hand in Israel's triumph, and this showed that they were unworthy to be chosen as His special instruments. Returning with the trophies of victory, they angrily reprimanded Gideon: " 'Why have you done this to us by not calling us when you went to fight with the Midianites?' "

Gideon Demonstrates Humility

" 'What have I done now in comparison with you?' " said Gideon. " 'Is not the *gleaning* of the grapes of Ephraim better than the *vintage* of Abiezer? *God* has delivered into your hands the princes of Midian, Oreb and Zeeb. And what was I able to do in comparison with you?' " Gideon's modest answer soothed the anger of the men of Ephraim, and they returned in peace to their homes. Gideon displayed a spirit of courtesy rarely seen.

In their gratitude for deliverance from the Midianites, the people of Israel proposed to Gideon that he become their king. This directly violated the principles of the theocracy. God was the King of Israel, and for them to place a man on the throne would be a rejection of their divine Sovereign. Gideon recognized this fact. His answer shows that his motives were true and noble: " 'I will not rule over you, nor shall my son rule over you; the LORD shall rule over you.' "

But Gideon fell into another error, which brought disaster on his family and on all Israel. The time of inactivity that follows a great struggle is often filled with greater danger than is the period of conflict. Gideon was now exposed to this danger. A spirit of unrest came over him. Instead of waiting for divine guidance, he began to plan for himself.

Because he had been commanded to offer sacrifice on the rock where the Angel appeared to him, Gideon concluded that he had been appointed as a priest. Without waiting for divine permission, he determined to establish a system of worship similar to the one carried on at the tabernacle.

With the strong popular feeling in his favor, he found no difficulty in carrying out his plan. At his request all the earrings of gold taken from the Midianites were given him as his share of the spoil. The people also collected other costly materials, together with the richly adorned garments of the princes of Midian. From these materials, Gideon made an ephod and a breastplate, in imitation of those worn by the high priest. These actions turned out to be a snare to himself and his family, as well as to Israel. The unauthorized worship led many of the people finally to turn from the Lord to serve idols. After Gideon's death, great numbers, including his own family, joined in apostasy. The people were led away from God by the very man who once overthrew their idolatry.

Those who stand in the highest positions may lead others astray. The wisest make mistakes; the strongest may hesitate and stumble. Our only safety lies in trusting our way completely to Him who has said, "Follow Me."

After the death of Gideon, the people of Israel accepted his illegitimate son Abimelech as their king, who, to shore up his power, murdered all but one of Gideon's lawful children. Israel's cruel way of dealing with the house of Gideon was what might be expected from a people who showed such great ingratitude to God.

More Backsliding and More Misery!

After the death of Abimelech, the rule of God-fearing judges served to restrain idolatry for a time. But before long the people returned to the practices of the heathen around them. Apostasy speedily brought punishment. The Ammonites conquered the eastern tribes of Israel and, crossing the Jordan, invaded the territory of Judah and Ephraim. On the west the Philistines came up from their plain beside the sea, burning and looting wherever they went. Israel seemed to be hopelessly under the power of unyielding foes.

Again the people looked for help from Him whom they had forsaken and insulted. "The children of Israel cried out to the LORD, saying, 'We have sinned against You, because we have both forsaken our God and served the Baals!' " But the people mourned not because they had dishonored God by breaking His holy law but because their sins had brought suffering on themselves. True repentance is a determined turning away from evil.

The Lord answered them through one of His prophets: " 'Did I not deliver you from the Egyptians and from the Amorites and from the people of Ammon and from the Philistines? . . . You cried out to Me, and I delivered you from their hand. Yet you have forsaken Me and served other gods. Therefore I will deliver you no more. Go and cry out to the gods which you have chosen; let them deliver you in your time of distress.' "

The Israelites now humbled themselves before the Lord. "So they put away the foreign gods from among them and served the LORD." And the Lord's heart of love "could no longer endure the misery of Israel." Oh, the long-suffering mercy of our God! When His people put away the sins that had shut out His presence, He heard their prayers and began at once to work for them. He raised up a deliverer in the person of Jephthah, who made war on the Ammonites and completely destroyed their power. At this time Israel had suffered under the oppression of her foes for eighteen years, yet again the people forgot the lesson taught by suffering.

As His people returned to their evil ways, the Lord permitted them to be oppressed by powerful enemies, the Philistines. For many years they were constantly harassed, and at times completely conquered, by this cruel and warlike nation. They had mingled with these idolaters, uniting in pleasure and in worship until they seemed to be one with them in spirit and interest. Then these professed friends of Israel became their bitterest enemies and tried to bring about their destruction.

The Bible plainly teaches that there can be no harmony between the people of God and the world. Satan works through the ungodly, under cover of pretended friendship, to entice God's people into sin. When their defense is removed, then he will lead his agents to turn against them and seek to destroy them.

Samson, the Strongest Yet Weakest Man*

Amid widespread apostasy, the faithful worshipers of God continued to plead with Him to deliver Israel. Though there was apparently no response, in the early years of the Philistine oppression a child was born through whom God planned to humble the power of these mighty enemies.

"The Angel of the LORD" appeared to the childless wife of Manoah with the message that she would have a son through whom God would begin to deliver Israel. The Angel instructed her concerning her own habits and also how to treat her child: " 'Be careful not to drink wine or similar drink, and not to eat any unclean thing.' " The child was also forbidden to take of these things. The Angel further instructed that his hair should not be cut, for he was to be consecrated to God as a Nazirite from his birth.

Importance of Prenatal Training

Fearful that they would make some mistake, the husband prayed, " 'Let the Man of God whom You sent come to us again and teach us what we shall do for the child who will be born.' "

When the Angel appeared again, Manoah asked, " 'What will be the boy's rule of life, and his work?' " The previous instruction was repeated—" 'Of all that I said to the woman let her be careful. . . . All that I commanded her let her observe.' "

To be sure the promised child was properly qualified for his important work, the habits of both mother and child needed careful regulation. The habits of the mother will affect the child for good or evil. She must be controlled by principle, practicing temperance and self-denial, if she wants the best development for her child. Unwise advisers will urge the mother to gratify every wish and impulse; but by command of God the mother is placed under solemn obligation to exercise self-control.

And fathers as well as mothers share in this responsibility. If the parents are intemperate, the children often lack physical strength and mental and moral power. Liquor drinkers and tobacco users may transmit their intense craving, inflamed blood, and irritable nerves to

---

* This chapter is based on Judges 13 to 16.

their children. The immoral often pass along a legacy of unholy desires and even loathsome diseases to their offspring. Each generation tends to fall lower and lower. To a great degree, parents are responsible for the afflictions of the thousands born deaf, blind, diseased, or idiotic.

Many have lightly regarded the effect of prenatal influence, but the instruction sent from heaven to those Hebrew parents shows how our Creator views this matter.

A good legacy from the parents must be followed by careful training and the formation of right habits. God directed that the future judge and deliverer of Israel should never, even as an adult, use wine or strong drink. Lessons of temperance, self-denial, and self-control are to be taught even from babyhood.

Why the Distinction Between Clean and Unclean Foods

The distinction between articles of food as clean and unclean was based on sanitary principles. To a great degree, one can trace the marvelous vitality that has distinguished the Jewish people for thousands of years to their observance of this distinction. Food that is stimulating and hard to digest often injures the health and in many cases sows the seeds of drunkenness. True temperance teaches us to do entirely without everything hurtful and to use wisely what is healthful. Few realize how much their dietary habits have to do with their health, their character, their usefulness in this world, and their eternal destiny. The body

should be servant to the mind, not the mind to the body.

Samson's Strength Depends on Faithfulness to God

In due time the divine promise to Manoah was fulfilled in Samson's birth. As the boy grew, all could see that he possessed extraordinary physical strength. As Samson and his parents well knew, this was not dependent on his good physique but on his status as a Nazirite, of which his uncut hair was a symbol. If Samson had obeyed the divine commands, his destiny would have been nobler and happier. But association with idolaters corrupted him.

Since his hometown of Zorah was near the country of the Philistines, Samson came to mingle with them on friendly terms. A young woman living in the Philistine town of Timnath caught Samson's interest, and he determined to make her his wife. His God-fearing parents tried to dissuade him, but his only answer was, " 'She pleases me well.' " At last the marriage took place.

Just as he was entering manhood, the time above all others when he should have been true to God, Samson connected himself with the enemies of Israel. He did not ask whether he could better glorify God when united with his chosen one. God has promised wisdom to all who seek first to honor Him. But there is no promise to those determined to please themselves.

How often emotions rule in the selection of husband or wife! The parties do not ask counsel of God nor have His glory in view. Satan is constantly seeking to strengthen his power over the people of God by leading them to unite with his subjects. To accomplish this, he tries to arouse unsanctified passions.

But the Lord has instructed His people not to join their lives with those who do not have His love abiding in them: "What accord has Christ with Belial? Or what part has a believer with an unbeliever? And what agreement has the temple of God with idols?" 2 Corinthians 6:15, 16.

At his wedding feast, Samson was brought into close social contact with those who hated the God of Israel. The wife betrayed her husband before the close of the feast. Furious at her treachery, Samson abandoned her for a time and went alone to his home at Zorah. Later, when he changed his mind, he returned for his bride only to find that she had married another. To take revenge, he destroyed all the fields and vineyards of the Philistines. This provoked them to murder her, although their threats had driven her to the deceit that started the trouble.

Samson had already demonstrated his marvelous strength by killing a young lion singlehanded and by killing thirty men of Ashkelon. Now, moved to anger by the barbaric murder of his wife, he attacked the Philistines and struck them "with a great slaughter." For a safe haven he retreated to "the rock Etam," in Judah.

The Philistines pursued him there, and in great alarm the inhabitants of Judah basely agreed to deliver him to his enemies. Three thousand men of Judah went up to take him captive. Samson permitted them to tie him with two new ropes, and he was led into the camp of his enemies amid demonstrations of great joy. But "the Spirit of the LORD came mightily upon him." He broke the strong new cords as if they had been flax burned in the fire. Then grasping the first weapon at hand, the jawbone of a donkey, he attacked the Philistines, leaving a thousand men dead on the field.

If the Israelites had been ready to join with Samson and follow up the victory, they might have freed themselves from their oppressors. But they had become discouraged and had neglected the work God commanded them to perform in driving out the heathen. They had united with them in their degrading practices. They tamely submitted to shameful oppression that they might have escaped if they had obeyed God. Even when the Lord raised up a deliverer for them, too often they would desert him and unite with their enemies.

Samson's Wrong Marriage

After his victory the Israelites made Samson judge, and he ruled Israel for twenty years. But Samson had disobeyed the command of God by taking a wife from the Philistines, and again he dared to go out among them—now his deadly enemies—to indulge unlawful passion. Trusting to his great strength, he went to Gaza to visit a prostitute. The inhabitants of the city learned he was there and were eager for revenge. Their enemy was shut safely within the walls of their most strongly fortified city. They felt sure of their victim and waited only till morning to complete their triumph.

At midnight the accusing voice of conscience filled Samson with remorse as he remembered that he had broken his vow as a Nazirite. But God's mercy had not forsaken him. His tremendous strength again served to deliver him. Going to the city gate, he wrenched it from its place and carried it to the top of a hill on the way to Hebron.

He did not venture among the Philistines again but continued to seek those sensuous pleasures that were luring him to ruin. "He loved a woman in the Valley of Sorek," not far from his birthplace. Her name was Delilah, "the consumer." Sorek's vineyards were also tempting to the wavering Nazirite who had already indulged in wine, thus breaking another tie that bound him to purity and to God. The Philistines determined to accomplish his ruin through Delilah.

They did not dare try to seize him while he possessed his great strength, but they were determined to learn the secret of his power. So they bribed Delilah to discover and reveal it.

A Weak Woman Subdues a Strong Man

As the betrayer kept on questioning Samson, he deceived her by saying that he would be as weak as other men if certain processes were tried. When she put the matter to the test, the cheat was discovered. Then she accused him of falsehood: " 'How can you say, "I love you," when your heart is not with me? You have mocked me these three times, and have not told me where your great strength lies.' " Three times Samson had the clearest evidence that the Philistines had plotted with his charmer to destroy him; but she treated the matter as a joke, and he blindly dismissed any fear.

Day by day a subtle power kept him by her side. Finally she overcame him, and Samson made known the secret: " 'No razor has ever come upon my head, for I have been a Nazirite to God from my mother's womb. If I am shaven, then my strength will leave me, and I shall become weak, and be like any other man.' "

Delilah immediately sent a messenger to the lords of the Philistines, urging them to come without delay. While the warrior slept, the Philistines lopped off the heavy masses of his hair from his head. Then Delilah called, " 'The Philistines are upon you , Samson!' " Waking up suddenly, he thought he would exert his strength as before, but his powerless arms refused to obey him. He knew that "the LORD had departed from him." Delilah began to annoy him and cause him pain, thus testing him for his strength, because the Philistines did not dare approach him until they were fully convinced that his power was gone. Then they seized him, put out both his eyes, and took him to Gaza. There they bound him with chains in their prison house and confined him to hard labor.

What a change! Weak, blind, imprisoned, degraded to the most menial service! God had been patient with him a long time. But when he had gone so far in sin as to betray his secret, the Lord left him. There was no special power in his long hair, but it was a sign of his loyalty to God. When the symbol was sacrificed in his indulgence of passion, the blessings that it represented were forfeited.

In suffering and humiliation, a laughingstock for the Philistines, Samson learned more of his own weakness than he had ever known before. His afflictions led him to repentance. As his hair grew, his power gradually returned. His enemies, regarding him as a chained and helpless prisoner, felt that he was no threat.

Samson's Final Repentance and Tragic Victory

The Philistines, boasting, defied the God of Israel. A feast was appointed in honor of Dagon, the fish god. Throngs of Philistine worshipers filled the vast temple and crowded the galleries around the roof. It was a scene of festivity and rejoicing.

Then, as the crowning trophy of Dagon's power, Samson was brought in. People and rulers mocked his misery and adored the god who had overthrown "the destroyer of their land." After a time, as if weary, Samson asked permission to rest against the two central pillars that supported the temple roof.

Then he silently prayed, " 'O Lord GOD, remember me, I pray! Strengthen me, I pray, just this once, O God, that I may at one blow take vengeance on the Philistines.' " With these words he encircled the pillars with his mighty arms, and crying, " 'Let me die with the Philistines!' " he bowed himself and the roof fell, destroying at one crash all that vast multitude. "So the dead that he killed at his death were more than he had killed in his life."

The idol and its worshipers, priest and peasant, warrior and noble, were buried together beneath the ruins of Dagon's temple. And among them was the giant form of him whom God had chosen to be the deliverer of His people.

The news was carried to the land of Israel, and Samson's relatives rescued the body of the fallen hero without opposition. They "buried him between Zorah and Eshtaol in the tomb of his father Manoah."

How dark and terrible is the record of that life which might have been a praise to God and a glory to the nation! If Samson had been true to his divine calling, he could have accomplished the purpose of God. But he yielded to temptation, and his mission to humble Israel's enemies was fulfilled in bondage and death.

Physically, Samson was the strongest man on earth, but in self-control, integrity, and firmness, he was one of the weakest. Whoever is mastered by the lower passions is weak. Real greatness is measured by the power of the feelings that we control, not by those that control us.

Those who are brought to the test while fulfilling their duty may be sure that God will preserve them; but any who willfully place themselves under the power of temptation will fall, sooner or later. Satan attacks us at our weak points, working through character defects to gain control of the whole person. He knows that if we cherish these defects, he will succeed.

But no one needs to be overcome. Help will be given to every soul who really wants it. Angels of God that ascend and descend the ladder that Jacob saw in vision will help everyone who chooses, to climb even to the highest heaven.

God Calls the Child Samuel*

Elkanah, a Levite of Mount Ephraim, was a wealthy and influential man who loved and feared the Lord. His wife, Hannah, was a woman of fervent piety and strong faith.

Their home was childless, so the husband took a second wife. But this step, prompted by lack of faith in God, did not bring happiness. Sons and daughters were added to the household, but the joy and beauty of the sacred marriage institution had been marred and the peace of the family broken.

Peninnah, the new wife, was jealous and narrow-minded and acted proud and contemptuous. To Hannah, hope seemed crushed and life a weary burden; yet she faced her pain with uncomplaining meekness.

At Shiloh Elkanah's services as a Levite were not demanded. Yet he went up with his family to worship and sacrifice at the appointed gatherings. Even during the sacred festivities connected with the service of God, the evil spirit that had cursed his home intruded. After presenting the thank offerings, all the family, according to the custom, united in a solemn yet joyous feast. Elkanah gave the mother of his children a portion for herself and for each of her sons and daughters. He gave Hannah a double portion to show that his affection for her was the same as if she had had a son. Then the second wife, fired with jealousy, claimed first place as one that God had highly favored, and she taunted Hannah about her childless condition.

This happened year by year until Hannah could no longer endure it. She wept uncontrollably and left the feast. Her husband tried to comfort her, but without success. " 'Why do you weep? Why do you not eat? And why is your heart grieved? Am I not better to you than ten sons?' "

Hannah made no accusations. She went to God with the burden she could share with no earthly friend. Earnestly she pleaded that He would grant her the gift of a son to train for Him. And she made a vow that if her request were granted, she would dedicate her child to God from his birth.

Hannah came near the entrance of the tabernacle and in the distress

_____
* This chapter is based on 1 Samuel 1; 2:1-11.

of her spirit "prayed . . . and wept in anguish." In those evil times, such scenes of worship were rare. Eli the high priest, watching Hannah, supposed that she was overcome with wine. Thinking he should give her a well-deserved rebuke, he said sternly, " 'How long will you be drunk? Put your wine away from you!' "

Startled and hurt, Hannah answered gently, " 'No, my lord, I am a woman of sorrowful spirit. I have drunk neither wine nor intoxicating drink, but have poured out my soul before the LORD. Do not consider your maidservant a wicked woman, for out of the abundance of my complaint and grief I have spoken until now.' "

The high priest was deeply moved, for he was a man of God. So instead of rebuke he uttered a blessing: " 'Go in peace, and the God of Israel grant your petition which you have asked of Him.' "

Hannah Gives Samuel to God

Hannah received the gift that she had earnestly asked for. As she looked on the child, she called him Samuel—"asked of God." As soon as the little one was old enough to be separated from his mother, she fulfilled her vow. He was her only son, the special gift of Heaven; but she had received him as a treasure belonging to God, and she would not withhold from the Giver what was His own.

Hannah went with her husband to Shiloh and presented her precious gift to the priest, saying, " 'For this child I prayed, and the LORD has granted me my petition which I asked of Him. Therefore I also have lent him to the LORD; as long as he lives he shall be lent to the LORD.' "
Eli, who was too lenient a father himself, was awed and humbled as he saw this mother's great sacrifice in parting with her only child so that she might devote him to the service of God. He felt condemned for his own selfish love, and in humiliation and reverence bowed before the Lord and worshiped. Hannah's heart was filled with joy and praise, and she poured out her gratitude to God.

From Shiloh, Hannah returned to her home at Ramah, leaving Samuel with Eli to be trained for service in the house of God. From his babyhood she had taught her son to regard himself as the Lord's. Every day he was the subject of her prayers. Every year she made a robe of service for him, and as she went up with her husband to worship at Shiloh, she gave the child this reminder of her love. Every fiber of the little garment had been woven with prayer that he would be pure, noble, and true. She earnestly pleaded that he would reach the greatness that Heaven values, that he would honor God and bless others.

What a reward was Hannah's! And what an encouragement to faithfulness is her example! There are opportunities committed to every mother. The humble round of duties that women regard as boring and tiresome should be looked upon as a grand and noble work. Through sunshine and shadow, the mother may make straight paths for the feet of her children, toward the glorious heights above. But it is only when she seeks to follow Christ in her own life that the mother can hope to form the character of her children after God's pattern. Every mother should go often to her Savior with the prayer, "Teach us, how shall we train the child, and what shall we do to him?" She will be given wisdom.

"The child Samuel grew in stature, and in favor both with the LORD and men." Samuel's youth was not free from evil influences or sinful example. The sons of Eli neither feared God nor honored their father; but Samuel did not seek their company nor follow their evil ways. He constantly tried to become what God wanted him to be.

The beauty of Samuel's character drew out the warm affection of the aged priest. Samuel was kind, generous, obedient, and respectful. Eli, pained by the evil ways of his own sons, found comfort and blessing in the presence of this child entrusted to him. No father ever loved his son or daughter more tenderly than Eli loved this youth. Filled with anxiety and remorse by the immoral behavior of his own sons, Eli turned to Samuel for comfort.

Every year saw more important trusts committed to him. While Samuel was still a child, Eli placed a linen ephod on him as a sign that he was set apart for the work of the sanctu-ary. Young as he was when he had been brought to minister in the tabernacle, Samuel had duties to perform, according to his ability. These were not always pleasant, but he performed them with a willing heart. He regarded himself as God's servant and his work as God's work. His efforts were accepted because they sprang from love to God and a sincere desire to do His will. Thus Samuel became a co-worker with the Lord of heaven and earth.

Integrity in Little Things

To perform every duty as something done for the Lord throws a charm around the humblest work and links the workers on earth with the holy beings who do God's will in heaven. Integrity in little things, doing little acts of fidelity and little deeds of kindness, will gladden the path of life. And when our work on earth is over, we will find that every one of the little duties faithfully performed has exerted an influence for good that can never perish.

The youth of our time may become as precious in the sight of God as Samuel was. By faithfully preserving their Christian integrity they may exert a strong influence to make the world better. God has a work for every one of them. Never did anyone achieve greater results for God and humanity than people may achieve today if they will be faithful to their God-given trust.

Eli and His Wicked Sons*

Eli, priest and judge in Israel, had a great influence over the tribes of Israel. But he did not rule his own household well. He was a permissive father. He did not correct the evil habits and passions of his children. Rather than have conflict with them, he would give them their own way.

The priest and judge of Israel had not been left in darkness about his duty to govern the children God had given to his care. But Eli shrank from this duty, because it involved crossing the will of his sons, and would require punishing and denying them. He let his children have whatever they desired and neglected the work of fitting them for God's service and the duties of life.

The father became subject to the children. His sons did not begin to understand the character of God or the sacredness of His law. From childhood they had been familiar with the sanctuary and its service, but they had lost all sense of its holiness and meaning. Eli had not restrained their disrespect for the solemn services, and when they reached manhood they were full of the deadly fruits of doubt and rebellion.

Though entirely unfit, they were placed as priests in the sanctuary to minister before God. These wicked men carried their rebellion into the service of God. The sacrifices, pointing forward to Christ's death, were designed to preserve the people's faith in the coming Redeemer. So it was absolutely essential to follow the Lord's directions concerning them to the letter. In the peace offerings only the fat was to be burned on the altar. A certain specified portion was reserved for the priests, but the greater part was returned to the offerer to eat in a sacrificial feast with friends. This would direct all hearts in gratitude and faith to the great Sacrifice that was to take away the sin of the world.

Not content with their share of the peace offerings, the sons of Eli demanded an additional portion. The priests took these sacrifices as an opportunity to enrich themselves at the expense of the people. They not only demanded more than their right, but refused to wait even until the fat had been burned as an offering to God. They claimed whatever portion pleased them, and, if denied, threatened to take it by force.

* This chapter is based on 1 Samuel 2:12-36.

This irreverence robbed the service of its sacred meaning, and the people "abhorred the offering of the LORD." They no longer recognized in the symbol the great Sacrifice to which they were to look forward. "Therefore the sin of the young men was very great before the LORD."

These unfaithful priests dishonored their sacred office by their vile, degrading practices. Many of the people were disgusted over the corrupt practices of Hophni and Phinehas, and they stopped coming to the place of worship. Ungodliness, immorality, and even idolatry gained ground to a fearful extent.

Eli had done great wrong in permitting his sons to minister as priests. Making excuses for them on one pretext and another, he became blinded to their sins. But at last he could no longer hide his eyes from the crimes of his sons. The people complained about their evil deeds, and the high priest did not dare any longer to remain silent. His sons saw the grief of their father, but their hard hearts were not touched. They heard his mild rebukes, but they were not impressed, and they would not change their evil course. If Eli had treated his wicked sons according to law, they would have been punished with death. Dreading to take any steps that would bring public disgrace and condemnation on them, he kept them in the most sacred positions of trust. He permitted them to corrupt the service of God and inflict an injury on the cause of truth that years could not undo. But God took the matter in hand.

Eli's Unfaithfulness Leads to Ruin

"A man of God came to Eli and said to him, 'Thus says the LORD: . . . "Why do you . . . honor your sons more than Me, to make yourselves fat with the best of all the offerings of Israel My people?" Therefore the LORD God of Israel says: "I said indeed that your house and the house of your father would walk before Me forever"; but now the LORD says: "Far be it from Me; for those who honor Me I will honor, and those who despise Me shall be lightly esteemed. . . . I will raise up for myself a faithful priest who shall do according to what is in My heart and in My mind. I will build him a sure house, and he shall walk before My anointed forever." ' "

Those whose blind affection for their children leads them to pamper them in their selfish desires, not rebuking sin and correcting evil, make it clear that they honor their wicked children more than they honor God. Eli should have attempted first to restrain evil by mild measures; but if these did not work he should have subdued the wrong even if by the severest means. We are just as responsible for evils that we might have stopped in others by parental or pastoral authority, as if the acts had been our own.

Eli overlooked the faults and sins of his sons in their childhood, fooling himself that after a time they would outgrow their evil tendencies. Many today make a similar mistake. They encourage wrong tendencies in their children, offering the excuse, "They are too young to be punished. Wait till they become older and we can reason with them." Thus the children grow up with traits of character that are a lifelong curse to them.

There is no greater curse on a home than to allow youth to have their own way. The children soon lose all respect for their parents, all regard for authority, and are led captive at the will of Satan. The influence of an out-of-control family is disastrous to society. It builds a tide of evil that affects families, communities, and governments.

Thousands of homes throughout Israel imitated Eli's family life. Actions speak louder than the most positive claim of godliness. The evils of parental unfaithfulness are great under any circumstances; they are ten times greater in the families of those who teach the people.

Effective Agents of Satan

When people use their sacred calling as a cover for selfish or sensual gratification, they make themselves effective agents of Satan. Like Hophni and Phinehas, they cause others to "abhor the offering of the LORD." They may do their evil deeds in secret for a time, but when their true character finally is exposed, the faith of the people receives a shock that often results in distrusting any-one who professes to teach the Word of God. The message of the true servant of Christ is received with doubt. The question constantly arises, "Won't this man prove to be like the one we thought so holy, and found so corrupt?"

Eli's reproof to his sons contains these solemn and fearful words: "If one man sin against another, the judge shall judge him: but if a man sin against the LORD, who shall intreat for him?" (KJV). If their crimes had injured only other people, the judge might have made reconciliation by setting a penalty and requiring restitution; and so the offenders might have been pardoned. But their sins were so interwoven with their ministry as priests of the Most High, the work of God was so profaned and dishonored before the people, that no atonement could be accepted for them. Their own father, though himself a high priest, dared not make intercession in their behalf; he could not shield them from the wrath of a holy God. Of all sinners, those are most guilty who cast contempt on the means that Heaven has provided for our redemption, who "crucify again for themselves the Son of God, and put him to an open shame." Hebrews 6:6.

Punishment, the Ark Taken*

God could not communicate with the high priest, Eli, and his sons. Their sins had shut out the presence of His Holy Spirit. But the child Samuel remained true to Heaven, and giving the message of condemnation to the house of Eli was Samuel's first task as a prophet of the Most High.

"While Eli was lying down in his place, and when his eyes had begun to grow so dim that he could not see, and before the lamp of God went out in the tabernacle of the LORD where the ark of God was, and while Samuel was lying down, . . . the LORD called Samuel."

Thinking that the voice was Eli's, the child hurried to the bedside of the priest, saying, " 'Here I am, for you called me.' " Eli answered, " 'I did not call; lie down again.' "

Three times Samuel was called, and three times he answered in the same way. Then Eli was convinced that the mysterious call was the voice of God. The Lord had passed by His chosen servant, the man of gray hairs, to speak with a child. This in itself was a bitter yet deserved rebuke to Eli and his family.

No envy or jealousy stirred in Eli's heart. He told Samuel to answer, " 'Speak, LORD, for Your servant hears.' "

Once more the voice came, and the child answered, " 'Speak, for Your servant hears.' "

"Then the LORD said to Samuel, 'Behold, I will do something in Israel at which both ears of everyone who hears it will tingle. In that day I will perform against Eli all that I have spoken concerning his house, from beginning to end. For I have told him that I will judge his house forever for the iniquity which he knows, because his sons made themselves vile, and he did not restrain them. . . . The iniquity of Eli's house shall not be atoned for by sacrifice or offering forever.' "

Samuel was filled with fear and amazement at the thought of having received so terrible a message. In the morning he went about his duties as usual, but with a heavy burden on his young heart. The Lord had not commanded him to reveal the fearful condemnation, so he remained silent. He trembled in the fear that some question would force him to

_____
* This chapter based on 1 Samuel 3 to 7.

declare the divine judgments against the one whom he loved and reverenced. Eli was confident that the message foretold some great calamity to him and his house. He called Samuel and told him to relate faithfully what the Lord had revealed. The youth obeyed, and the old man bowed in humble submission to the dreadful sentence. " 'It is the LORD,' " he said. " 'Let Him do what seems good to Him.' "

Eli Loses His Last Chance

Yet Eli did not show true repentance. He did not forsake his sin. Year after year the Lord delayed His threatened judgments. Eli might have done much to redeem the failures of the past, but the aged priest took no effective measures to correct the evils that were polluting the Lord's sanctuary and leading thousands in Israel to ruin. The patience of God caused Hophni and Phinehas to harden their hearts and become still bolder in transgression.

Eli made known to the whole nation the messages of warning and reproof to his family. By this means he hoped to undo the evil influence of his past neglect. But the people disregarded the warnings, as the priests had done. The people of surrounding nations also became bolder in their idolatry and crime. They felt no sense of guilt for their sins, as they would have felt if the Israelites had preserved their integrity. It became necessary for God to intervene, to maintain the honor of His name.

"Now Israel went out to battle against the Philistines, and encamped beside Ebenezer; and the Philistines encamped in Aphek." The Israelites undertook this expedition without counsel from God, without the agreement of high priest or prophet. "Then the Philistines put themselves in battle array against Israel. And when they joined battle, Israel was defeated by the Philistines, who killed about four thousand men of the army in the field." As the shattered, disheartened force returned to their camp, "the elders of Israel said, 'Why has the LORD defeated us today before the Philistines?' " They did not see that it was because of their own sins that this terrible disaster had occurred.

And they said, " 'Let us bring the ark of the covenant of the LORD from Shiloh to us, that when it comes among us it may save us from the hand of our enemies.' " The Lord had given no command or permission for the ark to come into the army. Yet the Israelites felt confident that victory would be theirs, and they gave a great shout when it was carried into the camp by the sons of Eli.

The Philistines considered the ark as the god of Israel. They said, " 'What does the sound of this great shout in the camp of the Hebrews mean?' Then they understood that the ark of the LORD had come into the camp. So the Philistines were afraid, for they said, 'God has come into the camp!' And they said, 'Woe to us! . . . These are the gods who struck the Egyptians with all the plagues in the wilderness. Be strong and conduct yourselves like men, you Philistines, that you do not become servants of the Hebrews, as they have been to you. Conduct yourselves like men, and fight!' "

The Philistines made a fierce attack, which resulted in great slaughter. Thirty thousand men lay dead on the field, and the ark of God was taken. The two sons of Eli died while fighting to defend it.

The most terrifying calamity that could happen had come on Israel. The ark of God was in the hands of the enemy. The symbol of the abiding presence and power of Jehovah was gone. In former days, miraculous victories had followed whenever it appeared. The visible symbol of the most high God had rested over it in the Holy of Holies. But now it had brought no victory, and there was mourning throughout Israel.

The law of God, contained in the ark, was a symbol of His presence, but they had shown contempt for the commandments and had grieved the Spirit of the Lord from among them. When the people did not honor God's revealed will by obedience to His law, the ark could help them little more than a common box. They looked to it the way the idolatrous nations looked to their gods. They violated the law it contained, for their worship of the ark led to hypocrisy and idolatry.

Tragic News Kills Eli

When the army went out to battle, Eli had stayed at Shiloh. With dread he waited for the result of the conflict, "for his heart trembled for the ark of God." Outside the gate of the tabernacle he sat by the highway day after day, anxiously expecting a messenger to come from the battlefield.

Finally a Benjamite, "with his clothes torn and dirt on his head," rushed to the town and repeated to eager crowds the news of defeat. The sound of wailing and crying reached Eli beside the tabernacle. The messenger came to him and said, " 'Israel has fled before the Philistines, and there has been a great slaughter among the people. Also your two sons, Hophni and Phinehas, are dead.' " Eli could endure all this, terrible as it was, for he had expected it. But when the messenger added, " 'and the ark of God has been captured,' " a look of extreme anguish passed over his face. The thought that his sin had dishonored God and caused Him to withdraw His presence from Israel was more than he could bear. He fell, "and his neck was broken and he died."

The wife of Phinehas feared the Lord. The death of her father-in-law and her husband, and above all, the terrible news that the ark of God was taken, caused her death. She felt that the last hope of Israel was gone. She gave the name Ichabod, or "inglorious," to the child born in this hour of adversity, with her dying breath mournfully repeating the words, " 'The glory has departed from Israel!' because the ark of God has been captured."

But the Lord had not cast His people aside entirely, and He used the ark to punish the Philistines. The divine presence, invisible, would still be with it to bring terror and destruction to those who transgressed His holy law. The wicked may triumph for a time as they see Israel being punished, but the time will come when they, too, must meet the sentence of a holy, sin-hating God.

Heathen Gods Cannot Stand Before the Ark of God

In triumph the Philistines took the ark to Ashdod and placed it in the house of their god Dagon. They imagined that the power that had gone with the ark would be theirs, and that this, united with the power of Dagon, would make them impossible to defeat.

But entering the temple the following day, they saw a sight that filled them with dismay and confusion. Dagon had fallen on his face before the ark of the Lord. The priests reverently lifted the idol and restored it to its place.

But the next morning they found it strangely mutilated, again lying on the earth before the ark. The upper part of this idol was like that of a man, and the lower part like a fish. Now every part that resembled the human form had been cut off, and only the body of the fish remained. Priests and people were horror-struck; they saw this as an evil sign, predicting destruction to themselves and their idols before the God of the Hebrews. They removed the ark from their temple and placed it in a building by itself.

The people who lived in Ashdod were struck with a distressing and fatal disease. Remembering the plagues inflicted on Egypt, the people blamed the presence of the ark among them for their afflictions. It was decided to take the ark to Gath. But the plague followed, and the people of that city sent it to Ekron. Here the people received it with terror, crying, " 'They have brought the ark of the God of Israel to us, to kill us and our people!' " The work of the destroyer went on, until "the cry of the city went up to heaven."

Afraid to keep the ark any longer among their homes, the people next placed it in the open field. A plague of mice followed, which infested the land, destroying the crops in the storehouse and in the field. Complete destruction now threatened the nation.

For seven months the ark remained in Philistia. The Israelites made no effort to recover it. But the Philistines were eager to get rid of it. Instead of being a source of strength to them, it was a burden and heavy curse. Yet they did not know what to do. The people called for the princes of the nation, with the priests and diviners, and asked, " 'What shall we do with the ark of the LORD? Tell us how we should send it to its place.' " They were advised to return it with a costly trespass offering. " 'Then,' " said the priests, " 'you will be healed.' "

The Ark Sent to Beth Shemesh

Based on a widespread superstition, the Philistine lords directed the people to make likenesses of the plagues that had afflicted them—" 'five golden tumors and five golden rats, according to the number of the lords of the Philistines. For,' " they said, " 'the same plague was on all of you and on your lords.' "

These wise men recognized that a mysterious power accompanied the ark. Yet they did not counsel the people to turn from their idolatry to serve the Lord. They still hated the God of Israel, though His judgments had compelled them to submit to His authority. Such submission cannot save the sinner. The heart must be yielded to God—must be subdued by divine grace—if God is to accept our repentance.

How great is God's patience toward the wicked! Ten thousand unnoticed mercies were silently falling on the pathway of the ungrateful and rebellious. But when they refused to listen to the voice of God in His created works and in the warnings and counsels of His word, He was forced to speak to them through judgments.

The priests and the diviners urged the people not to imitate the stubbornness of Pharaoh and the Egyptians and thus bring still greater afflictions on themselves. These religious leaders now proposed a plan that won the consent of all. The ark, with the golden trespass offering, was placed on a new cart, to avoid all danger of defilement. Two milk cows that had never worn a yoke were attached to the cart. Their calves were shut up at home and the cows were left free to go where they pleased. If the ark returned to the Is-raelites in this manner by way of Beth Shemesh, the nearest city of the Levites, the Philistines would take this as evidence that the God of Israel had done this great evil to them. " 'But if not,' " they said, " 'then we shall know that it is not His hand that struck us; it was by chance that it happened to us.' "

When they were set free, the cows turned from their young and took the direct road to Beth Shemesh. Guided by no human hand, the patient animals kept on their way. The divine Presence accompanied the ark safely to the very place designated.

The men of Beth Shemesh were reaping in the valley, "and saw the ark, and rejoiced to see it. Then the cart came into the field of Joshua of Beth Shemesh, and stood there; a large stone was there. So they split the wood of the cart and offered the cows as a burnt offering to the Lord." The Philistines had followed the ark "to the border of Beth Shemesh" and had seen its reception. The plague had stopped, and they were convinced that their calamities had been a judgment from the God of Israel.

The People of Israel Do Worse Than the Philistines

The people of Beth Shemesh quickly spread the news that the ark was in their possession, and many people from the surrounding country flocked to welcome its return. Sacrifices were offered. If the worshipers had repented of their sins, God's blessing would have rested on them. But while they rejoiced at the return of the ark as a good omen, they had no true sense of its sacredness. They let it remain in the harvest field. As they continued to look at the sacred chest, they began to wonder where its peculiar power came from. At last, overcome by curiosity, they removed the coverings and dared to open it.

Israel had been taught to regard the ark with awe and reverence. Only once a year was the high priest permitted to see the ark of God. Even the heathen Philistines had not dared to remove its coverings. Angels of heaven, unseen, always went with it in all its journeyings. The irreverent daring of the people at Beth Shemesh was speedily punished. Many were struck with sudden death.

This judgment did not lead the survivors to repent of their sin but only to regard the ark with superstitious fear. Eager to be free from its presence, the people of Beth Shemesh sent a message to the inhabitants of Kirjath Jearim, inviting them to take it away. With joy the people of this place welcomed the sacred chest and placed it in the house of Abinadab, a Levite. This man appointed his son Eleazar to take charge of it, and it remained there for many years.

The whole nation had come to acknowledge Samuel's call as a prophet. He had given proof of his allegiance by faithfully delivering the divine warning to the house of Eli, painful and difficult as the duty had been. "And the LORD was with him

and let none of his words fall to the ground. And all Israel from Dan to Beersheba knew that Samuel had been established as a prophet of the LORD."

Samuel visited the cities and villages throughout the land, hoping to turn the hearts of the people to the God of their fathers, and his efforts brought good results. After suffering the oppression of their ene-mies for twenty years, the Israelites "lamented after the LORD." Samuel counseled them, " 'If you return to the LORD with all your hearts, then put away the foreign gods and the Ashtoreths from among you, and prepare your hearts for the LORD, and serve Him only.' " Practical religion was taught in the days of Samuel, as Christ also taught it when He was on earth.

Repentance is the first step that all who would return to God must take. Individually we must humble our souls before God and put away our idols. When we have done all that we can do, the Lord will show us His salvation.

Samuel Becomes a Judge

A large assembly gathered at Mizpah. Here they held a solemn fast. With deep humiliation the people confessed their sins, and they gave Samuel the authority of judge.

The Philistines interpreted this gathering as a council of war and set out to scatter the Israelites before their plans could mature. News of their approach caused great terror in Israel. The people begged Samuel, " 'Do not cease to cry out to the

LORD our God for us, that He may save us from the hand of the Philistines.' "

While Samuel was in the act of presenting a lamb as a burnt offering, the Philistines drew near for battle. Then the Mighty One who had parted the Red Sea and made a way through Jordan for Israel showed His power again. A terrible storm burst on the advancing army, and the earth was littered with the bodies of mighty warriors.

The Israelites had stood trembling with hope and fear. When they saw the slaughter of their enemies, they knew that God had accepted their repentance. Though unprepared for battle, they took the weapons of the slaughtered Philistines and pursued the fleeing army. This victory came on the very field where, twenty years before, Israel had been defeated by the Philistines, the priests killed, and the ark of God taken. The Philistines were now so completely subdued that they surrendered the strongholds that they had taken from Israel, and they avoided any acts of hostility for many years. Other nations followed this example, and the Israelites enjoyed peace until the close of Samuel's lone administration.

So that they would never forget the occasion, Samuel set up a great stone as a memorial. He called it Ebenezer, "the stone of help," saying to the people, " 'Thus far the LORD has helped us.' "

The Schools of the Prophets

God had commanded the Hebrews to tell their children about His dealings with their ancestors. They were often to recount the mighty works of God and the promise of the Redeemer to come. Illustrations and symbols fixed the lessons firmly in the memory. The young mind was trained to see God both in the scenes of nature and the words of revelation. The stars, trees, and flowers, the mountains, the brooks, all spoke of the Creator. Worship at the sanctuary and the messages of the prophets were a revelation of God.

Such was the training of Moses in Goshen, of Samuel by Hannah, of David in Bethlehem, of Daniel before captivity separated him from his family, of Christ at Nazareth. Such was the training by which the child Timothy learned from his grandmother Lois and his mother Eunice. 2 Timothy 1:5; 3:15.

The schools of the prophets offered further provision for the instruction of the young. If a youth wanted to search deeper into truth so that he could become a teacher in Israel, these schools were open to him. Samuel founded the schools of the prophets to serve as a barrier against widespread corruption, to provide for the moral and spiritual welfare of youth, and to promote the prosperity of the nation by furnishing qualified leaders and counselors. He drew young men who were devout, intelligent, and studious. These were called the sons of the prophets. The instructors, well versed in divine truth, had themselves enjoyed communion with God and received of His Spirit. They had the respect and confidence of the people.

In Samuel's day there were two of these schools—at Ramah and at Kirjath Jearim. Others were established later.

The pupils supported themselves by farming or in some mechanical employment. In Israel it was thought to be a crime to allow children to grow up ignorant of useful work. Every child learned some trade, even if he was to be educated for holy office. Many religious teachers supported themselves by manual labor. Even as late as the time of the apostles, Paul and Aquila earned a livelihood by tentmaking.

The law of God, sacred history, sacred music, and poetry were the chief subjects of study in these schools. Instruction was different from the teaching in the theological schools of today, from which many students graduate knowing less about God and religious truth than when they entered. It was the aim of all study to learn the will of God and man's duty toward Him. In sacred history students traced the footsteps of Jehovah. Great truths set forth by the sanctuary symbols were brought to view, and faith grasped the focal point of all that system—the Lamb of God that was to take away the sin of the world.

Students were taught how to pray, how to approach their Creator, how to exercise faith in Him, and how to understand and obey the teachings of His Spirit. The presence of God's Spirit was evident in prophecy and sacred song.

Uplifting Music Taught

Music was made to lift the thoughts to what is pure and elevating, and to awaken devotion and gratitude to God in the soul. But how many use this gift to exalt self instead of to glorify God! A love for music becomes one of the most successful agencies that Satan employs to draw the mind from duty and from thinking on eternal things.

Music forms a part of God's worship in the courts above, and in our songs of praise we should try to approach as nearly as possible to the harmony of the heavenly choirs. Singing is as much an act of worship as is prayer. The heart must feel the spirit of the song to give it right expression.

Aren't there some lessons that the educators of our day might well learn from the ancient schools of the Hebrews? Real success in education depends on fidelity in carrying out the Creator's plan.

The true object of education is to restore the image of God in the soul. Sin has nearly erased the image of God in human beings. To bring them back to the perfection in which they were first created is the great purpose of life. It is the work of parents and teachers, in educating the youth, to cooperate with God's plan. Every ability, every attribute with which the Creator has endowed us, is to be used for His glory and for the uplifting of others.

If this principle were given the attention it deserves, there would be a radical change in some current methods of education. Instead of appealing to pride and selfish ambition, teachers would try to awaken love for goodness, truth, and beauty. The student would not seek to excel others but to fulfill the Creator's purpose and receive His likeness. Instead of being driven by the desire to exalt self, which dwarfs and debases the mind, the student would be directed to the Creator.

" 'The fear of the LORD is the beginning of wisdom, and the *knowledge of the Holy One* is understanding.' " Proverbs 9:10. To impart this knowledge and to mold the character in harmony with it should be the goal of the teacher's work. The psalmist says, "All Your commandments are righteousness"; and "through Your precepts I get understanding." Psalm 119:172, 104. Through the Bible and the book of nature we are to gain a knowledge of God.

The mind gradually adapts itself to the subjects on which it dwells. If occupied only with trivial matters, it will become dwarfed and weak. If never required to grapple with difficult problems, it will almost lose the power of growth. As an educating power the Bible has no rival. It came fresh from the fountain of eternal truth, and a divine hand has preserved its purity through all the ages. It lights up the far-distant past, where human research tries in vain to penetrate. Only here can we find a history of our race untarnished by human prejudice or pride. Here are recorded the struggles, defeats, and victories of the greatest people this world has ever known. Here the curtain that separates us from the unseen world is lifted, and we see the conflict of the opposing forces of good and evil, from the first entrance of sin to the final triumph of righteousness. All of this is to reveal the character of God. The student is brought into fellowship with the infinite mind. Such a study cannot fail to expand and invigorate the mental powers.

The Bible unfolds principles that are the cornerstone of society and the safeguard of the family. If studied and obeyed, the Word of God would give to the world men and women of strength and solid character, of keen perception and sound judgment— people who would be a blessing to the world.

All true science is an interpretation of God's handwriting in the material world. Scientific research brings only fresh evidences of the wisdom and power of God. Rightly understood, both the book of nature and the Written Word make us acquainted with God by teaching us something of the wise and beneficial laws through which He works.

Teachers should copy the example of the Great Teacher, who drew illustrations that simplified His teachings and impressed them more deeply on the minds of His hearers. The birds in the leafy branches, the flowers of the valley, the lofty trees, the fruitful lands, the growing grain, the barren soil, the setting sun gilding the skies with golden beams—all illustrated His lessons. He connected the visible works of the Creator with the words of life that He spoke.

Religion Promotes Health and Happiness

The things of nature speak to us of the Creator's love. This world is not all sorrow and misery. "God is love" is written on every opening bud, on the petals of every flower, and on every blade of grass. There are flowers on the thistles, and thorns are hidden by roses. Everything in nature testifies to God's desire to make His children happy. When He forbids something, it is not just to display His authority; He has the well-being of His children in view. He does not require them to give up anything that they would be better off retaining.

The opinion that religion does not promote health or happiness is one of the most harmful errors.

Scripture says: "The fear of the LORD leads to life, and he who has it will abide in satisfaction." Proverbs 19:23. The words of wisdom "are life to those who find them, and health to all their flesh." Proverbs 4:22.

True religion brings us into harmony with the laws of God: physical, mental, and moral. It teaches self-control, serenity, temperance. Religion ennobles the mind, refines the taste, and sanctifies the judgment. Faith in God's love and overruling guidance lightens the burdens of anxiety and care. It fills the heart with joy and contentment, whether one's lot in life is high or low. Religion tends to promote health, to lengthen life, and to heighten our enjoyment of all its blessings. It opens a never-failing fountain of happiness. No real joy can be found in the path forbidden by Him who knows what is best.

We may profitably study the physical as well as the religious training in the schools of the Hebrews. There is a close relationship between the mind and the body. In order to reach a high moral and intellectual standard, we must obey the laws that control our physical being.

And now, as in the days of Israel, every youth should learn some branch of manual labor. Young men and women should be taught to work, even if they could be certain of never needing to resort to manual labor for support. Without physical exercise, no one can have vigorous health. The discipline of well-regulated labor is essential to a strong and active mind and a noble character.

Every student should devote a portion of each day to active work. This would shield the youth from many evil and degrading practices that often result from being idle. Such a practice is in harmony with the primary purpose of education.

If the youth see the tender love the Father in heaven has extended toward them, and the dignity and honor to which He calls them—even to become the sons and daughters of God—thousands will turn away firmly from selfish aims and pleasures that have held their attention until then. They will learn to hate sin, not merely from hope of reward or fear of punishment, but from a sense of its inherent evil.

God does not ask the youth to lower their sights. By the grace of God they are to set their goals higher than mere selfish and earthly interests—as much higher as the heavens are higher than the earth.

And the education begun in this life will continue in the life to come. " 'Eye has not seen, nor ear heard, nor have entered into the heart of man the things which God has prepared for those who love Him.' " 1 Corinthians 2:9. We will reach the fullness of joy and blessing in the hereafter. Eternity alone can reveal the glorious destiny to which men and women, restored to God's image, may attain.

Saul, the First King of Israel*

The government of Israel was administered in the name of God. The work of Moses, of the seventy elders, of the rulers and judges, was simply to enforce the laws that God had given; they had no authority to legislate for the nation. This was the condition on which Israel was to exist as a nation.

The Lord foresaw that Israel would want a king, but He did not change the principles on which the state was founded. The king was to be the deputy of the Most High. God was the head of the nation. (See Appendix, Note 7.)

When the Israelites first settled in Canaan, the nation prospered under the rule of Joshua. But interaction with other nations brought a change. The people adopted many of the customs of their heathen neighbors and no longer appreciated the honor of being God's chosen people. Attracted by the pomp and display of heathen kings, they became tired of their own simplicity. Jealousy sprang up between the tribes. Internal disputes made them weak. They had to deal with invasion by heathen enemies, and the people were coming to believe that the tribes must be united under a strong central government. They wanted to be free from the rule of their divine Sovereign. The demand for a king became widespread throughout Israel.

Under Samuel's administration the nation had prospered, order had been restored, godliness promoted, and the spirit of discontent held back for the time. But when he got older, the prophet appointed his two sons to act as his assistants. The young men were stationed at Beersheba to administer justice among the people near the southern border of the land.

They did not prove worthy but "turned aside after dishonest gain, took bribes, and perverted justice." They had not copied the pure, unselfish life of their father. To some extent he had been too permissive with his sons, and the result was plain to see in their character.

This gave the people a pretext for urging the change they had secretly desired for a long time. "All the elders of Israel gathered together and came to Samuel at Ramah, and

---

* This chapter is based on 1 Samuel 8 to 12.

said to him, 'Look, you are old, and your sons do not walk in your ways. Now make us a king to judge us like all the nations.' " If Samuel had known about the evil course of his sons, he would have removed them immediately, but this was not what the people wanted. Samuel saw that their real motive was discontent and pride. No one had lodged a complaint against Samuel. Everyone acknowledged that he had governed with integrity and wisdom. The old prophet gave no rebuke, but he carried the matter to the Lord in prayer and sought counsel from Him alone.

The Lord Warns Israel of Their Mistake

The Lord said to Samuel: " 'Heed the voice of the people in all that they say to you; for they have not rejected you, but they have rejected Me, that I should not reign over them. According to all the works which they have done since the day that I brought them up out of Egypt, even to this day—with which they have forsaken Me and served other gods—so they are doing to you also.' "

Israel had prospered the most when they acknowledged Jehovah as their King, when they believed that the laws and the government that He had established were superior to those of other nations. But by straying from God's law the Hebrews had failed to become the people that God wanted to make them. Then they blamed God's government for all the evils that resulted from their own sin and foolish actions.

The Lord permitted the people to follow their own choice, because they refused to be guided by His counsel. When people choose to have their own way, He often grants their desires so that they may come to realize their folly. Whatever the heart desires contrary to the will of God will end up to be a curse rather than a blessing.

God instructed Samuel to grant the request of the people but to warn them of the Lord's disapproval and to make known what would be the result of their choice. He faithfully set before them the burdens that a king would lay upon them and the contrast between such oppression and their present freedom and prosperity. Their king would imitate the pomp and luxury of other monarchs. Heavy demands on themselves and their property would be necessary. The king would require the best of their young men for his service. They would be made charioteers and horsemen and runners before him. They must fill the ranks of his army and be required to work *his* fields, reap *his* harvests, and manufacture implements of war for *his* service. To support his royal state he would take the best of their lands. The most valuable of their servants and cattle he would take and " 'put them to his work.' " Besides all this, the king would require a tenth of all their income, the profits from their work or the products of the soil. " 'You will be his servants,' " concluded the prophet. " 'And the LORD will not hear you in that day.' " Once a monarchy was established, they could not set it aside whenever they pleased.

The People Reject God as King

But the people returned the answer, " 'No, but we will have a king over us, that we also may be like all the nations, and that our king may judge us and go out before us and fight our battles.' "

" 'Like all the nations.' " To be unlike other nations in this respect was a special privilege. God had separated the Israelites from every other people, to make them His own special treasure. But they wanted to imitate the heathen! As those who claim to be the people of God depart from the Lord, they become ambitious for the honors of the world. Many urge that by uniting with secular people and conforming to their customs they can exert a stronger influence over the ungodly. But all who take this path separate themselves from the Source of their strength. Becoming friends of the world, they are enemies of God.

Samuel listened to the people with deep sadness. But the Lord said to him, " 'Make them a king.' " The prophet had faithfully presented the warning, and they had rejected it. With a heavy heart he left to prepare for the great change in the government.

Samuel's life of purity and unselfish devotion was a rebuke both to self-serving priests and to the proud, sensual congregation of Israel. His work carried the seal of Heaven. He was honored by the world's Redeemer, under whose guidance he ruled the Hebrew nation. But the people, weary of his godliness, despised his humble authority and rejected him in favor of a man who would rule them as a king.

We see the likeness of Christ reflected in the character of Samuel. It was Christ's holiness that stirred up against Him the fiercest passions of hypocrites who only professed godliness. The Jews looked for the Messiah to break the oppressor's yoke, yet they cherished the sins that fastened it on their necks. If Christ had praised their piety, they would have accepted Him as their king, but they would not tolerate His fearless rebuke of their vices. It has been this way in every age of the world. When rebuked by the example of those who hate sin, false Christians become the agents of Satan to persecute the faithful.

God had reserved to Himself the right to choose their king. The choice fell on Saul, a son of Kish, of the tribe of Benjamin.

"There was not a more handsome person than he among the children of Israel." As someone with a noble and dignified bearing, good looking and tall, he appeared like one born to command. Yet Saul had none of those higher qualities that constitute true wisdom. He had not learned to control his thoughtless impulses. He had never felt the renewing power of divine grace.

Saul was the son of a wealthy chief, yet he was performing the humble duties of a farmer. Some of his father's animals had strayed on the mountains, and Saul went with a servant to look for them. As they were not far from Ramah, the home of Samuel, the servant suggested that they ask the prophet concerning the missing property.

As they approached the city, they were told that a religious service was about to take place and that the prophet had already arrived. Worship of God was now carried on throughout the land. With no services at the tabernacle, sacrifices for a while were offered elsewhere. The cities of the priests and Levites, where the people went for instruction, were chosen for this purpose. The highest points in these cities were usually selected as the place of sacrifice and hence were called the "high places."

King Revealed to Samuel

At the gate of the city Saul was met by the prophet himself. God revealed to Samuel that at that time the chosen king of Israel would appear before him. As they now stood face to face, the Lord said to Samuel, " 'There he is, the man of whom I spoke to you. This one shall reign over My people.' "

Assuring Saul that the lost animals had been found, Samuel urged him to stay and attend the feast, at the same time giving some hint of the great destiny before him. " 'On whom is all the desire of Israel? Is it not on you, and on all your father's house?' " The demand for a king had become a matter of absorbing interest to the whole nation, yet with modest self-depreciation, Saul replied, " 'Am I not a Benjamite, of the smallest of the tribes of Israel, and my family the least of all the families of the tribe of Benjamin? Why then do you speak like this to me?' "

Samuel took the stranger to the place of assembly. At the prophet's direction, the place of honor was given to Saul, and at the feast the best portion was set before him. When the services were over, Samuel took his guest to his own home and talked with him there, setting forth the great principles on which the government of Israel had been established, in this way seeking to prepare him for his high position.

When Saul left the next morning, the prophet went with him. After they had passed through the town, he directed the servant to go forward. Then he told Saul to stand still to receive a message sent him from God. "Then Samuel took a flask of oil and poured it on his head, and kissed him and said, 'Is it not because the LORD has anointed you commander over His inheritance?' " He assured Saul that he would be qualified by the Spirit of God for the role awaiting him. " 'The Spirit of the LORD will come upon you, and you will . . . be turned into another man. And let it be . . . that you do as the occasion demands; for God is with you.' "

As Saul went on his way, everything happened as the prophet had said. At Gibeah, his own city, a group of prophets returning from "the high place" were singing the praise of God to the music of the flute and the harp, a stringed instrument and a tambourine. As Saul approached them, the Spirit of the Lord came over him also, and he joined in their song of praise and prophesied with them. He spoke with great fluency and wisdom and joined earnestly in the service. Those who had known him exclaimed in astonishment, " 'What is this that has come upon the son of Kish? Is Saul also among the prophets?' "

The Holy Spirit worked a great change in him. The light of divine holiness shone in on the darkness of the natural heart. He saw himself as he was before God. He saw the beauty of holiness. He was called to begin the warfare against sin and was made to feel that in this conflict his strength must come wholly from God. The plan of salvation, which before this had seemed dim and uncertain, opened to his understanding. The Lord blessed him with courage and wisdom for his high position.

Saul Publicly Acclaimed King

The anointing of Saul as king had not been made known to the nation. God's choice was to be publicly revealed by lot. For this purpose Samuel called the people together at Mizpah. Prayer was offered for divine guidance, and then followed the solemn ceremony of casting the lot. In silence the multitude awaited the choice. One by one, the lot designated the tribe, the family, and the household, and then Saul, the son of Kish, was pointed out as the individual chosen.

But Saul was not in the assembly. Burdened with a sense of the great responsibility about to fall on him, he had secretly withdrawn. He was brought back to the congregation, who noticed with pride that he had a kingly bearing and noble form, being "taller than any of the people from his shoulders upward." Samuel exclaimed, " 'Do you see him whom the LORD has chosen, that there is no one like him among all the people?' " In response one long, loud shout of joy arose from the throng, " 'Long live the king!' "

Samuel then set before the people "the behavior of royalty," stating the principles upon which the monarchical government was based. The king was not to be an absolute monarch but to hold his power in obedience to the will of the Most High. This message was recorded in a book. Though the nation had despised Samuel's warning, the faithful prophet still tried to guard their liberties as far as possible.

While most of the people were ready to make Saul their king, there was a large group that was opposed. For a king to be chosen from Benjamin, the smallest tribe of Israel—and to neglect both Judah and Ephraim, the largest and most powerful—was a slight that they could not accept. Those who had been most urgent in their demand for a king were the ones who refused to accept the man God had appointed.

Saul returned to Gibeah, leaving Samuel to administer the government as before. He made no attempt to use force to claim the throne. He quietly occupied himself with the farm duties, leaving it entirely to God to establish his authority.

Soon after, the Ammonites invaded the territory east of Jordan and threatened the city of Jabesh Gilead. The inhabitants tried to secure peace by offering to pay tribute money to the Ammonites. The cruel king would not agree except on condition that he put out the right eye of everyone.

Messengers were sent at once to seek help from the tribes west of Jordan. Saul, returning at night from the field, heard the loud wail that told of some great calamity. When he learned the shameful story, all his dormant powers were roused. "The Spirit of God came upon Saul. . . . So he took a yoke of oxen and cut them in pieces, and sent them throughout all the territory of Israel by the hands of messengers, saying, 'Whoever does not go out with Saul and Samuel to battle, so shall it be done to his oxen.' "

Three hundred thirty thousand men gathered under the command of Saul. By a rapid night march, Saul and his army crossed the Jordan and arrived near Jabesh in "the morning watch." Dividing his force into three companies, he attacked the Ammonite camp at that early hour, when they were not suspecting danger and were least secure. In the panic that followed, they were defeated with great slaughter. "Those who survived were scattered, so that no two of them were left together."

The promptness and bravery of Saul, as well as his generalship, were qualities that the people of Israel wanted in a monarch, so that they might cope with other nations. They now greeted him as their king, giving the honor of the victory to human power and forgetting that without God's special blessing all their efforts would have been in vain. Some proposed putting to death those who had refused at first to acknowledge the authority of Saul. But the king interfered, saying, " 'Not a man shall be put to death this day, for today the LORD has accomplished salvation in Israel.' " Instead of taking honor to himself, he gave the glory to God. Instead of showing revenge, he modeled forgiveness. This is unmistakable evidence that the grace of God dwells in the heart.

Samuel now proposed that they call a national assembly at Gilgal to publicly confirm the kingdom to Saul. It was done, and "there they made sacrifices of peace offerings before the LORD, and there Saul and all the men of Israel rejoiced greatly."

On this plain, linked with so many thrilling associations, stood Samuel and Saul; and when the shouts of welcome to the king had died away, the old prophet gave his parting words as ruler of the nation.

Samuel had previously set forth the principles that should govern both the king and the people, and he wanted to add the weight of his own example to his words. From childhood he had been connected with the work of God, and during his long life he had always had one objective—the glory of God and the highest good of Israel.

As a result of sin Israel had lost their faith in God and their belief in

His power and wisdom to rule the nation—lost confidence in His ability to maintain His cause. Before they could find true peace, they must see and confess the sin of which they had been guilty.

Samuel reviewed the history of Israel from the day God brought them from Egypt. The King of kings had fought their battles. Often their sins had brought them under the power of their enemies, but no sooner did they turn from their evil ways than God's mercy raised up a deliverer. The LORD sent Gideon and Barak, and " 'Jephthah, and Samuel, and delivered you out of the hand of your enemies on every side; and you dwelt in safety.' " Yet when threatened with danger they had declared, " 'A king shall reign over us,' " when, said the prophet, " 'the LORD your God was your king.' "

In humiliation the people now confessed their sin, the very sin of which they had been guilty. " 'Pray for your servants to the LORD your God, that we may not die; for we have added to all our sins the evil of asking a king for ourselves.' "

Samuel did not leave the people in discouragement, for this would have prevented them from making any effort for a better life. To look on God as severe and unforgiving would expose them to many temptations. " 'Do not fear,' " was the message of God by His servant: " 'You have done all this wickedness; yet do not turn aside from following the LORD, but serve the LORD with all your heart. And do not turn aside . . . . For the LORD will not forsake His people.' "

Samuel spoke no word of rebuke for the ingratitude with which Israel had repaid his lifelong devotion, but he assured them of his unceasing interest for them. " 'Far be it from me that I should sin against the LORD in ceasing to pray for you; but I will teach you the good and the right way. Only fear the LORD, and serve Him in truth with all your heart; for consider what great things He has done for you.' "

Saul Makes a Terrible Mistake*

After the assembly at Gilgal, Saul disbanded the army that had come together at his call to overthrow the Ammonites. This was a serious error. His army was filled with hope and courage by the recent victory. If he had moved at once against other enemies of Israel, he could have struck a mighty blow for the liberties of the nation.

Meanwhile, the Philistines were active. They had still kept some hill fortresses in Israel, and now they established themselves in the very heart of the country. During their long oppressive rule, the Philistines had tried to strengthen their power by forbidding the Israelites to practice the trade of smiths, so they could not make weapons of war. Even in peacetime, the Hebrews still took such work to the Philistine garrisons. Dispirited by long oppression and controlled by love of ease, the men of Israel had largely neglected to provide themselves with weapons of war. The Israelites could obtain bows and slings, but none of them possessed a spear or sword except Saul and his son Jonathan.

Not until the second year of Saul's reign did he make an attempt to subdue the Philistines. The first blow was struck by Jonathan, who overcame their garrison at Geba. The exasperated Philistines got ready for a speedy attack on Israel. Saul declared war by the sound of the trumpet, calling all men of war, including the tribes across the Jordan, to assemble at Gilgal.

The Philistines had gathered an immense force at Michmash—"thirty thousand chariots and six thousand horsemen, and people as the sand which is on the seashore in multitude." Saul and his army at Gilgal were appalled at the mighty forces they would have to encounter in battle. Many were so terrified that they did not dare to come to the encounter. Others hid in caves and amid rocks in that region. As the time drew near, desertions rapidly increased, and those who did not leave were filled with terror.

When Saul was anointed king, Samuel had given him explicit directions about what he should do at this time. " 'You shall go down before me to Gilgal,' " said the prophet, " 'and

---

* This chapter is based on 1 Samuel 13; 14.

surely I will come down to you to offer burnt offerings and make sacrifices of peace offerings. Seven days
you shall wait, till I come to you and
show you what you should do.' "
1 Samuel 10:8.

Discouraged by Circumstance

Day after day Saul waited, but
without encouraging the people and
inspiring confidence in God. Before
the designated time had fully passed,
he allowed himself to be discouraged by his difficult circumstances.
Instead of trying to prepare the
people for the service that Samuel
was coming to perform, he indulged
in unbelief. To seek God by sacrifice
was a most solemn work; God required His people to search their
hearts and repent of their sins, so
that their offerings would be acceptable, and He could bless their efforts to conquer the enemy. But
Saul had grown restless; and the
people, instead of trusting in God
for help, were looking to the king to
lead and direct them.

Yet the Lord still cared for them
and did not abandon them. He
brought them into difficult places to
convict them of how foolish it is to
depend on human strength and that
they should turn to Him as their only
help. The time for testing Saul had
come. Would he depend on God and
patiently wait according to His command, showing that God could trust
him as the ruler of His people, even
under pressure? Or would he be unprincipled and unworthy of his sacred
responsibility? Would the king listen
to the Ruler of all kings? Would he

turn the attention of his fainthearted
soldiers to the One who has everlasting strength and deliverance?

With growing impatience he
waited for Samuel to arrive, blaming
the prophet's absence for the distress
and desertion of his army. The appointed time came, but the man of
God did not appear. God's leading
had delayed His servant. Feeling that
he must do something to calm the
people, Saul decided to call an assembly and offer sacrifice to seek divine aid. God had directed that only
the priests should present sacrifices
before Him. But Saul commanded,
" 'Bring a burnt offering,' " and he
approached the altar and offered the
sacrifice.

Saul's Presumption

"Now it happened, as soon as he
had finished offering the burnt offering, that Samuel came." Samuel saw
at once that Saul had violated the
clear directions given him. If Saul
had fulfilled the conditions for the
promised divine help, the LORD
would have worked a marvelous deliverance for Israel. But Saul was so
well satisfied with himself that he
went out to meet the prophet expecting approval rather than criticism.

Samuel asked, " 'What have you
done?' " and Saul offered excuses for
taking such liberties. " 'When I saw
that the people were scattered from
me, and that you did not come within the days appointed, and that the
Philistines gathered together at Michmash, then I said, "The Philistines
will now come down on me at Gilgal,

and I have not made supplication to the LORD." Therefore I felt compelled, and offered a burnt offering.'

"And Samuel said to Saul, 'You have done foolishly. You have not kept the commandment of the LORD your God, which He commanded you. For now the LORD would have established your kingdom over Israel forever. But now your kingdom shall not continue. The LORD has sought for Himself a man after His own heart, and the LORD has commanded him to be commander over His people.' . . . Then Samuel arose and went up from Gilgal to Gibeah of Benjamin."

Either Israel must cease to be the people of God, or the monarchy and the nation must be governed by divine power. In Israel no monarchy could prosper that did not acknowledge the supreme authority of God in all things.

In this time of trial, Saul's failure showed that he was unfit to be the representative of God to His people. He would mislead Israel. His will, rather than the will of God, would be the controlling power. Since he had failed, God's plans must be accomplished by someone else. The government of Israel must be committed to someone who would rule according to the will of Heaven.

The Reason for Saul's Sad Failure

Saul was out of favor with God but was unwilling to humble his heart in repentance. He was not ignorant of Israel's defeat when Hophni and Phinehas had brought the ark of God into the camp; and yet, knowing all this, he determined to send for the sacred chest and the priest who accompanied it. By doing so he hoped to reassemble his scattered army and give battle to the Philistines. Then he could do without Samuel and free himself from the prophet's unwelcome criticisms and reproofs.

The Holy Spirit had been granted to Saul to give him understanding and soften his heart. And yet how stubborn he was in choosing the wrong! That impulsive spirit, not trained to submission early in life, was always ready to rebel against divine authority. People cannot spend years perverting the powers God has given them and then, when they choose to change, find these powers fresh and free for an opposite course.

Saul's efforts to rally the people failed. His force reduced to six hundred men, he retreated to the fortress at Geba on the south side of a deep, rugged gorge a few miles north of Jerusalem. On the north side of the valley, at Michmash, the Philistine force had encamped, sending troops out in different directions to ravage the country.

Jonathan, the King's Son, Is Honored

God had permitted a crisis in order to rebuke Saul and teach His people a lesson of humility and faith. Because of Saul's sin in offering the sacrifice himself, the Lord would not give him the honor of defeating the Philistines. Jonathan, the king's son, who feared the Lord, was chosen. Moved by a divine impulse, he put forward a plan to his armor-bearer that they make a secret attack on the enemy's camp. " 'It may be,' " he urged, " 'that the LORD will work for us. For nothing restrains the LORD from saving by many or by few.' "

The armor-bearer, also a man of faith and prayer, encouraged the idea. Together they left the camp secretly to avoid opposition. With earnest prayer to the Guide of Israel, they agreed on a sign to help them know how to proceed. Going down into the gorge separating the two armies, they silently threaded their way under the cliff, partially hidden by the ridges of the valley. Approaching the fortress they came in sight of their enemies, who taunted them: " 'Look, the Hebrews are coming out of the holes where they have hidden. . . . Come up to us, and we will show you something,' " meaning that they would punish the two Israelites for their daring. This challenge was the sign that Jonathan and his companion had agreed to accept as evidence that the Lord would bless their efforts.

Choosing a secret and difficult path, the warriors made their way to a cliff that had been thought out of reach and was not strongly guarded. Thus they penetrated the enemy's camp and killed the sentinels, who, overcome with surprise and fear, offered no resistance.

Angels of heaven shielded Jonathan and his attendant; angels fought by their side, and the Philistines fell before them. The earth trembled as though a great multitude with cavalry and chariots were approaching. Jonathan recognized the signs of divine aid, and even the Philistines knew that God was working for the deliverance of Israel. Great fear seized the army. In the confusion the Philistines began to kill one another.

Soon the noise of the battle reached the camp of Israel. The king's sentinels reported great confusion among the Philistines and that their numbers were decreasing. Seeing that the Philistines were being driven back, Saul led his army to join the assault. The Hebrews who had deserted to the enemy now turned against them. Great numbers also came out of their hiding places. As the Philistines fled, Saul's army inflicted terrible havoc on the fugitives.

Again Saul Is Foolish

Determined to make the most of his advantage, the king rashly forbade his soldiers to partake of food for the entire day. " 'Cursed is the man who eats any food until evening, before I have taken vengeance on my enemies.' " The victory had already been gained without Saul's knowledge or cooperation, but he hoped to distinguish himself by the complete destruction of the defeated army. The command to refrain from food showed that the king was indifferent to the needs of his people when these conflicted with his desire to exalt himself. By his own declaration, his goal was not "that the Lord may take vengeance on *His* enemies" but that " '*I* have taken vengeance on *my* enemies.' "

The people had been engaged in warfare all day and were faint for lack of food. As soon as the hours of restriction were over, they rushed to the spoils and devoured meat with the blood, violating the law that prohibited the eating of blood.

Jonathan had not heard of the king's command, and during the day's battle he unwittingly offended by eating a little honey as he passed through some woods. Saul had declared that anyone violating his ban would be punished with death. Jonathan had not been guilty of a willful sin, and God had brought about deliverance through him, but the king declared that the sentence must be executed. " 'God do so and more also,' " was his terrible sentence; " 'you shall surely die, Jonathan.' "

Jonathan's Life Is Saved

Saul could not claim the honor of the victory, but he hoped to be honored for his zeal in enforcing the sacredness of his oath. The people refused to allow the sentence to be carried out. Braving the anger of the king, they declared, " 'Shall Jonathan die, who has accomplished this great salvation in Israel? Certainly not! As the LORD lives, not one hair of his head shall fall to the ground, for he has worked with God this day.' "

Jonathan's deliverance was a severe reproof to the king's rashness. Saul felt a premonition that his curses would return on his own head. He went back to his home, moody and dissatisfied.

Those who are most ready to excuse themselves in sin are often the most severe in condemning others. Many, like Saul, when convinced that the Lord is not with them, refuse to see the cause of their trouble in themselves. They indulge in cruel judgment of others who are better than they.

Often those who are seeking to exalt themselves are brought into situations where their true character is revealed. This is how it was in the case of Saul. Kingly honors were more important to him than justice, mercy, or benevolence. Thus the people were led to see their error. They had exchanged the godly prophet, whose prayers had brought down blessings, for a king who had prayed for a curse upon them. If the men of Israel had not intervened, Jonathan, their deliverer, would have died by the king's decree. Afterward, as the people followed Saul's guidance, what doubts they must have had! How bitter the thought that Saul had been placed on the throne by their own act!

Saul Rejected as King*

Saul's errors were not yet beyond remedy. The Lord would grant him another opportunity to learn the lesson of unquestioning faith in His word and obedience to His commands.

When Samuel had reproved him at Gilgal, Saul felt he had been treated unjustly and offered excuses for his error. Samuel loved Saul as his own son, but Saul resented Samuel's rebuke and from then on avoided him as far as possible.

But the Lord sent His servant with another message to Saul: " 'Thus says the LORD of hosts: "I will punish what Amalek did to Israel, how he laid wait for him on the way when he came up from Egypt. Now go and attack Amalek, and utterly destroy all that they have, and do not spare them. But kill both man and woman, infant and nursing child, ox and sheep, camel and donkey." ' " Through Moses the Lord had pronounced sentence on the Amalekites. The history of their cruelty toward Israel had been recorded with the command, " 'You will blot out the remembrance of Amalek from under heaven. You shall not forget.' " Deuteronomy 25:19.

For four hundred years God had postponed execution of this sentence, but the Amalekites had not turned from their sins. Now the time had come for the sentence, so long delayed, to be executed.

To our merciful God, punishment is a strange act. " 'As I live,' says the Lord GOD, 'I have no pleasure in the death of the wicked, but that the wicked turn from his way and live.' " The Lord is "merciful and gracious, long-suffering, and abounding in goodness and truth, . . . forgiving iniquity and transgression and sin, by no means clearing the guilty." Ezekiel 33:11; Exodus 34:6, 7. He does not delight in vengeance, but He will execute judgment on the transgressors of His law. He is forced to do this to preserve earth's population from complete depravity and ruin. In order to save some, He must cut off those who have become hardened in sin.

But while inflicting judgment, God remembered mercy. The Amalekites were to be destroyed, but the Kenites, who lived among them,

---

* This chapter is based on 1 Samuel 15.

were spared. These people were not completely free from idolatry, but they were worshipers of God and friendly to Israel.

King Saul Gets Another Chance

On receiving the orders against the Amalekites, Saul at once declared war. At the call to battle the men of Israel flocked to his banner. The Israelites were not to receive either the honor of the conquest or the spoils of their enemies; they were to engage in the war only as an act of obedience to God. God intended that all nations should see the doom of this people that had defied His rulership.

"Saul attacked the Amalekites. . . . He also took Agag [the] king. . . . But Saul and the people spared Agag and the best of the sheep, the oxen, the fatlings, the lambs, and all that was good, and were unwilling to utterly destroy them. But everything despised and worthless, that they utterly destroyed."

This victory rekindled the pride that was Saul's greatest danger. Eager to heighten the honor of his triumphal return, Saul dared to imitate the customs of the nations around him, and spared Agag. The people reserved for themselves the finest of the flocks, herds, and beasts of burden, excusing their sin on the ground that the cattle were to be offered as sacrifice to the Lord. They intended, however, to sacrifice these in place of their own cattle.

Saul's arrogant disregard of the will of God proved that he could not be trusted with royal power as the Lord's deputy. While Saul and his army were marching home enjoying the thrill of victory, there was anguish in the home of Samuel. He had received a message from the Lord: " 'I greatly regret that I have set up Saul as king, for he has turned back from following Me, and has not performed My commandments.' " The prophet wept and prayed all night that the terrible sentence might be changed.

God's regret is not like human regret. Human regret implies a change of mind. God's regret implies a change of circumstances and relations. People may change their relation to God by complying with the conditions of coming into the divine favor, or they may, by their own actions, place themselves outside the favoring condition. Saul's disobedience changed his relation to God, but the conditions of acceptance with God had not changed. With Him there "is no variation or shadow of turning." James 1:17.

With an aching heart the prophet set out the next morning to meet the disobedient king. Samuel cherished a hope that Saul might repent and be restored to the divine favor. But Saul, corrupted by his disobedience, came to meet Samuel with a lie on his lips: " 'Blessed are you of the LORD! I have performed the commandment of the LORD.' "

When the prophet asked the pointed question, " 'What then is this bleating of the sheep in my ears, and the lowing of the oxen which I hear?' " Saul answered, " 'They have brought them from the Amalekites;

for the people spared the best of the sheep and the oxen, to sacrifice to the LORD your God; and the rest we have utterly destroyed.' " In order to shield himself, he was willing to blame the people for his sin of disobedience.

The message of Saul's rejection had to be delivered in the hearing of Israel's army when they were filled with pride over a victory accredited to the heroics and generalship of their king, for Saul had not associated God with the success of Israel in this conflict. When the prophet saw the evidence of Saul's rebellion, he was stirred with indignation that he had led Israel into sin. With mingled grief and anger he declared, " 'I will tell you what the LORD said to me last night. . . . When you were little in your own eyes, were you not head of the tribes of Israel? And did not the LORD anoint you king over Israel?' " He repeated the Lord's command to destroy Amalek and demanded the reason for the king's disobedience.

Saul Proves His Rebellion

Saul persisted in self-justification: " 'But I have obeyed the voice of the LORD, and gone on the mission on which the LORD sent me, and brought back Agag king of Amalek; I have utterly destroyed the Amalekites. But the people took of the plunder, sheep and oxen, the best of the things which should have been utterly destroyed, to sacrifice to the LORD your God in Gilgal.' "

In solemn words the prophet swept away the cover of lies and pronounced the irrevocable sentence: " 'Has the LORD as great delight in burnt offerings and sacrifices, as in obeying the voice of the LORD? Behold, to obey is better than sacrifice, and to heed than the fat of rams. For rebellion is as the sin of witchcraft, and stubbornness is as iniquity and idolatry. Because you have rejected the word of the LORD, He also has rejected you from being king.' "

As the king heard this fearful sentence, he cried out, " 'I have sinned, for I have transgressed the commandment of the LORD and your words, because I feared the people and obeyed their voice.' " Terrified, Saul acknowledged his guilt, but he still persisted in blaming the people.

It was not sorrow for sin but fear of its penalty that moved the king of Israel as he begged Samuel, " 'Please pardon my sin, and return with me, that I may worship the LORD.' " If Saul had had true repentance, he would have confessed his sin publicly; but his chief concern was to maintain his authority and keep the allegiance of the people. He wanted the honor of Samuel's presence to strengthen his own influence.

" 'I will not return with you,' " was the answer of the prophet: " 'for you have rejected the word of the LORD, and the LORD has rejected you from being king over Israel.' " As Samuel turned to leave, the king, in an agony of fear, took hold of his robe to hold him back, but it tore in his hands. At this, the prophet declared, " 'The LORD has torn the kingdom of Israel from you today, and has given it to a neighbor of yours, who is better than you.' "

An act of justice, stern and terrible, still needed to be performed. Samuel commanded that the king of the Amalekites be brought before him. Agag, guilty and merciless, came at the prophet's command, supposing that the danger of death was past. Samuel declared: " 'As your sword has made women childless, so shall your mother be childless among women.' And Samuel hacked Agag in pieces before the LORD." With this done, Samuel returned to Ramah.

God Did All Possible to Help Saul

When called to the throne, Saul lacked knowledge and had serious defects of character. But the Lord granted him the Holy Spirit and placed him where he could develop the qualities that a ruler of Israel needed. If he had remained humble, every good quality would have grown stronger, while evil tendencies would have lost their power. This is the work that the Lord will do for all who consecrate themselves to Him. He will reveal to them their defects of character and will give them strength to correct their errors.

When he was first called to the throne, Saul was humble and self-distrustful, but success made him self-confident. The valor and military skill he displayed in delivering Jabesh Gilead roused the enthusiasm of the whole nation. At first he gave the glory to God, but afterward he took honor to himself. He lost sight of his dependence on God,

and his heart strayed from the Lord. This prepared the way for his sin of presumption at Gilgal. The same blind self-confidence led him to reject Samuel's reproof. If he had been willing to confess his error, this bitter experience would have become a safeguard for the future. If the Lord had separated Himself entirely from Saul at that time, He would not have spoken to him again through His prophet, entrusting him with a definite work to perform, so that he might correct the errors of the past.

When Saul persisted in stubbornly justifying himself, he rejected the only means God could use to save him from himself. At Gilgal, the religious service he performed in direct opposition to the command of God only placed him beyond the help that God was willing to grant. In the expedition against Amalek, the Lord was not pleased with partial obedience. God has never given us liberty to depart from His requirements.

Obedience, the Fruit of Faith

" 'To obey is better than sacrifice.' " Without patience, faith, and an obedient heart, sacrificial offerings were worthless. When Saul proposed presenting a sacrifice of the things that God commanded to be destroyed, he was showing open contempt for divine authority. The sacrifice would have been an insult to Heaven. Yet many are following a similar course. They offer up to God their formal services of religion while they refuse to believe and obey some requirement of the Lord. The Lord cannot accept them if they persist in willfully violating even one of His commands.

" 'Rebellion is as the sin of witchcraft, and stubbornness is as iniquity and idolatry.' " Those who set themselves against the government of God have entered into an alliance with the chief apostate. He will cause everything to appear in a false light. Like our first parents, those who are under his bewitching spell see only the great benefits to be received by transgression.

Many thus led by Satan deceive themselves with the belief that they are in the service of God. In the days of Christ the Jewish scribes and elders who professed great zeal for the honor of God crucified His Son. The same spirit still exists in the hearts of those who follow their own will in opposition to the will of God.

Saul's fatal presumption must be attributed to satanic sorcery. In his disobedience to the divine command he had been as really inspired by Satan as are those who practice sorcery; and when reproved, he added stubbornness to rebellion. He could have offered no greater insult to the Spirit of God if he had openly united with idolaters.

In Saul, God had given Israel a king after their own heart, as Samuel said, " 'Here is the king *whom you have chosen and whom you have desired.*' " 1 Samuel 12:13. His physical appearance matched their ideas of royal dignity. His personal bravery and ability to lead armies were qualities they regarded as most likely to secure respect from other nations. They did not ask for a king who had true nobility of character, who possessed the love and fear of God. They were not seeking God's way, but their own. Therefore God gave them such a king as they desired—one whose character was a reflection of their own.

If Saul had relied on God, God would have been with him. But when Saul chose to act independently of God, the Lord was forced to set him aside. Then he called to the throne "a man after His own heart" (1 Samuel 13:14)—one who would rely on God and be guided by His Spirit; one who, when he sinned, would submit to reproof and correction.

David Anointed
as King*

In the freshness of boyhood, David kept watch of his flocks as they grazed on the hills surrounding Bethlehem. The simple shepherd sang songs he composed himself, and the music of his harp made a sweet accompaniment to the rich melody of his young voice. The Lord was preparing David for the work He planned to commit to his trust in later years.

"Now the LORD said to Samuel, 'How long will you mourn for Saul, seeing I have rejected him from reigning over Israel? Fill your horn with oil, and go; I am sending you to Jesse the Bethlehemite. For I have provided Myself a king among his sons. . . . You shall anoint for Me the one I name to you.' So Samuel did what the LORD said, and went to Bethlehem. And the elders of the town trembled at his coming, and said, 'Do you come peaceably?' And he said, 'Peaceably.' " The elders accepted an invitation to the sacrifice, and Samuel called Jesse and his sons. All the household of Jesse were present except David, the youngest son, who had been left to guard the sheep.

Before eating of the offering feast, Samuel began his prophetic inspection of the noble-appearing sons of Jesse. Eliab was the eldest, and more nearly resembled Saul in height and good looks than the others. As Samuel looked at his princely bearing, he thought, "This is indeed the man whom God has chosen as successor to Saul," and waited for the divine permission to anoint him.

But Eliab did not fear the Lord. He would have been a proud, exacting ruler. The Lord's word to Samuel was, " 'Do not look at his appearance or at the height of his stature, because I have refused him. For the LORD does not see as man sees; for man looks at the outward appearance, but the LORD looks at the heart.' " We may learn from the mistake of Samuel how useless it is to judge people on beauty of face or nobility of stature. God's thoughts regarding His creatures are above our finite minds. But if they will submit their will to God, His children will be brought to fill the place for which they are qualified and enabled to accomplish the work committed to their hands.

---

* *This chapter is based on 1 Samuel 16:1-13.*

The Shepherd Boy Is Called to the Feast

Eliab passed from Samuel's inspection, and the six brothers who were at the service followed in succession for the prophet to observe them. But the Lord did not indicate that He had chosen any one of them. With painful suspense, Samuel had looked at the last of the young men. Perplexed and bewildered, he inquired, " 'Are all the young men here?' " The father answered, " 'There remains yet the youngest, and there he is, keeping the sheep.' " Samuel directed that he be called. " 'We will not sit down till he comes here.' "

The lonely shepherd was startled by the unexpected call of the messenger who announced that the prophet had come to Bethlehem and had sent for him. Why should the prophet and judge of Israel want to see him? But without delay he obeyed the call.

"Now he was ruddy, with bright eyes, and good looking." As Samuel saw the handsome, manly, modest shepherd boy, the voice of the Lord spoke: " 'Arise, anoint him; for this is the one.' " David had proved himself brave and faithful in the humble office of a shepherd, and now God had chosen him to be captain of His people. "Samuel took the horn of oil and anointed him in the midst of [from among] his brothers; and the Spirit of the LORD came upon David from that day forward." With a relieved heart the prophet returned to Ramah.

The ceremony of anointing David had been performed in secret. It was an indication to him of the high destiny awaiting him, that amid all the dangers of his coming years, this knowledge might inspire him to be true to the plans that God wanted to accomplish through his life.

The great honor conferred on David did not make him proud. As humble and modest as before his anointing, the shepherd boy returned to the hills and watched his flocks. But with new inspiration he composed his melodies and played his harp.

Before him lay a landscape of rich and varied beauty. He saw the sun flooding the heavens with light, like a bridegroom coming out of his chamber, and rejoicing "as a strong man to run its race." There were bold summits of the hills reaching toward the sky. And beyond was God. The light of day, gilding forest and mountain, meadow and stream, carried the mind up to glimpse the Author of every good and perfect gift. Daily revelations of his Creator's character filled the young poet's heart with adoration and rejoicing. The powers of David's mind and heart were developing and coming into a richer communion with God. His mind was constantly penetrating into new depths for fresh themes to inspire his song and to wake the music of his harp. The rich melody of his voice poured out on the air as if responsive to the angels' songs in heaven.

Who can measure the results of those years of toil and wandering among the lonely hills? The psalms of Israel's sweet singer would ever afterward kindle love and faith in the hearts of God's people, bringing them nearer to the loving heart of Him in whom all His creatures live.

David was preparing to take a high position with the noblest people of the earth. Clearer understandings of God opened before his mind. Obscure themes were illuminated, difficulties made plain, perplexities harmonized. Each ray of new light called forth sweeter songs of devotion to the glory of God and the Redeemer. As he saw the love of God in the events of his life, his heart throbbed with more fervent adoration and gratitude. His voice rang out in richer melody; he swept his harp with more exultant joy. And the shepherd boy developed from strength to strength, from knowledge to knowledge, for the Spirit of the Lord was on him.

David Kills Goliath*

When King Saul realized that God had rejected him, he was filled with bitter rebellion and despair. He had no clear understanding of his sin and did not reform his life. He brooded over what he thought was God's injustice in taking the kingdom away from his descendants. He constantly dreaded the ruin that he had brought on his house. He did not meekly accept the chastisement of God, but his haughty spirit became desperate, until he was on the verge of becoming insane.

His counselors advised him to seek a skilled musician, hoping that the soothing notes of a sweet instrument might calm his troubled spirit. David, as a skilled harpist, was brought before the king. His heaven-inspired music had the desired effect. The dark cloud over Saul's mind was charmed away.

Whenever necessary, David was called back to soothe the mind of the troubled king. Although Saul expressed delight in David and his music, the young shepherd felt a sense of relief when he went from the king's house to the fields and hills of his pasture.

David was growing in favor with God and man. He had been in the court of the king and had seen the responsibilities of royalty. He had understood some of the mysteries in the character of Israel's first king. He knew that in their private life the household of Saul were far from happy. These things troubled his thoughts. But he turned to his harp and called forth music that elevated his mind to the Author of everything good, and the dark clouds that seemed to shadow the future disappeared.

David's Special Educator

As Moses was trained for his work, so the Lord was fitting the son of Jesse to become the guide of His chosen people. Animal predators lurked in the lonely hills and wild ravines where David wandered with his flocks. Not infrequently lions or bears, fierce with hunger, came to attack the flocks. David was armed only with his sling and shepherd's staff, yet he protected his flock courageously. Describing these encounters later, he said: " 'When a lion or bear came and took a lamb out of

---

* This chapter is based on 1 Samuel 16:14-23; 17.

the flock, I went out after it and struck it, and delivered the lamb from its mouth; and when it arose against me, I caught it by its beard, and struck and killed it.' " His experience developed his courage, fortitude, and faith.

When Israel declared war against the Philistines, three of Jesse's sons joined the army under Saul, but David stayed at home. After a time, however, he went to visit the camp. His father gave him a message and a gift for his older brothers. But Jesse did not know that the armies of Israel were in danger and that an angel had directed David to save his people.

As David drew near to the army, Israel and the Philistines were drawn up in battle lines, army against army. Goliath, the champion of the Philistines, came out and with insulting language defied Israel to provide a man from their ranks who would fight with him. When David learned that the Philistine hurled his defiance at them day after day without any champion stepping forward to silence the boaster, he was fired up with zeal to preserve the honor of God.

The armies of Israel were depressed. They said one to another, " 'Have you seen this man who has come up? Surely he has come up to defy Israel.' "

Ashamed and indignant, David exclaimed, " 'Who is this uncircumcised Philistine, that he should defy the armies of the living God?' "

Even as a shepherd, David had revealed daring, courage, and strength rarely seen, and the mysterious visit of Samuel to their father's house had made the brothers suspicious of the real object of his visit. Their jealousy had been aroused.

And now Eliab regarded the question that David asked as a rebuke to his own cowardice in making no attempt to silence the giant. The elder brother exclaimed angrily, " 'Why did you come down here? And with whom have you left those few sheep in the wilderness? I know your pride and the insolence of your heart, for you have come down to see the battle.' " David's answer was respectful but firm: " 'What have I done now? Is there not a cause?' "

David Brought Before the King

The words of David were repeated to the king, who summoned the youth before him. The shepherd said, " 'Let no man's heart fail because of him; your servant will go and fight with this Philistine.' " Saul tried to talk David out of it, but the young man was not to be dissuaded. " 'The Lord, who delivered me from the paw of the lion and from the paw of the bear, He will deliver me from the hand of this Philistine.' And Saul said to David, 'Go, and the Lord be with you!' "

For forty days Israel had trembled before the Philistine giant. On his head was a helmet of bronze, he wore a metal coat that weighed five thousand shekels, and he had bronze armor on his legs. The coat was made of bronze plates that overlaid one another, like the scales of a fish, and no arrow could possibly penetrate the armor. The giant carried a huge javelin, also of bronze. "The staff of his spear was like a weaver's beam, and his iron spearhead weighed six hundred shekels; and a shield-bearer went before him."

Morning and evening, Goliath had challenged the camp of Israel, saying, " 'Choose a man for yourselves, and let him come down to me. If he is able to fight with me and kill me, then will we be your servants. But if I prevail against him and kill him, then you shall be our servants. . . . I defy the armies of Israel.' "

The king had little hope that David would be successful in his brave attempt. He gave command to clothe the youth in the king's own armor. The heavy bronze helmet was put on his head, and the coat of mail was placed on his body; the king's sword was at his side. Thus equipped, he started toward Goliath, but soon he began to come back. The worried spectators thought that David had decided not to risk his life. But this was far from what the brave young man was thinking. When he returned he took off the king's armor and in its place took only his staff and a simple sling. Choosing five smooth stones out of the brook, he put them in his bag, and with his sling in his hand, advanced toward the Philistine. The giant strode forward boldly, expecting to meet the mightiest of the warriors of Israel. His armor-bearer walked before him as if nothing could withstand him. As he came near he saw a mere youth. David's well-knit body, unprotected by armor, was impressive; yet there was a marked contrast between its youthful outline and the massive proportions of the Philistine.

Goliath Despises the Youthful David

Goliath was filled with amazement and anger. " 'Am I a dog,' " he exclaimed, " 'that you come to me with sticks?' " He heaped terrible curses on David then called scornfully, " 'Come to me, and I will give your flesh to the birds of the air and the beasts of the field!' "

David did not weaken. Stepping forward, he said to his antagonist: " 'You come to me with a sword, with a spear, and with a javelin. But I come to you in the name of the LORD of hosts, the God of the armies of Israel, whom you have defied. This day the LORD will deliver you into my hand, and I will strike you and take your head from you. And this day I will give the carcasses of the camp of the Philistines to the birds of the air and the wild beasts of the earth, that all the earth may know that there is a God in Israel. Then all this assembly shall know that the LORD does not save with sword and spear; for the battle is the LORD's, and He will give you into our hands.' "

This speech, given in a clear voice, rang out on the air, and the listening thousands heard it distinctly. In his rage Goliath pushed up the helmet that protected his forehead and rushed forward. "It was so, when the Philistine arose and came and drew near to meet David, that David hurried and ran toward the army to meet the Philistine. Then David put his hand in his bag and took out a stone; and he slung it and struck the Philistine in his forehead, so that the stone sank into his forehead, and he fell on his face to the earth."

The two armies had been confident that David would be killed. But when the stone went whizzing through the air straight to the mark, they saw the mighty warrior tremble and reach forth his hands as if struck with blindness. The giant staggered, and like a great oak fell to the ground.

David did not wait an instant. He jumped on the fallen form of the Philistine and took hold of Goliath's sword with both hands. He lifted it in the air, and the head of the boaster rolled from his body. A shout of joy went up from the camp of Israel.

The Philistines were terror-stricken, and the triumphant Hebrews rushed after their fleeing enemies "to the gates of Ekron." "Then the children of Israel returned from chasing the Philistines, and they plundered their tents."

David
Flees*

After Goliath was killed, Saul kept David with him and would not let him return to his father's house. And "the soul of Jonathan was knit to the soul of David, and Jonathan loved him as his own soul." Jonathan and David made a covenant to be united like brothers, and the king's son "took off the robe that was on him and gave it to David, with his armor, even to his sword and his bow and his belt." Yet David preserved his modesty and won the affection of the people as well as of the royal household. It was evident that the blessing of God was with him.

Saul felt that the kingdom would be more secure if someone could be connected with him who received instruction from the Lord. David's presence might be a protection to Saul when he went out with him to war.

The guiding hand of God had connected David with Saul. David's position at the royal court would give him a knowledge of statecraft and would enable him to gain the confidence of the nation. Hardships that he experienced through Saul's hostility would lead him to feel his de-

pendence upon God. And the friendship of Jonathan was also in God's plan, to preserve the life of Israel's future ruler.

When Saul and David were returning from battle with the Philistines, "the women had come out of all the cities of Israel, singing and dancing, to meet King Saul, with tambourines, with joy, and with musical instruments." One company sang, " 'Saul has slain his thousands,' " while another company responded, " 'And David his ten thousands.' " The king was angry because David was exalted above himself. Rather than subdue his envious feelings, he exclaimed, " 'They have ascribed to David ten thousands, and to me they have ascribed but thousands. Now what more can he have but the kingdom?' "

Saul's love of praise had a controlling influence over his actions and thoughts. His standard of right and wrong was popular applause; Saul's ambition was to be first in people's estimation. A settled conviction entered the mind of the king that David would obtain the heart of the people and take his throne.

---

* *This chapter is based on 1 Samuel 18 to 22.*

The Demon of Jealousy Enters Saul's Heart

Saul opened his heart to the spirit of jealousy that poisoned his soul. The king of Israel was opposing his will to the will of the Infinite One. He allowed his emotions to control his judgment until he was plunged into a fury of passion. He had fits of rage, times when he was ready to kill any who dared oppose him. From this frenzy he would lapse into despondency and self-contempt, and remorse would take possession of his mind.

He loved to hear David play the harp, and this seemed to charm the evil spirit away for the time. But one day when David was bringing sweet music from his instrument, accompanying himself as he sang praises to God, Saul suddenly threw a spear at him. God preserved David, and he fled from the rage of the maddened king.

As Saul's hatred of David increased, he watched all the more intently for an opportunity to take his life, but none of his plans were successful against the one anointed by the Lord. David trusted in Him who is strong to deliver. " 'The fear of the LORD is the beginning of wisdom' " (Proverbs 9:10), and David's prayer was that he might walk before God in a perfect way.

The people quickly saw that David was a competent person. With wisdom and skill he managed the matters entrusted to him. The counsels of the young man were safe to follow, while at times the judgment of Saul was unreliable.

Saul was afraid of him, since it was evident the Lord was with him. The king felt that the life of David cast reproach on him, since by contrast it presented his own character as inferior. Envy made Saul miserable. What great mischief this evil trait has worked in our world! Envy is the offspring of pride, and if it is allowed to remain in the heart, eventually it will lead to murder.

The king kept watch, hoping to find something to serve as an excuse to take the young man's life and still be justified before the nation for his evil act. He laid a trap, urging David to fight against the Philistines with still greater vigor, promising the oldest daughter of the royal house as a reward. David's modest answer to this offer was, " 'Who am I, and what is my life or my father's family in Israel, that I should be son-in-law to the king?' " The monarch showed his insincerity by marrying the princess to another.

Michal, Saul's youngest daughter, was offered to David on condition that he give evidence of having slaughtered a specified number of their enemies. "Saul thought to make David fall by the hand of the Philistines," but David returned as victor from the battle, to become the king's son-in-law. "Michal, Saul's daughter, loved him," and the enraged king was still more sure that this was the man whom the Lord had said was better than he and who would reign in his place. No longer concealing his feelings, he ordered his officers to take the life of the one he hated.

Jonathan recounted to the king

what David had done to preserve the honor and life of the nation, and what terrible guilt would rest on anyone who murdered the one whom God had used to scatter their enemies. The conscience of the king was touched. "And Saul swore, 'As the LORD lives, he shall not be killed.' " David was brought to Saul, and he served in his presence as in the past.

David Leads the Victorious Army

Again the nation declared war, and David led the army against their enemies. The Hebrews gained a great victory, and the people praised David's wisdom and heroism. This served to stir up the former bitterness of Saul against him. While the young man was playing, filling the palace with sweet harmony, Saul's anger overcame him and he hurled a javelin at David, but the angel of the Lord turned aside the deadly weapon. David escaped and fled to his own house. Saul sent spies to take him in the morning and put an end to his life.

Michal informed David of her father's intentions. She urged him to flee, and she let him down from the window to make his escape. He fled to Samuel at Ramah, where the prophet welcomed the fugitive. It was here, amid the hills, that the honored servant of the Lord continued his work. A company of prophets with him studied closely the will of God and listened reverently to Samuel's words of instruction. David learned precious lessons from the teacher of Israel. But David's

connection with Samuel aroused the jealousy of the king, who feared that the prophet would lend his influence to advancing Saul's rival. The king sent officers to bring David to Gibeah, where he intended to kill him.

God Restrains Evil

The messengers went on their way intent on taking David's life, but One greater than Saul controlled them. Met by unseen angels, they began to utter prophetic sayings and proclaimed the glory of Jehovah. Thus God revealed His power to restrain evil.

Saul, exasperated, sent other messengers. These also were overpowered by the Spirit of God and united with the first in prophesying. The king sent a third group, but the divine influence fell on them also, and they prophesied.

Saul then decided that he would go himself. As soon as he would come within reach of David, he intended to kill him with his own hand, whatever the consequences.

But an angel of God met him, and the powerful Spirit of God took control of him. He went forward uttering prayers to God, with predictions and sacred melodies. When he came to the prophet's home in Ramah, he laid aside the outer garments that indicated his rank and lay before Samuel and his pupils under the influence of the divine Spirit. The people were drawn together to witness this strange scene, and the experience of the king was reported far and wide.

Saul assured David that he was at peace with him, but David had little confidence in the king's change of heart. He longed to see his friend Jonathan once more. Conscious of his innocence, he found the king's son and made a touching appeal: " 'What have I done? What is my iniquity, and what is my sin before your father, that he seeks my life?' "

Jonathan believed that his father no longer intended to take the life of David. " 'By no means! You shall not die! Indeed, my father will do nothing either great or small without first telling me. And why should my father hide this thing from me? It is not so.' "

After the remarkable exhibition of God's power, Jonathan could not believe that his father would harm David. This would be rebellion against God.

David Hides From Saul

But David was not convinced. He declared to Jonathan, " 'As the LORD lives and as your soul lives, there is but a step between me and death.' "

At the time of the new moon, Israel celebrated a sacred festival. Both David and Jonathan would be expected to appear at the king's table. But David was afraid to come, and it was arranged that he would visit his brothers in Bethlehem. On his return he was to hide in a field not far from the banqueting hall, absenting himself from the presence of the king for three days. Jonathan would observe the effect on Saul. If the king made no angry demonstration, then it would be safe for David to return to court.

When David's place was vacant the second day, the king asked, " 'Why has the son of Jesse not come to eat, either yesterday or today?' So Jonathan answered Saul, 'David earnestly asked permission of me to go to Bethlehem. And he said, "Please let me go, for our family has a sacrifice in the city, and my brother has commanded me to be there. And now, if I have found favor in your eyes, please let me get away and see my brothers." Therefore he has not come to the king's table.' "

When Saul heard these words, his anger was uncontrollable. He declared that as long as David lived, Jonathan could not become king. David should be sent for immediately, that he might be put to death. Jonathan again pleaded, " 'Why should he be killed? What has he done?' " This only made the king more satanic in his fury, and he now hurled at his own son the spear intended for David.

The prince was sad and offended. Leaving his father's presence, he went at the appointed time to the spot where David was to learn the king's intentions. They wept bitterly. The king's dark passion cast its shadow on the young men, and their grief was too intense for expression. Jonathan's last words to David as they separated were: " 'Go in peace, since we have both sworn in the name of the LORD, saying, "May the LORD be between you and me, and between your descendants and my descendants, forever." ' "

David hurried to Nob. The tabernacle had been taken to this place from Shiloh, and here Ahimelech the high priest ministered. The priest looked at David in astonishment, as he came hurriedly and apparently alone. He inquired what had brought him there. In his desperation the young man resorted to deception. David told the priest he had been sent on a secret errand by the king.

David's Faith Fails

Here he showed a lack of faith in God, and his sin resulted in the death of the high priest. If he had stated the facts plainly, Ahimelech would have known what to do to preserve his life. God requires His people to tell the truth, even in the greatest peril.

Doeg, chief of Saul's herders, was fulfilling his vows in the place of worship. At the sight of this man, David determined to find another place of refuge quickly. He asked Ahimelech for a sword and was told that he had none except the sword of Goliath, kept as a relic in the tabernacle. David replied, " 'There is none like it; give it to me.' "

David fled to Achish, king of Gath; for he felt that there was more safety among the enemies of his people than in Saul's realm. But it was reported to Achish that David was the man who had killed the Philistine champion years before. This put David, who was seeking safety among these foes of Israel, in great peril. But, pretending to be insane, he deceived his enemies and thus made his escape.

David's first error was to distrust God at Nob; his second, to deceive Achish. As trials came upon him, his faith was shaken and human weakness appeared. Everyone looked like a spy and a betrayer to him. As he had been hunted and persecuted, perplexity and distress had nearly hidden his heavenly Father from his sight.

Every failure on the part of the children of God is due to their lack of faith. When shadows cloud the soul, we must look up; there is light beyond the darkness. David should not have distrusted God. He was the Lord's anointed. If he had just removed his mind from his distressing situation and had thought of God's power and majesty, he would have had peace even in the midst of the shadows of death.

David sought safety in the mountains of Judah. He escaped to the cave of Adullam, a place that he could defend with a small force against even a large army. "And when his brothers and all his father's house heard it, they went down there to him." The family of David could not feel secure, knowing that at any time Saul's unreasonable suspicions might be directed against them because of their relation to David. They had now learned what was becoming generally known in Israel, that God had chosen David as the future ruler of His people. They believed that they would be safer with him.

In the cave of Adullam, the family were united in sympathy and affection. The son of Jesse could make melody with voice and harp. He had tasted the bitterness of distrust from his own brothers, and the harmony that now replaced this discord brought joy to the exile's heart.

Many had lost confidence in the ruler of Israel, for they could see that he was no longer guided by the Spirit of the Lord. "And everyone who was in distress, everyone who was in debt, and everyone who was discontented" gathered to David, and "he became captain over them. And there were about four hundred men with him." Here David had a little kingdom of his own, and in it order and discipline prevailed. But he was far from safe, for he had ongoing evidence that the king had not given up his murderous purpose.

When a warning of danger came from a prophet of the Lord, David fled from his hiding place to the forest of Hereth. God was giving David a course of discipline to fit him to become a wise general as well as a just and merciful king.

Saul had been preparing to trap David in the cave of Adullam, and when it was discovered that David had left this hiding place, the king was furious. David's escape was a mystery. Had traitors in his camp informed the son of Jesse of his plans?

King Saul Orders a Terrible Massacre

Saul told his counselors that a conspiracy had been formed against him, and he bribed them with the offer of rich gifts and honor to reveal who among his people had befriended David. Doeg the Edomite turned informer. Moved by ambition and greed and by hatred of the priest who had reproved his sins, Doeg reported David's visit to Ahimelech in such a light as to ignite Saul's anger against the man of God. Insane with rage, Saul declared that the whole family of the priest should die. Not only Ahimelech, but the members of his father's house—"eighty-five men who wore a linen ephod"—were killed at the king's command by the murderous hand of Doeg. This is what Saul could do under the control of Satan.

This deed filled all Israel with horror. The king whom they had chosen had committed this outrage. The ark was with them, but the priests of whom they had inquired were killed with the sword.

What would come next?

The Largeheartedness of David*

O ne of the sons of Ahimelech the son of Ahitub, named Abiathar, escaped and fled after David. And Abiathar told David that Saul had killed the Lord's priests. So David said to Abiathar, 'I knew that day, when Doeg the Edomite was there, that he would surely tell Saul. I have caused the death of all the persons of your father's house. Stay with me; do not fear. For he who seeks my life seeks your life, but with me you shall be safe.' "

Still hunted by the king, David's brave group withdrew to the wilderness of Ziph. At this time, when there were so few bright spots in the path of David, he received an unexpected visit from Jonathan. These two friends told their varied experiences, and Jonathan cheered the heart of David, saying, " 'Do not fear, for the hand of Saul my father shall not find you. You shall be king over Israel, and I shall be next to you. Even my father Saul knows that.' " The hunted fugitive was greatly encouraged. "So the two of them made a covenant before the Lord. And David stayed in the woods, and Jonathan went to his own house."

The Ziphites sent word to Saul in Gibeah that they knew where David was hiding and that they would guide the king to his retreat. But David, warned of their intentions, changed his location, seeking safety in the mountains between Maon and the Dead Sea.

Again word came to Saul, " 'Take note! David is in the Wilderness of En Gedi.' Then Saul took three thousand chosen men from all Israel, and went to seek David and his men on the Rocks of the Wild Goats." David had only six hundred men in his company. In a secluded cave the son of Jesse waited for God's guidance about what to do.

As Saul was making his way up the mountains, he entered alone the very cave in which David and his people were hiding. When David's men saw this, they urged their leader to kill Saul. The king was now in their power—certain evidence that God Himself had delivered the enemy into their hand so that they could destroy him. David was tempted to take this view of the matter, but the voice of conscience spoke to him. "Touch not the anointed of the Lord."

---

* This chapter is based on 1 Samuel 22:20-23; 23 to 27.

David's men reminded their commander of the words of God, " ' "Behold, I will deliver your enemy into your hand, that you may do to him as it seems good to you." And David arose and secretly cut off a corner of Saul's robe.' "

Saul got up and went out of the cave to continue his search, when a voice came to his startled ears, " 'My lord the king!' " Who was addressing him? The son of Jesse, the man he had so long wanted to kill. David bowed, then addressed Saul: " 'Look, this day your eyes have seen that the LORD delivered you today into my hand in the cave, and someone urged me to kill you. But my eye spared you, and I said, "I will not stretch out my hand against my lord, for he is the LORD's anointed." Moreover, my father, see! Yes, see the corner of your robe in my hand! For in that I cut off the corner of your robe, and did not kill you, know and see that there is neither evil nor rebellion in my hand, and I have not sinned against you. Yet you hunt my life to take it.' "

Saul was deeply moved as he realized how completely he had been in the power of the man whom he was trying to kill. With softened spirit he exclaimed, " 'Is this your voice, my son David?' And Saul lifted up his voice and wept." Then he said to David: " 'You are more righteous than I; for you have rewarded me with good, whereas I have rewarded you with evil. . . . For if a man finds his enemy, will he let him get away safely? Therefore may the LORD reward you with good for what you have done to me this day. And now I know indeed that you shall surely be king, and that the kingdom of Israel shall be established in your hand.' " And David made a covenant with Saul that he would not cut off his descendants.

David could not rely on the assurances of the king, so when Saul returned home, he stayed on in the mountains.

After evil-minded men do and say wicked things against the Lord's servants, the Spirit of the Lord works with them, and sometimes they humble their hearts before those they have tried to destroy. But as they again open the door to the evil one, the old hatred rekindles and they return to the same work they repented of. Satan can use such souls with far greater power than before, because they have sinned against greater light.

The People Are Sorry They Asked for a King

"Then Samuel died; and the Israelites gathered together and lamented for him, and buried him at his home at Ramah." A great and good prophet and an eminent judge had fallen in death. From his youth up, Samuel had walked before Israel in the integrity of his heart. Although Saul had been king, Samuel had wielded a more powerful influence than he, because his record was one of faithfulness and devotion.

The people saw what a mistake they had made in desiring a king so that they would not be different from the nations around them. Many looked with alarm at the condition of society, fast becoming corrupted with godlessness. Well might Israel mourn that Samuel, the prophet of the Lord, was dead.

The nation had lost the one to whom the people had been used to going with their great troubles—lost one who had constantly interceded with God for the best interests of the people. His prayers had given them a sense of security, for "The effective, fervent prayer of a righteous man avails much." James 5:16. The king seemed almost a madman. Justice was perverted, and order was turned to confusion.

The people's thoughts were bitter as they looked on Samuel's quiet resting place and remembered their folly in rejecting him as their ruler, for he had had so close a connection with Heaven that he seemed to bind all Israel to the throne of Jehovah. Samuel had taught them to love and obey God, but now he was dead. The people felt that they were left to the mercies of a king who was joined to Satan and who would divorce the people from God and heaven.

David knew that Samuel's death had broken another bond of restraint on the actions of Saul, and he felt less secure than when the prophet lived. So he fled to the wilderness of Paran. In these desolate wilds, realizing that the prophet was dead and the king was his enemy, he sang:

He who keeps you will not slumber.
Behold, He who keeps Israel
Shall neither slumber nor sleep. . . .

The LORD shall preserve your going
   out and your coming in
From this time forth, and even for-
   evermore.
Psalm 121:3-8

Nabal, the Hard-Hearted Farmer

David and his men protected the flocks and herds of a wealthy man named Nabal, who had vast resources in Paran. Nabal's character was ill-tempered and stingy.

It was the time of sheep shearing, a season of hospitality. David and his men needed supplies, and the son of Jesse sent ten young men to Nabal, instructing them to greet him in their master's name: " 'Peace be to you, peace to your house, and peace to all that you have! Now I have heard that you have shearers. Your shepherds were with us, and we did not hurt them, nor was there anything missing from them all the while they were in Carmel. [Not Mount Carmel, but a place in the territory of Judah.] Ask your young men, and they will tell you. Therefore . . . . Please give whatever comes to your hand to your servants and to your son David.' "

From his abundance this rich man was asked to furnish some relief to the needs of those who had done him such valuable service. The answer Nabal returned showed his character: " 'Who is David, and who is the son of Jesse? There are many servants nowadays who break away each one from his master. Shall I then take my bread and my water and my meat that I have killed for my shearers, and give it to men when I do not know where they are from?' "

David was furious. He determined to punish the man who had denied him what was his right and had added insult to injury. This impulsive movement was more like the character of Saul than of David. The son of Jesse still had to learn patience.

Nabal's Wise Wife Saves the Household

Without consulting her husband, Abigail made up an ample supply of food, which she sent forward in the care of servants, and started out herself to meet David. When Abigail saw David, "she hastened to dismount from the donkey, fell on her face before David, and bowed down to the ground. So she fell at his feet and said, 'On me, my lord, on me let this iniquity be! And please let your maidservant speak in your ears.' " Abigail addressed David with as much reverence as though she were speaking to a crowned monarch. With kind words she tried to soothe his irritated feelings. Full of the wisdom and love of God, she made it plain that the unkind course of her husband was certainly not premeditated but simply the outburst of an unhappy, selfish nature. She then offered her rich provision as a peace offering to the men of David.

She said, " 'The LORD will certainly make for my lord an enduring house, because my lord fights the battles of the LORD, and evil is not found in you throughout your days.' " Abigail implied that David ought to fight the battles of the Lord. He was not to seek revenge for personal wrongs, even though persecuted as a traitor. " 'And it shall come to pass, when the LORD has done for my lord according to all the good that he has spoken concerning you, and has appointed you ruler over Israel, that this will be no grief to you, nor offense of heart to my lord, either that you have shed blood without cause, or that my lord has avenged himself.' "

The piety of Abigail, like the fragrance of a flower, breathed out all unconsciously in face and word and action. The Spirit of God was abiding in her soul. Her speech, seasoned with grace, carried a heavenly influence. David trembled as he thought of his rash intentions. "Blessed are the peacemakers; for they shall be called the children of God." Matthew 5:9, KJV. May there be many more like this woman of Israel who would soothe irritated feelings, prevent rash impulses, and stop great evils by words of calm wisdom.

David's anger died away under the power of Abigail's influence and reasoning. He was convinced that he had lost control of his own spirit. With humble heart he received the rebuke, in harmony with his own words, "Let the righteous strike me; it shall be a kindness. And let him reprove me; it shall be as excellent oil." Psalm 141:5. He gave thanks and blessings because she advised him righteously. How few take reproof with gratitude and bless those who try to save them from following an evil course.

Remorse and Fear Take Nabal's Life

When Abigail returned home she found Nabal and his guests in a drunken celebration. Not until the next morning did she tell her husband what had happened in her meeting with David. When he realized how near his folly had brought him to sudden death, he seemed struck with paralysis. He was filled with horror and sank down in a helpless stupor. After ten days he died. In the midst of his making merry, God had said to him, as to the rich man of the parable, " 'This night your soul will be required of you.' " Luke 12:20.

Later David married Abigail. He was already the husband of one wife, but the custom of the nations of his time had perverted his judgment. Throughout all the life of David, he felt the bitter result of marrying many wives.

The Ziphites, hoping to win favor with the king, informed him again of David's hiding place. Once more Saul summoned his men of arms and led them in hunting David. But friendly spies brought word to the son of Jesse, and with a few of his men, David started out to learn the location of his enemy.

It was night when they came upon the tents of the king and his attendants and saw, unobserved, the camp quiet in sleep. David asked, " 'Who will go down with me to Saul in the camp?' " Abishai promptly responded, " 'I will go down with you.' "

Hidden by the shadows of the hills, David and his attendant entered the camp. They came upon Saul sleeping, his spear stuck in the ground and a jug of water at his head. Beside him lay Abner, his chief commander, and all around them were the soldiers, locked in slumber. Abishai raised his spear. " 'God has delivered your enemy into your hand this day. Now therefore, please, let me strike him at once with the spear, right to the earth; and I will not have to strike him a second time!' " He waited for permission, but instead he heard the whispered words: " 'Do not destroy him; for who can stretch out his hand against the LORD's anointed, and be guiltless? . . . As the LORD lives, the LORD shall strike him, . . . or he shall go out to battle and perish. The LORD forbid that I should stretch out my hand against the LORD's anointed. But please, take now the spear and the jug of water that are by his head, and let us go.' . . . And no man saw it or knew it or awoke . . . because a deep sleep from the LORD had fallen on them."

When David was a safe distance from the camp, he called with a loud voice to Abner, " 'Are you not a man? And who is like you in Israel? Why then have you not guarded your lord the king? For one of the people came in to destroy your lord the king. This thing that you have done is not good. As the LORD lives, you are worthy to die, because you have not guarded your master, the LORD's anointed. And now see where the king's spear is, and the jug of water that was by his head.' Then Saul knew David's voice, and said, 'Is that your voice, my son David?' David said, 'It is my voice, my lord, O king.' And he said,

'Why does my lord thus pursue his servant? For what have I done, or what evil is in my hand?' "

Again King Saul Confesses He Is Wrong

Again the king acknowledged: " 'I have sinned. Return, my son David. For I will harm you no more, because my life was precious in your eyes this day. Indeed I have played the fool and erred exceedingly.' "

David answered, " 'Here is the king's spear. Let one of the young men come over and get it.' " Although Saul had made the promise, " 'I will harm you no more,' " David did not place himself in his grasp.

Saul exclaimed as they parted, " 'May you be blessed, my son David! You shall both do great things and also still prevail.' " But the son of Jesse had no hope that the king would continue very long in this frame of mind.

David despaired of a reconciliation with Saul. It seemed that he would finally fall victim to the hatred of the king. With the six hundred men under his command, he went over to Achish, the king of Gath.

David's conclusion that Saul would accomplish his murderous intent was formed without the counsel of God. Even while Saul was plotting his destruction, the Lord was working to secure the kingdom for David. Looking at appearances, people interpret the trials and tests that God permits as things that will only bring their ruin. David looked on appearances and not at the promises of God. He doubted that he would ever come to the throne. Long trials had worn down his faith and exhausted his patience.

The Lord did not send David for protection to the Philistines, the most bitter foes of Israel. Yet, having lost all confidence in Saul and in those who served him, David threw himself on the mercies of his people's enemies. God had appointed him to plant his flag in the land of Judah, and it was lack of faith that led him to forsake his post of duty.

Another of David's Mistakes

The Philistines had feared David more than Saul. By placing himself under the protection of the Philistines, David revealed to them the weakness of his own people. Thus he encouraged these determined enemies to oppress Israel. David had been anointed to stand in defense of the people of God. The Lord does not want His servants to give encouragement to the wicked by disclosing the weakness of His people.

Further, the Israelites received the impression that he had gone to the heathen to serve their gods. By this act, many were led to be prejudiced against him. The very thing Satan desired to have him do, he was led to do. David did not renounce his worship of God nor devotion to His cause, but he sacrificed his trust in Him for his personal safety.

The king of the Philistines received David cordially. The king admired him and was flattered to have a Hebrew seek his protection. David brought his family, his household, and all his possessions, as his men did also. To all appearances he had come to settle permanently in the land of Philistia. This flattered Achish, who promised to protect the fugitive Israelites.

At David's request, the king graciously granted him Ziklag as a possession. In a town wholly separated for their use, David and his men could worship God with more freedom than in Gath, where heathen rites might become a source of evil.

While living in this isolated town David made war on the Geshurites, the Girzites, and the Amalekites, and left none alive to bring the report to Gath. He led Achish to believe that he had been warring against his own nation, the men of Judah. By these lies he strengthened the hand of the Philistines, for the king said, " 'He has made his people Israel utterly abhor him; therefore he will be my servant forever.' " David was not

walking in the counsel of God when he practiced deception.

"Now it happened in those days that the Philistines gathered their armies together for war, to fight with Israel. And Achish said to David, 'You assuredly know that you will go out with me to battle, you and your men.' " David answered the king evasively, " 'Surely you know what your servant can do.' " Achish pledged his word to bestow on David a high position at the Philistine court.

But although David's faith had faltered somewhat regarding the promises of God, he still remembered that Samuel had anointed him king of Israel. He reviewed the mercy of God in preserving him from Saul and determined not to betray a sacred trust. Even though the king of Israel had sought his life, he would not join his forces with the enemies of his people.

Saul Takes His Own Life*

The Philistines gathered themselves together, and came and encamped at Shunem," while Saul and his forces encamped a few miles away at the foot of Mount Gilboa. Saul felt alone and defenseless, because God had forsaken him. As he looked around at the Philistine army, "he was afraid, and his heart trembled greatly."

Saul had expected that David would take this opportunity to get revenge for the wrongs he had suffered. The king was in great distress. His own mindless zeal to destroy the man chosen by God had put the nation in great danger. While pursuing David, he had neglected the defense of his kingdom. The Philistines, taking advantage of its unguarded condition, had penetrated into the very heart of the country. While Satan had been urging Saul to destroy David, the same hateful spirit inspired the Philistines to try to ruin Saul. How often Satan moves upon some unconsecrated person to start a quarrel in the church, and then, taking advantage of the divided condition of God's people, he stirs up his agents to bring about their ruin.

The next day Saul must fight the Philistines. Dark shadows of impending doom gathered about him. He longed for guidance, but even though he sought counsel from God, "the LORD did not answer him, either by dreams or by Urim or by the prophets."

The Lord never turned away anyone who came to Him in sincerity. Why did He turn Saul away unanswered? The king had rejected the counsel of Samuel the prophet; he had exiled David, the chosen of God; he had killed the priests of the Lord. Could he be answered when he had cut off the channels of communication that Heaven had established? It was not pardon for sin and reconciliation with God that Saul wanted but deliverance from his enemies. By rebellion he had cut himself off from God. He could return only by confessing and forsaking his wrongs.

"Then Saul said to his servants, 'Find me a woman who is a medium, that I may go to her and inquire of her.' " The Lord had forbidden attempts to talk with the dead, and the sentence of death

---

* This chapter is based on 1 Samuel 28; 31.

was pronounced against anyone who practiced such unholy arts. Saul had commanded that all wizards and those who arranged spirit contact should be put to death. But now, in desperation, he resorted to that which he had condemned as an abomination.

A woman who had an evil spirit was living in hiding at Endor. She had promised Satan to fulfill his purposes and, in return, the prince of evil revealed secret things to her.

Pretending to be someone else, Saul went by night with two other men to find the sorceress. Oh, pitiable sight! The king of Israel led captive by Satan! Trust in God and obedience to His will were the only conditions on which Saul could be king of Israel. If he had complied with these conditions, his kingdom would have been safe; God would have been his guide, the Almighty his shield. Although his rebellion and stubbornness had nearly silenced the divine voice in his soul, there was still opportunity for him to repent. But when Saul, facing danger, turned to Satan, he cut the last tie that bound him to his Maker. He placed himself fully under the control of the satanic power that for years had brought him to the verge of destruction.

Under cover of darkness, Saul and his companions safely passed the Philistine host. They crossed the mountain ridge to the lonely home of the sorceress of Endor. Even though he was disguised, Saul's unusual height and kingly bearing showed that he was no common soldier. The rich gifts that he offered strengthened her suspicions. To his request the woman answered, " 'Saul has . . . cut off the mediums and the spiritists from the land. Why then do you lay a snare for my life, to cause me to die?' " Then "Saul swore to her by the LORD, saying, 'As the LORD lives, no punishment shall come upon you for this thing.' " And when she said, " 'Whom shall I bring up for you?' " he answered, " 'Samuel.' "

After performing her magic rites, she said, " 'I saw a spirit ascending out of the earth. . . . An old man is coming up, and he is covered with a mantle.' And Saul perceived that it was Samuel, and he stooped with his face to the ground and bowed down."

It was not God's prophet that appeared. Samuel was not present in that den of evil spirits. Satan could as easily take the form of Samuel as he could assume that of an angel of light when he tempted Christ in the wilderness.

The message to Saul from the pretended prophet was, " 'Why have you disturbed me by bringing me up?' " Saul answered, " 'I am deeply distressed; for the Philistines make war against me, and God has departed from me and does not answer me anymore, neither by prophets nor by dreams. Therefore I have called you, that you may reveal to me what I should do.' "

When Samuel was alive, Saul had despised his counsel. But now, in order to communicate with Heaven's ambassador, he had gone to the messenger of hell! Saul had placed himself fully in Satan's power, and now he whose only pleasure is found in making people miserable and destroying them made the most of his opportunity to ruin the unhappy king. In answer came the terrible message, supposedly from the lips of Samuel:

" 'The LORD has departed from you and has become your enemy. . . . The LORD has torn the kingdom out of your hand and given it to your neighbor, namely, David. Because you did not obey the voice of the LORD nor execute His fierce wrath upon Amalek, therefore the LORD has done this thing to you this day. Moreover the LORD will also deliver Israel with you into the hand of the Philistines.' "

Satan had led Saul to justify himself in defying Samuel's reproofs and warning. But now he turned on him, hoping to goad him to desperation by presenting the enormity of his sin and the impossibility of pardon. Nothing could better drive him to despair and self-destruction.

Saul was faint with fasting, terrified, and conscience-stricken. His body swayed like an oak in a storm, and he fell flat to the earth.

The sorceress was filled with alarm. The king of Israel lay before her as if dead. She begged him to eat some food, urging that since she had risked her life in granting his desire, he should give in to her request in order to preserve his own. Saul yielded, and the woman set before him the fatted calf and bread prepared quickly.

What a scene! In the wild cave of the sorceress, in the presence of Satan's messenger, the man who had been anointed of God as king over Israel sat down to eat, getting ready for the day's deadly battle.

By consulting that spirit of darkness, Saul had destroyed himself. Depressed by feelings of despair, it would be impossible for him to inspire his army with courage. He could not lead the minds of Israel to look to God as their helper. Thus the prediction of evil would help to bring about those very events.

The Sad End of the "Anointed of the Lord"

The armies of Israel and the Philistines came together in deadly combat. Though the frightening scene in the cave of Endor had driven all hope from his heart, Saul fought with heroic courage. But it was in vain. "The men of Israel fled from before the Philistines, and fell slain on Mount Gilboa." Saul had seen his soldiers falling around him and his three princely sons cut down by the sword. He himself was wounded and could neither fight nor run. Escape was impossible, so, determined not to be taken alive by the Philistines, Saul took his own life by falling on his sword.

Thus the first king of Israel died, with the guilt of self-murder on his soul. His life had been a failure, and he went down in dishonor and despair.

The news of defeat spread far and wide, creating terror in all of Israel. The people fled from the cities, and the Philistines took possession without fighting. Saul's reign, independent of God, had almost proved the ruin of his people.

On the next day, the Philistines discovered the bodies of Saul and his three sons. They cut off Saul's head and stripped him of his armor. Then they sent the head and the armor, reeking with blood, to the country of the Philistines as a trophy of victory, "to proclaim it in the temple of their idols and among the people." Thus the glory of victory was credited to the power of false gods, and the name of Jehovah was dishonored.

In Beth Shan the bodies of Saul and his sons were hung up in chains, to be eaten by birds of prey. But the brave men of Jabesh Gilead, remembering Saul's deliverance in earlier and happier years, now showed their gratitude by rescuing the bodies of the king and princes and giving them honorable burial. Thus the noble deed performed forty years before secured for Saul and his sons a burial by tender and pitying hands in that dark hour of defeat and dishonor.

Ancient and Modern Spiritualism

The Scripture account of Saul's visit to the woman of Endor puzzles many students of the Bible. Some take the position that Samuel was actually present. But the Bible furnishes ground for the opposite conclusion.

If Samuel was in heaven, he must have been called from there either by God or by Satan. No one can believe for a moment that Satan had power to call the prophet from heaven to honor the magic spells of a lawless woman. Nor can we conclude that God summoned him to the witch's cave, for the Lord had already refused to communicate with Saul by dreams, by Urim, or by prophets.

The message itself shows where it came from. Its purpose was not to lead Saul to repent but to urge him on to ruin. This is not the work of God but of Satan. Furthermore, Scripture cites the act of Saul in consulting a sorceress as one reason why he was rejected by God: "Saul died for his unfaithfulness which he had committed against the LORD, because he did not keep the word of the LORD, and also because he *consulted a medium for guidance.* But he did not inquire of the LORD; there-fore He killed him, and turned the kingdom over to David the son of Jesse." 1 Chronicles 10:13, 14. Saul did not communicate with Samuel, God's prophet, but with Satan. Satan could not present the real Samuel, but a counterfeit that served his purpose of deception.

In ancient times sorcery and witchcraft were founded upon a belief that one could talk with the dead. Those who practiced these arts claimed to obtain a knowledge of future events through departed spirits. "When they say to you, 'Seek those who are mediums and wizards, who whisper and mutter,' should not a people seek their God? *Should they seek the dead on behalf of the living?*" Isaiah 8:19.

The gods of the heathen were believed to be the spirits of departed heroes who had risen to the level of gods. Thus the religion of the heathen was a worship of the dead. Speaking of the apostasy of the Israelites, the psalmist says, "They joined themselves also to Baal of Peor, and *ate sacrifices made to the dead*" (Psalm 106:28), that is, offered to the dead.

In nearly every system of heathenism, the dead were believed to reveal their will to human beings, and also, when consulted, to give them counsel. Even in professedly Christian lands, the practice of talking with beings claiming to be the spirits of the dead has become widespread. Spirit beings sometimes appear in the form of deceased friends and relate personal experiences from their lives and do things that they did while alive. In this way they lead people to believe that their dead friends are angels. With many their word has greater weight than the Word of God.

Many regard spiritualism as a hoax and its phenomena as frauds. But while it is true that the results of trickery have often been palmed off as genuine, there have also been striking evidences of supernatural power. And many who reject spiritualism as human deceit will be led to acknowledge its claims when they are confronted with manifestations that they cannot explain.

Modern spiritualism and ancient witchcraft—both holding communion with the dead as their vital principle—are based on that first lie by which Satan deceived Eve in Eden: " 'You will not surely die. For God knows that in the day you eat of it . . . you will be like God.' " Genesis 3:4, 5. Based on falsehood, both are from the father of lies.

God said: "The dead know nothing. . . . Nevermore will they have a share in anything done under the sun." Ecclesiastes 9:5, 6. "His breath goeth forth, he returneth to his earth; in that very day his thoughts perish." Psalm 146:4, KJV. The

Lord declared to Israel: " 'The person who turns after mediums and familiar spirits, to prostitute himself with them, I will set My face against that person and cut him off from his people.' " Leviticus 20:6.

The "familiar spirits" were not the spirits of the dead but evil angels, the messengers of Satan. The psalmist, speaking of Israel, says that "they even sacrificed their sons and their daughters to demons," and in the next verse he explains that they sacrificed them "to the idols of Canaan." Psalm 106:37, 38. In their supposed worship of the dead, they were actually worshiping demons.

Identity of Spiritualism Revealed

Modern spiritualism is a revival of the witchcraft and demon worship that God condemned long ago. The Scriptures foretold it, declaring that "in latter times some will depart from the faith, giving heed to deceiving spirits and doctrines of demons." 1 Timothy 4:1. In the last days there will be false teachers. 2 Peter 2:1, 2. Spiritualist teachers refuse to acknowledge Christ as the Son of God. Concerning such teachers the beloved John declares: "Who is a liar but he who denies that Jesus is the Christ? He is antichrist who denies the Father and the Son. Whoever denies the Son does not have the Father either." 1 John 2:22, 23. Spiritualism, by denying Christ, denies both the Father and the Son, and the Bible calls it the manifestation of antichrist.

Spiritualism's lure to attract the multitudes is its pretended power to reveal the future. In His Word God has opened before us the great events of the future—all that is essential for us to know. But Satan wants to destroy our confidence in God, lead us to seek a knowledge of what God has wisely veiled from us, and to reject what He has revealed in His Holy Word.

Many become restless when they cannot know how things will turn out. They cannot stand uncertainty and refuse to wait to see the salvation of God. They give way to rebellious feelings and run here and there in desperate grief, trying to get information that God has not revealed. If they would only trust in God and persist in prayer, they would receive divine comfort.

This impatience to unveil the future reveals a lack of faith in God, and Satan inspires confidence in his power to foretell things to come. By experience gained through long ages, he can often forecast, with a degree of accuracy, some future events to deceive misguided souls and bring them under his power.

God Himself is the light of His people. He invites them to fix their eyes by faith on the glories that are hidden from human sight. They have light from the throne of heaven and have no desire to turn to the messengers of Satan.

The demon's message to Saul was not meant to reform him but to goad him to despair and ruin. More often, however, the tempter uses flattery to lure people to destruction. Truth is lightly regarded, and impurity permitted. Spiritualism declares that there is no death, no sin, no judgment, no punishment; desire is the highest law, and human beings are accountable only to themselves. Such views break down the barriers that God has set up to guard truth, purity, and reverence, and many are thus emboldened in sin.

God is leading His people out from the abominations of the world, that they may keep His law. Because of this, the anger of "the accuser of our brethren" knows no limits. "The devil has come down to you, having great wrath, because he knows that he has a short time." Revelation 12:10, 12. Satan is determined to destroy the people of God and cut them off from their inheritance. The admonition, " 'Watch and pray, lest you enter into temptation' " (Mark 14:38), was never more needed than now.

David's Heavy Trial*

D avid and his men had not taken part in the battle between Saul and the Philistines, though they had marched with the Philistines to the field of conflict. As the two armies prepared to join battle, the son of Jesse found himself in great perplexity. Achish expected him to fight for the Philistines. Should he leave the post assigned him and withdraw from the field with ingratitude and treachery to Achish, who had protected him? Such an act would give him a bad name and expose him to the wrath of enemies who were more to be feared than Saul.

Yet he could not for a moment consent to fight against Israel and become a traitor to his country—the enemy of God and of His people. It would forever bar his way to the throne of Israel. And if Saul was killed in the battle, many would charge David with his death.

Far better would it have been to find refuge in God's strong fortress of the mountains than with the sworn enemies of His people. But the Lord in His great mercy did not punish His servant by leaving him in his distress and perplexity. Though David, losing his grasp on divine power, had left the path of strict integrity, it was still the purpose of his heart to be true to God. Angels of the Lord moved upon the Philistine princes to protest against having David and his force with the army in the approaching conflict.

" 'What are these Hebrews doing here?' " cried the Philistine lords, crowding around Achish. He replied, " 'Is this not David, the servant of Saul king of Israel, who has been with me these days, or these years? And to this day I have found no fault in him since he defected to me.' "

David Sent Back to Ziklag

But the princes angrily persisted: " 'Make this fellow return, that he may go back to the place which you have appointed for him, and do not let him go down with us to battle, lest in the battle he become our adversary. For with what could he reconcile himself to his master, if not with the heads of these men? Is this not David, of whom they sang one to another in dances, saying: "Saul has slain his thousands, and David his ten thousands"?' " They

---

* This chapter is based on 1 Samuel 29; 30; 2 Samuel 1.

did not believe that David would fight against his own people. In the heat of battle he could inflict greater harm on the Philistines than all of Saul's army.

Achish, calling David, said, " 'Surely, as the LORD lives, you have been upright. . . . For to this day I have not found evil in you since the day of your coming to me. Nevertheless the lords do not favor you. Therefore return now, and go in peace, that you may not displease the lords of the Philistines.' " Thus the snare entangling David was broken.

After three days' travel David and his band of six hundred men reached Ziklag, their Philistine home. But a scene of desolation met their view. The Amalekites had avenged themselves for David's invasions into their territory and had surprised the city while it was unguarded. They sacked and burned it and departed, taking all the women and children as captives, and much plunder.

In horror and amazement, David and his men stared silently at the smoldering ruins. Then as a sense of their terrible loss burst upon them, those battle-scarred warriors "lifted up their voices and wept, until they had no more power to weep."

Here again David was reaping the sad results of his lack of faith that led him to place himself among the enemies of God and His people. David's followers turn on him as the cause of their calamities. He had angered the Amalekites by his attack against them; yet, too confident of security in the midst of his enemies, he had left the city unguarded. Maddened with grief and rage, his soldiers threatened to stone their leader.

David's Great Temptation to Discouragement

All that David held dear on earth had been swept from him. Saul had driven him from his country; the Amalekites had plundered his city; his wives and children had been made prisoners; and his friends had threatened him with death.

In this time of utmost desperation, David looked earnestly to God for help. He "strengthened himself in the LORD," recalling many evidences of God's favor. "Whenever I am afraid, I will trust in You" (Psalm 56:3), was the language of his heart. Though he could not see a way out of the difficulty, God would teach him what to do.

Sending for Abiathar the priest, "David inquired of the LORD, saying, 'Shall I pursue this troop? Shall I overtake them?' " The answer was, " 'Pursue, for you shall surely overtake them and without fail recover all.' "

David and his soldiers set out at once to catch their fleeing foe. So rapid was their march that two hundred of their number were too exhausted to continue and had to stop and rest. But David pressed forward with the remaining four hundred.

Advancing, they came on an Egyptian slave, apparently about to die of weariness and hunger. When he received food and drink he revived. He had been left to die by the invading force. After David promised that he would not be killed or delivered to his master, he agreed to lead the men to the camp of their enemies.

As they came near the encampment, they saw a scene of drunkenness and merrymaking. The victorious host were "spread out over all the land, eating and drinking and dancing, because of all the great spoil which they had taken from the land of the Philistines and from the land of Judah." David ordered an immediate attack. The Amalekites were surprised and thrown into confusion. The battle was continued until nearly all the enemy were killed. "David recovered all that the Amalekites had carried away, and David rescued his two wives. And nothing of theirs was lacking, either small or great, sons or daughters, spoil or anything which they had taken from them; David recovered all."

If it had not been for the restraining power of God, the Amalekites would have killed the people of Ziklag. They decided to spare the captives, thinking to heighten the triumph by leading home a large number of prisoners to sell as slaves. Thus, unwittingly, they fulfilled God's purpose, keeping the prisoners to be restored to their husbands and fathers.

God Is Ever at Work to Counteract Evil

With great rejoicing the victorious fighters began their homeward march. The more selfish and unruly of the four hundred urged that those who had had no part in the battle should not share the spoils.

But David did not agree and would permit no such arrangement. " 'My brethren, you shall not do so,' " he said, " 'with what the LORD has given us. . . . As his part is that goes down to the battle, so shall his part be who stays by the supplies; they shall share alike.' "

David and his men had captured extensive flocks and herds belonging to the Amalekites. These were called "David's spoil," and upon returning to Ziklag he sent presents from this spoil to the elders of his own tribe of Judah. All were remembered who had helped and supported him and his followers in the mountain refuges when he had been forced to flee for his life.

As David and his warriors worked to restore their ruined homes, they watched for news of the battle fought between Israel and the Philistines. Suddenly a messenger entered the town, "with his clothes torn and dust on his head." He was at once brought to David, and he bowed before him as if David were a powerful prince whose favor he desired. The messenger reported Saul's defeat and death and the death of Jonathan. But he went beyond a simple statement of facts. He hoped to secure honor to himself as the one who had killed the king. With an air of boasting the man related that he found the monarch of Israel wounded, and that at his own request the messenger had killed him. Then he gave David the crown from Saul's head and the golden bracelets from his arms. He confidently expected a rich reward for the part he had acted.

David Grieved for Saul

But "David took hold of his own clothes and tore them, and so did all the men who were with him. And they mourned and wept and fasted until evening for Saul and for Jonathan his son, for the people of the Lord and for the house of Israel, because they had fallen by the sword."

After the first shock of the terrible news wore off, David's thoughts returned to the stranger who had brought the news and the crime of which, according to his own statement, he was guilty. " 'Where are you from?' " And he answered, " 'I am the son of an alien, an Amalekite.' So David said to him, 'How was it you were not afraid to put forth your hand to destroy the Lord's anointed?' " Twice David had refused to lift his hand against him who had been consecrated by the command of God to rule over Israel. Yet the Amalekite had accused himself of a crime worthy of death. David said, " 'Your blood is on your own head, for your own mouth has testified against you, saying, "I have killed the Lord's anointed." ' "

David's grief at the death of Saul was sincere and deep, revealing the generosity of a noble nature. He did not rejoice in the fall of his enemy. The barrier that had kept him from taking the throne of Israel was removed, but this brought him no joy. Now he thought of nothing in Saul's history except that he was noble and kingly. The name of Saul was linked with that of Jonathan, whose friendship had been so true and unselfish.

The song in which David expressed the feelings of his heart became a treasure to his nation and to the people of God in all subsequent ages. See 2 Samuel 1:19-27.

David at Last Crowned King*

The death of Saul removed the dangers that had made David an exile. The way was now open for him to return to his own land. "David inquired of the LORD, saying, 'Shall I go up to any of the cities of Judah?' And the LORD said to him, 'Go up.' David said, 'Where shall I go up?' And He said, 'To Hebron.' "

David and his followers immediately prepared to obey. As the caravan entered the city, the men of Judah were waiting to welcome David as the future king of Israel. Arrangements were made at once for his coronation. "And there they anointed David king over the house of Judah." No effort was made to establish his authority over the other tribes.

When David heard of the brave deed of the men of Jabesh Gilead in rescuing the bodies of Saul and Jonathan and giving them honorable burial, he sent the message, " 'You are blessed of the LORD, for you have shown this kindness to your lord, to Saul, and have buried him. And now may the LORD show kindness and truth to you. I also will repay you this kindness.' "

The Philistines were not upset by the action of Judah in making David a king. They hoped that because they had been kind to David, the increase of his power would work to their advantage. But David's reign was not to be free from trouble.

God had chosen David to be king of Israel, yet hardly had the people of Judah accepted his authority when Ishbosheth, the son of Saul, was made king on a rival throne in Israel. Ishbosheth was a weak, incompetent representative of the house of Saul, in contrast to David who was supremely qualified. Abner, the chief agent in raising Ishbosheth to kingly power, was the most distinguished man in Israel. He knew that the Lord had appointed David to the throne, but he was not willing for the son of Jesse to come into possession of the kingdom.

Abner was ambitious and unprincipled. Saul had influenced him to detest the man whom God had chosen to reign over Israel. His hatred had been increased by the cutting rebuke that David had given him

---

* This chapter is based on 2 Samuel 2 to 5:5.

when the king's jug of water and spear had been taken from the side of Saul as he slept.

Determined to create division in Israel by which he himself might be exalted, he used Ishbosheth, the representative of the previous king, to advance his own selfish ambitions. He knew that the army had not forgotten Saul's first successful campaigns. With determination, this rebellious leader went forward to carry out his plans.

First, he chose Mahanaim, on the farther side of Jordan, as the royal residence. Here Ishbosheth's coronation took place. His reign extended over all Israel except Judah. For two years this son of Saul enjoyed his honors in his secluded capital. But Abner, intent on extending his power over all Israel, prepared for aggressive warfare. And "there was a long war between the house of Saul and the house of David. But David grew stronger and stronger, and the house of Saul grew weaker and weaker."

At last Abner, becoming angry with the incompetent Ishbosheth, deserted to David, offering to bring over to him all the tribes of Israel. David accepted his proposals. But David's favorable reception of so famed a warrior as Abner excited the jealousy of Joab, commander-in-chief of David's army. There was a blood feud between the two men, Abner having killed Asahel, Joab's brother, during the war between Israel and Judah. Now Joab basely waylaid and murdered Abner.

When David heard of this treacherous assault, he exclaimed, " 'My kingdom and I are guiltless before the LORD forever of the blood of Abner the son of Ner. Let it rest on the head of Joab.' " In view of the unsettled state of the kingdom and the power of the murderers, David could not punish the crime properly, but he publicly showed his shock and disapproval. The king followed Abner's coffin as chief mourner, and at the grave he pronounced an elegy that was a cutting rebuke of the murderers.

"Should Abner die as a fool dies? . . . As a man falls before wicked men, so you fell."

David's tribute to one who had been his bitter enemy won the admiration of all Israel. "For all the people and all Israel understood that day that it had not been the king's intent to kill Abner the son of Ner." In the private circle of his trusted counselors and attendants, the king recognized his own inability to punish the murderers as he desired. He left them to the justice of God. " 'The LORD shall repay the evildoer according to his wickedness.' "

When Ishbosheth "heard that Abner had died in Hebron, he lost heart, and all Israel was troubled." Soon another act of treachery completed the downfall of the weakened, rival power. Ishbosheth was murdered by two of his captains who, cutting off his head, rushed with it to the king of Judah, hoping by this to gain his favor.

David Punishes the Murderers of His Enemy

But David did not want the help of foul play to establish his power. He told these murderers of what happened to the man who boasted that he had killed Saul. " 'How much more,' " he added, " 'when wicked men have killed a righteous person in his own house on his bed? Therefore, shall I not now require his blood at your hand and remove you from the earth?' So David commanded his young men, and they executed them."

After the death of Ishbosheth, there was a general desire among the leading men of Israel for David to become king of all the tribes. They declared, " 'You were the one who led Israel out and brought them in; and the LORD said to you, "You shall shepherd My people Israel, and be ruler over Israel." ' " So all the elders of Israel came to the king at Hebron, and King David made a covenant with them at Hebron before the LORD." Thus through the leading of God the way had opened for him to come to the throne.

The change in the people's sentiments was decisive. The revolution was quiet and dignified, in keeping with the work they were doing. Nearly half a million people, the former subjects of Saul, thronged Hebron and its environs. The hour for the coronation was appointed. David—the man who had been expelled from the court of Saul, who had fled to the mountains and hills and to the caves of the earth to preserve his life—was about to receive the highest honor that human beings can confer on a person. Priests and elders, officers and soldiers with glittering spear and helmet, and strangers from long distances stood to witness the coronation.

David was arrayed in the royal robe. The high priest put the sacred oil on his brow, for the earlier anointing by Samuel had been prophetic of what would take place at the king's inauguration. The time had come, and David was consecrated to his office as God's representative. The scepter was placed in his hands. The covenant of his righteous sovereignty was written, and the people gave their pledges of loyalty. Israel had a king by divine appointment.

He who had waited patiently for the Lord saw the promise of God fulfilled. "So David went on and became great, and the LORD God of hosts was with him." 2 Samuel 5:10.

The Prosperous Reign of David*

Twenty miles from Hebron a place was selected as the future capital of the kingdom. It had been called Salem. Eight hundred years before, it had been the home of Melchizedek, priest of God Most High. It was almost in the center of the country and was protected by hills. On the border between Benjamin and Judah, it was close to Ephraim and easily reached by the other tribes.

To secure this location, the Hebrews must drive out a remnant of the Canaanites who held a fortified position on the mountains of Zion and Moriah. This stronghold was called Jebus, and its inhabitants, Jebusites. For centuries no one thought Jebus could be conquered. But it was besieged and taken under the command of Joab, and as a reward he was made commander-in-chief of the armies of Israel. Jebus became the national capital, and its heathen name was changed to Jerusalem.

Hiram, king of Tyre, now provided help to David in erecting a palace at Jerusalem. He sent ambassadors from Tyre, accompanied by architects and workmen and costly material.

The increasing strength of Israel, united under David, stirred the hostility of the Philistines, and they again invaded the country, taking up their position only a short distance from Jerusalem. David withdrew with his men of war to the stronghold of Zion. "And David inquired of the LORD, saying, 'Shall I go up against the Philistines? Will You deliver them into my hand?' And the LORD said to David, 'Go up, for I will doubtless deliver the Philistines into your hand.' "

David attacked at once, defeated them, and took from them the gods that they had brought to ensure victory. Frustrated because of their defeat, the Philistines gathered a larger army and returned to the conflict. Again David asked the Lord for guidance, and the great I AM took direction of the armies of Israel.

God instructed David: " 'You shall not go up; . . . come upon them in front of the mulberry trees. And . . . when you hear the sound of marching in the tops of the mulberry trees, then you shall advance quickly. For then the LORD will go out before you to

---

* This chapter is based on 2 Samuel 5:6-25; 6; 7; 9; 10.

strike the camp of the Philistines.' " If David, like Saul, had chosen his own way, he would not have been successful. But he did as the Lord commanded, and he "drove back the army of the Philistines from Gibeon as far as Gezer. Then the fame of David went out into all lands, and the LORD brought the fear of him upon all nations." 1 Chronicles 14:16, 17.

The Ark Returned to Jerusalem

Now that David was established on the throne, he turned to accomplish a cherished purpose—to bring the ark of God up to Jerusalem. It was fitting that the capital of the nation should be honored with the ark, the token of the divine Presence.

David's purpose was to make the occasion a scene of great rejoicing and impressive display. The people responded gladly. The high priest and the princes and leading men of the tribes assembled at Kirjath Jearim. David's spirits were brimming with holy zeal. The ark was brought out from the house of Abinadab and placed on a new cart drawn by oxen, while two of the sons of Abinadab accompanied it.

The people of Israel followed with shouts and songs of rejoicing, a multitude of voices joining in melody with the sound of musical instruments. "David and the house of Israel played music before the LORD . . . on harps, on stringed instruments, on tambourines, on cymbals, and with trumpets." With solemn joy the vast procession wound its way along the hills and valleys toward the Holy City.

But "when they came to Nachon's threshingfloor, Uzzah put out his hand to the ark of God and took hold of it, for the oxen stumbled. Then the anger of the LORD was aroused against Uzzah, and God struck him there for his rashness [KJV marginal reading]; and he died there by the ark of God." Terror fell on the rejoicing crowd. David was greatly alarmed, and in his heart he questioned the justice of God. Why had that fearful judgment been sent to turn joy into grief and mourning? Feeling that it would be unsafe to have the ark near him, David let it stay where it was. They found a place for it nearby, at the house of Obed-Edom.

God Requires Precise Obedience

The fate of Uzzah was a divine judgment for disobeying a most explicit command. None but the priests, the descendants of Aaron, were to touch the ark or even look on it unless it was covered. The divine direction was, " 'The sons of Kohath shall come to carry them; but they shall not touch any holy thing, lest they die.' " Numbers 4:15. The priests were to cover the ark, and then the Kohathites must lift it by the rods that were placed in rings on each side of the ark. They should bear the ark *"on their shoulders."* Numbers 7:9. There had been an inexcusable disregard of the Lord's directions.

David and his people had engaged in a sacred work with glad and willing hearts, but they had not done it in keeping with the Lord's directions. The Philistines, who knew nothing of God's law, had placed the ark on a cart when they returned it to Israel. But the Israelites had a plain statement of the will of God in these matters, and their neglect of these instructions was dishonoring to God. Since God's law had been ignored, Uzzah had a lessened sense of its sacredness. With unconfessed sins upon him, in face of the divine prohibition, he had presumed to touch the symbol of God's presence. God cannot accept partial obedience or lax ways of treating His commandments. The death of Uzzah, by leading the people to repentance, might prevent judgments on thousands.

The Ark Brings Blessings to Those Who Love the Lord

Feeling that his own heart was not entirely right with God, and seeing what had happened to Uzzah, David feared the ark, lest some sin bring judgments on him. But Obed-Edom welcomed the sacred symbol as the promise of God's favor to people who obey. All Israel watched to see what would happen to his household. "And the LORD blessed Obed-Edom and all his household." David was led to realize as never before the sacredness of God's law and the necessity of strict obedience.

At the end of three months he decided to make another attempt to move the ark, and this time he was very careful to carry out the directions of the Lord. Again a large crowd gathered around the home of Obed-Edom. With reverent care the ark was placed on the shoulders of men appointed by God, and with trembling hearts the vast procession set out. By David's direction sacrifices were offered. Rejoicing now took the place of trembling and terror. The king had laid aside his royal robes and dressed himself in a plain linen robe as worn by the priests. (This robe was sometimes worn by others besides the priests.) In this holy service David would take his place before God on the same level as his subjects. Jehovah was to be the sole object of reverence.

Again the music of harp and cornet, trumpet and cymbal, floated heavenward, with the melody of many voices. "Then David danced before the LORD," keeping time to the measure of the song.

David's dancing in reverent joy before God has been used to justify the modern dance, but in our day dancing is associated with folly and reveling. Morals are sacrificed to pleasure. God is not an object of thought; prayer would be out of place. Amusements that weaken love for sacred things are not to be sought by Christians. The music and dancing in joyful praise of God when the ark was moved had not the faintest resemblance to the corrupting influence of modern dancing. One exalted God's holy name; the other is a device of Satan to cause people to forget and dishonor God.

The triumphal procession approached the capital. Then a burst of song demanded of the watchers upon the walls that the gates of the Holy City be thrown open:

Lift up your heads, O you gates!
And be lifted up, you everlasting
　　doors!
And the King of glory shall come in.

A band of singers and players answered:

Who is this King of glory?

From another company came the response:

The LORD strong and mighty,
The LORD mighty in battle.

Then hundreds of voices, uniting, swelled the triumphal chorus:

Lift up your heads, O you gates!
And lift them up, you everlasting
　　doors!
And the King of glory shall come in.

Again was heard, "Who is this King of glory?" And the voice of the great multitude, like "the sound of many waters," was heard in rapturous reply:

The LORD of hosts,
He is the King of glory.
Psalm 24:7-10

Then the gates were opened wide, and with reverent awe the ark was placed in the tent prepared for it. As the service ended, the king himself pronounced a blessing on his people.

This celebration was the most sacred event yet in the reign of David. As the last beams of the setting sun bathed the tabernacle in holy light, the king's heart was uplifted in gratitude to God that the blessed symbol of His presence was now so near the throne of Israel.

But there was one who saw the scene of rejoicing with a very different spirit. "As the ark of the LORD came into the City of David, Michal, Saul's daughter, looked through a window and saw King David leaping and whirling before the LORD; and she despised him in her heart." She went out to meet him and poured forth a torrent of bitter words, sharp and cutting:

" 'How glorious was the king of Israel today, uncovering himself today in the eyes of the maids of his servants, as one of the base fellows shamelessly uncovers himself!' "

David felt that Michal had despised the service of God, and he answered: " 'It was before the LORD, who chose me instead of your father and all his house, to appoint me ruler over the people of the LORD, over Israel. Therefore I will play music before the LORD. And I will be even more undignified than this, and will be humble in my own sight. But as for the maidservants of whom you have spoken, by them I will be held in honor.' " To this rebuke by David was added that of the Lord. Because of her pride and arrogance, Michal "had no children to the day of her death."

Nation Freed From Idolatry

The removal of the ark had made a lasting impression on the people of Israel, igniting anew their zeal for Jehovah. David tried to deepen these impressions. He made song a regular part of religious worship, and he composed psalms for the people to sing as they traveled to the annual feasts. The influence of these things resulted in freeing the nation from idolatry. Many of the surrounding peoples came to think favorably of Israel's God who had done such great things for His people.

David had built a palace for himself, and he felt that it was not fitting for the ark of God to be housed in a tent. He determined to build a temple for it beautiful enough to show how much Israel appreciated the abiding presence of Jehovah their King. When he told the prophet Nathan about his plans, he received the response, " 'Do all that is in your heart, for the LORD is with you.' "

But that same night the word of the Lord came to Nathan, giving him a message for the king: " 'The LORD tells you that He will make you a house. . . . I will set up your seed after you. . . . He shall build a house for My name, and I will establish the throne of his kingdom forever.' "

God explained the reason David was not to build the temple: " 'You have shed much blood and have made great wars; you shall not build a house for My name. . . . Behold, a son shall be born to you, who shall be a man of rest; and I will give him rest from all his enemies. . . . His name shall be Solomon [peaceful], for I will give peace and quietness to Israel in his days. He shall build a house for My name.' " 1 Chronicles 22:8-10.

Though the cherished purpose of his heart had been denied, David was grateful for the message. He knew that it would be an honor to his name to perform the work he had planned to do, but he was ready to submit to the will of God. How often those who have passed the strength of manhood cling to the hope of accomplishing some great work that they are not fitted to perform! God's providence may declare that they are to prepare the way for someone else to accomplish it. But instead of gratefully submitting to divine direction, many draw back as if offended. If they cannot do the one thing they want to do, they will do nothing. Many try without success to accomplish a work of which they are incapable, while what they might do lies neglected. And because of this the greater work is hindered.

In his covenant with Jonathan, David had promised that he would show kindness to the house of Saul. Remembering this, the king asked, " 'Is there still anyone who is left of the house of Saul, that I may show him kindness for Jonathan's sake?' " He was told of a son of Jonathan, Mephibosheth, who had been lame from childhood. The nurse of this child had let him fall, making him a lifelong cripple. David now invited the young man to come to the palace, and gave him the private possessions of Saul for the support of his household; but beyond this, the son of Jonathan was to be the constant guest of the king. Mephibosheth had been led to cherish a strong prejudice against David as one who had no right to the throne; but the monarch's continued kindness won the heart of the young man. Like his father Jonathan, he felt that his interest was one with that of the king whom God had chosen.

After David had been established on the throne of Israel, the nation enjoyed a long period of peace. The surrounding peoples soon thought it wise to end open hostilities, and David refrained from aggressive war. At last, however, he made war against Israel's old enemies, the Philistines and Moabites, and subjugated them.

Hostile Nations Plot Against David

Then a vast coalition of surrounding nations formed against David. Out of it grew the greatest wars and greatest victories of his reign and the biggest increases of his power. He had done nothing to provoke this hostile alliance. The circumstances were these:

News had come to Jerusalem about the death of Nahash, king of the Ammonites, who had shown kindness to David when he was fleeing from Saul. Wanting to express his appreciation of the favor shown him in his distress, David sent a message of sympathy to Hanun, son of the Ammonite king.

Hanun's counselors misinterpreted David's message. They "said to Hanun their lord, 'Do you think that David really honors your father because he has sent comforters to you? Has David not rather sent his servants to you to search the city, to spy it out, and to overthrow it?' " They could not comprehend the generous spirit that inspired David's message. Believing that his counselors were right, Hanun regarded David's messengers as spies and loaded them with scorn and insult.

God permitted the Ammonites to carry out the evil purposes of their hearts so that their real character might be clear to David. It was not His will that Israel enter into an alliance with this heathen people.

Knowing that David would surely avenge the insult to Israel, the Ammonites prepared for war. The inhabitants of the region between the River Euphrates and the Mediterranean Sea joined with the Ammonites to crush Israel.

The Hebrews did not wait for the invasion. Under Joab they advanced toward the Ammonite capital. The united forces of the enemy were overcome in the first engagement, but the next year they renewed the war. David took the field in person, and by the blessing of God inflicted a defeat so disastrous that the Syrians, from Lebanon to the Euphrates, not only gave up the war, they became subject to Israel.

The dangers that threatened the nation with destruction proved to be the means by which it rose to greatness. Commemorating his deliverance, David sang:

Blessed be my Rock!

Let the God of my salvation be ex-
alted.
It is God who avenges me,
And subdues the peoples under me;
He delivers me from my enemies.
Psalm 18:46-48

Throughout the songs of David, the thought was impressed on his people that Jehovah was their strength and deliverer:

Some trust in chariots,
and some in horses;
But we will remember the name of the
LORD our God.
Psalm 20:7

The kingdom of Israel had now reached the full extent of what God had promised to Abraham: " 'To your descendants I have given this land, from the river of Egypt to the great river, the River Euphrates.' " Genesis 15:18. Israel had become a mighty nation, respected and feared by surrounding peoples. As few other sovereigns in history, David commanded the affections and allegiance of his people. He had honored God, and God was now honoring him.

But in the time of his greatest outward triumph, David met his most humiliating defeat.

David's Sin of Adultery and His Repentance*

The Bible has little to say in praise of human beings. All the good qualities that people possess are the gift of God; their good deeds are performed by the grace of God through Christ. They are only instruments in His hands. All the lessons of Bible history teach that it is dangerous to praise people, for if one comes to lose sight of his or her entire dependence on God, one is sure to fall. The Bible teaches distrust of human power and encourages trust in divine power.

The spirit of self-exaltation prepared the way for David's fall. Flattery, power, and luxury had their effect on him. According to the customs prevailing among Eastern rulers, crimes that were not tolerated in subjects were overlooked in the king. All this tended to lessen David's sense of the exceeding sinfulness of sin. He began to trust to his own wisdom and might.

As soon as Satan can separate a person from God, he will arouse the unholy desires of man's carnal nature. The work of the enemy does not begin with something sudden and startling. It begins in apparently small things—neglect to rely fully on God, the inclination to follow the practices of the world.

David returned to Jerusalem. The Syrians had already surrendered, and the complete defeat of the Ammonites appeared certain. David was surrounded by the fruits of victory and the honors of his wise rule. Now the tempter seized the opportunity to occupy his mind. In ease and self-security, David yielded to Satan and brought upon himself the stain of guilt. He, the Heaven-appointed leader of the nation, chosen by God to uphold His law, himself trampled on its precepts. By his own act, he who should have been a terror to evildoers strengthened their hands.

Guilty and unrepentant, David did not ask guidance from Heaven but tried to disentangle himself from the dangers in which sin had involved him. Bathsheba, whose fatal beauty had proved a snare to the king, was the wife of Uriah the Hittite, one of David's bravest and most faithful officers. The law of God pronounced the adulterer guilty of death, and the proud-spirited soldier, so shamefully

* This chapter is based on 2 Samuel 11; 12.

wronged, might avenge himself by taking the life of the king or by leading the nation in revolt.

Every effort that David made to hide his guilt was unsuccessful. He had betrayed himself into the power of Satan; danger surrounded him, and dishonor more bitter than death loomed before him. There appeared to be only one way of escape—to add the sin of murder to that of adultery. David reasoned that if Uriah were killed in battle, the guilt of his death could not be traced to the king. Bathsheba would be free to become David's wife, he could avoid suspicion and maintain the royal honor.

Uriah was made the bearer of his own death warrant. In a letter sent by his hand to Joab, the king commanded, " 'Set Uriah in the forefront of the hottest battle, and retreat from him, that he may be struck down and die.' " Joab, already stained with the guilt of one murder, did not hesitate to obey the king's instructions, and Uriah was killed by the sword of the Ammonites.

David Temporarily Becomes the Agent of Satan

David's record as a ruler had won the confidence of the nation. But as he departed from God, he became for the time the agent of Satan. Yet he still held the authority that God had given him, and because of this he claimed obedience that would imperil the soul of his commander if he cooperated. But Joab had given his allegiance to the king rather than to God, and he transgressed God's law because the king commanded it.

When David commanded what was contrary to God's law, it became sin to obey. "The authorities that exist are appointed by God" (Romans 13:1), but we are not to obey them contrary to God's law. The apostle Paul sets forth the principle by which we should be governed: "Be ye followers of me, even as I also am of Christ." 1 Corinthians 11:1 KJV.

Joab sent news to David that his order had been carried out, but it was so carefully worded that it did not implicate either Joab or the king. " 'Your servant Uriah the Hittite is dead.' "

The king's answer was, " 'Thus you shall say to Joab, "Do not let this thing displease you, for the sword devours one as well as another." ' "

According to custom, Bathsheba mourned for her husband an appropriate number of days, and at their close, "David sent and brought her to his house, and she became his wife." He who would not, even when his life was in danger, put forth his hand against the Lord's anointed, had so fallen that he could wrong and murder one of his most faithful, brave soldiers, and hope to enjoy undisturbed the reward of his sin.

Happy are they who, having strayed from the path of right, learn how bitter are the fruits of sin, and turn from it. God in His mercy did not leave David to be lured to complete ruin by the deceitful rewards of sin.

How God Intervened

It was necessary for God to step in. David's sin with Bathsheba became known, and many suspected that he had planned Uriah's death. The Lord was dishonored. He had exalted David, and David's sin brought disgrace on His name. It tended to lower the standard of godliness in Israel, to lessen in many minds the perception that sin is hateful.

Nathan the prophet was given a message of reproof for David. Though it was terrible in its severity, Nathan delivered the divine message with such heaven-born wisdom that it engaged the sympathies of the king, aroused his conscience, and called from his own lips the sentence of death upon himself. The prophet told a story of wrongdoing and injustice that simply had to be made right.

" 'There were two men in one city,' " he said, " 'one rich and the other poor. The rich man had exceedingly many flocks and herds. But the poor man had nothing, except one little ewe lamb which he had bought and nourished; and it grew up together with him and with his children. It ate of his own food and drank from his own cup and lay in his bosom; and it was like a daughter to him. And a traveler came to the rich man, who refused to take from his own flock and from his own herd to prepare one for the wayfaring man who had come to him; but took the poor man's lamb and prepared it for the man who had come to him.' "

The king became angry. " 'As the Lord lives, the man who has done this shall surely die! And he shall restore fourfold for the lamb, because

he did this thing and because he had no pity.' "

Nathan fixed his eyes on the king, then solemnly declared, " 'You are the man! . . . Why have you despised the commandment of the Lord, to do evil in His sight?' " The guilty may attempt, as David had, to conceal their crime from others, to bury the evil deed forever from human sight, but "all things are naked and open to the eyes of Him to whom we must give account." Hebrews 4:13.

Nathan declared: " 'You have killed Uriah the Hittite with the sword; you have taken his wife to be your wife, and have killed him with the sword of the people of Ammon. Now therefore, the sword shall never depart from your house. . . . Behold, I will raise up adversity against you from your own house; and I will take your wives before your eyes and give them to your neighbor. . . . For you did it secretly, but I will do this thing before all Israel, before the sun.' "

The prophet's rebuke touched David's heart; conscience was aroused, and he saw how great was his guilt. With trembling lips he said, " 'I have sinned against the Lord.' " David had committed a terrible sin against both Uriah and Bathsheba, but infinitely greater was his sin against God.

David Punished for His Sin

David trembled, being afraid that he would be cut down, guilty and unforgiven, by the swift judgment of God. But the message was sent him by the prophet, " 'The LORD also has put away your sin; you shall not die.' " Yet justice must be maintained. The sentence of death was transferred from David to the child of his sin. Thus the king was given opportunity to repent, while the suffering and death of the child, as a part of his punishment, was far more bitter to him than his own death could have been.

When his child was stricken, David pleaded for its life with fasting and deep humiliation. Night after night he lay in heartbroken grief interceding for the innocent one suffering for his guilt. When he heard that the child was dead, he quietly submitted to the decree of God. The first stroke had fallen of the very punishment that he himself had declared just.

Reading the history of David's fall, many have asked, "Why did God see fit to throw open to the world this dark chapter in the life of one so highly honored by Heaven?" Atheists and unbelievers have pointed to the character of David and have exclaimed with a sneer, "This is the man after God's own heart!" Thus God and His word have been blasphemed, and many, while professing to be religious, have become bold in sin.

But the history of David provides no approval for sin. It was when he was walking with God and following His counsel that David was called a man after God's own heart. When he sinned, this stopped being true of him until by repentance he had returned to the Lord. "The thing that David had done was evil in the eyes of the LORD" (KJV). Though David repented of his sin, he reaped the deadly harvest of the seed he had sown. The judgments upon him testify how much God hates sin.

David himself was broken in spirit by the consciousness of his sin and its far-reaching results. He felt humbled in the eyes of his subjects. His influence was weakened. Now his subjects, knowing about his sin, would be led to sin more freely. His authority in his own household was weakened. His guilt kept him silent when he should have condemned sin. His evil example exerted its influence on his sons, and God would not step in to prevent the result. Thus David was severely punished. No repentance could help him escape the agony and shame that would darken his whole earthly life.

People who point to the example of David to try to lessen the guilt of their own sins should learn from the Bible record that the way of transgression is hard. The results of sin, even in this life, will be found bitter and hard to bear.

God intended that the history of David's fall would serve as a warning that even those whom He has greatly blessed are not to feel smugly secure. And it has served this purpose to all who in humility have sought to learn the lesson He designed to teach. The fall of David, one so honored by the Lord, has awakened in them distrust of self. Knowing that their strength and safety was in God alone, they have feared to take the first step onto Satan's ground.

Even before the divine sentence was pronounced against David, he had begun to reap the fruit of transgression. The agony of spirit he then endured is brought to view in the thirty-second psalm:

When I kept silent, my bones grew old
Through my groaning all the day long.
For day and night Your hand was heavy upon me;
My vitality was turned into the drought of summer.
Psalm 32:3, 4

And the fifty-first psalm is an expression of David's repentance, when the message of reproof came to him from God:

Create in me a clean heart, O God,
And renew a steadfast spirit within me.
Do not cast me away from Your presence,
And do not take Your Holy Spirit from me. . . .
Deliver me from bloodguiltiness, O God,
The God of my salvation,
And my tongue shall sing aloud of Your righteousness.
Psalm 51:10, 11, 14

Thus the king of Israel told of his sin, his repentance, and his hope of pardon through the mercy of God. He wanted others to be instructed by the sad history of his fall.

More Than Pardon

David's repentance was sincere. He did not try to make his crime look less serious, nor did he desire to escape the judgments threatened. He saw the defilement of his heart. He hated his sin. It was not for pardon only that he prayed, but for purity of heart. In God's promise to repentant sinners he saw the evidence of his pardon and acceptance: "The sacrifices of God are a broken spirit, a broken and a contrite heart—These, O God, You will not despise." Psalm 51:17.

Though David had fallen, the Lord lifted him up. In the joy of his release he sang, "I acknowledged my sin to You, and my iniquity I have not hidden. I said, 'I will confess my transgressions to the LORD,' and You forgave the iniquity of my sin." Psalm 32:5. David humbled himself and confessed his sin, while Saul, in contrast, despised reproof and hardened his heart in justifying himself.

This passage in David's history is one of the most forcible illustrations given to us of the struggles and temptations of humanity, and of genuine repentance. Through all the ages, thousands of the children of God who have been betrayed into sin have remembered David's sincere repentance and confession and have taken courage to repent and try again to walk in the way of God's commandments.

All who will humble themselves with confession and repentance, as David did, may be sure that there is hope for them. The Lord will never cast away one truly repentant soul.

The Rebellion of Absalom, David's Son[*]

He shall restore fourfold," had been David's unwitting sentence upon himself after hearing the prophet Nathan's parable. Four of his sons must fall, and the loss of each would be a result of the father's sin.

David permitted the shameful crime of Amnon, his firstborn, to go unpunished. The law pronounced death upon the adulterer, and the unnatural crime of Amnon made him doubly guilty. But David, self-condemned for his own sin, failed to bring the offender to justice. For two years Absalom, the natural protector of the sister so terribly wronged, concealed his purpose of revenge, but by his orders, at a feast the drunken, incestuous Amnon was killed.

The king's sons returned in panic to Jerusalem and told their father that Amnon had been killed. And they "lifted up their voice and wept. Also the king and all his servants wept very bitterly." But Absalom fled. David had neglected his duty to punish Amnon, and the Lord allowed events to take their natural course. When parents or rulers neglect the duty of punishing evil, a train of circumstances will follow that will punish sin with sin.

Absalom's alienation from his father began here. David, feeling that Absalom's crime demanded punishment, refused to let him return. Shut out by his exile from the affairs of the kingdom, Absalom occupied his time with dangerous scheming.

At the close of two years Joab determined to reconcile the father and son. He got a woman of Tekoah, known for her wisdom, to help him. The woman presented herself to David as a widow whose two sons had been her only comfort and support. In a quarrel one had killed the other, and now the relatives demanded that the surviving son be given up to the avenger of blood. And so, said the mother, " 'they would extinguish my ember that is left, and leave to my husband neither name nor remnant on the earth.' " The king's feelings were touched, and he assured the woman that he would protect her son.

Then, asking for the king's permission to say more, she pointed out that he was at fault in not bringing his

* This chapter is based on 2 Samuel 13 to 19.

banished son home again. " 'For,' " she said, " 'we will surely die and become like water spilled on the ground, which cannot be gathered up again. Yet God does not take away a life; but *He devises means, so that His banished ones are not expelled from Him.'* " This tender and touching portrayal of the love of God toward the sinner is striking proof that the Israelites were familiar with the great truths of redemption. The king could not resist this appeal. He gave the command, " 'Go therefore, bring back the young man Absalom.' "

The Sad Results of David's Sin

Absalom was permitted to return to Jerusalem, but not to appear at the court or to meet his father. Tenderly as he loved this beautiful and gifted son, David felt it necessary to show abhorrence for the crime he had committed. Absalom lived two years in his own house, banished from the court. His sister's presence kept alive the memory of the irreparable wrong she had suffered. In the public's eyes, the prince was a hero rather than an offender, and he put himself in a position to gain the hearts of the people.

His personal appearance was enough to win the admiration of all. "In all Israel there was no one who was praised as much as Absalom for his good looks. From the sole of his foot to the crown of his head there was no blemish in him." David's decision permitting him to return to Jerusalem while refusing to admit him to his presence enlisted the people's sympathies for him.

Before his sin David had been courageous and decided. Now he was weak and hesitating. This worked in favor of his son's plans.

Through the influence of Joab, Absalom was again admitted to his father's presence. He continued his scheming, diligently courting popular favor and artfully turning every cause of dissatisfaction to his own advantage. Day by day this man of noble appearance could be seen at the city gate, where a disgruntled crowd waited to present their wrongs for remedy. Absalom listened, expressing sympathy with their sufferings and regret at the inefficiency of the government. " 'Oh, that I were made judge in the land, and everyone who has any suit or cause would come to me; then I would give him justice.' And so it was, whenever anyone came near him to bow down to him, that he would put out his hand and take him and kiss him."

Rebellion Grows Underground

Discontent with the government was fast spreading, stirred up and encouraged by the prince. Absalom was generally regarded as heir to the kingdom, and many wanted him to occupy the throne. "So Absalom stole the hearts of the men of Israel." Yet the king suspected nothing. David thought the princely role that Absalom had assumed was intended to do honor to his court.

Absalom secretly sent chosen men throughout the tribes to lay plans for revolt. And now he used religious devotion as a covering to conceal his traitorous plans. Absalom said to the king, " 'Please, let me go to Hebron and pay the vow which I vowed to the LORD. For your servant vowed a vow while I dwelt at Geshur in Syria, saying, "If the LORD indeed brings me back to Jerusalem, then I will serve the LORD." ' "

The fond father, comforted with this appearance of piety in his son, sent him away with his blessing. Absalom planned his crowning act of hypocrisy not only to blind the king but to secure the confidence of the people. In this way he would lead them on to rebellion against the king whom God had chosen.

Absalom set out for Hebron, and with him "two hundred men invited from Jerusalem. . . , and they went along innocently and did not know anything." These men went, never thinking that their love for the son was leading them into rebellion against the father. At Hebron, Absalom called for Ahithophel, a man famous for wisdom. Ahithophel's support made Absalom's cause appear certain to succeed, attracting many influential men to his ranks. As the trumpet of revolt sounded, the prince's spies throughout the country spread the news that Absalom was king, and many of the people gathered to him.

David Finally Acts

Meanwhile the alarm was carried to Jerusalem. David suddenly saw that rebellion was breaking out close beside his throne. His own son had been plotting to seize his crown and doubtless take his life. In his great danger David shook off the depression that had long engulfed him and prepared to meet this terrible emergency. Absalom was only twenty miles away. The rebels would soon be at the gates of Jerusalem.

David shuddered at the thought of exposing his capital to bloodshed and devastation. Should he permit Jerusalem to be deluged with blood? He made his decision. He would leave Jerusalem, and then test his people, giving them opportunity to rally to his support. It was his duty to God and to his people to maintain the authority that Heaven had given him.

In humility and sorrow, David went out of the gate of Jerusalem. The people followed in long, sad procession, like a funeral train. David's bodyguard of Cherethites, Pelethites, and Gittites, under the command of Ittai, accompanied the king. But with characteristic unselfishness, David could not consent to involve these strangers in his calamity. Then said the king to Ittai, " 'Why are you also going with us? . . . You are a foreigner and also an exile. . . . In fact, you came only yesterday. Should I make you wander up and down with us today, since I go I know not where? Return, and take your brethren back. Mercy and truth be with you.' "

Ittai answered, " 'As the LORD lives, and as my lord the king lives, surely in whatever place my lord the king shall be, whether in death or life, even there also your servant will be.' " These men had been converted from paganism, and nobly they now proved their loyalty to God and their king. David accepted their devotion to his apparently losing cause, and all passed over the brook Kidron, toward the wilderness.

Some Are Loyal to David in the Crisis

Again the procession stopped. "There was Zadok also, and all the Levites with him, bearing the ark of the covenant of God." To the people with David the presence of that sacred symbol was a pledge of deliverance and victory. Its absence from Jerusalem would bring terror to Absalom's followers.

At sight of the ark, for a brief moment joy and hope thrilled the heart of David. But soon other thoughts came. The glory of God and the good of his people were to be uppermost in his mind, for he was the appointed ruler of God's heritage. God had said of Jerusalem, " 'This is my resting place' " (Psalm 132:14), and neither priest nor king had a right to remove the symbol of His presence from the city. And David's great sin was ever before him. It was not for him to remove from the nation's capital the sacred statutes that embodied the will of their divine Sovereign, the constitution of the realm and the foundation of its prosperity.

He commanded Zadok, " 'Carry the ark of God back into the city. If I find favor in the eyes of the LORD, He will bring me back and show me both

it and His habitation. But if He says thus: "I have no delight in you," here I am, let Him do to me as seems good to Him.' "

When All Looks Dark, David Prays

As the priests turned back toward Jerusalem, a deep shadow fell over the people with David. Their king a fugitive, themselves outcasts, forsaken even by the ark of God—the future was dark! "So David went up by the ascent of the Mount of Olives, and wept as he went up; and he had his head covered and went barefoot. And all the people who were with him covered their heads and went up, weeping as they went up. Then someone told David, saying, 'Ahithophel is among the conspirators with Absalom.' " Again David was forced to recognize the results of his own sin. The defection of Ahithophel, the most talented of political leaders, was prompted by revenge for the wrong to his granddaughter, Bathsheba.

"And David said, 'O LORD, I pray, turn the counsel of Ahithophel into foolishness!' " Upon reaching the top of the mountain, the king bowed in prayer, casting the burden of his soul on God and humbly pleading for divine mercy.

Hushai the Archite, a wise and able counselor and a faithful friend to David, now came to cast in his fortunes with the dethroned and fugitive king. As if by a divine enlightenment, David saw that this man was the one needed to serve the interests of the king in the capital's councils. At David's request, Hushai returned to Jerusalem to offer his services to Absalom and defeat the crafty counsel of Ahithophel.

With this gleam of light in the darkness, the king and his followers continued down the eastern slope of Olivet, through a rocky and desolate wasteland toward the Jordan River. "Now when King David came to Bahurim, there was a man from the family of the house of Saul, whose name was Shimei the son of Gera. . . . And he threw stones at David and at all the servants of King David. . . . And Shimei said thus when he cursed: 'Come out! Come out! You bloodthirsty man, you rogue! The LORD has brought upon you all the blood of the house of Saul, in whose place you have reigned; and the LORD has delivered the kingdom into the hand of Absalom your son. So now you are caught in your own evil, because you are a bloodthirsty man!' "

When David was prosperous, Shimei had not shown that he was disloyal. He had honored David on his throne, but now he cursed him in his humiliation. Inspired by Satan, he gave vent to his wrath on him whom God had punished.

David had not been guilty of wrong toward Saul or on any of his family. He had spent much of his life amid scenes of violence; but of all who have passed through such an ordeal, few have been so little hardened and demoralized by it as was David.

David's nephew, Abishai, could not listen patiently to Shimei's insulting words. He exclaimed, " 'Why should this dead dog curse my lord the king? Please, let me go over and take off his head!' " But the king said No. " 'My son . . . seeks my life. How much more now may this Benjamite? Let him alone, and let him curse; for the LORD has ordered him. It may be that the LORD will look on my affliction, and that the LORD will repay me with good for his cursing this day.' "

David Knows This Trouble Is the Consequence of His Sin

While King David's faithful subjects were amazed at his sudden reverse of fortune, it was no mystery to him. He had often had forebodings of an hour like this. He had marveled that God had so long tolerated his sins. And now in his hurried and sorrowful escape, he thought of his loved capital, the place that had been the scene of his sin. As he remembered the patience of God, he felt that the Lord would still deal with him in mercy.

David had confessed his sin and had tried to do his duty as a faithful servant of God. He had worked to build up his kingdom. He had gathered supplies of material for building the house of God. And now must the results of years of consecrated toil pass into the hands of his reckless, traitorous son?

He saw the cause of his trouble in his own sin. And the Lord did not forsake David. Under cruel wrong and insult he showed himself humble, unselfish, generous, and submissive. Never was the ruler of Israel more truly great in the sight of heaven than at this hour of his deepest humiliation.

In the experience through which He caused David to pass, the Lord shows that He cannot tolerate or excuse sin. David's history enables us to trace the working out of His purpose of mercy, even through darkest judgments. He caused David to be punished, but He did not destroy him. The furnace is to purify, not to consume.

God Does Not Give Absalom Wisdom

Soon after David left Jerusalem, Absalom and his army took possession of that stronghold of Israel. Hushai was among the first to greet the newly-crowned monarch, and the prince was pleased that his father's old friend and counselor had joined him. Absalom was confident of success. Eager to secure the confidence of the nation, he welcomed Hushai to his court.

Absalom was surrounded by a large force, but it was composed mostly of men untrained for war. Ahithophel well knew that a large part of the nation was still true to David and that he was surrounded by tried warriors commanded by able and experienced generals. Ahithophel knew that after the first burst of enthusiasm in favor of the new king, a reaction would come. If the rebellion should fail, Absalom and his father might reconcile. Then Ahithophel, as his chief counselor, would be held most guilty; upon him the heaviest punishment would fall.

To prevent Absalom from giving up his rebellion, Ahithophel devised a plan that would make reconciliation impossible. With hellish cunning, this unprincipled statesman urged Absalom to add the crime of incest to that of rebellion. In the sight of all Israel he was to take to himself his father's concubines, by this act declaring that he had succeeded to his father's throne. And Absalom carried out the vile suggestion. This fulfilled the word of God to David by the prophet, " 'Behold, I will raise up adversity against you from your own house; and I will take your wives before your eyes and give them to your neighbor. . . . For you did it secretly, but I will do this thing before all Israel, before the sun.' " 2 Samuel 12:11, 12. Not that God prompted these acts, but He did not exercise His power to prevent them.

Ahithophel was totally without divine enlightenment, or he could not have used the crime of incest to make a success of treason. People of corrupt hearts plot wickedness, as if there were no overruling Providence to disrupt their schemes.

Having succeeded in securing his own safety, Ahithophel urged, " 'Now let me choose twelve thousand men, and I will arise and pursue David tonight. I will come upon him while he is weary and weak, and make him afraid. And all the people who are with him will flee, and I will strike only the king. Then I will bring back all the people to you.' " If this plan had been followed, David would surely have been killed. But "the Lord had purposed to defeat the good advice of Ahithophel, to the intent that the LORD might bring disaster on Absalom."

Hushai had not been called to the council. But after the assembly had dispersed, Absalom, who had a high regard for the judgment of his father's counselor, submitted Ahithophel's plan to him.

Hushai saw that if the plan were followed, David would be lost. So he said, " 'The advice that Ahithophel has given is not good at this time. For,' " said Hushai, " 'you know your father and his men, that they are mighty men, and they are enraged in their minds, like a bear robbed of her cubs in the field; and your father is a man of war, and will not camp with the people. Surely by now he is hidden in some pit, or in some other place.' " If Absalom's forces were to pursue David, they would not capture the king; and if they suffered a reverse, it would dishearten them and work great harm to Absalom's cause. " 'For,' " he said, " 'all Israel knows that your father is a mighty man, and those who are with him are valiant men.' "

Hushai Suggests an Alternate Plan

Hushai suggested a plan that appealed to a vain and selfish nature: " 'I counsel that all Israel be fully gathered to you, from Dan to Beersheba, like the sand that is by the sea for multitude, and that you go to battle in person. So we will come upon him in some place where he may be found, and we will fall on him as the dew falls on the ground. And of him and all the men who are with him there shall not be left so much as one. Moreover, if he has withdrawn into a city, then all Israel shall bring ropes to that city; and we will pull it into the river, until there is not one small stone found there.'

"So Absalom and all the men of Israel said, 'The advice of Hushai the Archite is better than the advice of Ahithophel.' "

But one person clearly foresaw the result of this fatal mistake of Absalom's. Ahithophel knew that the cause of the rebels was lost. And he knew that whatever might be the fate of the prince, there was no hope for the counselor who had masterminded his greatest crimes. Ahithophel had encouraged Absalom in rebellion; he had counseled him to the most abominable wickedness, to the dishonor of his father; he had suggested a plan to kill David; he had cut off the last possibility of being reconciled himself with the king; and now Absalom was looking to someone else before him. Jealous, angry, and desperate, Ahithophel "went home to his house, . . . and hanged himself, and died." Such was the result of the wisdom of one who did not make God his counselor.

Hushai lost no time in warning David to escape beyond Jordan without delay: " 'Do not spend this night in the plains of the wilderness, but speedily cross over, lest the king and all the people who are with him be swallowed up.' "

David, worn out with toil and grief after that first day of fleeing, received the message that he must cross the Jordan that night, for his son was seeking his life. What were the feelings of the father and king in this dangerous, terrible time? In the hour of his darkest trial, David's heart was fixed upon God, and he sang:

LORD, how they have increased who
　　trouble me!
Many are they who rise up against
　　me.
Many are they who say of me,
"There is no help for him in God."
But You, O LORD, are a shield for
　　me,
My glory and the One who lifts up
　　my head.
I cried to the LORD with my voice,
And He heard me from His holy hill.
I lay down and slept;
I awoke, for the LORD sustained me.
I will not be afraid of ten thousands of
　　people
Who have set themselves against me
　　all around.
Psalm 3:1-6

In the darkness of night, David and all his company crossed the deep, swift-flowing river. "By morning light not one of them was left who had not gone over the Jordan."

David and his forces fell back to Mahanaim, which had been the royal seat of Ishbosheth. It was a strongly fortified city set in mountains favorable for retreat in case of war. The country had abundant sup-

plies and the people were friendly to David.

Absalom, the rash and impetuous prince, soon set out in pursuit of his father. His army was large, but it was undisciplined and poorly prepared to cope with the battle-hardened soldiers of his father.

David divided his forces into three battalions under the command of Joab, Abishai, and Ittai.

The Battle That Defeated the Rebellion

From the walls of Mahanaim, the long lines of Absalom's army were in full view. The rebel was accompanied by a vast host; David's force seemed only a handful in comparison. As the army filed out from the city gates, David encouraged his faithful soldiers, urging them to go out trusting that the God of Israel would give them victory. But as Joab, leading the column, passed his king, the conqueror of a hundred battlefields stooped his proud head to hear the monarch's last message, " 'Deal gently *for my sake* with the young man Absalom.' " And Abishai and Ittai received the same instruction. But the king's plea, seeming to say that Absalom was dearer to him than the subjects faithful to his throne, only increased the anger of the soldiers toward the unnatural son.

The place of battle was a woods near the Jordan. Among the thickets and marshes of the forest, the great numbers of undisciplined troops of Absalom's army became confused and unmanageable. And "the people of Israel were overthrown there before the servants of David, and a great slaughter of twenty thousand took place there that day."

Absalom, seeing that the battle was lost, had turned to flee, and his head became caught between the branches of a widespreading tree. His mule, going out from under him, left him hopelessly suspended, a prey for his enemies. He was found by a soldier, who spared him but reported to Joab what he had seen.

Joab was held back by no scruples. He had befriended Absalom, having twice reconciled him with David, and the trust had been shamelessly betrayed. If Joab had not obtained advantages for Absalom, this rebellion could never have occurred. "And he took three spears in his hand and thrust them through Absalom's heart. . . . And they took Absalom and cast him into a large pit in the woods, and laid a very large heap of stones over him."

God's Judgment on the Rebellion

Thus perished the instigators of rebellion in Israel. Ahithophel had died by his own hand. The princely Absalom, whose beauty had been the pride of Israel, had been killed in his youth, his dead body thrown into a pit and covered with a heap of stones, to represent everlasting reproach.

With the leader of the rebellion dead, Joab at once sent two messengers to carry the news to the king.

The second messenger announced, " 'There is good news, my lord the king! For the LORD has avenged you this day of all those who rose against you.' " From the father's lips came the question, " 'Is the young man Absalom safe?' " Unable to conceal the bad news, the herald answered, " 'May the enemies of my lord the king, and all who rise against you to do you harm, be as that young man.' " David questioned no further, but with bowed head "went up to the chamber over the gate, and wept. And as he went, he said thus: 'O my son Absalom—my son, my son Absalom—if only I had died in your place! O Absalom my son, my son!' "

The victorious army approached the city, their shouts of triumph echoing on the hills. But as they entered the city gate the shout died away and their banners drooped in their hands, for the king was not waiting to welcome them. From the chamber above the gate his wailing cry was heard, " 'O my son Absalom—my son, my son Absalom—if only I had died in your place! O Absalom my son, my son!' "

Joab was filled with anger. God had given them reason for triumph and gladness. The greatest rebellion ever known in Israel had been crushed. Yet this great victory was turned to mourning for Absalom whose crime had cost the blood of thousands of brave men. The rude, blunt captain pushed his way into the presence of the king and boldly said, " 'Today you have disgraced all your servants who today have saved your life, the lives of your sons and daughters, . . . in that you love your enemies and hate your friends. For you have declared today that you regard neither princes nor servants; for today I perceive that if Absalom had lived and all of us had died today, then it would have pleased you well. Now therefore, arise, go out and speak comfort to your servants. For I swear by the LORD, if you do not go out, not one will stay with you this night. And that will be worse for you than all the evil that has befallen you from your youth until now.' "

Though the reproof was harsh and cruel, David did not resent it. Seeing that his general was right, he went down to the gate, and with words of commendation greeted his brave soldiers as they marched past him.

A Man After God's Own Heart[*]

Absalom's overthrow did not bring peace at once. So much of the nation had joined in revolt that David would not return to his capital and take up the kingship again without an invitation from the people. There was no prompt, firm action to recall the king, and when the tribe of Judah finally set about to bring David back, the action roused the jealousy of the other tribes. A counterrevolution followed, but it was speedily put down, and peace returned to Israel.

Dangers threaten the soul from power, riches, and worldly honor. God had designed that David's early life—with a shepherd's lessons of humility, patient toil, and tender care for his flocks; with the scenes of nature in the solitude of the hills directing his thoughts to the Creator; with the long discipline of his wilderness life—would prepare him for the throne of Israel. And yet, worldly success and honor weakened the character of David so much that he was overcome by the tempter.

David Falls Again to the Sin of Pride

Dealings with heathen peoples led to a desire to follow their national customs and awakened ambition for worldly greatness. To extend his conquests, David determined to increase his army by requiring military service from all who were of proper age. To make this happen, he needed to take a census of the population. Pride and ambition prompted this action. The numbers would show the contrast between the weakness of the kingdom when David came to the throne and its strength and prosperity under his rule. The Scripture says, "Satan stood up against Israel, and moved David to number Israel." The prosperity of Israel under David had been due to the blessing of God. But increasing the kingdom's military resources would give surrounding nations the impression that Israel's trust was in her armies, not in Jehovah.

The people of Israel did not approve of David's plan for greatly extending military service. The proposed census caused much dissatisfaction, so military officers were used in place of the priests and magistrates who had formerly taken the census. The purpose was

---

* This chapter is based on 2 Samuel 24; 1 Kings 1; 1 Chronicles 21; 28; 29.

directly contrary to the principles of a theocracy. Even Joab protested: " 'Why . . . does my lord require this thing? Why should he be a cause of guilt in Israel?' Nevertheless the king's word prevailed against Joab. Therefore Joab departed and went throughout all Israel and came to Jerusalem."

David was convicted of his sin. Self-condemned, he "said to God, 'I have sinned greatly, because I have done this thing; but now, I pray, take away the iniquity of Your servant, for I have done very foolishly.' "

Next morning the prophet Gad brought a message: " 'Thus says the LORD, "Choose for yourself, either three years of famine, or three months to be defeated by your foes with the sword of your enemies overtaking you, or else for three days the sword of the LORD—the plague in the land, with the angel of the LORD destroying throughout all the territory of Israel." ' "

David Chooses Punishment From the Lord

The king's answer was, " 'I am in great distress. Please let me fall into the hand of the LORD, for His mercies are very great; but do not let me fall into the hand of man.' "

The land was struck by a pestilence that destroyed seventy thousand in Israel. "David lifted his eyes and saw the angel of the LORD standing between earth and heaven, having in his hand a drawn sword stretched out over Jerusalem." The king pleaded with God in behalf of Israel: " 'Was it not I who commanded the people to be numbered? I am

the one who has sinned and done evil indeed; but these sheep, what have they done? Let Your hand, I pray, O LORD my God, be against me and my father's house, but not against Your people that they should be plagued.' "

The people had cherished the same sins that prompted David's action. As the Lord brought judgment on David through Absalom's sin, so through David's error He punished the sins of Israel.

The destroying angel had stood on Mount Moriah, "on the threshing floor of Ornan the Jebusite." Directed by the prophet, David went to the mountain, "and offered burnt offerings and peace offerings, and called on the LORD; and He answered him from heaven by fire on the altar of burnt offering." "So the LORD heeded the prayers for the land, and the plague was withdrawn from Israel."

The spot where the altar was built, regarded from that time on as holy ground, was the place where Abraham had built the altar to offer up his son. Later it was chosen as the site of the temple.

David had reached the age of seventy. The hardships and exposures of his early wanderings, his many wars, and the afflictions of later years had sapped the fountain of life. Feebleness and age, with his desire to be alone, kept him from seeing quickly what was happening in the kingdom, and again rebellion sprang up in the very shadow of the throne.

The one who now wanted the throne was Adonijah, "very good-looking," but unprincipled and reck-less. In his youth "his father had not rebuked him at any time by saying, 'Why have you done so?' " Having been subjected to little restraint, he now rebelled against the authority of God, who had appointed Solomon to the throne.

Solomon was better qualified than his older brother, but although the choice of God had been clearly indicated, Adonijah did not fail to find sympathizers. Joab, up to that time loyal to the throne, now joined the conspiracy against Solomon, and so did Abiathar the priest.

The rebellion was ripe. The con-spirators had assembled at a great feast to proclaim Adonijah king, when their plans were defeated by the prompt action of Zadok the priest, Nathan the prophet, and Bathsheba the mother of Solomon. They told the king about the situa-tion, reminding him that God had said that Solomon should come to the throne next. David at once abdi-cated in favor of Solomon, who was immediately anointed and pro-claimed king. The conspiracy was crushed.

Abiathar's life was spared out of respect to his office and former loy-alty to David, but he was demoted from the office of high priest, which passed to the family of Zadok. Joab and Adonijah were spared for the time, but after David's death they suffered the penalty of their crime. The execution of the sentence on the son of David completed the four-fold judgment that testified to God's hatred of the father's sin.

David Unselfishly Gathers Money and Material for the Temple

From the opening of David's reign, one of his most cherished plans had been to construct a tem-ple to the Lord. He had provided an abundance of costly materials—gold, silver, onyx stones, and stones of various colors, marble, and pre-cious woods. And now other hands must build the temple—the house for the ark, the symbol of God's presence.

Knowing that he was soon to die, the king called representative men from all parts of the kingdom to receive this legacy in trust. Be-cause of his physical weakness, no one had expected him to make this transfer in person, but the inspira-tion of God came upon him, and with fervor and power he was able to address his people for the last time. He told them of his own desire to build the temple and of the Lord's command that the work be com-mitted to Solomon his son. " 'Now therefore,' " David said, " 'in the sight of all Israel, the congregation of the Lord, and in the hearing of our God, be careful to seek out all the commandments of the Lord your God, that you may possess this good land, and leave it as an inheritance for your children after you forever.' "

David's whole soul was moved with deep concern that the leaders of Israel should be true to God and that Solomon should obey God's law, avoiding the sins that had weak-ened his father's authority, embit-tered his life, and dishonored God.

Turning to his son, already acknowledged as his successor, David said: " 'My son Solomon, know the God of your father, and serve Him with a loyal heart and with a willing mind; for the LORD searches all hearts and understands all the intent of the thoughts. . . . Consider now, for the LORD has chosen you to build a house for the sanctuary.' "

David gave Solomon detailed directions for building the temple. Solomon was still young and shrank from the weighty responsibilities involved in constructing the temple and governing God's people. David said, " 'Be strong and of good courage, and do it; do not fear nor be dismayed, for the LORD God—my God—will be with you. He will not leave you nor forsake you.' "

Again David appealed to the congregation: " 'My son Solomon, whom alone God has chosen, is young and inexperienced; and the work is great, because the temple is not for man but for the LORD God.' " He said, " 'For the house of my God I have prepared with all my might,' " and he went on to list the materials he had gathered. " 'Who then,' " he asked of the assembled multitude that had brought their generous gifts, " 'who then is willing to consecrate *himself* this day to the LORD?' "

There was a ready response from the assembly. "Then the people rejoiced, for they had offered willingly, because with a loyal heart they had offered willingly to the LORD; and King David also rejoiced greatly.

"Therefore David blessed the LORD before all the congregation; and David said: 'Blessed are You, LORD God of Israel, our Father, forever and ever. . . . Now therefore, our God, we thank You and praise Your glorious name. But who am I, and who are my people, that we should be able to offer so willingly as this? For all things come from You, and of Your own have we given You. . . . Give my son Solomon a loyal heart to keep Your commandments and Your testimonies and Your statutes, to do all these things, and to build the temple for which I have made provision.' "

David's Example Is No Excuse for Sin Today

With deepest interest the king had gathered the rich material for building and beautifying the temple. He had composed the glorious anthems that in future years would echo through its courts. Now his heart rejoiced in God. The chief of the fathers and the princes of Israel swelled the offerings, giving of their own possessions into the treasury. It was God alone who had made His people generous. He, not man, must be glorified. His Spirit had made them willing. If His love had not moved on the hearts of the people, the temple never would have been built.

When he felt that death was approaching, the burden of David's heart was still for Solomon and for Israel, whose prosperity must so largely depend on her king's integrity and loyalty to God. "And he charged Solomon his son, saying: 'I go the way of all the earth; be strong, therefore, and prove yourself a man. And keep the charge of